MW00755867

BAROQUE TIMES IN OLD MEXICO

BAROQUE
TIMES
IN OLD
MEXICO

Seventeenth-Century Persons, Places, and Practices

by Irving A. Leonard

Ann Arbor Paperbacks
The University of Michigan Press

Copyright © by the University of Michigan 1959
All rights reserved
ISBN 0-472-06110-0
Published in the United States of America by
The University of Michigan Press
Manufactured in the United States of America

1993   14   13   12

To the memory of
HARRY A. LEONARD

(1869–1941)

De la famosa México el asiento,
origen y grandeza de edificios,
caballos, calles, trato, cumplimiento,
letras, virtudes, variedad de oficios,
regalos, ocasiones de contento,
primavera inmortal y sus indicios,
gobierno ilustre, religión, estado,
todo en este discurso está cifrado.
—Bernardo de Balbuena.

PREFACE

WHEN historians of Hispanic America meet, their discussions occasionally turn to the origins of the republics in the southern reaches of the Western Hemisphere. Then the remark is sometimes heard that, in comparison to the Age of Discovery and Conquest and the later period of intellectual ferment foreshadowing the political separation from Spain, the intervening seventeenth century is a "forgotten" or "neglected" era. It seems a sort of night's rest, as it were, between two strenuous days of history, but thoughtful students of things past have an uneasy feeling that history does not really take these respites and that historical processes continue during such quiet moments; indeed, times of quiescence may effect powerful, if subtle, transformations that shape the character of a people and condition subsequent events. The stormy record of Europe in the same age, with its interminable wars, dynastic struggles, commercial rivalries, emerging nationalisms, and developing science, has established the traditional pattern of modern historical writing in which the concept is implicit that the history of the West is the history of the world. Though largely an extension of western culture, colonial Hispanic America, with its isolation, its nearly three centuries of peace, its religious orthodoxy, and its heterogeneous inhabitants, hardly fits into so narrow a scheme. By comparison its evolutionary trend appears scarcely perceptible, uneventful, and quite insignificant. But if for Europe that part of the globe provided little more than its quota of fuel to the current conflagrations of nationalism devastating the Continent, for the peoples who lived out their days in these remote regions of the New World it was a formative period of ethnic and cultural consolidation. It was a quiet era, comparatively speaking, when the processes of hybridization, cultural absorption, and psychological growth shaped the matrix whose imprint on the human elements of present-day Hispanic America is recognizable. Hence, to understand these Western Hemisphere neighbors today it is needful to peer behind the curtain that separates the colonial and national periods and glimpse their social, cultural, and intellectual beginnings. This effort may well be more fruitful for comprehension than the scrutiny of military and political aspects that conventional history so often prefers.

Systematic investigation of this less glamorous nature presents difficulties. Lacking the massive and specific documentation that great issues, battles, and personalities usually provide, sources of a more scattered and disparate nature must be located, and their utilization calls for delicate discrimination. The general absence of striking events shifts attention to more minute and intangible elements of history, and the scholar perforce works more in the climate of feeling of the time than among the flora and fauna of historical evidence. It is not easy to penetrate the inner reality of an era whose anachronistic spirit deliberately strove to conceal substance behind an elaborate façade of intricately ornate design. The comparative success of that decorative effort obliges the investigator to map his course, not so much by the bearings which significant events or the movements of ideas ordinarily supply, as by the prevailing attitudes, principles, and beliefs of the period. These imponderables often reveal themselves in trivial incidents and seemingly unimportant details. This inwardly pulsating and externally inactive stage of historical evolution in New Spain or Old Mexico is conveniently called "the Baroque age."

The broader use of the term "Baroque" is comparatively recent and its definition is controversial. Earlier applied to a style of architecture and plastic arts, it has come to designate a historical epoch and, subsequently, a way of life. For Hispanic America in general and Old Mexico in particular, where its artistic expression was so complex and its spirit so enduring, the semantic extension seems especially logical. The efflorescence of colonial Baroque art is better known through well-conceived studies, but the Baroque as an historical epoch and a way of life is incompletely assessed. The present work does not claim to fill, in any substantial fashion, this gap in historiography, nor does it undertake a profound analysis or interpretation. For such ends the need for more systematic research is still pressing, and a well-founded synthesis awaits fuller information. This account seeks only to give an impression of the cultural, literary, and intellectual aspects of a relatively neglected period of Mexican history. It is, indeed, a kind of mosaic composed of bits of incident and anecdote and of larger pieces of personalistic and customary detail; it is in itself a kind of Baroque design. Like the motifs of a contemporary sculptured retable, the life and culture of Old Mexico present an elaborate pattern of "whorls within whorls," and the whole cannot be fully comprehended in a glance. By focusing on a few "persons, places and practices," and by magnifying a few details of existence a better understanding of the general may emerge.

In a measure the career of the Archbishop-Viceroy, Fray García Guerra, treated in the first chapter, symbolizes the Baroque age in Spanish America, which, in less personal terms, the second chapter seeks to describe. Since profusion of detail, hierarchy, and contrast are among the dominant traits of the Baroque, their human expression appears marked in a description of colonial society offered in the third chapter. An intricate pattern of class, caste, race, and hybridization demonstrates these tendencies. The sections following concern themselves mainly with cultural mores, literary habits, and intellectual concepts of the ruling elements of a neomedieval civilization. The evolution in this last respect is epitomized to a certain extent in two conspicuous figures, the nun-poetess, Sister Juana Inés de la Cruz, and the Creole scholar, Don Carlos de Sigüenza y Góngora, of whom "profiles" are offered in the concluding chapters. In conjunction with the Archbishop-Viceroy Fray García Guerra, they point up, or personalize, the gradual change in thought and attitude discernible in the course of the seventeenth century. Through these and other personalities introduced one dimly perceives the rudimentary shaping of a psychological pattern of a people becoming a nation. Foreshadowed, too, is an ideological revolution destined to undermine the neo-orthodoxy of the Baroque age.

Of even more significance is the fact that these figures reveal that, over the decades of the century, the Creole was identifying himself more and more with the land of his birth, and increasingly he was aware of his separate and unique personality. This dawning nationalism, discreetly obscure at first, asserts itself more boldly in writings of the late seventeenth century. If the American-born Spaniard rarely considered the Indian, Negro, and mixed elements of the proletariat as partners in a new body politic, he did not differ so greatly in this kind of patriotism from the aristocratic and bourgeois classes dominant in the more advanced nations of contemporary Europe with respect to their peasantry. From 1600 to 1700 the Creole acquired a perceptible consciousness of his individuality and a faith in his latent, if not actual, parity with his kinsmen in the old country. His improving economic, social, and political status gave him increased assurance and it nurtured his ambition to take the reins of power from the faltering grasp of the Peninsulars.

In the intellectual sphere the two distinguished Creoles mentioned, Sister Juana Inés de la Cruz and Don Carlos de Sigüenza y Góngora, exemplify the incipient decline of scholasticism and the beginnings of the critical spirit so much more discernible in the Europe of their time. If their reflection of seventeenth-century scientific thought seems hazy and remote, and if their enlightenment appears as only the pallid glow of a false dawn, they heralded, nonetheless, the coming of the modern age in Mexico and in Hispanic America, and indirectly they prepared the soil for the seedling of political independence by challenging authority in the intellectual realm. Because the nun-poetess is so widely known for her literary distinction, emphasis is here placed on the mental qualities of this brilliant woman. Her preoccupation with ideas clearly places her at the side of the Creole scholar as a precursor of eighteenth-century rationalism in Mexico.

To point up further the element of contrast, which is an important component of the Baroque, side glances are occasionally cast at circumstances and developments to the north of Old Mexico, particularly in English America. The more recently planted British colonies, cruder and far less opulent than the Spanish establishments that were older by a century, presented curious similarities in the seventeenth century, as well as differences. An interesting instance, set forth in Chapter XI, concerns the respective reading habits of the dour Pilgrims of New England and the mercurial Creoles of New Spain.

In several chapters I have drawn extensively on my own studies and previously published articles, but in each case new data are added and, in varying degrees, the text is rewritten.

I am grateful to the University of Michigan for a sabbatical leave that permitted an uninterrupted period for writing a substantial part of this book. For help in assembling illustrations I am indebted to Mr. Christian M. F. Brun of the William L. Clements Library, Ann Arbor, Michigan, to my student, Mr. Edward H. Worthen, and to Dr. Paul Murray, Mexico City.

Irving A. Leonard

Heathbrook
South Tamworth (East Sandwich)
New Hampshire

CONTENTS

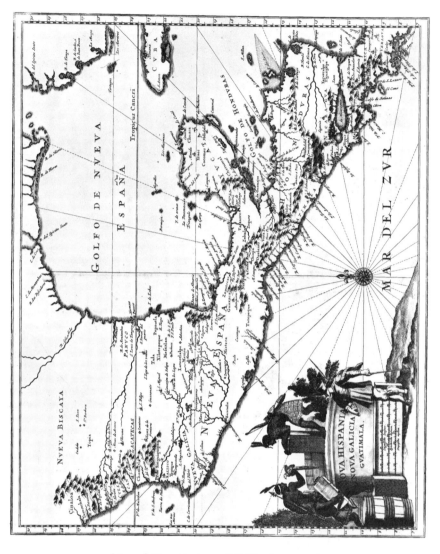

Map of New Spain or Old Mexico, *ca.* 1620
(From Ogilby, *America,* London, 1671)

DOMÍNUS. FRATER. GARCÍAS. GUERRA. ARCHIEPÍSCOPUS MEXÍCANUS PROREX E. DUX 12, GE-
NERALÍS. 1611.

Archbishop-Viceroy Fray García Guerra

(From Rivera Cambas, *Los gobernantes de México,*
Mexico City, 1872)

Mexico City, 1628

(From S. de Educación Pública, Mexico City)

NOVA MEXICO

Mid-Seventeenth Century Mexico

(From Ogilby, *America*, London, 1671)

Sor Juana Ines De La Cruz
(From the Museo Nacional, Mexico City)

Don Carlos De Sigüenza Y Góngora
(From *The Mercurio Volante*, Los Angeles, 1932)

BAROQUE TIMES IN OLD MEXICO

I

A BAROQUE
ARCHBISHOP-VICEROY

TWO heavy cannon shots boomed dully across the murky waters of the roadstead at Vera Cruz, port of entry of Old Mexico, as the first clumsy galleons of the annual fleet from Spain gingerly rounded the island fortress of San Juan de Ulloa, a good musket-shot distance from the shore. Further reports of ordnance hurled echoes landward as more ships limped through the exposed north channel toward the comparatively safe anchorage of the fort's south wall. For the sixty-two vessels that had sailed from Cádiz on June 12, 1608 it had been a good crossing, notably free of the customary threats of storms and pirates. The size of the fleet had shrunk considerably after sighting the islands of the Caribbean as units seceded from the group to deliver cargoes and passengers at Puerto Rico, Santo Domingo, Cartagena, Havana, Honduras, Jamaica, and Yucatan. But the bulk of the flotilla was now putting in at its terminal port, gateway of the spacious realm of New Spain. It was August 19, well over two months since the coast of Spain had faded into the haze, and both crew and passengers were weary of the anxious monotony of cramped and comfortless life on shipboard. These last few days at sea, with the voyage end so near, had tantalized everyone to the point of exasperation. An inopportune calm had delayed arrival and the sun's heat, both by direct rays and reflections on the bright, blue water, had frayed tempers already ragged. Perspiration ran from every pore of unwashed

1

bodies and the pitch fairly oozed from every plank of the small, crowded ships. The tiny, coffinlike cabins below were suffocating and passengers, partly disrobed, sought relief at night among the boxes, crates, and casks littering the decks. Hence a thrill of joy and relief ran through the fretting travelers when suddenly they heard a loud shout "Land! Land! Land!" These glad tidings seemed to stir into action even the offshore breezes, and not a few individuals knelt to give thanks for beholding the continent of the New World and a happy conclusion of the journey.

One by one the tiny vessels, with all but the midsail lowered, awkwardly maneuvered into the shelter of the great wall of the fortress. Its four-hundred foot length presented rows of large, bronze rings which provided mooring and protection from the north winds that so often pounded the open coast. But these installations seldom equaled the number of units composing the fleet and the expedient was frequently necessary of forming parallel chains of two, three, or more ships that tended to sway back and forth with the tide like ponderous streamers. This arrangement was a perilous one, especially when the fierce "northers" raised heavy seas, for the adjacent series of sailing craft sometimes battered each other disastrously or broke loose from their moorings.[1]

Surrounded by a numerous retinue and mountainous luggage, an imposing figure, in the panoply of high ecclesiastical office, stood on the foredeck of one of the ships slowly picking its way toward this precarious haven. Among the swarm of expectant inhabitants lining the shore word had quickly passed that the conspicuous personage was no less than a great Prince of the Church, the Archbishop newly appointed to the See of Mexico, Fray García Guerra by name and renowned for his vast learning and stirring eloquence. Increasingly visible to these eager onlookers, as the vessel hove to, was the commotion on deck caused by the obsequious crew and personal servants who scurried about to initiate the formidable task of lightering ashore the distinguished dignitary and his multitudinous effects.

Even before the laborious process of mooring the many ships began, customs officials of the crown and inspectors of the Holy Office of the Inquisition had put out from the mainland in small boats, and soon they clambered up the sides of the vessels to the cluttered decks. Neither the boatmasters nor the sea-weary passengers greeted these emissaries with enthusiasm, for their presence presaged annoying delays in landing and possibly embarrassing investigations. The commissioners themselves had no illusions regarding their shipboard popularity but this realization did not lessen the mutual jealousy which disposed them to quarrel over matters of jurisdiction. The captains of the arriving ships had learned by experience that, with suitable discretion, both delegations could, therefore, be bribed into a most cursory exercise of their functions. But on this occasion the presence of the highest ecclesiastical authority in the realm moved the inspectors to a more faithful performance of duty and they bustled about their tasks with ostentatious efficiency, exempting from their scrutiny only the possessions of the Archbishop and his attendants. Not even the more distinguished passengers basking in episcopal favor, including a famous Spanish novelist, Mateo Alemán, escaped inconvenience.

The Vera Cruz, at which the travelers were disembarking, had an aspect of raw newness for, indeed, it was not yet a decade old. An earlier site of the port farther south was abandoned at the close of the sixteenth century because the fortified rock of San Juan de Ulloa offered better protection from the heavy gales which descended from the north and from the fierce pirates who might descend from anywhere. Otherwise, there was little to commend the location for human habitation and, important as the settlement was as a trading center and entrance to an opulent viceroyalty, its population barely exceeded two thousand. Situated in a dreary stretch of sand broken by tiny, sluggish streams, swampy bogs, and shallow pools of stagnant water, the moist heat, swarms of mosquitoes, gnats, and other noxious insects made the vicinity singularly unhealthy. The frequent, heavy downpours during the long rainy season, now approaching its end when the fleet put in, left a humid, dank atmosphere that was almost suffocating, and in it every sort of pest and repulsive creature seemed to proliferate. "When it rains, every drop produces a toad, and some are as big as a hat," wrote an early chronicler.[2] The flora and fauna were proportionately lush, while crocodiles and alligators lolled conspicuously on the banks of the marshy estuaries. The rude habitations of rough boards and crude timbers scattered about gave the seaport an unkempt look. The shelters of the rich merchants and of the wretched poor were hardly distinguishable one from the other; the drabness of all the buildings, whether dwellings, churches or convents, was unrelieved by whitewash or other embellishment, and every structure had a rotted, waterlogged appearance in the wet season, while they shook, rattled, and rumbled as the gusty winds beat against them. During the dry months the wood was like tinder and an easy prey to devastating fires that now and then leveled the community.[3]

On that August day of 1608, however, the dismal town strove to offer a more alluring appearance. The coming of the annual fleet was a great event of the year, and on this occasion it was anticipated with more than normal excitement. Preparations, as elaborate as the meager resources of the community permitted, had been arranged, and the whole motley population was on the waterfront to welcome the great prelate. The *cabildo,* or council, of the Cathedral in Mexico City had already sent down two of its eldest and most distinguished canons to greet this illustrious personage, though advanced age compelled one of them to remain in the more salubrious vicinity of Jalapa. The hardier clergyman was already in Vera Cruz, to which he had brought an ample supply of tasty foods and fruits along with forty servants, saddlehorses, mules, and other animals to convey the Archbishop's retinue and the enormous quantity of baggage to the highland capital. For the ease and comfort of this ecclesiastical prince, the Cathedral council had also provided a spacious carriage drawn by well-trained mules.[4]

The prosperous merchants and the clergy of the port town had no wish to be outdone in the homage paid to this powerful minister of God whose esteem they craved, and they spared no effort to insure the comfort and pleasure of the temporary guest. The priests and canons of the local cathedral in their vestments, and the religious orders in their dusty gray, black, and brown habits, had formed a procession, each with an upraised Cross at the head of its column. Chanting a *Te Deum Laudamus,* they picked their way through the muddy streets where scrawny fowls pecked about the refuse, mud-caked pigs rooted in the offal, and spectral *zapilotes,* or vultures, fed on carrion. This solemn parade moved slowly toward the beach, passing raucously braying donkeys protesting under heavy burdens of faggots which almost concealed them, and lumbering, ox-drawn carts, called *chirriones,* whose tortured axles filled the air with shrill squeaks and strident squeals.

Small, naked children, and slightly more clothed adults, mulattoes and Negroes for the most part, ran along the line of friars, or brought up the rear. The ebony skin of these inhabitants glistened with sweat in the humid sunlight, while the marching members of the religious orders perspired profusely beneath their heavy vesture. The dank air seemed oppressive, and its steamy vapor was redolent of the mingled odors of decaying fruit, carrion, excrement, and the sweaty bodies of man and beast.

Now safely on the waterfront Fray García Guerra, in resplendent vestments, stood under an ornate pallium to receive the obeisance of clergy and laymen, while cannon shots resounded sharply from the anchored ships and from the island fortress. Looking slightly harried by the intensity of the obsequious throng, the Archbishop and his servitors who surreptitiously mopped their brows, were slowly conducted through the miry streets amidst further chanting and responses to the rude church and convent of the Dominicans, of which order the honored guest was a member. In due course the friars of other congregations returned to their cloisters while their superiors entertained the prelate in a more private manner.

Fray García Guerra hardly wished to linger in these unhealthy surroundings and, as everything was in readiness for his journey to Mexico City, he began the slow advance inland accompanied by a long caravan of horses, pack mules, coaches, litters, creaking carts, and pedestrians. It was a triumphal march and the progress of his carriage was deliberately slow to permit all his flock along the way to behold the majesty of a Prince of the Church and to pay homage to this intermediary of God. Well over a month elapsed before he made his ceremonious entry into the viceregal capital.

Meanwhile, the bright-hued caravan halted at each Indian village and hamlet where the natives, doubtless prompted by the local *cura,* or parish priest, proffered their most colorful entertainments, often a curious mixture of aboriginal folkloric elements and those acquired from the Spaniards. These festivities were unfailingly accompanied by a noisy salute of fireworks. Between these stops the Archbishop's carriage passed under an endless series of floral arches, erected scarcely a musket-shot distance apart. As the episcopal conveyance approached these Indian communities a small band of villagers came forth to meet it, each individual bedecked in the peculiar attire of the locality and blowing odd strains on trumpets and other wind instruments. Escorted in this manner the Archbishop's coach rolled into the tiny village square invariably adorned with floral chains and varicolored bunting, and there its occupant witnessed the colorful *mitotes,* the most solemn of the ceremonial dances and songs of the natives. Fray García Guerra vastly enjoyed these strange interludes in which these primitive members of his flock, arrayed in picturesque costumes and adornments, performed the most ritualistic of their pagan rites, for he had a special fondness for music in all its forms, and the novelty of these curious strains left him undisturbed by their non-Christian origins. In his train were clergymen from Castile who were gifted instrumentalists, and the Cathedral council, doubtless informed of the new prelate's predilection, had thoughtfully sent down skilled musicians from Mexico City to lighten the tedium of his journey. Thus the Archbishop found delight in the variety of harmonies that charmed his ears along the way.

In this pleasant fashion Fray García Guerra neared his destination. Scarcely a dozen leagues from Mexico City he paused briefly in the small Indian town of Apa where a personal representative of the viceroy, in behalf of that magistrate, welcomed the new head of the Mexican church. Only the fact that his feet hurt, so ran the message, prevented Don Luis de Velasco, viceroy for the second time of this great realm of the Spanish empire, from coming in person to kiss the ring of the chief primate and place himself unreservedly at the Archbishop's disposal. Despite his gouty extremities Don Luis de Velasco assured the prelate that he would not fail to meet him in person before the triumphal entry into the capital.

Mexico City, situated amidst lakes in the lofty valley of Anahuac, suffered periodic inundations that had long called for drastic remedy. Only the year before so destructive a flood had descended upon this administrative center that a transfer of the municipality to another site was seriously contemplated. Commercial and other interests, however, strongly resisted this solution and the viceroy, on the advice of a German cosmographer, Enrico Martínez, and of others, had authored a gigantic engineering project designed to carry off the excess waters in a series of cuts and channels. The most ambitious part of this undertaking was a huge notch in the hills near the village of Huehuetoca. It occurred to Don Luis de

Velasco that a joint inspection of this work would be an admirable occasion for the first meeting of the respective heads of Church and State, and necessary arrangements were, accordingly, made. In due course Fray García Guerra alighted from his carriage at the viceroy's temporary quarters whereupon the king's surrogate in New Spain hobbled out to the front staircase and demonstratively welcomed the new prelate. After dining together the two most powerful dignitaries in the land drove away to inspect the progress made on the large cut. It was on this excursion that the first of an ominous series of mishaps befell the proud Fray García Guerra.

The rise of this Dominican clergyman to the eminence he now claimed in one of the richest archbishoprics in Spain's enormous empire had been foreordained and rapid. Singularly propitious were the auguries of the stars at his birth in 1560 in a village of Old Castile. Of noble ancestry, it was soon apparent that his studious temperament admirably equipped him for the verbalistic intellectualism of the age and culture in which he lived. His native talents splendidly adapted him for a luminous career in the Church, then so powerful in the affairs of man, and at the age of fifteen he sought to don the Dominican habit. In May, 1578, he was duly admitted to the order of his choice at the Convent of St. Paul in Valladolid, and almost immediately he gained distinction in philosophy, metaphysics, and theology. His extraordinary gifts as a dialectician and his consummate skill as an orator quickly brought wide acclaim. His brilliance as an expounder of the doctrines then hardening under the pressures of the Counter Reformation brought recognition from the secular rulers of the land as well as from his Dominican superiors. After filling chairs of theology in monasteries at Ávila, Burgos, Segovia and Valladolid, he became prior of the convent where he had taken his first vows. When the weak monarch, Philip III, was induced to transfer his Court from Madrid to Valladolid in 1600, Fray García Guerra attracted the approving eye of the king's influential favorite, the Duke of Lerma, who soon elevated the talented clergyman to the lofty eminence of the *Patronato* of Castile. After the birth of a royal prince destined, as Philip IV, to preside over the dissolution of the political glory that was Spain, Fray García Guerra officiated at the baptism.

With Madrid once again the capital a few years later, Philip III did not forget the churchman whose eloquence and administrative ability he had admired in Valladolid. When death created a vacancy in the archbishopric of Mexico, it was the royal will that Fray García should accept it. If the clergyman's hesitation was sincere, his Dominican superiors soon convinced him that it was a duty to fulfill his destiny. After papal confirmation Fray García was consecrated on April 5, 1608, and, two months later, he embarked for his New World post. Fate had smiled steadily upon this son of Old Castile and now had placed him in one of the most important offices to which a clergyman might aspire.[5]

The shift of activities from the Old to the New World seemed to mark, however, the turning point in the unbroken good fortune which had attended his career from birth. Almost imperceptibly portents of the future began to gather like clouds on the horizon, and the brightness of the day slowly dimmed until the darkness of death blotted all. The first of these omens, which hardly seemed to have any import, occurred when the new Archbishop and the Viceroy of New Spain rode together to inspect the drainage project at Huehuetoca. The road through the pass, over which they were driving, had been traveled again and again without mishap of any sort, and it appeared free of any hazards to the safety of these heads of the absolute government of the land. Suddenly and without warning their carriage turned completely over, spilling the august occupants by the wayside in a most undignified manner. Attendants hurried to their aid. Though both victims of the accident were badly shaken and slightly injured, they were able to resume the journey the next day. This incident seemed insignificant enough, but Fray García was to remember it as the beginning of his misfortunes.

Again his caravan took up the slow pilgrimage toward Mexico City, stopping in each of the intervening villages for the customary ceremonies of fealty, homage, and entertainment so obsequiously provided by the inhabitants. Meanwhile, the viceroy sped ahead to oversee the final arrangements for the sumptuous reception of the Archbishop in the capital. Even slower than before was Fray García's progress, for he was repeatedly administering the sacrament of confirmation, and the festive journey from Vera Cruz had stretched into a full month. But at last he reached Santa Ana, a suburb of the city, where he alighted from his ornate carriage and mounted a mule to make his entry with the simulated humility of the Founder of Christianity. A group of municipal officials, in brightest livery and astride gaily caparisoned horses, had come out to accompany the Archbishop on this final stage of his travels.

As the small procession entered the outskirts of the capital it stopped at the Dominican monastery. Near a platform, erected by the members of this religious body to do honor to a distinguished brother of their Order, Fray García dismounted from his mule and climbed upon the shaky staging where the Dean, councilors of the Cathedral, and other dignitaries were seated. Scarcely had the Archbishop begun to acknowledge the rejoicing of the assembly when the improvised rostrum trembled ominously and, with a loud crash, the entire structure collapsed, flinging its respected occupants to the ground and crushing a luckless Indian beneath it. Once again, as when he was thrown from the carriage at Huehuetoca, Fray García was badly shaken but received no severe injury, and presently the interrupted ceremonies were resumed. There were those, however, who, having heard of the earlier mishap, shook their heads gravely. These signs did not augur well for the new prelate.

The arrangements for the crowning event went forward—the magnificent spectacle of the entry into the Cathedral under the episcopal pallium. The liveried magistrates, who had met Fray García on the outskirts of the city, now took positions as a guard of honor. Each held an ornate staff supporting the purple and gold pallium with brocade trimmings which sheltered the Archbishop robed in glittering vestments. So massive was this canopy that it required twenty-two of the uniformed *regidores* to hold it aloft in this fashion. This dazzling tableau moved slowly through the streets lined with the awed populace. From the walls, windows, and balconies of the buildings on either side hung rich tapestries and bright-hued bunting. At length the procession halted in front of the Cathedral, still far from completion. Before the ponderous portal stood a gigantic arch with a Baroque profusion of sculptural details, of complex symbols, of ornamental figures, and of erudite quotations.

Leaving the pallium on the Cathedral steps the Archbishop, with attendant priests and acolytes, moved majestically into the gloomy splendor of the interior and advanced toward the gleaming effulgence of the candlelit altar while the great nave resounded with

the swelling paeans of the *Te Deum Laudamus,* sung by an aug-
mented choir. To the edification of all assembled this mighty
Prince of the Church prostrated himself before the Cross with ostentatious humility. After an appropriate pause in this position
Fray García Guerra slowly arose to his feet and the profound
solemnity of the moment yielded to an almost gay burst of melodious song, secular and festive in character. This sudden transition heightened the emotional effect and drama of the scene, filling
the audience with a kind of rapture. The Archbishop, a dazzling
figure in the magnificence of his episcopal robes, then seated himself near the high altar to witness a brief, allegorical play in-
geniously staged in the chancel. Elaborately costumed performers,
in witty dialogues of prettily worded phrases, explained and interpreted the fanciful designs and symbols embellishing the enormous
arch at the Cathedral door. At the conclusion of this sprightly
interlude the Dean, prebendaries, and other ecclesiastical dignitaries approached the prelate in single file to offer their obeisance
with impressive humility. The object of this adulation was now
more than ever the cynosure of admiring and reverent eyes.

For Fray García it was a supreme moment. His fortunate career
had brought him to a pinnacle of glory in the neomedieval world
that Spain was expending its blood and treasure to maintain and
that it passionately believed was the fulfillment of God's will on
earth. But like the civilization that he personified, he was already
an anachronism and his own fate epitomized the destiny of that
age. Unforeseen by all that throng was the certainty that, in a few
brief years, his dissected and decomposing body would lie interred
in the very place where he now sat amid so much pomp and circumstance. Long after in the same century a distinguished citizen
of Mexico City, moved by other portents, would exclaim: "O sacred
and most just God, how removed from human reason are Thy
incomprehensible and venerable judgments! And how true are the
Scriptures when they state that laughter is mingled with tears
and that sorrow follows upon the greatest joys!"[6]

The newly inaugurated Archbishop did not fail to display the
piety, benevolence, and oratorical gifts that so clearly justified his
designation to the richest See of the New World. To his flock he
seemed the perfect embodiment of an exemplary minister of the
Gospel and a saintly administrator of the Church of God. In those

first months of his office he appeared to strive for justice for all with an impartiality, a lack of precipitation, and a compassionate rectitude. His varied duties he performed with punctuality, and so zealous was he in distributing alms personally from his vast income that his meals were often delayed. Faithfully he visited all parts of his broad diocese, and in the churches he preached with that moving eloquence and great learning that unmistakably marked him as one set apart to do God's work.

All who came into the presence of this ecclesiastical Prince acquired a conviction that Fray García was, indeed, an inspired person happy in fulfilling a great destiny. Yet a close observer might have perceived that, with all the homage daily bestowed upon him, with all the Croesus-like wealth at his disposal, and with all the assurance of an eternal reward at the end of his earthly existence, a disquieting urge vaguely stirred deep within his consciousness. Omnipotent as he was in the social and economic as well as the spiritual lives of his flock, an unspoken longing, which was growing in intensity, possessed him to dominate the political affairs of the realm as well. Don Luis de Velasco, the reigning viceroy, was a great proconsul of his Majesty who had served with great distinction in both Mexico and Peru. His long experience, proven skill, and sound judgment were indispensable to the weak and vacillating Philip III, sorely needing in Spain such able administrators to manage an empire already betraying symptoms of decay and disintegration. It was but a matter of time before royal summons would compel the return of Don Luis to the homeland. In such an eventuality the viceregal office commonly devolved upon the Archbishop as an interim appointment at least, and Fray García found himself dwelling on this possibility with increasing insistency.

Like most at the summit of human institutions, the prelate's existence was essentially a lonely one. As the accepted instrument of God he was the recipient of obsequious demonstrations of awe, veneration, and fear wherever he went. Nowhere did his basically gregarious nature find the intimate companionship and confidence that it craved. With all his appearance of piety and of a dedicated servant of the Lord, and with all his ascetic ostentation, he longed for the milder sensual delights of his flock. He loved the sweet melody of instrumental music, the singing of ballads and folk songs, the gustatory pleasures of the table, and the strong tonic of spectacles of the bull ring. To satisfy the first of these tastes Fray García had fallen into the habit of dropping into the Royal Convent of Jesus and Mary in the afternoon to visit Sister Mariana de la Encarnación and Sister Inés de la Cruz, whose company he found especially congenial. Both nuns were skilled instrumentalists and singers who infallibly charmed the Archbishop by lively renditions of popular airs. With perfect mastery they played liturgical music on the convent organ, and with effortless ease they shifted to the guitarlike *laúdes* and *rabeles,* strumming accompaniments to worldly songs that told of sentimental longings, of blighted loves, and of forsaken hopes. This musical potpourri they interlarded with sprightly chatter most relaxing to a prelate surfeited by the ceremonious formality of his daily life. The culinary arts of these talented ladies, manifested in sweetmeats and dainty dishes, added delight to these restful occasions, and rarely did Fray García miss these agreeable afternoon visits.

This was a common practice of clergymen noted a few years after this time by Thomas Gage, the "English American" who reported: "It is ordinary for the Fryers to visit their devoted Nuns, and to spend whole days with them hearing their musick, feeding on their sweet-meats. And for this purpose they have many chambers, which they call Loquitorios, to talk in, with wooden bars between the Nuns and them, and in these chambers are tables for Fryers to dine at; and while they dine, the Nuns recreate them with their voices. Gentlemen and citizens gave their daughters to be brought up in these Nunneries, where they are taught to make all sorts of conserves and preserves, all sorts of musick, which is so exquisite in that City, that I dare be bold to say, that the people are drawn to their churches more for the delight of their musick, than for any delight in the service of God."[7]

Even this gentle and harmless association did not exempt Fray García entirely from the solicitation and importunity that often beset the powerful and influential, for the hospitable nuns were not wholly without guile. They, too, had dreams and ambitions. Long cherished was their hope of founding a new convent under the rule of the reformed Carmelites, and already a wealthy patron had willed a sufficient sum for a building and given part of the endowment. This benefactor had named the Archbishop an executor, and only the approval and a supplementary grant of funds by Fray García were needed to convert a dream into reality. Hence the devout ladies exerted themselves to charm their opulent guest who remained curiously immune to their overtures. This intimate communion with the nuns, however, had brought forth a confession of his own aspirations of becoming the viceroy of Mexico, and whenever pressed for action on the beloved project of his hostesses he invariably put them off by exclaiming: "Ah, my dear sisters, if God is pleased to bestow upon me the office of viceroy, I shall surely help you to start the convent that you so rightly desire! And what a splendid one I shall make it!"

"Must we wait until then, Sire?" the anxious nuns pleaded.

"Yes, my dears," was his constant answer. "It can only be when I become the viceroy."

Fray García's afternoon visits continued regularly and with equal regularity, as they plied him with appetizing tidbits, melody, and conversation, the nuns repeated their pleas. Invariably the obdurate Archbishop vouchsafed the same reply: "When I am the viceroy . . ." Even when Sister Inés de la Cruz professed to have had a vision in which the viceregal office was bestowed upon the ambitious prelate, Fray García remained unmoved. Until the prophecy was fulfilled he would make no commitment, and the impatient nuns could only pray more fervently for divine intercession.[8]

Another favorite diversion of the Archbishop were the drives in his ornate, mule-drawn carriage to outlying churches and congregations. The upset near Huehuetoca, when he had accompanied the viceroy on a tour of inspection, had in no way diminished his enjoyment of such excursions, which were of frequent occurrence. One day, however, in returning from the Santa Monica monastery it happened that the well-trained mules suddenly took fright and dashed pell-mell through the streets of the city. Frantically the coachman tried to bring the careening carriage under control, and a few bystanders bravely attempted to check the flight of the maddened beasts. Fray García clung desperately to his seat in an effort to ride out the fury of the mules but, as his equipage plunged wildly about the thoroughfare, panic seized him. In a convulsive attempt to save himself he started to leap. Unfortunately, his foot caught in the carriage step, hurling him to the ground where he lay senseless. Though in time he seemed to recover from this mishap, so much more severe than the preceding ones, it had fatal consequences.

Fateful for Fray García was the year 1611 which witnessed his greatest triumph and greatest disaster. It was as if the Fates, having bestowed their bounties so generously on the Spanish clergyman, were growing weary of his claims on their prodigality. His gnawing desire for secular power, after rising so high in the ecclesiastical sphere, appeared to turn his wheel of fortune downward. The series of accidents befalling him were unheeded warnings and now Nature itself was offering disturbing admonitions.

The spring of that year brought the long-expected summons to Don Luis de Velasco to vacate his viceregal office and return to Spain to serve as president of the Royal Council of the Indies. The same decree formally designated Fray García Guerra as his successor in Mexico. The prayerful and seemingly modest acquiescence of the Archbishop did not wholly conceal his inner delight, and his ostentatious humility hardly veiled his keen pleasure in supervising the elaborate plans for a second triumphal entry into the capital, this time with the full panoply of the viceregal office. He gave his closest personal attention to the details of erecting an ornate arch, of selecting the sonorous verses and Latin inscriptions to adorn it, of preparing the magnificent display of fireworks and the illuminations of the façades of public buildings by night, of rehearsing the *Te Deum Laudamus* and the lighter music that so delighted him, and of the construction of the grandstands along the line of march. Absorbed in these pleasurable activities all thought of his promises to the hospitable nuns at the Convent of Jesus and Mary fled from his mind. Indeed, the financial assistance pledged for the new Carmelite establishment was diverted to a pastime close to Fray García's heart—bullfights. To celebrate his elevation to the supreme rank of Archbishop-Viceroy he decreed that these taurine spectacles should take place every Friday for an entire year. And presently he prevailed upon a reluctant city council to construct a private bull ring within the Palace since it hardly seemed fitting for one of his ecclesiastical eminence to attend such functions in public places.

The first of these *corridas* occurred on Good Friday. The choice of the date, curiously symptomatic of the juxtaposition of the sensate and the spiritual in the Baroque age, apparently inspired no adverse comment except from one source. Sister Inés de la Cruz, whose protest possibly arose as much from disappointed hopes as from scandalized disapproval, begged the Archbishop-Viceroy in a note not to encourage such diversions on the day commemorating the Passion of Jesus Christ. But Fray García was too elated to heed this plea and the spectacle took place as scheduled. But a similar event the following Friday brought possible signs of divine displeasure. Just before the appointed hour of the bullfight earth tremors shook the city so severely that the *corrida* was postponed. Undaunted by this warning Fray García comfortably seated himself the following week to witness his favorite sport. Hardly was the first bull charging into the ring when the city experienced another earth spasm so violent that the grandstand and the neighboring houses collapsed. The stone coping of the balcony where the Archbishop was sitting suddenly cracked and a portion of it fell, narrowly missing him and killing several onlookers below. But even so pointed a hint did not deter Fray García, who refused to revoke his decree calling for a weekly exhibition of the popular pastime.

Before assuming his new office Fray García had retired to an outlying village to await formal notification of the departure of his predecessor from Vera Cruz and to make a ceremonial entry into Mexico City as viceroy. When the welcome word arrived that Don Luis de Velasco had sailed the Archbishop's first act was to abase himself publicly before the shrine of the Virgin of Guadalupe. This rite performed, he permitted his attendants to address him by the coveted secular title "Your Excellency."

The inaugural march into the capital on June 19, 1611, duplicated the pomp and splendor of his earlier entry as Archbishop with, however, features of a more secular character. This time he rode a beautiful mare of the most pure blooded stock of the realm, the gift of the city council. Beneath the episcopal pallium supported by the *regidores* on foot, who were dressed in velvet uniforms of brilliant crimson, the Archbishop-Viceroy presented a gallant figure. Next in order came the judges of the Royal Audiencia, the magistrates of other tribunals, and the flower of the viceregal aristocracy, each group vying with the other in theatrical splendor. Slowly the pageantlike procession filed through the streets hung with garlands and past the bordering houses almost concealed by the tapestries and hangings draped from their balconies. But again, as Fray García tasted anew the wine of earthly fame and glory, a tragic note jarred the festive moment.

On the little Santiago square, the Indian community had erected a tall pole called a *volador* from which, as a feature of the celebration, acrobatic members swung high in the air as if from a lofty merry-go-round. This circus-like performance was a death-defying act which thrilled the spectators and added a note of expectancy to the general excitement. Just as the Archbishop-Viceroy drew abreast of this plaza a performer, whirling through the air, lost his grip on the rope and fell, his body horribly shattered, almost at the feet of Fray García. Once again in the midst of rejoicing and at a moment of proud fulfillment tragedy struck, a sinister warning, perhaps, that the Fates were losing patience with the excessive ambition of a favored mortal.

But this macabre incident scarcely interrupted the colorful inauguration. The glittering procession resumed its course toward the triumphal arch which simulated a huge fortress gate decorated by an intricate pattern of symbolic figures painted on its façade. Here the Corregidor administered a ceremonious oath to the new viceroy and handed him a large golden key. The ponderous doors of the imitation stronghold then swung open and the bright column, with Fray García in the lead, wended its way to the Cathedral where the thunderous *Te Deum Laudamus* reverberated through the nave. Presently the Archbishop-Viceroy, accompanied by the city's principal magistrates, departed by another door and entered the viceregal Palace on the east side of the central square. There his accompaniment of judges of the Royal Audiencia and other officials obsequiously took their leave and Fray García retired into the chambers of his secular predecessors to relish the first moments of his ascent to the supreme authority of the State as well as of the Church in the fairest of Spanish realms. Outside, in the plaza, deafening explosions of bombs and artillery-pieces saluted the new viceroy. That night the whole city seemed ablaze with lanterns in doorways and windows and roaring bonfires in the streets and squares.

These noisy demonstrations and the general rejoicing found the Archbishop-Viceroy vaguely troubled. His satisfaction was tinged with disillusionment, a sort of *desengaño*. Realization, somehow, fell short of anticipation. The series of mishaps had engendered haunting forebodings, and already a recurrence of physical pain depressed his spirits. Ever since that dreadful day when he had leaped from the carriage drawn by runaway mules, the pain in his side had become increasingly severe. Also a series of strange phenomena of nature in recent months had filled him and his subjects with uneasiness. Were they harbingers of impending disaster? Oppressed by bodily discomfort and superstitious fears, he confronted with deepening anxiety the heavier obligations which his pride and ambition had thrust upon him.

The disturbing aberrations of nature did not cease as Fray García took up his duties. The very month of his inauguration witnessed a total eclipse of the sun which terrified the masses. An unnatural darkness engulfed the city at noon, and it seemed to deepen as the afternoon advanced. "This phenomenon," wrote a chronicler, "which the astronomers had predicted, produced an effect upon Spaniards and Indians such that both raced frantically to the shelter of the churches to implore God's mercy, and they did not venture out until nightfall."[9] The seismic disturbances coinciding with Fray García's bullfights were followed in August by the severest earthquake in the memory of the oldest inhabitant. With seeming pointedness it wreaked heavy damage on religious establishments where many inmates were crushed beneath the rubble. To everyone this disaster appeared especially terrifying because an inordinate number of tremors had preceded it. More than forty were experienced within thirty hours and all were exceedingly violent.

Weeks and months passed without dissipating the dread and anxiety that pervaded the city. Christmas day brought even more menacing indications of divine displeasure. About half past two in the afternoon the whole sky over the Valley of Mexico turned a dark, reddish black and a shower of ashes fell, sifting a thin layer over the houses and the fields. This strange manifestation lasted until the great, crimson bowl of the sun dipped over the western rim. Just as it disappeared, a frightful downpour of rain deluged the city, transforming its streets into rushing torrents of water.[10] Clearly, these were unmistakable signs of heavenly wrath and inexorable summonses to repentance, most of all, perhaps, for the ailing Archbishop-Viceroy.

Fray García Guerra's symptoms, meanwhile, had worsened, and it was clear that he was gravely ill. Attacks of pain alternated with high fever and confined him to his bed. The best physicians in the land, whose medical knowledge derived almost wholly from the ancients, Galen and Hippocrates, could prescribe no other remedies than repeated purges and bloodletting which further weakened the afflicted prelate. Early in January, 1612, a stormy dispute arose among the doctors in consultation regarding the necessity of an operation. Three of them were promptly dismissed while the others performed some crude surgery which doubtless hastened the patient's demise. In sick despair Fray García had even turned to his good friend, Sister Inés de la Cruz, whose hopes for a new convent he had so long defrauded, and he begged for her prayers. He assured her of his deep repentance and pledged himself to keep his promise to her if he could but be restored to health. The response of the disappointed nun was hardly consoling to the doomed Archbishop-Viceroy, for she merely urged him to prepare for death and to voice thanks to God that his sorrow was only in the temporal realm. Fray García now knew that he must resign himself to the inevitable. Calling his confessor, he received the last Sacrament and thereafter, with the feeble strength left to him, he performed such acts of humility and contrition as he could. Further bloodletting doubtless shortened his period of suffering. With Christian fortitude he endured his afflictions until "he surrendered his spirit to the Lord on February 22, 1612."

The chronicler gives a gruesome account of the autopsy performed upon the noble cadaver hardly had life departed. With morbid satisfaction he describes the advanced decomposition of various organs and the removal of the skull top and the emptying of the brains into a container for separate burial. This writer seemed to share the view of a contemporary Baroque poet Jerónimo de Cáncer that "también en lo horrible hay hermosura" (there is also beauty in the horrible). These repellent details, following almost immediately the recital of the colorful pageantry of the Archbishop-Viceroy's years in Mexico, provide an abrupt transition. Sharpening the contrast still further is the rapid shift from the vital, dynamic scenes of Fray García's existence to the minute description of the veritable orgy of mourning at the public funeral. With morose zest the eulogist tells of streets and public buildings draped in black, of the mournful monotony of endlessly tolling bells, of the almost exuberant frenzy of the chapel decorations, and of the corpse lying in state, of the interminable processions of dignitaries, nobles, officials, monks, and soldiers marching to the rhythm of muffled drums and hoarse fifes, of downcast throngs of the kaleidoscopic society of Mexico, and of the all-pervading solemnity of Death and the futility of things mortal.[11] All of this tremendously heightened the tragic sense of drama infusing the spirit of that age.

The death of the chief of Church and State and the ensuing funeral obsequies increased the mounting tension and anxiety of the inhabitants of the capital. Scarcely were the remains of Fray García deposited beneath the altar by which, a few short years before, he had sat at his episcopal installation flushed with the joy of adulation, when dread rumors and alarms gripped the nervous citizenry. With no successor to wield the absolute power of government to which all were accustomed, the more privileged elements of society especially fell prey to a panic fear. Like a noisome vapor, dark threats against law and order seemed to rise from every quarter. The judges of the Royal Audiencia assumed the executive functions, but their collective rule failed to offer the security that the single figure of the Archbishop-Viceroy, endowed with the legal sanction of the distant Spanish monarchy and, seemingly, of God Himself, embodied in the minds of all. The apprehension of the upper classes spawned vague intimations of plots against the regime, of uprisings in the provinces, particularly of Negroes who had escaped from slavery and had taken refuge in the hills. These *cimarrones* were ever suspected of conspiring with the exploited Indian masses to throw off white supremacy. So great was the terror of Europeans and Creoles that they did not dare to venture out upon the streets and they barricaded themselves within their homes.

This community neurosis became acute one night when a herd of hogs was heard rooting and squealing about the city thoroughfares. These sounds were interpreted as an assault launched by runaway Negroes and they created near panic among the judges of the Royal Audiencia as well as the citizenry. Even the coming of daylight failed to dissipate the general hysteria, and fear-ridden officials rounded up twenty-nine Negro men and four women as alleged conspirators. In a desperate effort to deter subversive elements, the authorities barbarously executed the wretched suspects in the public square before a huge gathering. The severed heads were conspicuously displayed on pikes until the stench of decomposition caused their removal.[12] Similar spasms of uncontrollable fear had shaken Europeans before between the terms of viceroys, but the simultaneous disappearance of both the head of the State and of the Church in one person had let loose a more violent wave of unreasoning fright and terror. Thus, in death as in life, this Spanish Archbishop-Viceroy singularly epitomized an aspect of that strange spirit of the Baroque which subtly dominated the entire seventeenth century and long after.

⚜ II

THE BAROQUE AGE

WITH the prescience of hindsight, posterity sees a kind of boundary between two epochs of western history in the quartet of years
which witnessed Fray García's rise to supreme ecclesiastical and
political office in New Spain. When that illustrious Dominican embarked in 1608 for the New World he could not realize that the
Europe he was leaving was turning into a new world of politics,
economics, social organization, and science. Already, in parts of the
Continent, these changes were so far advanced that they rendered
impossible the recovery of the lost unity of Christendom and the
medieval tradition that the Archbishop-Viceroy so conspicuously
personified. If to him the "kingdom of God" was an empire composed of principalities acknowledging a supreme prince and bol-
stered by an aristocracy enjoying feudal privileges, with the whole
structure cemented by an adherence to the one true Faith, elsewhere in Europe many were beholding the "kingdom of man"
emerging from a set of ideas quite different. Among these other
peoples the conviction was growing that human will might determine human destiny, and that mankind need not regard itself as
a helpless pawn of an all-powerful deity. They glimpsed earthly
existence as something more than a painful preparation for eternity,
and they were increasingly reluctant to abdicate the mind completely to the dogmatic prescriptions of a medieval Church. The
opposing pressures of the Reformation and Counter Reformation
had cracked the mortar of orthodoxy and, particularly in the north
where new political entities were assuming importance, they had

21

perceptibly loosened a solidarity inherited from the Middle Ages. The great Schism had split the Continent into two Europes, Protestant and Catholic, and the breach was widening. Irreparably sundered already were the bonds of religion and tradition that had promised a unified order, and the process of fragmentation would go on.

In the divided Europe of Fray García's closing years the policies of statesmen were no longer influenced by the *Philosophia Christi,* or the achievement of a perfect universal state, which had conditioned the utopianism of the late Renaissance. While religious affiliations clearly colored the issues of the time, secular concerns were taking precedence over ecclesiastical, though the Catholic South, reacting to the contemporary ferment, was growing more inflexible in its adherence to orthodoxy. But emerging national states in the Protestant North were subordinating spiritual matters to commercial activities, and in public affairs merchant adventurers, trading companies, and the like were outweighing the organized Church in influence. Shifting and multiplying trade routes were expanding mercantilism, revolutionizing society, and facilitating the rise of new kinds of imperialism, capitalism, and colonialism. A class of *nouveaux riches* was slowly usurping the power of the agrarian aristocracy, and an expanding *bourgeoisie* was acquiring a larger measure of political control. Confidence was growing that men could, indeed, shape destiny.

In the very years that Fray García was rising to fame a seed was germinating which would strengthen the conviction that mankind could master its fate. The most portentous discovery of the moment was a new approach to truth destined to transform the western world, and, in time, the entire globe. This was modern science. The Ptolemaic universe, with the earth its center and pivotal point, was yielding, still imperceptibly perhaps and quite precariously as Galileo was experiencing, to the Copernican universe with the earth a mere peripheral planet of an immense solar system. A newer freedom of speculation and experimentalism was undermining the traditional verbalistic methods of scholasticism, and it would lead to discoveries dwarfing the miracles of medieval lore.

If this fundamental divergence of intellectual methodology was hardly discernible at the outset of the seventeenth century, within a few decades it was changing the conceptions of many concerning the world, and it was posing a threat to medieval cosmology and religious orthodoxy. As the methods of analysis and measurement were applied, a new search was underway for the divine plan of the universe; as this endeavor began to create new values, the time-worn monopoly of theology and scholasticism as the avenue to truth was shattered and the infallibility of dogmas was doubted. Already, as the seventeenth century dawned, confirmation of the heliocentric theory of Copernicus (1543) had appeared. Tycho Brahe (1546-1601), intending to reconstitute the Ptolemaic system, had recorded the position of the planets with precision, unaided by the invention of the telescope; Johannes Kepler (1571-1630) was determining the elliptic orbit of these planets by mathematical analysis; and in the very moment that Fray García was symbolizing medieval authoritarianism in Mexico, Galileo Galilei (1564-1642) was making the first use of the telescope, invented in 1608, to demonstrate the validity of the Copernican theory. This positive refutation of age-long assumptions of cosmology was a threat to authority and, in 1616, it moved the Church belatedly to place the Copernican treatise on the Index of Prohibited Works. And even before this Giordano Bruno (1548-1600) was burned at the stake for his belief in the plurality of worlds and populated planets.

As the seventeenth century advanced, startling discoveries in other fields shook orthodox conceptions. William Gilbert (1540-1603) had made systematic observations of the phenomenon of magnetism; William Harvey (1578-1657) demonstrated the circulation of blood; Robert Boyle (1627-1691) would contribute laws of chemistry and gaseous pressures; and Marcello Malpighi (1628-1694) and others would make important findings through the microscopic analysis of living organisms.

Even more direct threats to the older methodology would create tension and harden conservative resistance. In 1605 Francis Bacon (1561-1626), after subjecting medieval science to a close scrutiny, branded it "contentious learning." René Descartes (1596-1650) was still a boy when Fray García was parading his scholastic erudition and watching his bullfights in Mexico City, but this Frenchman, in his *Discourse on the Method of Rightly Conducting the Reason and Seeking for Truth in the Sciences* (1637), would presently deal a body blow to the dialectical verbalism that had carried the Spanish Dominican to such heights of power. And still later the great English mathematician, Isaac Newton (1642-1727), carrying forward Descartes' work, would wreck beyond repair the remaining underpinnings of the medieval world view represented by the Archbishop-Viceroy of Mexico.

As the spiritual, intellectual, and social solidarities of Europe melted in the heat of revolutionary changes, the conservatism of the Catholic South hardened into a reactionary intransigence. Spain, which had become a mighty empire under the sixteenth century Hapsburgs, assumed the role of champion of orthodoxy, and its rulers took an uncompromising stand on the side of traditionalism. This resolute attitude dominated the Council of Trent and set the tone of the Counter Reformation, thus defeating the hope of reconciliation with the Protestant North. The enormous extent of the Spanish empire, scattered over the Old and New Worlds like a sprawling league of nations, seemed to point clearly to a universal hegemony under Hispanic auspices as the divine plan. The large populations threatened by heresy in Europe and awaiting the illumination of Christian doctrine in America were clearly a trust which Providence had bestowed exclusively on the peoples of the Spanish Peninsula. Christianity must be restored to its pristine state on the one hand and, on the other, diffused in its purest form. There could be no temporizing with heterodoxy at home or abroad and hence free inquiry, which had enjoyed relative immunity during the early sixteenth century in Spain, was soon halted. The desperate fear of heretical infection was unhappily withdrawing doctrine after doctrine in both natural and moral philosophy from the possibility of rational proof and relegating them to the sphere of unquestioned dogma. Simple belief and the complete acceptance of authority in every field of thought made for righteousness in the Hispanic view, and they offered the best guarantee of salvation. "In the seventeenth century you do not breathe a 'normal' air of belief," observes a modern Spanish scholar, "but, rather, something like an oxygen of faith."[1]

In this situation ideas, whether secular or religious, were carefully screened in Spain and excluded, as far as possible, from the New World so as to protect the incompletely Christianized natives from contamination. Thus reason fell under the sway of rigid authority and conclusions reached through rational processes were predetermined; the initiative of thinkers was confined to formal details in the treatment of a thesis rather than to any revaluation of the thesis itself. Truth was accessible only through verbalistic methods of scholasticism, and knowledge acquired through the senses was unreliable and potentially dangerous. Under Spanish influence Catholic Europe was becoming stranded in the shallows of authoritarianism and ecclesiastical learning, while other parts of the Continent were slowly moving into the freer currents of experimentalism sweeping onward into modern science and technology.

In the New World realms the preservation of traditional thought was facilitated by a remoteness from Europe's turmoil and by a more solidified feudal pattern of society in which a small white minority dominated large populations of submissive Indians for whom ignorance increasingly appeared to be a blessing. However, for the intelligentsia of the Spanish Indies, the insulation from the changing world and the revolutionary ideas of Europe was much less hermetic than often asserted, and various American-born intellectuals during the course of the seventeenth century displayed a surprising familiarity with contemporary thought. But clearly the climate of opinion in those distant possessions was hardly propitious for overt dissenters from the traditional orthodoxy and scholasticism to which the motherland was passionately committed. Intellectual activity centered almost exclusively in the universities and seminaries of the colonial cities where a decadent neo-scholasticism prevailed and where thinkers of an experimental turn of mind were notably absent. Since this purely verbalistic rationalism dominated Hispanic intellectualism during the so-called Baroque period, and especially in the American realms, a brief description is appropriate.

Scholasticism was, of course, essentially ecclesiastical in origin and, as philosophy grew out of theology, the methods of the latter carried over into secular learning. The basic premise of scholasticism was that God was the source of all truth and that, in His wisdom, this truth, or portions of it, was divinely revealed to chosen individuals as the human agencies of transmission. Their writings were revelation and hence the final authority of all learning. As the product of God's inspiration, the writings of the Church Fathers were the highest court of appeal, and they were held to contain within themselves the refutation of any and every argument advanced by human reason. This concept of knowledge obviously stressed memory rather than rational powers, since the pages of these books afforded an answer to every question. Consequently, intellectual brilliance was manifested by dialectics and by a deftness in quoting authorities. Doctrinal matters were established by disputation and logic, and conclusions were reached by verbal rationalization—not by experimental demonstration perceived through the senses as in modern science. Intellectual activity, then, put stress on arguments based on memorized material from accepted sources. Thus, the supreme equipment for superior knowledge was a photographic memory and a dialectical skill in exploiting it. An impressive example of this kind of mental legerdemain is offered by a record of a prodigious feat performed publicly at the University of Mexico.

Having learned by heart the voluminous writings of St. Thomas Aquinas, a Dominican friar, Father Francisco Naranjo, conducted himself so brilliantly in a contest for a professorship in 1635 that he was induced to give a repeat performance before a "plenary session of learned Doctors, the students of the different faculties, the prebendaries of the Cathedral, and other ecclesiastics and members of different Orders as well as a large number of distinguished laymen, both military and civilian." Selecting at random four out of one hundred and fifty-four difficult questions drawn from a theological work, "He began by addressing a dissertation to the audience on four controversial points of theology which had fallen to him by lot, linking them up one to another with much grace, lucidity, distinction, and learning. He then proceeded to the second part of the test, dictating to four lay brothers, one after the other, four separate theses on the four points of theology, one passage at a time to each clerk, doing so without hesitation or mistake, as if he were dictating a single continuous thesis."[2] His ability to cite readily any appropriate passage from the vast work of St. Thomas Aquinas made possible this extraordinary feat "which seems beyond the powers of the human brain," and to his audience it demonstrated the highest form of cerebration that a mortal mind could achieve.

This neo-scholasticism, of which Father Naranjo gave such a prodigious exhibition, especially re-emphasized certain other peculiarities of the earlier scholasticism. In secular philosophy the writings of Aristotle were almost as infallible as the Holy Writ, and for more than three centuries the works of that ancient Greek reigned supreme in European thought, though the Schoolmen, as the exponents of scholasticism were called, failed to heed, especially in colonial Spanish America, their master's teachings with respect to the need of experimentation in seeking truth. Applying the same procedure to his writings as to theology, the Schoolmen accepted Aristotle as superior to all other pagan masters and the last word in varied fields of knowledge.

Chief among the tools of the scholastics, and virtually regarded as the exclusive method of argumentation, was the syllogism, and the conclusions obtained by this device were regarded as truth. The syllogism consisted of a major premise, a minor premise, and the conclusion deduced from them. An example will illustrate:

Major premise: No finite being is exempt from error.
Minor premise: All men are finite beings.
Conclusion: Therefore, no man is exempt from error.

Such rigid exercises in logic could lead to absurdities and, in time, inspired crude parodies. But scholasticism as a whole was not as sterile as this oversimplified discussion may suggest, though it lent itself to the excessive abuse evident in the striving for cleverness which beset the Baroque intellectualism of colonial Spanish America. It could and did sharpen the wits to the subtleties of expression, it gave rigorous training in logic, and it afforded valuable experience in deductive reasoning, though again in practice the end sought was too often a dazzling verbal dexterity. Its legacy, perhaps, is a predilection for florid rotundity and high-flown rhetoric, still discernible in much public oratory of modern Hispanic America, and in the general disposition, at least until recently, to cultivate philosophy and metaphysics in preference to natural and physical sciences.

In contrast to the more northerly parts of Europe the Hispanic people reacted to humanism by trying to reintegrate a medieval religiosity and science, but the end result was largely a blend of the two intellectual movements. A neo-scholasticism became the methodology of a neo-orthodoxy without diminishing the dilemma of Christendom. Medieval thinkers, for whom science was ancillary to theology, had endeavored to understand how the order of human

existence illustrated divine goodness; they sought to determine the
objectives, purposes, or final causes toward which things seemed to
be striving, but they made little effort to analyze physical conditions of existence, and a quantitative approach to the causes of behavior in matter appeared quite irrelevant. The vain quest of the
ultimate undertaken by medieval science yielded to the more mundane and feasible aims of humanism, and the effort to reinstate that
intellectual orthodoxy only restored considerable futility. The resulting frustration caused an unconscious substitution of the intellectual devices of scholasticism as ends in themselves and a
forsaking of the ultimate objectives.[3] The effect was a tendency to
shift from content to form, from ideas to details, to give new sanc-
tions to dogmas, to avoid issues, and to substitute subtlety of language for subtlety of thought; it served to repress rather than
liberate the human spirit, and to divert by spectacles, by overstate-
ment, and by excessive ornamentation. Such, in essence, was the
spirit of the so-called "Baroque Age" as manifested in the Hispanic
world.

There is some mystery about the origin of the term "Baroque,"
but it is generally agreed that it derives from a nonsense word by
which humanists of the Renaissance derided medieval scholasticism. In mockery of that early disputatiousness "Baroco" became a
synonym of confused and unclear thinking; later it assumed the
meaning of "decadent" and "in bad taste." Not until the nineteenth
century did the term acquire a more dignified usage as a historical
and technical designation applied successively to the arts and later
to a chronological period.[4] Few living in the "Baroque Age" had
ever heard the word, and probably no one applied it to his own time.
It is, in fact, an unsolicited gift of posterity needing labels to comprehend the stages of evolution through which pass the activities
of mankind.

In the long course of western history an alternation of conflicting
moods and divergent attitudes toward existence appears, each one
extending for varying lengths of time from centuries and generations to decades, or even shorter spans, and to these periods names
are subsequently bestowed. In retrospect perceptible oscillations appear in social, moral, and creative life between attitudes of intellectual restraint and emotional freedom, or between conformity or
nonconformity to self-imposed restrictions. Greek and Roman

antiquity, the Renaissance, and the so-called Neo-Classic eighteenth
century were eras noted for a tendency to abide by classic rules; the
Middle Ages, the Baroque period, usually associated with the seventeenth century, and the Romanticism of the nineteenth century
seem times of more uninhibited feeling.[5] This classification over-
simplifies, of course, since opposing tendencies operate at all times
to produce tension and conflict. Indeed, some epochs are distinguished more by paradox than consistency, and perhaps none so
much as the Baroque Age. Hence arise difficulties of comprehension and definition.

The chronological limits of the Baroque period are roughly set
from the mid-sixteenth to the mid-eighteenth centuries, reaching a
peak around the middle of the seventeenth. Its intensity was relatively brief in some parts of Europe, and elsewhere it was of much
longer duration. Closely linked with the Counter Reformation it
proved more durable in the south of the Continent. The Baroque
is described as "a continuous polemic on the Catholic way of life
with a mixture of the ideals of the Middle Ages and the Renaissance."[6] It is not surprising, therefore, that it lasted longest and its
manifestations were most extreme in the Hispanic world. "The
Baroque is Spain's true form and fulfillment," it has been said, and
indeed the passionate, individualistic genius of the Spaniard, reacting to historical circumstances, points to its truth.

That bizarre age witnessed the mystical exaltation of Santa
Teresa de Ávila and of St. John of the Cross expressed in classic
prose and verse and a sordid materialism set forth in the abundant
picaresque literature of the time. The excessive license in public
morals was paralleled by the asceticism of seared consciences, and
the intellectual strait jacket of neo-scholasticism accented the un-
fettered sway of emotion. Through medieval religiosity chaotic
feelings vented themselves in a fierce fanaticism which spawned an
arid dogmatism, an uncompromising intolerance, an implacable
persecution, and a degrading superstition. Through a degenerate
chivalry, a tawdry relic of the Middle Ages, an explosive fervor
fathered a morbid punctilio in personal relations and a specious
code of honor which prolifically begot vengeful feuds and murder-
ous duels. Baroque passion stimulated an urge to action, an obsession to wield power, and, from the deep recesses of the unconscious,
it conjured up an extraordinary vitality and a forward thrust of

energy which found no adequate outlet or satisfying release. Unlike the Promethean spark of the Renaissance, it was a vitality which denied life and expended itself in trivia. Having briefly experienced the emancipation of a fecund humanism, the distraught spirit now fell prey to a deep despondency on finding its medieval chains restored. Like Segismund in Calderón's famous play *Life's a Dream,* it pondered on whether the Renaissance vision of life, so fleetingly beheld, was but a dream. Thwarted impulses engendered a restlessness which sought relief from frustration by applying to the accepted verities of orthodox existence an ornamental patina worked in startling combinations of detail, in intricate patterns, in multicolored designs, and in complex arrangements. But these activities failed to ease tensions completely, and they allowed slight sense of fulfillment. Instead, they seemed to induce a vague *desengaño,* a brooding disillusionment which, in turn, provoked moods of pessimism and fatalism and a resurgence of the stoicism so profoundly embedded in the Hispanic psyche. There was a withdrawal within oneself, a closing of the frontiers to newer ideas, much as Spain was closing its geographical frontiers to the rest of Europe and retreating into tradition. And intimately associated with this essential negativism was a morbid concern with death and decay. In "a world of extreme contrasts, of arrogant magnificence and hopeless misery, of carnal indulgence and ecstatic asceticism,"[7] life was not real but a drama, a tragedy enacted upon a stage, a spectacle to be watched.

Yet this strange agitation, this peculiar disquiet, this frustrating dilemma underlying the Baroque attitude released a prodigious creativity in Spain and ignited a pyrotechnic display of artistic genius. A dazzling constellation of stars of the first magnitude emerged. The masterworks of Cervantes, Lope de Vega, Tirso de Molina, Quevedo, Góngora, Gracián, Velázquez, El Greco, and of many more rivaled the finest achievements of the Renaissance itself and made the early seventeenth century an artistic Golden Age. Indeed, the most famous literary work of all, *Don Quixote de la Mancha,* might not have come into being but for the profound preoccupations of the Baroque age in which it appeared. After the Council of Trent the anti-Platonic moralists censured the optimistic belief of humanists in the perfectibility of man. This utopian idea was contrary to the doctrine of original sin. But the genius of Cervantes fused these conflicting concepts into a synthesis formed by the contrasting figures of the Manchegan hidalgo and Sancho Panza.

Such triumphs of imagination, however, appear in retrospect like mountain peaks scattered about a monotonous plain of dense and tangled verbiage. The clarity of the Humanists surrendered to the Baroque pursuit of the less clear and the opaque, and the aesthetic techniques of *culteranismo* and *conceptismo* facilitated the desired obscurity of expression. The first achieved this result by involved syntax, words invented from Greek and Latin roots, and strained figures of speech, while the second, aiming at verbal economy, subordinated meaning to cleverness by ingenious antitheses, paradoxes, and word-play. These contrary currents fused in the Baroque style and shifted importance from content to form. Writing, like the plastic and pictorial arts, tended to become a crowded spectacle rather than a vehicle of thought, and the repressed vitality of the age produced a lush foliage which choked out much of the fruit of true inspiration. Excess energy expended itself chiefly in allegory of obscure symbolism and in an exaggerated verbalism, relieved now and then by savage satire. But the Baroque was a time-spirit with its own aesthetic and ethical canons and only within these, perhaps, can it be fairly judged.

When Fray García journeyed across the Atlantic to become a Prince of the State as well as of the Church he dramatically symbolized the transfer of the Baroque to the New World, and the viceroyalty, over which he presided, offered singularly propitious soil for the growth of the new spirit as the final grand flourish of feudalism. The sixteenth century fusion of Romanesque, Gothic, Renaissance and indigenous elements, particularly in architecture, had prepared the ground for Baroque innovations. If these were manifestations of a "time-spirit," it is more accurate to assert, perhaps, that they expressed a "time-spirit-place," for the exotic Baroque plant soon blossomed in the Spanish Indies into an amazing variety of regional species as the Indian and mestizo shoots were grafted upon it. "A full blooded Baroque spread to even the less accessible regions of Latin America," writes an art critic,[8] "and, with its vast register of variations, developed such regional expressions as the 'Andean Mestizo' and the 'Mexican poblano' style." This blending process in a relatively immobile society placed so indelible a stamp on Hispanic America that the Baroque pattern lingered long after the close of the colonial period and traces of it are visible today.

Numerous factors account for the comparative permanence of this culture and its medieval character. Spain's determination to isolate the American realms from European centers of infection, as already suggested, was aided by the immense distance of the seas and by the inland location of the important aggregations of population. All but the few inhabitants of the coastal towns were immune to the increasing attacks of Protestant pirates. Racial, linguistic, and cultural differences divided the elements of a feudal society in which a tiny European minority ruled as an aristocracy over a large primitive mass of aborigines hardly capable of comprehending the theological issues that had torn the Continent asunder. These oppressed natives retained much of the half-barbarous culture which contrasted sharply with the ultrarefinement that wealth and leisure permitted the governing class. The incomplete task of proselyting among the Indian charges of the crown allegedly justified an enormous staff of clergymen who, in turn, required innumerable churches, seminaries, and convents. Much wealth poured into the coffers of the Church, which exercised as pervasive an influence in the secular affairs of these overseas realms as its parent organization had in the Middle Ages of Europe. Besides economic and political power the riches at its disposal enabled this institution to be the patron of the arts, particularly of architecture in which the Baroque fervor was most clearly manifest. Thus a neomedieval regime had emerged, and it survived as an anachronism in which, it seemed, theology could prevail over history. The Indian majority had, in fact, lost its historical past, while the mixed elements resulting from racial fusion had not yet made any history. Only the small European minority could have an active role in the historical process, but even the participation of this group was severely restricted by the reactionary policies of the motherland. Hence, in a community of such social and cultural immobility, the Baroque vitality could only develop deeper tensions and frustration, particularly when bitter jealousies and rivalries divided the dominant white elements. To win favors in this static society the Creole, or the American-born Spaniard, was obliged to cloak his bitter resentment in a hypocritical adulation of the more privileged class, the

European-born Spaniard, and, in an unsatisfying dilettantism, he often frittered away his talents on pageant-like ceremonies, ceremonious functions, and versified panegyrics designed to flatter its vanity. These false and artificial exercises readily carried the Baroque emphasis on form to its most extreme manifestations.[9]

Thus it is that the brief career and varied experience of Fray García in the viceroyalty of New Spain epitomize the Baroque age in the distant realms of Spanish America. Embodying the absolute power of a combined Church and State, this Peninsular Spaniard came in medieval pomp and splendor to rule a kingdom as Archbishop-Viceroy. From the moment of his arrival at Vera Cruz to his entombment in the Cathedral of Mexico City he was the object of the theatrical adulation of his subjects in every form of colorful pageantry and exaggerated ceremony. The passion for drama in public spectacles almost reached a delirium in the macabre magnificence of the funeral obsequies. And the morbid recital of the progressive disintegration of the ailing ecclesiastical potentate, and the meticulous description of the autopsy performed on his cadaver written by a celebrated author of the time, all testify to the pathological concern with death and decay that preoccupied the Baroque mind. Similarly typical of this spirit is the juxtaposition of Fray García's excessive alms-giving and his sensual excitement in the sanguinary spectacle of the bull ring; of his great piety in religious practices and his keen delight in secular music and the pleasures of the palate; of his devotion to his ecclesiastical duties and his insatiable ambition for secular power; and of his position at the pinnacle of his world and his restless *querer más* or vague yearning for still loftier heights. Likewise suggestive of Baroque feeling is the strange coincidence of accidental injury and death and of ominous natural phenomena occurring at proud moments of glory which seemed to confirm its superstition, fatalism, and negativism. In all these aspects of the Archbishop-Viceroy's career the shadow rather than the substance prevails, and form, with its infinite profusion of detail, appears to obliterate the underlying reality. Such were the elements of the spiritual and intellectual climate of the New World centers of Hispanic civilization even long after the seventeenth century had vanished into the mists of the past.

Those years in which Fray García was sealing the triumph of the Counter Reformation in Mexico and setting the tone of its

Baroque age were, as earlier noted, of increasing political complexity in a changing Europe. It was a moment of uneasy lull in the stormy decades of war and disorder that had wracked the Continent in the sixteenth century and would soon resume in the holocaust of the Thirty Years' War and the subsequent clashes of rising nationalism. Hardly comprehending the revolutionary alterations already in movement, the chancellories of Europe were haunted by a sense of impending doom. From Spain the Netherlands had finally wrung a truce in 1609 which recognized the success of Holland's struggle for independence and enabled the Dutch to seize a commanding place in European affairs. This little nation was even beginning to threaten the Caribbean approaches to the Spanish empire in America. In England the wily Queen Elizabeth had recently died, and the first of the Stuart dynasty was pursuing a policy of appeasement with the weakening monarchy of Spain. Across the Channel in France the assassination of the absolutist Henry IV in 1610 frustrated his "Grand Design" for a federal unification of Europe to replace the vanished medieval unity. A feudal reaction weakened centralizing tendencies until Richelieu and Mazarin would organize the "modern state absolute," destined to elevate France to a great continental power. The loose aggregation of principalities composing the Holy Roman Empire of the Hapsburgs had virtually shrunk to the Germanies, and these weak entities were grouped in a series of alliances called the Protestant Union and the Catholic League. The devastation of the Thirty Years' War would soon insure the liquidation of the medieval concept of imperial organization to which Spain obstinately clung. In Italy the Pope, Paul V, stimulated by Cardinal Bellarmine's theory of papal sovereignty, was vigorously asserting the temporal authority of the Papacy against violations of ecclesiastical jurisdiction committed by the Italian republics. Far to the north, in the Baltic region, the ascendancy of Sweden under Gustavus Adolphus was about to get underway, and deep in Eastern Europe, and almost unnoticed, Russia was beginning to emerge from its "time of troubles." In 1613 a grand-nephew of Ivan the Terrible ascended the throne as the first Romanov.[10]

Externally Spain still appeared a powerful and splendid empire despite the successive defeats of the Armada, the deadlocked struggle in France, and the humiliating armistice in the Netherlands. But internally continuous wars, emigration, and withdrawal to monasteries had depleted its manpower and bled the nation white. Materially it was nearly bankrupt. Its weak, vacillating, and bigoted monarch, Philip III, lacked the stern resolution of his father and willingly he delegated his rule to the first of a series of irresponsible favorites who would speed the Spanish people to ruin. The martial qualities of the Spaniards no longer sufficed to maintain an imperial hegemony over a Europe visibly moving from medievalism to a new political and social order. Inflexibly arrayed on the side of religious orthodoxy and tradition, Spain's leaders failed to muster the still tremendous resources of the empire even to bolster the reactionary policies to which they were irrevocably committed. As Brooks Adams later wrote: "[The Spaniards] never emerged from the imaginative period, they never developed the economic type, and in consequence they never centralized as the English centralized. Even as early as the beginning of the seventeenth century this peculiarity had been observed, for the Duke of Sully remarked that with Spain the legs and arms are strong and powerful, but the heart is infinitely weak."[11]

Even as Fray García seemed to personify the unassailable might of the neomedieval Spanish system to the inhabitants of New Spain and to give assurance of the secure isolation of that realm, a great era of European expansion was already threatening Hispanic holdings in the Western Hemisphere. Holland, France and England were openly flaunting the Spanish theory of *mare clausum* which claimed for itself the exclusive possession of all western lands washed by the Atlantic. These rivals were boldly asserting the conflicting right of ownership based on effective occupation. By seizing islands of the West Indies and footholds in Guiana and Brazil the Dutch were threatening to make the Caribbean a Dutch sea. On the north mainland Hollanders settled in the Hudson Valley, and in 1614 founded New Amsterdam, the later day New York. In time they pushed southward to imprint their personality on the countryside of later Pennsylvania. Meanwhile, they were effectively relieving the Portuguese of their richest possessions in the East Indies.

Still farther north on the American mainland Samuel de Champlain, who had allegedly visited Vera Cruz at the turn of the century, was reconnoitering the St. Lawrence Valley region and strengthening the foundations of New France in the following decades. And no less active were the English who, just before Fray García's arrival in Mexico, had planted a feeble colony at Jamestown, and others soon followed in New England. Of more immediate danger to Spanish supremacy were the footholds gained by the English in Bermuda and in the Caribbean area. The neomedieval society of New Spain was but dimly aware of these perils, which, as the seventeenth century advanced, would grow more serious and deepen the vague anxiety and disquiet that haunted the inhabitants of the realm.

Such, briefly, were the circumstances that the pomp and pageantry of Fray García's few years and those following sought to conceal from the subjects of the Spanish crown. Resolutely fixing its gaze on the past, the Hispanic world contrived an illusory stability in a changing universe. For the moment it seemed to succeed, for those were "the sultry years of precarious power"[12] in Europe offering a short interval of equilibrium before accumulating forces precipitated the downward course of peoples dedicated to preserving the old. As inevitable defeat slowly overtook its dream of a neomedieval unity the Court at Madrid blinded itself to reality in the refulgent splendor of the Baroque art and letters created by the amazingly fecund genius of the nation. And even longer, if less brilliantly, Mexico City and other viceregal capitals of the New World would preserve the illusion possessing the motherland, thanks to the latter's protection, to the precariously maintained isolation, and to the rich silver mines that fed their economy. In the intricacy and profusion of a Baroque pattern the frustrated dynamism of Old and New Spain alike found its most enduring expression in life and thought.

✕ III

A BAROQUE SOCIETY

IT WAS the inhabitants of New Spain who offered the most vital expression of the Baroque complexity of their time and place. From the very beginning of Spanish rule a stratified society developed, the ethnic roots of which reached back to Asia through the Indians, to Africa through the Negroes, and to Europe through the Spaniards. The existence of these disparate elements side by side and the inevitable fusion resulting from association soon produced a strange ethnic conglomerate of almost kaleidoscopic diversity. Within this unequal partnership arose a complex system of tensions between men, colors, classes, and races that in ". . . all this inner unsteadiness, seething within a world kept in a thrice secular peace and security from European wars, everything contributed to make the soul of the Indies something strange and rare, almost unique in the annals of the human spirit."[1]

If profusion of detail and hierarchy are among the typical characteristics of the Baroque, they were increasingly present in the ethnic composition of the neomedieval communities of the New World. As the seventeenth century advanced Hispanic civilization sank its roots so deeply in the Spanish American soil that its patterns are discernible three centuries later. Ever more intricate did the constellation of class and caste grow as a prolific miscegenation progressed. And the very fluidity of this ethnic process, which was creating entirely new human species, helped to insure the stability of a neomedieval order. The multiplicity of racial types emerging from a sort of Baroque melting pot gave a sociological expression of

37

the political maxim "divide and rule" to which Spanish policy was securely wedded. By diligently fostering a kind of "pigmentocracy," with caste distinctions based largely on the amount of white blood in an individual's veins, the possibility was slight that sufficient cohesion might develop among the exploited masses to tempt them to challenge the control of the privileged white minority. But a closer scrutiny of the components of this Baroque society is in order.

The basic racial elements, as already indicated, were American, African, and European, together with resulting mixtures. Within each of these groups, however, social and psychological differences tended to compound mutual antagonisms, though prejudice stemmed much less from differences of pigment than in the English and French colonies. Blood played a part in determining position in the Spanish American hierarchy, but antipathies sprang more from the social discrimination maintained by rigid barriers which persons of color occasionally scaled. Though the Indian was the original and numerically the largest element of this New World cosmos, his lowly status in the social organism suggests a more inverted approach to the discussion by considering first the dominant white minority.

All too often the term "Spaniard" implies a collective identity, or a fairly precise national type. It is usually assumed that all individuals so designated have, in general, a common appearance, psychology, and language that give them a recognized national pattern. While such simplification is at all times hazardous, it is peculiarly unsafe when applied to the highly individualistic peoples of the Spanish Peninsula, particularly when nationalism itself was still in swaddling clothes. Shaped into more or less isolated compartments by its irregular topography and moulded by historical circumstances, Spain has long been characterized by a regionalism so pronounced as to endow its inhabitants with striking contrasts of temperament, appearance, and language. The gay Andalusian of the south, the sober Castilian of the central north, the laborious Gallician of the northwest, the enterprising Catalan of the east, the alien, industrious Basque of the northeast, are all "Spaniards" who present traits of character, psychology, and speech so diverse and so dissimilar as to form distinct peoples. This almost Baroque profusion of ethnic detail among the Peninsulars has played a part in retarding national unification in Spain down to the present time.

Owing to the celebrity of Cortés, Alvarado, Pizarro, and many other conquistadors, together with a certain similarity of the Spanish spoken in America to that in Andalucía, a belief was long current that the conquerors and early settlers came almost exclusively from southern Spain. This theory is no longer tenable, particularly when applied to the Baroque seventeenth century. While the men who accompanied Columbus on his first two voyages were probably all from Andalucía, as early as 1506 it was plainly evident that, politically at least, the Aragonese were dominant in Hispaniola, or Santo Domingo. Early chronicles and passenger lists indicate that about forty-two per cent of the emigration was from the southern region of the Peninsula. Nearly an equal percentage came from Castile; the balance originated in other parts of Spain bordering on these central provinces, including Portugal, the Balearic and Canary islands.[2] This early preponderance of Castilians and Andalusians is explained by the monopoly exercised by Castile from the outset in the affairs of the Indies. It is unfortunate, perhaps, that this policy tended to restrict the migration of Basques, Galicians, and Catalans whose thrift and industry admirably equipped them for the task of developing economically the new colonies. But well before the seventeenth century these restrictions were so far relaxed that immigration in the New World represented a cross section of the peoples of Spain.

So strong were linguistic bonds and provincial affinities of these groups, however, that they tended to reproduce in the New World much of the regionalism of the mother country by congregating in certain localities and in *barrios* or districts of the larger towns and cities. In the new environments old world jealousies and antagonisms acquired renewed vitality, occasionally exploding into open feuds and violent clashes attended by loss of life.[3] These enmities were visible even in the military phase of the Conquest. When the troubled Aztec monarch, Montezuma, held captive by Cortés, was informed that other Spaniards under Narváez had come to arrest his captor, he was doubtless puzzled by the explanation offered him. ". . . We came from Castile itself, which is called Old Castile, and we called ourselves Castilians, and the Captain (Narváez), who was now at Cempoala, and the people he had brought with him, came from another province, named Biscaya and they called themselves Biscayans, and spoke like the Otomis of this land of Mexico."[4] This last phrase clearly implied that the Basque language used by Narváez' followers was as outlandish as the Indian language mentioned was to Montezuma. These festering antipathies of Spanish regionalism brought much dissension and disunity among the dominant whites throughout the colonial era, including the religious communities in which the particularism of the old country was occasionally stronger than the vows of Christian brotherhood.

The frequent absence of cordiality among Spaniards of different provincial origin was only one of the discords afflicting the relations of the ruling classes. Even more widespread and vehement was the disaffection traceable to differing official status and social strata. The top administrative and judicial posts were uniformly reserved for Court favorites of the King in Madrid, and many of the lesser offices of a swollen colonial bureaucracy went to Peninsular-born individuals by appointment or, as the financial affairs of the Hapsburgs worsened, by purchase irrespective of merit. Each viceroy usually arrived with a populous retinue of servants, relatives, friends, and hangers-on for whom sinecures were procured or the acquisition of choice property was facilitated. The bait of a title, or the prestige accruing from the mere fact of being European-born, enabled many Spaniards in impecunious circumstances to contract marriages with daughters of wealthy families who willingly bestowed fabulous dowries. Not all new arrivals were so fortunate, and the failure to fulfill similar anticipations left them singularly incapable of admiring the luckier ones. But even more bitter was the resentment of the American-born descendants of the conquistadors and first settlers called Creoles. With envy and anger they saw the fruits of the blood, sweat, and swords of their ancestors consumed by haughty adventurers and newly powerful parvenus. The get-rich-quick philosophy of this parasitic upperclass inevitably poisoned the relations of the dominant whites, and the comparatively small minority of Europeans and American-born burned with passionate feelings of hostility and contempt.

The futile efforts of Hapsburg Spain to check the tide of heterodoxy in Europe by endless wars were destroying its solvency and depopulating its fields. The drain on manpower was not caused by the armies alone, but by the emigration of the more energetic of the humbler classes who, increasingly in the seventeenth century, poured into the Indies. These immigrant peasants and artisans frequently began life in the new environment as itinerant peddlers and small tradesmen. By dint of industry and frugal habits they often amassed a small fortune in a relatively short time. Though many were nearly illiterate and possessed none of the social graces, their thrift and stability, added to a European origin, gave them a certain luster in the eyes of the American-born Spanish women who found their own men much too fickle and irresponsible. Occasionally these *nouveaux riches* of male persuasion presumed on these favors and contracted unions which brought down upon them and their offspring the wrath of relatives with aristocratic pretensions but often of less pure white blood. Where marriages of daughters of genteel families in reduced circumstances to prosperous humble immigrants from Spain took place, the common effect was to produce rancorous antipathies which turned children against parents and cousin against cousin.

If upper-class Spaniards from the Peninsula often gained material and social advantages by favoritism and nepotism, and humbler representatives of the master race prospered through diligence and the better opportunities of the New World, many individuals in both categories were less successful. These self-proclaimed *hidalgos,* who had not found fortune or favor with the powerful, were little disposed to remedy matters by exerting themselves in useful occupations. Their scorn of manual labor and of trades soon reduced them to roving vagabonds on the highways or to loafers, ne'er-do-wells, pickpockets, and the like on the streets and squares of the larger towns and cities—the New World *picaros* of contemporary literary fame in Spain. These renegade Spaniards wandered about the countryside preying upon the browbeaten Indians and mixed elements, and it was their common practice to note some particularly desirable piece of land for a farm, ranch, or millsite held by an Indian community and report its existence to an influential official or member of the viceroy's retinue. The luckless natives were soon deprived of their property by forced sale at a mere pittance while the knavish Spaniards received an acceptable commission for their dubious services.[5]

In the cities these disreputable whites often became leaders in the dark underworld of half-caste, Indian, and Negro criminals and perverts. Still other unregenerate Spaniards resembled outcasts

later called "beachcombers." Both species were termed *zaramullos*
in the seventeenth century, and a contemporary Mexican writer
describes them as "knaves, rascals, and cape-snatchers [who], in
falling away from their [white] allegiance, are the worst of all in
such a vile rabble."[6] The habitués of local dives and *pulquerías,*
they were ever ready to incite the wretched Indians, Negroes, and
miscegenated masses to riots and tumults, and take advantage of
such upheavals to loot and plunder the shops and homes of countrymen.

The most profound and enduring cleavage among the dominant
white classes was undoubtedly between those born in Spain and
those born of Spanish parentage in America. The latter, called
Creoles, had appeared on the New World scene before the sixteenth century conquistadors had finished their work, and within a
generation they formed a well-defined type acutely sensitive and
continually afflicted by feelings of inferiority. Though it is often asserted that the first conquerors, having left their wives at home in
Spain, quickly consorted with women of the vanquished Indians
and produced a hybrid race, it is clearly evident that white representatives of the feminine sex were by no means absent in the stormy
days of conquest and early settlement. Hence, a generation of
American-born Spaniards promptly emerged upon the scene to receive, in due course, the originally unflattering designation by
which they are known.

The repressed feeling of this class, frequently exacerbated by the
condescension of the Peninsulars, remained one of the most deep-
seated of the Baroque tensions afflicting colonial society, and ultimately it resulted in secession from the Spanish empire. The hated
gachupines, as the European Spaniards were dubbed, deliberately
excluded the Creoles from the higher and more remunerative offices
of the viceregal State and Church, and permitted them only subordinate roles in their own government. This discrimination was,
in part, a calculated policy of the Spanish crown which feared
separatist tendencies in the overseas realms, and also, in part, because it needed to appease importunate office-seekers swarming
about the royal Court at Madrid. It rationalized this injustice by
embracing the popular belief that the climate and environment of
the New World had an enervating effect on children born of Europeans there. These offspring, it was assumed, matured early in a

sort of "rotten ripe" fashion, and quickly entered upon a physical and mental decline which, of course, clearly disqualified them for the heavy responsibilities of high office. Few, indeed, were the American-born whites appointed viceroys, archbishops, and judges of the higher tribunals during the three colonial centuries.

This situation was naturally galling to the Creole, in the veins of whom flowed the undiluted blood of the proud hidalgo and often that of the first conquerors and settlers, and this imputed inferiority filled him with a loathing of the *gachupines* that he was compelled to veil. Denied an outlet for his talents and energies in his own government, and endowed with a fierce pride that regarded the countinghouse and factory as beneath the dignity of a gentleman, he too often turned to a life of indolence and outright vice. Frequently a member of the landowning aristocracy, he preferred to live as an absentee proprietor in the cities and larger towns where his vanity was equalled by his lofty ignorance. Other Creoles, who were virtually landless, strove to keep up the appearances and arrogance of the well-to-do. Thomas Gage described one of these types whom he professed to have seen in Chiapas, a southern province of Mexico, but it would seem that his inspiration was the pathetically vain Squire portrayed in the famous Spanish picaresque tale, *Lazarillo de Tormes.*

"And thus, Reader, by this Don Melchor's wit and ability would I have thee judge of the gentlemen Creoles or natives of Chiapa; and yet as presumptuous they are and arrogant as if the noblest blood in the Court of Madrid ran through their veins. It is a common thing amongst them to make a dinner only with a dish of frijoles in black broth, boiled with pepper and garlic, saying it is the most nourishing meat in all Indies; and after this so stately a dinner they will be sure to come out to the street-door of their houses to see and to be seen, and there for half an hour will they stand shaking off the crumbs of bread from their clothes, bands (but especially from their ruffs when they use them) and from their mustachios. And with their toothpickers they will stand picking their teeth, as if some small partridge bone stuck in them; nay if a friend pass by at that time, they will be sure to find out some crumb or other in the mustachio . . . . and they will be sure to vent out some non-truth, as to say: Ah Señor que linda perdiz he comido hoy, 'O Sir, what a dainty partridge have I eat today,' whereas they pick out nothing from their teeth but a black husk of a dry frijole or Turkey bean."[7]

Open to this Creole class were the professions of law, medicine and theology, but the majority was temperamentally unsuited to sustained intellectual effort and its ample leisure was rarely productive of more than a certain dilettantism and an unrestrained flow of bombastic verse. The neo-scholasticism of the Baroque age stimulated the shallow erudition and hollow verbalism in which some members of this group sought a compensatory superiority. But few escaped a deepening sense of frustration and a festering dislike of their fellowmen of whatever race or color.

Another sector of this neomedieval society, predominantly white though including persons of mixed blood and even Indians, was the clergy. Since the sixteenth century Conquest this ecclesiastical element had increased rapidly in number and influence as the Church grew more wealthy and powerful. The continued presence of a large body of pagan and half-Christianized natives appeared to justify the ever-enlarging staff of clergymen until, by the seventeenth century, they constituted a considerable fraction of the population. The Church's forces were divided into the secular priests entrusted with administering the Sacraments and preventing backsliding among the faithful, and the religious orders such as the Franciscans, Dominicans, Augustinians, Jesuits, and the like, upon whom devolved primarily the tasks of education and proselyting among the heathen. As the crusading fervor of the Conquest died away and as more settled conditions prevailed jurisdictional disputes and doctrinal differences tended to replace the earlier zeal of both groups of clergymen. The acquisition of lands and the existence of a labor supply in the docile neophytes and the Indian peasantry rapidly increased the Church's wealth, and multiplying monasteries and convents dotted the land, particularly in the more populous areas. These institutions in turn drew off a growing number of men and women from more productive pursuits and attracted a steady stream of clergymen from Spain, usually to the higher levels of the hierarchy. The number of priests, monks, and nuns became disproportionate to the needs of the New World society and a heavy drain upon its resources. Inevitably, the weight of this burden fell hardest upon the exploited Indian population.

When Fray García Guerra ruled as Archbishop-Viceroy of

Mexico the Franciscans were said to maintain one hundred and seventy-two monasteries and religious houses, the Augustinians ninety, and the Dominicans sixty-nine, to which were added those of the various other orders. In 1611 the excessive number of these establishments moved the Pope, Paul V, to issue a bull suppressing convents not occupied by at least eight friars, but little respect greeted this papal decree. Many of these institutions amassed large properties in lands and goods which enabled them to conduct highly profitable business ventures of a capitalistic character. It was this wealth that made possible the Baroque splendor of so many ecclesiastical edifices and the luxurious manner of living for so many of the expanding membership of the orders. These circumstances inevitably brought in their train a relaxation of monastic ideals, rules, and morals, notorious in the Baroque age and later.

It is, perhaps, a little questionable to summon again the apostate Thomas Gage to give evidence on conditions in seventeenth century Mexico, particularly on matters relating to clergymen, yet undoubtedly his *New Survey of the West Indies* contains much truth. In relating his journey inland from Vera Cruz around 1625 he professes to be shocked by the gambling, drinking, and the profanity of the mendicant friars in the Franciscan monastery at Jalapa where he was a temporary guest. Especially horrifying to him was the hypocrisy of a monk playing cards with his confreres. "Though formerly he had touched money," wrote the scandalized Gage, "and with his fingers had laid it to the stake on the table, yet sometimes to make the company laugh, if he had chanced to win a double vie . . . then would he take the end of one sleeve of his habit and open wide the other broad sleeve, saying: I have vowed not to touch money, nor keep any . . . but my sleeve may touch it, and my sleeve may keep it."[8]

The Baroque age witnessed much constructive missionary activity on the frontiers of New Spain and in the founding of schools; still other endeavors testified to the zeal of the clergy. Unhappily these positive contributions were more than counterbalanced by a moral laxity and a parasitism afflicting many religious establishments. Throughout Spanish America, as in Spain itself, the rules of many monastic orders so far relaxed that numerous members lived outside convent walls and maintained illegal families and dependents in private houses.[9] Nunneries offered commodious refuge for large numbers of unmarriageable daughters who spent their lives in comfortable cells surrounded by conveniences and attended by personal servants and slaves. This idleness was not always conducive to the expected decorum, and permanent confinement sometimes brought antipathies into the open. Friction between inmates hailing from different provinces of Spain, between Peninsulars and Creoles, and between representatives of varied social classes not infrequently produced enough heat to flame into unseemly disturbances, and the quarrels over the election of priors and superiors often assumed such violent proportions that secular authorities of the State found it necessary to intervene. Particularly vexatious for the viceroys and their coadjutors were the rivalries of the religious orders who, with little of the otherworldly piety and concern suggested by their vows, jockeyed for power and preference in the affairs of the universities and even in more political agencies.

Still other human elements entered the white composite, increasing its diversity. Too readily is it assumed that the restrictive policies of the Spanish crown limited emigration to the colonies to approved nationals and excluded other Europeans. Records of licenses and permits issued to passengers embarking for the Indies plainly reveal the presence of Italians, Flemings, Germans, Austrians, Greeks, Irishmen, and even Dutchmen and Englishmen on Atlantic crossings of the merchant ships and galleons. As the Spanish Empire decayed, leaving its overseas possessions more vulnerable to piratical attacks, the king's ministers authorized the sending of skilled artisans, metallurgists, engineers, and other technicians, most of whom were aliens, to modernize fortifications and improve mining and other industries. Similarly, Italians, Flemings, Frenchmen and others, apparently more zealous for martyrdom in the frontier missions than either the Spanish or Creole clergymen, were subsidized for this purpose and sent to America. Spain's restrictive policy with respect to emigration stemmed from a religious rather than an antiforeign bias. Its essential requirement was that non-Spanish Europeans be orthodox Catholics.

If the number of authorized foreigners was fairly considerable, those entering without credentials of any sort were probably more numerous. Seaports such as Vera Cruz invariably harbored subjects of other nations who had deserted their ships, or were left by passing vessels. Though Spanish captains were severely enjoined to carry no unlicensed crewmen or passengers, and port officials were cautioned to prevent illegal entries, many undesirables, like forbidden books, found their way past these barriers and into the interior of the viceroyalties. Though now and then the net of the police-minded Inquisition ensnared them, many more remained inconspicuous in the heterogeneous population. Those who lingered in the seaports sometimes found themselves impressed as sailors in the returning fleets or in maritime expeditions fitted out for explorations.

Such extraneous elements were not always of European origin. Between the West Coast port of Acapulco and Manila in the Philippine Islands a freight and passenger service lasted for nearly two and a half centuries. The annual galleons plowing their tortuous course across the vast Pacific injected a slight admixture of Asiatic blood into the ethnic complexity of the Baroque society of Old Mexico. These clumsy crafts, sometimes the largest ships of the time, carried crews of Filipinos, Malays, and Chinese who, if they survived the arduous voyage of six or more months, settled somewhere along the coast or drifted into the interior to mingle with the varied inhabitants. Some brought technical skills useful to the economy. In commenting on the exquisite workmanship of the goldsmiths, Thomas Gage reports that: "The Indians, and the people of China that have been made Christians and every year come thither, have perfected the Spaniards in that trade."[10]

At the opposite extreme of the ethnic spectrum appeared the Negroes who, from the Conquest itself, had played an active role in the military and economic subjugation of the land. From the outset the Spaniards had displayed an enthusiasm for wealth with a minimum of labor and, as the Indians of the West Indies proved unsatisfactory workers, African slavery was introduced almost at once. Around 1441 the Portuguese had begun this traffic in human beings during their explorations along the Dark Continent, but it scarcely seemed likely to develop into a large-scale operation. The discovery of America and the opportunity offered by its rich soil to satisfy the newly whetted sweet-tooth of Europe by sugar cultivation soon placed a premium on Negro field hands. Even before the death of the discoverer of the New World the Spanish governor of the island of Hispaniola begged that no more Africans be shipped because many were escaping into the hills and joining the Indi-

ans.[11] Thus, almost coincident with the advent of the blackman in
the colonies, arose a menace that endured until final emancipation.
These fugitive slaves, called *cimarrones,* reverted to their tribal
ways, formed wilderness communities, and preyed upon the white
man's commerce.

The high mortality of West Indian workers in the mines and on
the plantations made the governor's protest ineffective and by 1510
the traffic had increased. Eight years later the Spanish crown permitted the shipping of 4,000 Negroes to the Caribbean area, and
by 1540 some 10,000 were imported annually into the mainland;
by the seventeenth century the total each year probably reached
75,000.[12] The year 1522 saw the first recorded Negro insurrection
when twenty blacks owned by Diego Columbus, son of the Discoverer, revolted and killed several of the outnumbered Spaniards
on Hispaniola.[13] But, almost at the same time, Africans were accompanying the conquistadors on their conquests of Mexico and
Peru as burden-bearers. In April, 1533, the Spanish king received
word that, within five months, more than six hundred whites and
four hundred black bondsmen had passed through Panama en
route to the former empire of the Incas, and Cortés' restless lieu-
tenant, Alvarado, also led an army to Quito in present-day Ecuador
which included two hundred Negro servitors.[14] As centers of
wealth and luxury developed in Mexico and elsewhere, Africans
became domestic servants and found their way into crafts and
trades. More enterprising, in general, than the fatalistic Indians,
they practiced ingenious forms of racketeering on the dominant
classes in the cities and large towns where they congregated in such
numbers as to cause profound anxiety among the white overlords.
But their economic contribution was great and their labor provided
the base of many fortunes made by their masters. The Negro's
talent for organization and leadership occasionally brought comparative prominence, while his gifts enriched the arts of music,
dance, folklore, sculpture, and carving.

Like the whites, the Negro also offered variations in the human
spectrum of a Baroque society. Just as the Europeans presented
shades from the alabaster whiteness of some Spanish women to the
dark swarthiness of Peninsular southerners, so the African varied
from jet black to the lighter tints of *café au lait.* Slave-trading activities had extended from the Senegal and Gambia rivers of the

African west coast to Guinea to the eastward and south to Angola, and the traders took captives from the Ashanti, Fanti, Minas, and Dahomean tribes of the Gold Coast and the Yoruba of Nigeria. These Negroes differed as much among themselves in temperament, skills, language, and pigmentation as did the whites, and among them existed vague castes of an undefined pattern. The third racial group, the Indian, was, of course, of fundamental importance sociologically. Despite recurring plagues and harsh exploitation which, in the early seventeenth century, had severely reduced the aboriginal population, it far outnumbered that of the Europeans. While the social structure of the remarkably advanced civilizations encountered by the Spaniards was largely crushed under the weight of the Conquest, representatives of the Indian nobility did retain some feudal rights and enjoyed a certain eminence. In the more thickly populated districts of the south, members of the conquered race were prosperous merchants. In this region Thomas Gage reports that: ". . . Indians live there who traffic to Mexico [City] and about the country with twenty or thirty mules of their own, chopping and changing, buying and selling commodities, and some of them are thought to be worth ten, or twelve, or fifteen thousand ducats, which is much for an Indian to get among the Spaniards . . ." He also describes a rich Indian in Chiapas with a title of Don, a fine stable of horses, and a mode of living as ostentatious as a Spaniard, who served as governor of a town.[15] But the lot of most Indians was clearly much less fortunate. Their status as a subjugated people tended to compress individual differences into a faceless mass and reduce them to a collective serfdom. Their sedentary nature included a certain passivity and fatalism which facilitated Spanish control and perpetuated a feudal relationship between conquerors and conquered, but these qualities enabled the Indians to preserve many of their characteristics which subtly affected the culture imposed upon them. Their artistic instinct served to enrich the complex patterns of Baroque expression, quietly imbuing them with a character distinct from the contemporary manifestations in Spain and, perhaps, accounting for the longer duration of this intricate style in Mexico and Spanish America generally.

On the outermost fringes of Spanish settlement roamed nomadic, warlike tribes little disposed to abandon a wild, free manner of living. Foiled in the efforts to vanquish these barbarous aborigines by swift, dramatic conquest, the Spaniards were obliged to engage in sporadic guerrilla warfare with these elusive foes. It was particularly aggravating because this resistance excluded the whites from regions which, though uninvitingly arid, might still fulfill their dreams of rich mines and sudden wealth. Courageous friars, with less materialistic motives, penetrated this forbidding hinterland to establish missions and reduce these fierce tribes to a Christian way of life. The seventeenth century witnessed heroic efforts of this sort in the far north and west, in New Mexico, Arizona, Lower California, Sinaloa and Sonora, but success was limited and the effect on the older settlements was negligible.

Where the ethnic pattern of colonial society acquired its most Baroque complexity was among its components of mixed blood. The association of white, red, and black races soon produced a strange conglomerate of humanity which included entirely new species of *homo sapiens*. This miscegenation coincided with the Conquest itself in the basic fusions of European and Indian, European and Negro, and Indian and Negro. By the time that the consolidation of Spanish civilization was giving the populous centers of New Spain a distinct character—and this was clearly visible by the end of the sixteenth century—the progressive mixing of diverse elements had created a veritable kaleidoscope of shades, complexions, and social castes. As time went on the pattern of old and new species became labyrinthine, almost defying analysis and forming a unique composite of human types, pigments, and psychology.

The generally enlightened laws promulgated by the Spanish crown took cognizance of this racial amalgamation by recognizing as prototypes the mestizos, offspring of Indian and white mating, mulattoes, and the *zambaigos* or *zambos*, as the products of Indian and Negro unions were called. But these were, of course, merely rudimentary combinations, and the lawmakers found the ensuing mixtures a bewildering problem of classification. Successive generations of crossbreeding created a confusing maze and a baffling system of nomenclature to identify each variation. Literally scores of designations were invented or applied to the different gradations of color and blood whose varieties taxed the resources of the language. Most of the names were based on shades of complexion, but other anatomical features, such as the shape of the nose, thickness or thinness of lips, body structure and the like, furnished inspiration.[16] Since these appellations were mostly bestowed by the dominant white castes they were intended to be humorous or downright insulting. The progeny of a *mestizo* couple, for example, was commonly called *tente en el aire* (suspended in the air), chiefly because it indicated no advance toward the white ancestry or no retrogression, as it was conceived, toward the Indian blood. If a *mestiza* woman married an Indian, the offspring might be called a *salta atrás* (a throwback) because the trend was toward the less-esteemed indigenous progenitor.

In the more intricate fluctuations of such advances and retreats of a mongrel population, and especially in mixtures in which Indian and Negro blood was dominant, the names bore connotations of scorn, contempt, mockery, and sneers. *No te entiendo* (I don't get you), for example, was the offspring of a *tente en el aire* and a mulatto woman, while an *Ahí te estás* (there you are) was the child of a *mestiza* mother and a *coyote* father, who, in turn, was the product of the union of a *mestizo* and an Indian.[17] Appellations of a zoological origin were deliberately derogatory such as: mule, coyote, wolf, cow, and the like. Each country, and even regions, had names of its own for the multitudinous mixtures, and a given designation might be used for a different combination of genes. The heterogeneous nature of this large segment of society is abundantly clear, a condition accentuated by a confusing array of castes into which it divided. Mutual jealousy and lack of cohesion kept this proletarian mass asunder as similar negative impulses did the more privileged groups, which fact largely explains why the restiveness of these overseas subjects of Spain, occasionally evident, was not translated for centuries into active opposition to the crown's authority.

Social position, based mainly on white blood, determined to a considerable extent the occupation of the individual in the more genteel pursuits, with idleness preferred, particularly in Creole circles. The large hybrid population, with its own complex hierarchy, had callings suited to its varying status. The upper strata with preponderant white blood were scarcely distinguishable from the Creoles or humbler Europeans and might pass as such; the lower approached the lowly condition of the Indians and Negroes and shared much the same destiny. The *mestizo* tended to find a place at the top of the mixed groups; in the sixteenth century the Spaniards accorded him paternal treatment. As his number increased a larger measure of discrimination was his lot—this prejudice often sprang from his "illegitimacy" and was more political and economic than ethical. It was, perhaps, a by-product of the hostile feeling in Spain for the remaining *Moriscos* and the mistrust of the so-called "new Christians" common in the days of the Counter Reformation. The military profession still remained one of the most honored in the contemporary culture, and the *mestizo* could find a place in it. The term "Spaniards," so frequently used in the reports of campaigns against pirates and the Indians on the frontiers, mostly referred to persons of diluted white blood. The trades and crafts were also open to this group, though usually the more menial tasks. The Indians were early taught such practical pursuits and might engage in these activities as well but, in the main, like the Negroes, they found themselves in the *obrajes* or the sweatshops of textile manufacture, in domestic service, or condemned to the hard work of agriculture and the heavy labor of the mines—slaves in fact though not in theory.

The misery and utter ignorance of this variegated and exploited proletariat were extreme. Their neglect and superstition made them a ready prey to a swarm of sorcerers and quacks who practiced magic rites and the black arts inherited from African and Indian barbarism. Faith in witchcraft, illuminati, animism, omens, charms, astrology and the occult flourished in all castes and classes, including the dominant whites. Baroque, indeed, does this profusion of ethnological detail, intricate hierarchy, and superstitious credulity of a New World society appear in retrospect during the "long siesta of the seventeenth century"!

✺ IV

LITERARY MIGRANTS

AS THE Baroque age lengthened, the culture and civilization of Old and New Spain tended to resemble each other more closely. But there were also sharp contrasts. While futile wars, an unbalanced economy, fiscal bankruptcy, and irresponsible monarchs and their favorites were depleting the manpower and irretrievably ruining the Spanish nation, a settled order was developing in the Mexican realm where, comparatively speaking, peace and tranquility flourished despite the coincidence of a part of the "century of depression."[1] Remote from the bloody conflicts devastating Europe and with an economy achieving greater equilibrium between mining, agriculture, and artisan crafts, Old Mexico, despite the ever-increasing taxation to support the follies of the Spanish crown, was enjoying a measure of prosperity that permitted refinement and luxury for many of the white minority, and tolerable conditions for at least some of the masses. It is hardly strange, then, that these trans-Atlantic domains beckoned Peninsular Spaniards, nobles and plebians alike, as a land of opportunity. Already, before the seventeenth century began, Cervantes had written that the New World was a "refuge and haven of all the poor devils of Spain." Though emigration often proved disillusioning, it was also "an incomparable remedy for the few." One of the more pragmatic minds of Mexico City wrote, in 1604: "It happens that the majority of the people coming to these parts are fetched by poverty and necessity. As this realm has been and is," he went on, "by God's mercy rich, fertile and abundant, those who come and wish to apply

53

themselves industriously are able to get an honest living by very modest effort . . ."[2]

Among the Spaniards hoping to better their lot by emigration were writers, artists, and thinkers of which Spain, in its political and moral decline, produced an astonishing array. An unknown number merely contemplated this solution of their problems, others made brief sojourns, a few wandered widely over the New World in a restless quest, and a smaller number found permanent abode there. Cervantes himself had applied vainly for a variety of posts in the overseas realms, and even the great mystic, Saint John of the Cross, was preparing to depart for the same destination when death barred the way. Other men of letters, including two dramatists, Juan de la Cueva (1550?-1610) and Tirso de Molina (1583?-1648), and a witty writer, Eugenio de Salazar (1530?-1608?), actually spent varying numbers of years in the new lands. Now and then an artist added his permanent presence to the influence his imported works were exerting on the Baroque culture of New World centers. The existence of material wealth, a privileged aristocracy, a strong feudal tradition, and a viceregal court even rivaling that of Madrid in opulence and located in such splendid isolation, all provided a propitious atmosphere for the perpetuation of the neomedieval ideals of the Counter Reformation, and an attractive environment for economically-harassed writers.

For the native-born in these seemingly favorable conditions, however, inhibiting factors hampered the lush growth of genius so notably present in contemporary Spain. If the orthodoxy of the Peninsula was rigid under the threat of heretical doctrines abroad on the Continent, it was scarcely less so in the overseas centers surrounded by pagan, or partially Christianized Indians. Moreover, the ruling whites there grappled with a profound sense of inferiority which reduced artistic expression to a servile imitation of the models of the motherland. Almost nowhere did local works compete in genius with those of Spain, though considerable originality appeared in Baroque architecture, design, and related manifestations. But if no colonial work of art equals the supreme achievements of the Peninsula, now and then one rivaled the products of the secondary creators of the homeland.

From the collapsing economy of Spain the pleasure-loving monarchs rescued sufficient resources to maintain a luxurious court at

Madrid which attracted and held most of the first-rate creative spirits of the so-called Golden Age. One of the major writers, and chief rival of Cervantes, however, sought to remedy his fortunes by a permanent transfer of residence to Old Mexico. This figure was the dyspeptic author of the celebrated picaresque tale, *Guzmán de Alfarache* (1599), Mateo Alemán, who arrived on the Mexican shore in 1608 to pass his few remaining years. The popularity of his long novel and its sequel probably helped to destroy the age-long enthusiasm for the adventurous romances of chivalry quite as much as did *Don Quixote,* and Alemán's narrative of low life long remained a "best seller" along with Cervantes' masterpiece. If the Archbishop-Viceroy, Fray García Guerra, in the entourage of whom Mateo Alemán formed an intimate part, seemed the active incarnation of the Baroque *zeitgeist* in his sensate love of pomp and splendor, his *querer más,* and his morbid preoccupations, the Spanish writer arriving with him left a more enduring record of the more passive characteristics of the Baroque attitude—pessimism, frustration, and *desengaño,* or disillusionment.

Guzmán de Alfarache is a rambling, humorless tale of the sordid adventures of a runaway lad on the highways of Spain and Italy and in the underworld of their cities. Each incident enables the author to expatiate on the evilness of human nature which he finds singularly corrupt. Hatred and disgust of life exude from its often dreary pages written, however, in a lean, repressed style that, somehow, possesses a strangely moving power. Clearly it spoke to the Baroque generations of the Hispanic world who read it avidly, to judge by its many editions. Its sixty chapters, amply padded with tedious moralizing, make it almost seem, as a critic expresses it, "a dissertation upon original sin"[3] in a wicked and hostile world from which man's corrupted nature can only be redeemed by conversion and submission to the Church. In fictional form it seemed to express, with extraordinary fidelity, the prevailing philosophy of the Counter Reformation Catholic world which explains, perhaps, the ecclesiastical approval of the novel and its wide circulation. Though Alemán did not initiate the picaresque genre—the short, masterly *Lazarillo de Tormes* had done so nearly a half century before—his *Guzmán de Alfarache* most completely assembled all the characteristics of this type of fiction. It ushered in the seventeenth century vogue of similar novels which, in varying ways, reaffirmed the Baroque pessimism regarding human existence. So it was that Old Mexico harbored in his last obscure years one of the most influential writers of Spain's great literary age.

The years 1547 and 1616 may well form a parenthesis of exceptional significance in the history of the Spanish novel, for they represent exactly the life span of the creator of *Don Quixote*. With less certainty, but offering a tempting coincidence, those years may also mark the bounds of Mateo Alemán's existence. The birth date appears to be correct but that of his demise requires a question mark. Neither the time nor place of his death is known, though presumably he died in Mexico. Other similarities in the careers of these foremost novelists include a common struggle against penury despite phenomenal successes in literature, intermittent and poorly compensated government positions, desperate hopes for a better fortune in the New World, spurious second parts of their masterworks, and the consequent stimulation of authentic sequels. Both spent unpleasant but possibly fruitful sojourns in jails. Alemán, upon release from debtors' prison in 1582 sought to migrate, and about this time the same thought occurred to Cervantes. Alemán's journey was long deferred while that of Cervantes, probably fortunately, never took place.

The decision of the author of *Guzmán de Alfarache* to depart to Mexico at the age of sixty arouses curiosity. His application for a permit to sail in 1607 reminded his Majesty of many services rendered on financial commissions, and asserted that he had "spent most of his life studying humane letters and had written several books; now he is unemployed and desires to continue in the royal service in the Indies where the viceroys and other administrative officers need persons of his training (in accountancy)." Then as if an afterthought, he adds: "and also because he has a very wealthy cousin, a mine owner of San Luis, New Spain, who has sent for him."[4]

To reach that "haven of refuge for the poor devils of Spain," as Cervantes had called the New World, was for the aging, poverty haunted novelist, seemingly, a last desperate resort on which he had staked his remaining earthly possessions in the Peninsula. He had signed over his properties in Madrid to a government officer, later granting him a power of attorney and transferring all rights of publication and sale of the second part of *Guzmán de Alfarache* in Castile and Portugal "for the period of ten years left to me by his Majesty's favor." And to the same individual he also made a similar donation of his pious *Life of Saint Anthony of Padua.* The recipient of these assets of the Spanish writer was a Pedro de Ledesma, "secretary of the king, our Lord, in his Royal Council of the Indies . . . which bestowal I make and grant because of the many kind acts which I have received from the said secretary . . ."[5] This assignment of his worldly effects to a functionary of the bureau in charge of imperial affairs overseas invites speculation. It has been suggested that one of these "kind acts" may have enabled Alemán to evade the ban against the emigration to the colonies of individuals with a taint of Jewish blood.[6]

This voluntary stripping of his possessions and the bold decision, for a misanthropic man of his years, to start life anew across the Atlantic hardly seem the result of blind impulse. The explanation lies, perhaps, in the reference to a "wealthy cousin" in his application. Who, then, was the moneyed relative in Mexico who had allegedly sent for him? Since the impecunious novelist fails to mention his name and it has not come to light in any other document, the identity of the would-be benefactor remains obscure. Circumstantial evidence, however, strongly suggests a prominent citizen of Mexico City, Dr. Alonso Alemán. This man of affairs had obtained a law degree in 1567 at Seville (birthplace of the creator of *Guzmán de Alfarache*) and, four years later, had sailed with a brother to New Spain. There, as a *gachupín,* or Peninsular Spaniard, he had married, with the ease that so exasperated the American-born Spaniards, a wealthy Creole heiress, daughter of a conquistador, and thus acquired a fortune, possibly in mines. His legal and business talents were, apparently, exceptional, and he filled various chairs and administrative offices in the University of Mexico. Though retiring as a professor in 1597, he continued to manage the financial affairs of that institution. These and other activities, together with his extensive law practice, undoubtedly increased a substantial fortune and reputation. His distinction seems apparent in existing documents where his name invariably appears as simply "Dr. Alemán," while all other cosigners give theirs in full. In 1604 a viceroy, the Count of Monterrey, referred to this individual "as one of the most learned men and ablest lawyer in Mexico City." He also reported this fiftyish jurist as in excellent health, an observation that hardly prepares one for the fact of Dr. Alemán's death in 1605.[7]

If, as seems likely, this prominent citizen was the *primo hermano* to whom, in his petition, the Spanish writer referred, the latter gives the impression that, in 1607, his relative was still alive. It is possible, of course, that the novelist had received an invitation earlier and was unaware of the death of the sender. Communications between Spain and the Indies were slow by any modern standards, but the news could have reached Mateo Alemán by early 1606, or sooner, on the annual fleet returning from Vera Cruz, or by a dispatch boat. Was it, rather, the possibility of a legacy that prompted the sacrifice of his effects in Spain and emigration so late in life? Obtaining the necessary permit was, apparently, not a simple matter for the famous author, and the knowledge that a well-to-do kinsman awaited his arrival carried more conviction than an expected inheritance that he would not become destitute. Hence the wording of his application. That he did not seek a credential in 1606 for the spring sailing was, possibly, because the word of Dr. Alemán's death arrived too late and, consequently, he had to apply for the fleet of the following year.

Menacing activities of Dutch pirates on the Spanish coast prompted the canceling of the 1607 sailing which obliged the despondent author to wait another twelvemonth for his departure. At last, on June 3, 1608, he embarked at Seville with three alleged children: Francisca de Alemán, a young woman of twenty-four who was, in reality, Doña Francisca Calderón, his mistress; Margarita and Antonio, his illegitimate offspring aged three and eight respectively; a forty-year-old niece, Catalina de Alemán, and two servants, Alonso Martín and María de Gálvez.[8]

At Cádiz the fleet added further units and passengers, including Archbishop Fray García Guerra, and his large retinue. With a total of sixty-two vessels it began the long crossing on June 30. Whether Alemán knew the prelate before, or won his favor on this voyage is unclear, but it is certain that a friendship was established of inestimable advantage to the immigrant writer in the new land. The lugubrious *Sucesos de Fray García Guerra, Arzobispo de México* ... (Events concerning Friar García Guerra, Archbishop of Mexico ...) written by the novelist after the death of its subject in 1613 and the last known product of his quill testifies to this intimate association and the protection received. This short work was a sort of extended obituary in which, with true Baroque feeling, the brilliant scenes of the Archbishop-Viceroy's triumphs contrasted with the macabre details of his fatal illness and the excessively somber spectacle of his funeral.

The record is silent concerning the success of Alemán's quest in Mexico, but he seems to have acquired the desired economic security that had induced him to abandon Spain. Not long after his arrival he published in Mexico City a treatise on Castilian orthography to which, apparently, he attached greater importance than to his well-known novel. The satisfactory outcome of his decision to come to the New World seems confirmed by the grateful tone of its preface. "Now receive, O generous and illustrious city," he wrote, "this rejoicing and lucky pilgrim whose good fortune brought him to your charitable embrace and who, like the worker wearied by the rigor of the summer sun, desires to rest his tired limbs in the comfort of your welcome shade . . ." But a prolonged illness during the first months of his residence and his failing eyesight had diminished, no doubt, these happier feelings and immersed him even more deeply in his habitual pessimism and despondency.

Only one document on the Spanish author's life in Mexico has so far come to light to supplement the meager personal data available in his two works printed there. It is a scribal record of a prosaic transaction, and its uniqueness lends an interest out of proportion to its importance. It is merely a small docket pertaining to a lease taken by Alemán on a house which reflects some of the difficulties confronted by tenants of the time.[9] A few details are illuminating.

Two residents of the viceregal capital, Juan and García Cabezas, had inherited a run-down dwelling in the district of San Angel, on the edge of the Pedregal, which they listed for renting with the business manager of the nearby *colegio* of the Carmelite order. On December 6, 1609 this agent of the religious community drew up a lease with "the accountant Mateo Alemán, a citizen of the City of Mexico" who, it appears, was already lodged in the house. The agreement stipulated that the Spanish author might occupy the premises during a three-year period from December 1, 1609 to the end of November, 1612, for an annual rental of three hundred pesos, payable in advance in four months' installments. The cost of repairs needed to make the dwelling habitable was deductible from the first payment. These improvements included rebuilding the wall separating the yard from the neighbor's property, and the installation of new doors and windows. The ecclesiastical agents shrewdly inserted an "escape clause" permitting them to cancel the lease on two months' notice, a privilege not shared, apparently, by the distinguished tenant. Doubtless harassed by a housing shortage, Alemán accepted these conditions without protest.

It appears likely that the Carmelite real estate dealers were slow in arranging for the needed repairs, or possibly labor was in short supply. At any rate, nothing was done, and the Spanish novelist probably found the windowless and doorless shelter rather too drafty for comfort in the chilly month of December. After waiting for things to happen, he decided to take action. He had been a landlord himself in Madrid and Seville and was handy in such matters. So he offered to attend to these repairs personally. On January 31, 1610, therefore, a clause was attached to the original lease authorizing ". . . the said accountant Mateo Alemán to undertake freely the said repairs . . . necessary for the occupancy of the said dwelling." On completing these improvements the tenant was to render a sworn statement of the expense incurred, which total would be credited to his account. This supplementary agreement, seemingly unnotarized, ends the short docket and no further information is vouchsafed. Presumably, the illustrious tenant remained in this house until his lease expired in late 1612. His account of Fray García Guerra, published the next year, indicates that he was living in the capital at that time, and two years later he was reported at Chalco, a nearby village.[10] Here all trace ends of the writer whose novel still rivaled *Don Quixote* in popular favor.

The symbolic significance of Fray García Guerra's arrival in Mexico in 1608 is heightened by the presence in the same fleet of two of the foremost figures of the Golden Age of Spanish literature. One was, of course, Mateo Alemán, whose misanthropic view of life harmonized so intimately with the prevailing Baroque spirit. The other was a squat and ugly humpback, a Mexican Creole by the name of Juan Ruiz de Alarcón y Mendoza, who was returning to his native land after a somewhat unsatisfactory sojourn in the Peninsula. The contrasts presented by these two men of letters, who traveled on different vessels and probably did not meet, were striking. More prepossessing in appearance and with an established reputation, Alemán had easy access to the circle about the Archbishop and to the special favor that a *gachupín* enjoyed in colonial society. Alarcón, whose physical deformities made him the butt of cruel jeers and whose literary distinction was still to be achieved, was prey to a Creole inferiority complex which moved him to seek compensation in a proud display of aristocratic pretensions. Alemán was already in the enjoyment of his prestige as a leading novelist of the time; Alarcón had yet to achieve a greatness in the Spanish theater that would place him in the front rank of European dramatists, though little recognition would come to him in his own lifetime. If Alemán was the most distinguished creative writer of the Peninsula to migrate to the New World during the colonial centuries, his fellow passenger in the fleet was the most talented author that that New World gave to Spain and to Europe during the same period.

The tone of their writings, the techniques employed, and the attitude toward life reflected in them differed sharply. If in *Guzmán de Alfarache* the succession of incidents is "set down in a casual sequence with little art or invention and with no attempt either to make the characters live or the circumstances revealing,"[11] and if they serve as an excuse for dreary disquisitions on the baseness of human nature, the plays of Alarcón display careful workmanship in plot, characterization, and language, and they exude a more optimistic tone. While the playwright's intention is also didactic, his moralizing is less protracted and reveals less of the cynical distrust of mankind that possessed the Spanish novelist. Perhaps the more tranquil and unruffled atmosphere of New Spain in which Alarcón had begun life had engendered a more wholesome outlook than Alemán could acquire in the disintegrating world of Old Spain, but doubtless it was a matter of temperament. Cervantes, whose experience more nearly paralleled that of Alemán, had developed, as his masterwork clearly shows, a far more charitable understanding of human frailty.

Much less prolific than the fecund geniuses of the Spanish theater of his time—only about twenty of his plays are known—Alarcón nevertheless demonstrated a versatility within this score or so of compositions. Most highly regarded are his comedies of contemporary manners in Madrid in which he gently but firmly excoriates, one by one, the common vices of lying, gossiping, ingratitude, fickleness, selfishness, and the like. This is accomplished by excellent delineation of character, natural dialogue, usually free of rhetorical flourishes, and by flowing verse in well woven plots. The most famous of these comedies is *La verdad sospechosa* (Truth Suspect) which delightfully depicts the confusions that result from an imaginative disregard of the truth. The adroit handling of the theme aroused the admiration of the great French playwright, Pierre Corneille, who is reported to have declared that he would give two of his own best works for the privilege of having written that Spanish masterpiece. Proof of his appreciation is offered in the flattery of imitation present in his justly famous *Le Menteur*. Alarcón's ethical intention was an important part of his originality which won him little popularity in his own time, a fact to which his own unprepossessing aspect and his quality as a Creole in Spain probably contributed.

With greater cause than Alemán had for a misanthropic view of his fellow men, who made his misshapen body the unceasing subject of ridicule, Alarcón's reflection of the *mal de siècle* is chiefly apparent in a slight thread of melancholy and a certain subtlety that run through his work. Overshadowed by the towering genius of Lope de Vega (1562-1635) and Tirso de Molina (1583?-1648) in his own lifetime, the truly Baroque splendor of the drama of Pedro Calderón de la Barca (1600-1681) entirely eclipsed his plays which were nearly forgotten for two centuries. Today his realistic portrayal of manners and analysis of character make him seem more modern than his contemporaries, and his comedies offer more reading pleasure than the pessimistic chapters of the novel written by his morose fellow passenger in the Mexico-bound fleet of 1608.

Ruiz de Alarcón was born in Mexico City about 1581 into a family of distinguished connections and his formative years were spent in that viceroyalty. In 1600 he sailed to Spain and studied law at the University of Salamanca, later practicing his profession in Seville. Possibly this experience moved him to conclude that a Creole might fare better after all in his native heath, for he returned to New Spain in 1608.

Once again in his homeland the hunchback Creole's efforts to find a rewarding career were unsuccessful. He resumed his studies at the University of Mexico, acquiring the degree of *licenciado* and working toward a doctorate which, apparently, he did not receive. He did prepare a dissertation, however, which, in the fond hope, perhaps, of winning the recognition of the Archbishop, Fray García Guerra, he dedicated to that celebrity.[12] There is no evidence that the ambitious prelate took any notice of the implied honor, or ever bestowed attention on this unattractive fellow passenger of his voyage from Spain. Repeatedly Alarcón entered contests to win a university professorship but failed in every attempt. Meanwhile, he practiced law in the viceregal capital without enhancing appreciably either his fame or fortune. As true of Alemán, few documents have come to light to reveal his activities in Mexico City during these years, and none permits any real glimpse of his personality. For both distinguished writers and residents of "the literary metropolis of the New World," this period of their respective careers remains the most obscure.[13]

About the time of Fray García's death the disappointed Creole abandoned his native land once again, for 1614 found him back in Madrid and launching on his calling as a playwright. Whether he had dabbled in this kind of writing before his return to Spain, or began there while trying to find more regular employment, is not at all clear. What is most curious about his plays is the slight indication in any of them of his Mexican origin, and few indeed are the allusions to his homeland. The most clearly discernible appear in a comedy El Semejante de sí mismo (So Like Himself), which imitates the models of the contemporary giants of the Spanish theater, Lope de Vega and Tirso de Molina. It contains a brief description of the departure of the fleet from Spain, probably based on personal recollection, a few verses sketching the location of Mexico City, and some laudatory comments on the drainage project that Fray García Guerra and the viceroy, Luis de Velasco, had inspected. Scarcely anything more tangibly Mexican can be distilled from Alarcón's theater, which was written while he held various governmental posts. His death occurred in 1639 at the Spanish capital.

During the years of Alarcón's return to Mexico, a youth from Spain paused briefly in that realm who was also to produce plays for the theaters of Madrid, though they would lack the originality and genius of the American Creole. This Spaniard, Luis Belmonte Bermúdez (1587-1650?), sharing the restlessness of his times, sought fortune first in New Spain, from which he presently moved on to Peru and joined the adventurous expeditions of Pedro Fernández de Quirós to the Solomon Islands, the Moluccas, and other parts of the Far East. There is no evidence that he met Alarcón, but he did strike up an acquaintance with a fellow townsman and expatriate, Mateo Alemán. Despite the disparity in age—Belmonte Bermúdez was a stripling of twenty-two in 1609—a warm friendship budded between the two Spanish-born literary figures. As the older novelist had testified to his orthodoxy by writing a pietistic *Life of Saint Anthony of Padua,* so the future dramatist and poet had already composed a *Life of Saint Ignatius of Loyola,* to which Alemán wrote a laudatory foreword: "It is not the passion of friendship, and let it not seem that I speak with exaggerated approval because [its author] is a fellow countryman, and we were born in the same part of Seville," the ailing author of *Guzmán de Alfarache* protests in explaining his encomiums.[14] Belmonte Bermúdez later achieved minor distinction in Spain for his epic poems and some twenty-five plays, the best known of which was *El Diablo Predicador* (The Devil a Preacher).[15] With themes of the supernatural and fantastic, mingled with elements of religiosity and satire, his plays contained the ingredients desired in the popular theater of the Baroque age.

Another adventurous Spaniard with literary pretensions, whose errant career brought him to Mexico after extensive travels, was Mateo Rosas de Oquendo (1559?-1613?). A sort of cultured *pícaro,* he had been a soldier in Italy and France. Seeking quicker fortune, like many another Spaniard of his time, he transferred activities to the New World. His bloodless participation in the conquest of Tucuman, now in Argentina, netted him unimpressive rewards and he drifted on to Lima, the metropolis of South America, where his engaging personality and talents gained him entry into the Viceroy of Peru's household. Possibly his sardonic wit displayed in satiric verses gained him more enemies than friends, making it expedient to move on. About 1598 his roving disposition brought Oquendo to Mexico which he favored with his presence apparently for the remainder of his life. Here his nimble quill caricatured in verse various social and ethnic types, notably the mestizo, but now and then it depicted the Mexican landscape with a sober charm and lyric melancholy.[16] But the author was too imbued with a hidalgo distaste for useful work and too disillusioned by his failure to acquire easy wealth to devote himself to sustained effort of any sort, and he remained a kind of polished *zaramullo,* substituting versified quips for cape-snatching.

The turn of the seventeenth century saw distinct changes in the art of literary expression which were promptly reflected in Mexico. Indeed, this opulent realm gave to the Spanish world of that time one of the greatest poets in Castilian, Bernardo de Balbuena (1561?-1627), who, with so much resonant elegance, marks a transition from the Renaissance to Baroque poetry. The sixteenth century had produced epic poems and chronicles full of action and penned with narrative verve, but toward the close of this period a shift was perceptible from dramatic content to profuse decoration. The color and music of words were claiming attention and the ornamental qualities of form were becoming more and more the pretext for literature. The spirited recounting of deeds was giving way to a detailing of the picturesque and a classic simplicity was yielding to a mannered style. Baroque patterns were emerging in literature as in art and, of the new fashion, Mexico would contribute some of the best and many of the worst exhibits.[17]

Somewhat accidentally, it appears, Balbuena was born a Peninsular Spaniard. His father was on a visit to Spain at the time and soon brought his infant son back to the viceroyalty of Mexico where he grew up in Guadalajara. Though the poet spent a number of his adult years in the mother country studying in its universities, his career was chiefly in the New World where he occupied various offices in the Church. In his youth he had attended the University of Mexico, later serving as a *cura* in a remote village. The quiet leisure of this rural life permitted a cultivation of his poetic gifts, of which he had already given substantial evidence, and his major works had their beginnings at this time. Of these the first, though not in the order of publication, was the *Siglo de Oro en las Selvas de Erífile* (The Golden Age in the Groves of Eriphyle), a notable collection of eclogues, written in the highly stylized prose and verse of the current pastoral novels, though with somewhat more realism than appears in the similar fictions of Lope de Vega and Cervantes.

The second and most imposing of Balbuena's works, *Bernardo o Victoria de Roncesvalles* (Bernard, or the Victory at Roncesvalles) was in the epic tradition inspired by the Italian poets Ariosto, Tasso, and others, and imitated by Spanish and Portuguese bards such as Alonso de Ercilla in *The Araucana* and Camoens in *The Lusiads*. With tedious results uninspired poetasters had made efforts to glorify Cortés and the Spanish Conquest in this manner, but Balbuena, with superb lyric talent, drew upon the rich storehouse of medieval Spain and from its legends produced a Baroque epic of some five thousand octaves. Complex in structure, broad in scope, his *Bernard* possessed an ornate intricacy, lush detail, and the richness of imagery of an immense tapestry. Among its shortcomings are: its enormous length; excessive number of episodes and personages, some poorly developed and often digressive; an abuse of allegory and of the marvellous; and occasional pedantry. Balancing these defects are its remarkable imaginativeness and invention, its musical verses, and extraordinary power of colorful description. The whole glitters with the sparkling splendor of a great diadem, a Baroque extravaganza which moved a beloved Spanish American critic to exclaim that it was "a delight for the eyes, a delight for the ears, and a delight for the mind."[18] Its vast profusion of ornamental details, over which Balbuena labored until near the end of his life, suggests the Baroque façades, altars, and retables of so many Mexican churches.[19]

As literary forms the pastoral narrative and the epic poem are long out of fashion, and the excessive length of most examples makes unlikely any revival. Balbuena's chief compositions, therefore, share with many classics the distinction of being more respected than read. But one of his poems, shorter and more spontaneous, retains an audience. *La Grandeza Mexicana* (Grandeur of Mexico City) is a lyrical description of the viceregal capital, its climate, surroundings, churches and public buildings, gardens, centers of learning, government, diversions, theater, women, horses, intellectuals, clergy, and the like. These altisonant verses, in tercets after the manner of Dante, are strewn with colorful adjectives, intricate metaphors, alliterations, ingenious wordplay, and verbal catalogues which, despite a pyrotechnic effect, convey a sincere admiration for the colonial metropolis. It would be idle, of course, to seek realism in this mellifluous description, yet it does give an impression of what life was like in the Mexican capital which, in

its own way, could rival the interest and charm of many cities of
Old Spain.

The intellectual activities of the community centered largely in
the University of Mexico and the seminaries of the various religious
orders scattered about the municipality. The learning was almost
wholly neo-scholastic, theological in substance, as already described, in harmony with the ideology of the Catholic Counter
Reformation. Its stimulation came mostly from the missionaries and
travelers passing through the city on their journeys between Europe
and the outposts of empire in other parts of the hemisphere, or in
the Far East. Many fine minds with extensive experience and
knowledge enlivened discussions often as animated as those in
contemporary Spain, but there was little opportunity for the development of more secular philosophies. As in most of Europe, the
Ptolemaic concept of the universe remained undisturbed, and the
superstitions of astrology, alchemy, and medical lore pervaded the
secular mind, though now and then an individual with a more
technical type of intellect applied his thought to more practical
matters.

The ambitious engineering project to relieve Mexico City from
periodic inundation, which the viceroy, Luis de Velasco, had
initiated and Fray García Guerra had inspected, brought into
prominence a German resident named Heinrich Martin, better
known in the castilianized form of Enrico Martínez. His was probably the foremost scientific mind in the viceroyalty during the first
decades of the seventeenth century. Born a Protestant in Hamburg
some time between 1550 and 1560, his family took him to Spain
at the age of eight where he became a Catholic. In his youth he
traveled widely in Europe and studied mathematics in France and
Germany where he also developed a knowledge of mechanics. Returning to the Spanish peninsula, he lived for varying periods in
Madrid, Toledo, and Seville, departing from the latter city in
1589 to become a royal cosmographer in Mexico. This designation
implied a scientific capacity for assembling geographical data,
compiling maps, measuring longitude and latitude, observing
eclipses and movements of the stars, and a knowledge of applied
mathematics. Enrico's command of languages also made him useful
to the Inquisition as an interpreter, and his wide-ranging interests
and technical skills moved him to acquire a printing press in 1599

for general work and the publication of his own writings such as almanacs and occasional treatises.[20]

In 1606 appeared an important item from his press which he had composed. It was his *Repertorio de los tiempos y Historia Natural desta Nueva España* (Almanac and History of New Spain) which was a potpourri of geographical data, astronomical and astrological observations, and historical facts concerning Mexico and Castile from 1520 to 1590. Of interest are its reflections of the scientific ideas of the time. He was a geocentrist, which is hardly surprising when Galileo was being punished about then for the "crime" of espousing the Copernican theory in the comparatively more enlightened Italy. If Enrico's astronomy sounds more like astrology, he was, at least, attempting to draw a line between the two kinds of study. And in the light of the concern with predestination in the Spanish Counter Reformation, the bold assertion of his belief in free will is significant. "Human acts depending on free will are not subject to celestial influences . . ." Even more striking is his declaration that ". . . kings and potentates may reduce realms, provinces, and cities with their thousands of population to their dominion, but the free will of man cannot be coerced"—a rather surprising assertion in an imperial, overseas realm steeped in a neomedieval orthodoxy and a royal absolutism. As an immigrant himself he was convinced that the different food and benign climate of Mexico sharpened the intelligence of the European born and tended to improve the natural gifts that he brought with him. Why this environment did not operate on the native-born Creole with similarly beneficial effect, he does not make clear.

Enrico Martínez' direction of what was a gigantic engineering undertaking for the time—the drainage of the valley of Mexico—brought him only sorrow, failure, and imprisonment. Highly controversial was the plan proposed, and it soon proved exceedingly costly in lives and money. The crown had sent inspectors to appraise the project who added their disapproval to the criticism emanating from local sources concerning the scheme and the work of construction. Some of this opposition stemmed from a provincial dislike of foreigners, especially non-Hispanic foreigners entrusted with conspicuous responsibilities whose technical superiority seemed a reflection on the national character. And this condemnation of the operation seemed justified by its failure to meet the test in subsequent occasions. In 1615, in 1623, and again in 1629 seasons of heavy rain inundated the capital, and these successive demonstrations of the ineffectiveness of the expensive undertakings resulted in the imprisonment of Enrico as its chief promoter. It was too vast an enterprise for the existing facilities, and its final achievement had to await the improved techniques and experience of the nineteenth century. The last days of the German engineer were embittered by a heavy sense of defeat and the harsh denunciations of which he was so long the object. Disillusionment and despondency crushed his spirit, and death followed in December, 1632, thus closing a career which, despite its limitations, had brought to the intellectual atmosphere of Mexico the first feeble intimations of the dawning age of science and technology.

V

SCENES, WRITERS, AND READING, 1620

WHEN the new Archbishop, Fray García Guerra, made his triumphal entry into Mexico City in 1608, the isolation of the rich realm of New Spain seemed complete and singularly propitious for the security of orthodoxy and the integrity of the Spanish empire in North America. Yet a heretical nation had already gained a foothold on the mainland of this continent and, in the course of the century, its aggressive intrusions would increase. At the moment it hardly formed a cloud speck on the horizon, but a new instrument of expansion unfamiliar to Spanish authority—the joint stock company—was accelerating a more openly economic imperialism than the messianic crown of Spain had envisaged. The new British dynasty of the Stuarts had bestowed a charter for a New World settlement on the Virginia Company of London which, in 1607, planted the first English colony on a malarial coast north of the Florida outpost at St. Augustine. But, however different this venture might seem, its objectives curiously resembled those of the Spanish conquistadors of the preceding century—discovery of gold and, incidentally, the conversion of Indian inhabitants to Christianity. The English gentlemen-adventurers at Jamestown were displaying as mild an enthusiasm for manual labor as their more vigorous Spanish counterparts had before them, and they were no less ready to exploit the native population in the name of religion. If the disconcerting absence of mines and submissive Indians in

Virginia deprived the English Conquest of the glamor of the Iberian enterprises, it assured the less profitable undertaking a more virtuous renown in history.

While Fray García was viewing the abundance of his bishopric from the Baroque splendor of his episcopal palace, disillusioned neighbors at distant Jamestown were dying by the hundreds in the "starving time," though the surrounding woods teemed with game and the rivers were choked with fish. And it was during those trying times that an Indian maiden, Pocahontas by name, served as intermediary between redskins and white invaders as another, less romanticized daughter of the New World, Doña Marina, had done for the Spaniards nearly a century before.

Another event of portentous significance to the northern region marked 1608. A resolute band of Englishmen departed that year from the homeland to the asylum of Holland. A dozen years later one hundred and two of its members crowded into a small vessel, poetically named "Mayflower," and crossed the Atlantic in sixty-five storm-stressed days to challenge further Spanish monopoly of the New World. These stern-faced immigrants found none of the prodigality of New Spain on landing on a harsh, rock-bound coast late in 1620. The grim, chill harbor of Plymouth, with its Indian-infested backlands, presented an even less hospitable aspect than the hot, vermin-ridden port of Vera Cruz in which Spanish pilgrims debarked only to hurry to the benign hinterland.

No one could foresee that these precarious footholds on the North Atlantic coast were the beginnings of a nation destined to surpass the opulence and power of the Spanish viceroyalty and eventually to seize a great part of its domain. The contrasts presented by that pathetic band, voluntarily marooned on the bleak, gray shore of Massachusetts Bay that dismal winter of 1620-1621, and the teeming population of the sunlit Valley of Mexico put such prophesies far beyond the boldest seers. The dull drabness of the rough settlements on the forbidding northern coast seemed the very antithesis of the polychromatic animation of the southern inland city.

Almost a century before the Massachusetts colony began, the beauty of the Aztec capital had moved to wonder the redoubtable soldier of Cortés, Bernal Díaz del Castillo, and now, when the English footholds were merely dreary scatterings of wattle huts, a less valiant traveler in Mexico, Thomas Gage, recorded a similar, if more sophisticated, enthusiasm for the same locality long transformed into a Spanish viceregal city. What stirred both observers as they had approached the municipality was the fair prospect of a broad, green valley, broken by sparkling stretches of water, lying in a pleasing bowl formed by circling mountains. As they descended to the margins of the lake surrounding the great city its details enhanced the impression of beauty and the variety of contrasts. "The situation of this city is much like that of Venice," wrote the seventeenth-century English visitor, "but only differs in this, that Venice is built upon the sea water, and Mexico upon a lake which, seeming one, indeed is two." Even in these waters embracing the capital he noted the element of contrast for ". . . one part is standing water, the other ebbeth and floweth according to the wind that bloweth."[1] The brackish Lake Texcoco was about forty-five miles in circumference, and fringing its shores were thirty or more villages and hamlets which, like the metropolis of Mexico City, now and then experienced the floods that Enrico Martínez so unsuccessfully sought to control. The viceregal capital stood upon an island reclaimed from the lake and, as if to hold the city in position, three causeways reached out to the mainland like mooring ropes over which travelers entered. The one from the west was about a mile and a half long, another from the north was three miles in extent, and the longest projected five miles from the southern mainland.

The insular city appeared spacious within its circumference of two leagues, or about six miles. Its streets were remarkably straight and broad, permitting three carriages to drive abreast in the narrowest ones and six or more in the widest. Low but imposing houses, often enclosed in gardens, lined the main thoroughfares together with neat shops, and ornate structures of stone and brick. Fifteen thousand Spanish families resided in these precincts, while eighty thousand Indians, and possibly fifty thousand Negroes and mulattoes, slaves and freedmen, crowded the barrios, and at almost any hour of the day motley throngs filled its avenues. These avenues varied in character from normal roadways of solid earth and cobbled pavements to mingled land and waterways along which the population moved in vehicles, on mounts, on foot, and afloat.[2]

There were seven of these *acequias* or canals which, after flow-

ing across the city like parallel arteries, emptied into the salty
waters of Lake Texcoco. To insure drainage a series of *compuertas*
or floodgates were lifted each morning to release water impounded
in the canals. In rainy seasons they remained open to carry off the
excess precipitation.[3] Over these waterways a thousand canoes and
scows brought from the mainland the city's supplies of bread, meat,
fish, game, firewood, *zacate* (forage), and the like, while daily over
the causeways more than three thousand mules plodded patiently
beneath heavy burdens of wheat, corn, sugar and other staples to
join the water-borne provisions at the market place and the gran-
aries.

"A thousand lovely canals, teeming with long, narrow boats,
veritable mine-hoards of supplies, goods, and singular articles for
the shops, twist and turn delightfully like crystalline serpents
through its spacious streets" rhapsodized Bernardo de Balbuena in his
lyric *Grandeur of Mexico City*. His panegyric suggests that he had
no eyes—or nostrils—for the unpoetic reality of these often sluggish, stagnant, and nauseous waterways, whose murky shallows
were befouled by corpses of animals—and sometimes of human
beings—excrement, and the varied refuse of a congested city.
The canals were open sewers as well as a means of floating multitudinous craft. As if to reflect the sharp contrasts of the Baroque
age, elongated flatboats, nearly hidden under bowers of sweet-
scented flowers or loads of bright-hued fruit and vegetables, glided
over these fetid waters and past the foul-smelling banks to the
markets. On festive occasions larger barges, gaily decorated with
pennants and bunting, conveyed the aristocratic society of the
capital, including the viceroy and his family, along these odorifer-
ous passages to places of recreation.

Widely scattered about the city were splendid public buildings
and ecclesiastical establishments built of neatly quarried stone of
brilliant hues and presenting façades of sculptured design, each
rivaling the other in intricate patterns of carvings, niches, statues,
and pillars. Impressive exhibits of ornate architecture were the
palaces of the viceroy, the archbishop, the Royal Audiencia, the
Town Council, the structures that housed the busy mint, daily
melting the silver bars from the Zacatecas mines, and the University, its lecture halls buzzing with the dull drone of neo-
scholastic verbalism. Most elaborately decorated of all were the

fifty or more churches, temples, convents, monasteries, and hospitals distributed broadly within the confines of the capital. Dominicans, Franciscans, Augustinians, Carmelites, and Jesuits all vied with each other in the number and magnificence of these buildings and the luxury of their furnishings. The Convent of St. Dominic was counted one of the richest in all the Spanish Indies, while six similar institutions of the Franciscans competed in brilliant ornamentation which seemed strangely at variance with the simplicity and poverty preached by the saintly founder of the Order. Almost as many monasteries with ornate cloisters, dormitories, and refectories housed monks of other communities. And the altars, marble pillars, and interiors of the adjoining chapels glittered with wrought gold and the jewels of images garbed in richest fabrics.

At least sixteen nunneries provided refuge for unmarried daughters of families able to supply dowries, and these cloistered females learned such skills as cooking, needlework, and playing musical instruments as well as routine obligations. If constricted, life for these "brides of Christ" could be pleasantly social. Not all such inmates, however, led quiet, inactive lives, nor were all religious establishments devoted solely to worship and comfortable living. Numerous were the charitable institutions which included some nine hospitals for the care of the sick, the poor, the aged, and the orphans of the community. One of these infirmaries, founded by a viceroy, the Count of Monterrey, was for the Indians. It derived its support partly from the proceeds of the local *corral de comedias,* or theater, where the public attended daily performances of plays by contemporary Spanish dramatists. Cortés, the conqueror, had endowed the Hospital de la Concepción for indigent sufferers, while the Hospital of Saint Hippolytus, one of the wealthiest in the Indies, was an insane asylum. In these institutions many nuns and clergymen spent their lives in noble service, their piety and sacrifice contrasting sharply with the moral laxity and luxury of other ecclesiastics.

The center of the city was the Plaza Mayor, now the Zócalo, a spacious though littered square which served as an important market place. Lining the south and western sides were buildings with arcades through which, sheltered from sun and rain, pedestrians idly sauntered to inspect the silks and fine wares of the bazaars. Often they stopped to haggle with Indian, Negro, or mulatto women squatting by mats covered with fruits, vegetables, and trinkets, offered as wares. Across the square on the east side was the viceroy's palace which, with its gardens and the stout stone prison adjacent, occupied almost the entire length. Its two stories had the appearance of a fort with small towers at the corners, regularly spaced loopholes in the walls, and two great gateways with massive doors. On the north side of the plaza was rising the great mass of the Cathedral, begun in the late sixteenth century. The viceroy preceding Fray García reported that the walls of this rectangular structure, with interior dimensions of 387 by 177 feet, were half of the planned height and that the vaulting of four of the chapels was complete.[4] The long, slow progress of construction was subjecting the original design to changes which marred its architectural unity. Begun when the severely classic spirit exemplified in Philip II's El Escorial prevailed, the lush manner of the Baroque had now modified the plan. Presently the architects reverted to classic influences and the massive pile, though majestic and splendid, would acquire a labored grandeur as it dominated the Plaza Mayor.

If this central square was the focal point of the worship of God and Mammon, several blocks west lay the favorite place of recreation of the aristocratic classes. Called the Alameda, it was a pleasant park of shady trees and walks which lured fine ladies in decorated carriages and sedan chairs, accompanied by slave attendants, and young gallants, mounted on mettlesome steeds, about four o'clock in the afternoon for the much cherished *paseo*. The Viceroy, attended by a stately retinue outshowing all others, frequently honored these occasions by his presence. Everyone came to see and be seen, to consume endless quantities of sweetmeats and drinks, and to promote flirtations and amorous intrigues. These gay and airy moments occasionally experienced violent transitions as jealous swains, contending for a lady's favor, drew swords or daggers and wounded a rival sometimes fatally. The Alameda was often the breeding place of bitter feuds and bloody skirmishes growing out of trivial causes exaggerated out of all proportion by hot-blooded individuals. Yet this park long remained a favorite place for the ostentatious display of luxury in dress, carriages, horses, and servants in which the wealthy indulged their excessive vanity.

The streets leading away from the Plaza Mayor were lined by

shops where goods were manufactured and sold. Certain crafts like, for example, silversmithing monopolized whole blocks which often bore the name of the predominant occupation. Thus there were sections which produced objects of gold as well as silver, precious stones, and feather work, all of exquisite workmanship, while others provided more practical wares such as saddles, ironwork, candles, pastry, furniture, and the like. As a halfway station between Europe and the Far East, and a point of convergence of the trade with outlying provinces of New Spain, including Guatemala, Yucatan, Tabasco, Nueva Galicia, Nueva Vizcaya, and others, Mexico City was an emporium of the most assorted goods, from the fine laces and textiles of Europe to the silks and chinaware of Asia, and from the exotic fruits and herbs of the provinces to the expertly wrought handicrafts of its own artisans.

The transplanted Spaniard, like his kinsmen at home, lived much of his life in the streets, enjoying the continuous jostle and animation of bustling activity and of endless throngs. At almost any hour of the day gilded coaches of the gentry, attended by brocaded lackeys, passed by. Thomas Gage alleged that in 1625 there were some fifteen thousand of these vehicles whose trimmings of gold, silver, and Chinese silk outshone anything that the Court of Madrid had to offer. In this busy traffic mingled sedan chairs, whose bejeweled occupants swung rhythmically to the trotting pace of the uniformed bearers, squeaking carts with ponderous, solid wheels, haughty riders on horseback with silver-studded saddles on gay yellow blankets, and raucously braying donkeys laden with faggots, charcoal, chicken coops, and strings of red-clay pottery. Weaving about these vehicles, mounts, and beasts of burden moved a throng of pedestrians representing the whole spectrum of a society of class, caste, and race. Clergymen and friars in black, brown, and grey habits of plain cloth strode among the crowd as ladies in bright *basquiñas* or petticoats, their faces plastered with powder, lipstick, and artificial beauty spots, picked their way over the cobblestones or rutted surface in satin high-heeled *chapines* or slippers, followed by pages holding parasols over their mistresses. Lordly gentlemen strutted under large plumed hats, displaying silver or pearl-hilted swords as insignia of their rank. With an easy disdain they ignored the submissive, ragged Indians in rough sandals and dirty *sarapes;* the garrulous *léperos,* or beggars, even more ragged and bare, who wandered aimlessly about reciting incoherent ballads, whining out their ills, or muttering prayers; the old hags with wrinkled faces hardly visible under their *rebozos,* or shawls, counting the beads of a rosary, or patting *tortillas* with rhythmic precision, or mutely vending pitiful wares spread out on straw mats; and the cursing muleteers guiding their docile but occasionally obdurate animals through this maze. Now and then these haughty gentlemen dropped the mask of disdain to turn and leer at a buxom mulatto wench passing by, her black and shiny breasts bare under strings of beads, a small bodice revealing her midriff, and a tight, flaming petticoat emphasizing the enticing movement of her hips. Lascivious Spaniards and Creoles preferred these blackamoor Jezebels to their white wives, and many a dusky Thais thus won her freedom and wore finery and jewels rivaling those of the *grandes dames* of the viceregal court. Indeed, in this strange Baroque society, where moral looseness jostled with ascetic practices, it was not rare to observe a dark-skinned strumpet prancing along the public way in a fetching array of silk, lace and ribbon, while a patched *zaramullo,* or ragged Creole, slunk miserably by, ignored and despised.

An almost continuous counterpoint of the street noises was the sound of bells. Life seemed ruled by an infinite tintinnabulation which filled the air day and night, usually loud and clamorous, sometimes lugubrious and mournful. From churches and chapels came melancholy tones of *Ave Marías* and the solemn notes of the Angelus, but more clangorous bells seemed to pick up these slow strains and accelerate them with rapid, resonant strokes maintained interminably. At times the din rose to a hammered crescendo calculated to deafen the ears and shatter the nerves of the most impassive. In the vicinity of the convents the tinkling of smaller bells regulating the routine of inmates day and night might be heard against the clanging cacophony of the belfries. Even after the ten o'clock curfew, which emptied the streets of all save an occasional furtive figure and the *ronda,* or police, making the rounds with lighted lanterns, the comparative silence was broken by the low pealing of bells summoning friars and nuns to nocturnal devotions. In days of public mourning the racket of pounding yielded to a slow, measured, and lugubrious tolling whose melancholy monotony worked its own tensions on distraught hearers by inspiring

morbid reflections on the inexorable destiny of mortals and the
need for repentance.[5]

Cultural life in this animated community, at least for the privileged few, was rich. The abundance of the realm permitted ample
leisure for the arts and letters, a fact, as already evident, which
attracted writers from abroad and stimulated local talent. Indeed,
seventeenth century Mexico City was "the Athens of America"
and, as a distinguished Spanish critic wrote, it ". . . continued being
the literary metropolis of the New World, famed for the learning
of its schools, the cultivation of its citizens, and for the care and
distinction with which our Spanish was spoken."[6] The Mexican
Court, as in contemporary Madrid and Lima, teemed with poets of
minor stature whose lyric and satiric effusions, much of which
proved ephemeral and have, perhaps happily, disappeared, constituted the bulk of the literature produced.

If lacking in genius a few local writers, some of whom were
mestizos or even Indians, produced enduring works. Conspicuous
as a chronicler and collector of the Aztec lore of the Lake Texcoco
region was Don Fernando de Alva Ixtlilxochitl (1568-1648), whom
William H. Prescott in his *Conquest of Mexico* called "the Livy
of Anahuac." He was a descendant of the only Texcocan chieftain
who remained loyal to Cortés during the siege of Mexico City, and
for this fidelity his heirs had enjoyed aristocratic privileges in the
viceregal community. When Fray García Guerra, for whom he
served as interpreter, arrived in 1608, De Alva was compiling his
Chichimecan History, a record of the achievements of his native
forebears. His assiduous collection of the data, legends, and lore of
the pre-Hispanic peoples of the Valley of Mexico inspired Lew
Wallace, author of the popular nineteenth century novel, *The
Fair God,* to attribute his tale to a chronicle allegedly found among
De Alva Ixtlilxochitl's papers, thus employing a timeworn device of
storytellers. This Indian nobleman also left much verse called
"mestizo elegies" because they incorporated into Castilian themes
elements of Nahuatl poems coming down from the Texcocan
emperor, Netzahualcoyotl. A nostalgic and melancholy charm in-
fuses much of this poetry whose hybrid nature was genuinely
Mexican.

More widely esteemed is a famous sonnet attributed to an obscure Augustinian clergyman living at Tiripitío in Michoacán

about 1620, by name Miguel de Guevara (1585?-1646?). Celebrated as a perfect example of Christian poetry, it reads:

TO CHRIST CRUCIFIED

I am not moved to love Thee, O my Lord,
By any longing for Thy Promised Land;
Nor by the fear of hell am I unmanned
To cease from my transgressing deed or word.
'Tis Thou Thyself dost move me,—Thy blood poured
Upon the cross from nailed foot and hand;
And all the wounds that did Thy body brand;
And all Thy shame and bitter death's award.
Yea, to Thy heart am I so deeply stirred
That I would love Thee were no heaven on high,—
That I would fear, were hell a tale absurd!
Such my desire, all questioning grows vain;
Though hope deny me hope I still would sigh,
And as my love is now, it should remain.[7]

Closer to the Court of Mexico and enjoying a sort of poet laureateship was a native of Spanish Extremadura, Árias de Villalobos (1568- ?), whose life passed almost entirely in Mexico. His precocious way with words won him a contract to compose the annual morality play, and the Royal Audiencia of the capital commissioned him to write a versified *jura,* or oath, of submission to Philip IV on his accession in 1621. Árias de Villalobos, in a similar manner, signalized the centennial of the Spanish Conquest, and was a conspicuous participant in many poetic contests of the time. These literary activities temporarily brought him a distinction which exceeded that of his contemporary, Bernardo de Balbuena, whose latter years were spent in Jamaica and Puerto Rico. Though Árias de Villalobos' subject matter was usually Mexican, his art reflected too faithfully the artificiality of Baroque fashion.

Four printing presses functioned in 1620, but few of their products were more than utilitarian "job-printing." One of the more literary publications of that year was a curious work entitled *Los Sirgueros de la Virgen,* quite possibly inspired by Cervantes' pastoral novel, *Galatea.* Written by Francisco Bramón, a counselor of the Royal University of Mexico, it vaguely resembled its model, though preoccupied by the theme of the Immaculate Conception which, in New Spain, had the force of dogma, rather than by the customary mournful amours of rustics. Combining musical prose and lyric verse, this short narrative is sometimes considered a rudimentary novel.

As a center of varied cultural life Mexico City did not lack books, nor was the available printed literature limited to the professional requirements of the clergy who were important book buyers of the community. In an age when religion was the dominant thought of men, works of this nature, whether from the local presses or imported from Spain, overshadowed all others and constituted the chief stock in trade of the local booksellers. Yet the latter sold surprising quantities of purely secular writings, fiction, poetry, plays, history, and other nonfiction, not only to the substantial lay public of the viceregal capital and outlying regions, but also to the many churchmen who found relaxation in popular works. Many of the convents and monasteries possessed rich libraries which steadily grew in size and variety, while the lordly officials of the state, merchants, wealthy Creoles, and even individuals in humbler categories, owned book collections of impressive proportions. Much evidence of their existence emerges from notarial records of the period, such as inventories, wills, promissory notes, and the like, and even from the surviving archives of the overly maligned Inquisition.

The efforts of the Holy Office to combat the spread of heresy have left an impression that it severely censored, or excluded, all literature save that of orthodox theology. This institution did, of course, adopt precautionary measures against the admission and circulation of heretical writings in the viceroyalty, and for its files it did demand from time to time lists of books in private and commercial hands. Most often, however, this requirement was a mere checking and not a confiscation, and the resulting records provide valuable, if incomplete, indications of the literature being read. In 1620, for example, a certain Simón García Becerril of Mexico City submitted to the Inquisition an inventory of his small personal library, supplying abbreviated titles.[8] Nothing in this document suggests that he was the object of criminal proceedings, or that his book collection was confiscated. Rather, it appears a merely routine check-up on the part of the policing agency. The identity of García Becerril is obscure, for the list bears only his signature, rubric, and the succinct statement: "These are the books which I possess and declare." Other sources mention a schoolmaster named Juan García Becerril at the time, possibly a relative. Of more significance, however, are his books.

A recent Spanish scholar has remarked: "If a personal library reveals the spirit of its owner, how much more true this is in periods when the scarcity of accessible book collections, the rarity of books themselves, and their excessive cost, oblige the collector to make his purchases with greater care and at larger sacrifice than is the case nowadays."[9] Hence, even so small a group of volumes may be representative of the reading preferences of ordinary citizens in Old Mexico during the first decades of the seventeenth century.

Omitting from consideration the religious writings which, in this layman's library, were unusually few, it will suffice to notice an occasional item of nonfiction while commenting on the purely creative literature that probably entertained the owner. Of special interest among belles-lettres is the variety of Italian works present, several in the original language, which testifies to the close cultural and political ties of the Spanish and Italian peninsulars since the fifteenth century and earlier. The importance of these works of Italianate origin in García Becerril's collection lies in the fidelity with which it reflects the current tastes of the mother country in a remote center of the New World.

Besides a *Dictionary of the Tuscan Language,* the *De Claris Mulieribus,* and *The Labyrinth of Love,* a prose satire against the widows of Florence—the last two being works of Boccaccio— there appear *La Cortegiana* (1524), a comedy by the sardonic and sometimes pornographic Pietro Aretino;[10] the *Tragedy of Phedra,* by the less known Francesco Boza Candioto; and the *Arcadia* of Sannazaro, a pastoral novel and the inspiration of so much falsification of rural life in European literature. All these García Becerril possessed in Italian, with a Spanish version accompanying the last named work.

Even more celebrated representatives of Italian letters are present in Castilian garb. Aside from the Latin poet Vergil, the most prominent is the often reprinted rendition of Ariosto's *Orlando Furioso,* an epic poem which fascinated readers everywhere and influenced writers of Spain's Golden Age. Of scarcely less renown is the *Jerusalem Liberated* of Torquato Tasso, who helped to mould the expression of many Spanish poets. Perhaps the most robust exemplar of Italian influences was Alonso de Ercilla (1533-1594), whose vigorous *La Araucana* drew inspiration from the author's participation in the campaigns against the Araucanian Indians of Chile. Considered the best historical poem in Castilian, it was certainly a popular success. Its three parts are present in the Mexican collection along with the Portuguese epic of Luis de Camoëns (1525-1580), *The Lusiads*, which recounts the exploits of his nation in another part of the globe during the great Age of Discovery. Local pride as well as a taste for lyric verse probably account for the copy of *The Grandeur of Mexico City*, which Bernardo de Balbuena had written in the tercets of Dante.

García Becerril was evidently partial to such devout verse as the *Vergel de Flores Divinas* (1582), (Garland of Divine Flowers) by a sixteenth century native of Toledo, Juan López de Úbeda, and the more interesting *Flores de Poetas Ilustres de España* (1605), (Garland of Illustrious Poets of Spain) which, in some respects, opened the era of Baroque verse. It was compiled by Pedro Espinosa (1578-1650), one of the minor poets of his time who, crossed in love, gave evidence of the enduring influence of romances of chivalry by becoming a hermit after the manner of Amadis of Gaul on the Peña Pobre, and so suggests that Cervantes had contemporary objects for his satire in *Don Quixote*. Espinosa's poetry had the sensuous, decorative, and ornate character, and the relative absence of content, that characterized much Baroque expression.

Miscellaneous works in the less esteemed medium of prose formed about two-thirds of García Becerril's collection. The most notable title was *The Tragi-comedy of Calixto and Melibea*, the first genuinely European novel which appeared in 1499. Written in dialogue form by a converted Jew, Fernando de Rojas, this Romeo and Juliet-like tale is eclipsed by the lifelike portrayal of minor characters, particularly the old procuress, Celestina, who so far overshadows the other protagonists that the novel is best known by her name. Its realistic depiction of low life and the contrast of idealistic and erotic love captured a permanent audience at home and abroad. Translated in 1631 by James Mabbe as *The Spanish Bawd*, it exerted an influence on English literature. Though its subject matter and frank language might have incurred the displeasure of the Inquisition as a work contrary to good morals—

rules laid down by the Council of Trent were fairly explicit on this head—it is significant that specific expurgation was first required in the *Index of Prohibited Books* issued in 1632, a dozen years after García Becerril reported his copy to the Holy Office.

Only one other novel appeared in the collection, the greatly inferior *Desengaño de Celos* (Jealousy Undeceived) by Bartolomé López de Enciso. It reflects the current taste for the unreality of pastoral fiction, mingling artistic prose and verse. Cervantes had sardonically consigned this narrative to the bonfire in the court-yard consuming so many of Don Quixote's bibliographical treas-ures with little immediate effect, apparently, on the reading public. That same year of 1620 it was still read from one end of the Spanish empire in America to the other, judging by a notarized sale of one hundred and forty books on the public square of Lima which were destined for the still more remote outpost at Concepción in Chile. On September 19, 1620—only three days after the Pilgrims embarked for the rock-bound coast of New England—the trans-action was completed and the volumes started for the scarcely less inhospitable settlement in South America, still beset by attacks of savage Indians, and where leisure for reading seemed unlikely. The shipment contained volumes of pious verses as well, four copies of Mateo Alemán's *Guzmán de Alfarache,* and a copy of *Jealousy Un-deceived,* whose artificiality must have contrasted sharply with the harsh reality of pioneer life in Chile.[11]

If prose fiction was rare in this Mexican library, essays were numerous. These varied from *El Estudioso Cortesano* (The Learned Courtier), a collection of proverbs by the Erasmist scholar, Lorenzo Palmireno, to the translated *Epistles* of Cicero, noted for their fluid style, and the *Familiar Epistles* of one of the most influential six-teenth century writers, Antonio de Guevara (1480?-1545). His mannered style and lavish imagery foreshadowed the Baroque fash-ions clearly evident in 1620.

García Becerril's inventory clearly suggests that music as well as reading was a hobby. There he listed four different manuals on guitar-playing, the *Músicas de Vihuela* of four leading authorities, Luis Milán, Enríquez de Valderrávano, Fuenllana, and Narváez. Classic as well as popular music was an art universally cultivated in colonial Mexico, and perhaps never more devotedly than during the seventeenth century. Both the conquered Indians and the

Spanish masters had musical aptitudes of high order, and between 1530 and 1680 at least three major composers flourished in New Spain. The most notable was Juan Gutiérrez de Padilla (d. 1664), originally a singer in the Puebla Cathedral whose great talent was developing in 1620. He was soon to prove the equal of any Peninsular composer in manipulating the sonorities and in investing his music with the somber magnificence of famous masses and magnificats. Every musical form of the Baroque he essayed, arranging impressive works for double choirs, and composing masses, motets, Marian antiphons, and carols that have been preserved.[12] But, while the naves of cathedrals and chapels resounded with the exalted strains of liturgical music by the best composers at home and abroad, outside these majestic walls the strumming of melodic and rhythmic improvisations, more plaintive than gay, on guitars was heard on every street corner and square. Somewhere in the city the obscure García Becerril apparently added his notes and flourishes with a skill which he strove to improve by the help of the best manuals available.

The inventory of this seemingly intelligent layman of a rudimentary middle class of the viceregal capital presents some curious omissions. The classics of antiquity, for example, have merely a token representation in translated versions of Vergil and Cicero. Is this symptomatic of declining interest in a Renaissance humanism? The complete absence of plays is surprising when the Spanish theater was in the full flush of Baroque splendor, and the drama in printed form was popular reading. And one looks in vain for any appreciation of the supreme genius of Cervantes, so recently deceased. On the other hand, the abundance of poetry, lyric and epic, much of it written under Italian influence, appears a more authentic index of prevailing tastes which clearly leaned toward the mannered expression of the late Renaissance and the early Baroque. But whatever other deductions may be drawn from this book list it is clear that, in the year of 1620, the inhabitants of the century-old realm of New Spain could indulge a fancy for polite letters of far wider range than could the struggling settlers of contemporary Jamestown, or the new arrivals at Plymouth who had little to solace their hardships besides their Bibles and Captain John Smith's inadequate *Description of New England*.[13]

THE STRANGE CASE
OF THE CURIOUS
BOOK COLLECTOR

FRAY GARCÍA GUERRA, arrayed in his episcopal robes, stood by an altar in the partially constructed Cathedral of Mexico. He was fulfilling a routine obligation as primate of the viceregal Church—administering the sacrament of Confirmation to members of his flock deemed fit to enter upon the privileges of the Faith. Those presented at this solemn rite were mostly small children dressed in white and accompanied by proud parents and *padrinos,* or godfathers. There is no reason to suppose that, among these eager young aspirants, Fray García took particular notice of an awed little boy, baptized Melchor Pérez de Soto, nor is it likely that the thought passed through the Archbishop's mind that presently this tiny lad, as an architect and builder, would help to further the construction of the unfinished Cathedral in which he was officiating. And much less could any one present at this ceremony have foretold that this child of such touching innocence would die tragically in the dungeons of the Inquisition accused of being remiss to the Faith into which he was being formally ushered.[1]

Melchor Pérez de Soto was born in 1606 under the shadow of the great Indian pyramid at Cholula near the city of Puebla. His father, a mason by trade, had come from Galicia in Spain, the son of humble peasants, and had married the daughter of a Creole

85

family of aristocratic pretensions. Her father, Sebastián de Espinosa, was the alleged descendant of a hidalgo and conquistador of Cholula, while her mother hailed from Guatemala. Shortly after Melchor's birth the family moved to Mexico City where, presumably, his father could profitably work at his craft. The child early learned to read and write in the private schools of Francisco Clavijo and Juan García Becerril, the latter possibly related to Simón García Becerril, owner in 1620 of a small book collection. Later young Melchor began to study Latin but soon abandoned this effort and apprenticed himself to his father's trade. This failure to master the current language of learning had unforeseen consequences which cost him dearly. But if this Creole builder never acquired the formal education of a scholar and gentleman of his time, he did develop a passion for books. In due course his house was cluttered with the boxes and trunks in which he stored his many volumes on almost every subject. These purchases must have absorbed no small part of his modest income judging by the comment of a later colonial figure who stated: "There is another matter worthy of mention which . . . clearly testifies to the love and affection of Mexicans for literature. I refer to the high cost of books, so excessive indeed that they cost us (imported) three and four times as much, and even more, as they do in Europe . . ."[2] Pérez de Soto probably did not read all of his collection—many volumes were in the Latin that he never mastered—and it is likely that, with the true ardor of a bibliophile, he bought many for the sheer delight of possession.

At what stage in his career he began to acquire his library, which now appears one of the finest of seventeenth century Mexico in private hands, is unknown, but the recorded total of 1,663 volumes must have been the result of many years of assembling, given his meager means and busy life as a workman. In 1628 he married Leonor de Montoya, a native of Florida. Illiterate like the majority of the women of her time, her husband's mania must have seemed incomprehensible. She bore him eight or nine children, all of whom died in infancy or childhood. Perhaps it was his extravagant devotion to his hobby that obliged her to supplement his wages by opening their home to roomers, an economic measure which inadvertently contributed to her spouse's undoing. The household also included two young girls, admittedly products of extramarital pursuits of the bookish Melchor.

In the years following his marriage his life appears uneventful. While his wife's energies must have been wholly absorbed by domesticity, the architect-builder immersed himself more deeply in his bibliographical interests. Seemingly, however, the year 1643 provided a break in this quiet routine. Lively rumors of pearl fisheries along the coasts of Lower California caused considerable excitement in the capital, and a maritime expedition under Admiral Pedro Porter de Casanate was organized to reconnoiter the region. This distinguished officer, a Knight of the Spanish Order of Saint James, possessed an intellectual curiosity that moved him to peep into odd corners of knowledge, some quite unorthodox. Perhaps it was a mutual concern for curious bits of learning that drew this gentleman and Pérez de Soto together, for he appointed the latter a captain of one of the ships with a crew of thirty men. Among other things the Admiral liked to cast horoscopes, in which prohibited exercise he had developed considerable skill. The three months together on what proved a fruitless undertaking apparently stirred in Pérez de Soto a desire to venture into the dangerous shallows of Astrology into which his influential companion had piloted him.

Upon his return from Lower California the architect-builder had little opportunity to pursue this fascinating subject, for his well established professional reputation caused the viceroy to send him on a mission of inspection to the damaged fort at San Juan de Ulloa. Scarcely back in Mexico City from this assignment he departed on a trip to some mines at Tetela with his brother-in-law. These interruptions possibly diverted his mind temporarily from his new interest but a seed was planted that would grow and presently involve him in fatal consequences.

After these various excursions in 1643, Pérez de Soto resumed the quiet tenor of his way, spending much time with his books and acquiring many more in varied fields. His extensive knowledge and studious habits doubtless impressed those about him, perhaps arousing suspicions among his uncultivated fellow craftsmen, jealous of the reputation which had won him the coveted appointment of chief mason on the uncompleted Cathedral and other important buildings. There was something queer, it seemed, about a person who spent his spare time poring over strange tomes and perhaps dabbling in occult matters.

And it was true, as the inventory of his book collection later revealed, that this capable artisan was allowing his curiosity to carry his mind over a wide range of secular subjects, most of them well removed from the "divine science" of theology and religion. Of special significance was a group of a hundred or more volumes pertaining to astrology, astronomy, and related subjects. It seemed as if the inquisitive, exploring mind of Pérez de Soto, after wandering about the intellectual map, had found astrology, palmistry, and similar black arts a congenial resting place for his curiosity and enthusiasm.

These pseudo sciences, with their associations of sorcery, necromancy, and magic, possessed a morbid fascination for the superstitious classes of a neomedieval society, and many dark practices found adherents even among the literate and more cultivated elements.[3] Some stealthily cast horoscopes, read palms, and made predictions by unhallowed means of divination despite the efforts of the Holy Office to stamp out all such forbidden practices. Even clergymen were known to dabble in these matters, and the Chair of Mathematics at the University of Mexico included formal instruction in astrology as an aid to the compilation of almanacs. Particularly seductive was "judiciary" astrology which sought to read the future in the stars. This activity the Church vigorously assailed through its secular arm, the Inquisition, which institution, as recently as 1616, had issued an edict forbidding, on pain of total excommunication, illicit practices, including the casting of horoscopes. "There is no human art or science capable of manifesting the things which are to come," the Holy Office had declared, "when they are dependent on the will of man, for this has been reserved by God our Lord for Himself, with His eternal wisdom."[4] Even so stern a stricture did not discourage clandestine interest and the book-loving Pérez de Soto found its fascination irresistible.

About 1650 it appears that he aroused the suspicions of the Inquisitors who began to form a dossier on him. That year they had arrested a freed mulatto named Gaspar Rivero Vasconcelos, whom they charged with possible heresy, defamation of the Holy Office, and practicing astrology. As usual in such matters these judicial authorities urged the accused to do his "Christian" duty both by confessing his misdeeds and by informing on persons known to him to have committed sins of any sort. Doubtless hoping that compliance would soften the severity of the judges, Rivero gave testimony against several individuals, among them Pérez de Soto. This person, he alleged, on more than one occasion had loaned him treatises on astrology; moreover, he had even employed the mulatto to translate some of them from Latin to Spanish. And earlier, before starting on a journey to Yucatan, Rivero had left all his papers with the architect; subsequently, when he returned to Mexico City and demanded their return, Pérez de Soto coolly reported that he had lost them.

Whatever importance the Inquisitors attached to these statements it evidently was not enough for them to take action, and two years elapsed without adding anything to the dossier. Then it was that a former roomer in Pérez de Soto's house made damaging disclosures. He was a scribe, named Nicolás de Robles, who had also made translations from Latin for the architect. Halfway through one of the volumes he came across a discussion of free will and the prediction of the future. Fearing that the book was heretical, Robles had confided his misgivings to a clergyman who urged him to report the matter to the Inquisition. He decided, however, to finish the translation first as otherwise his quick-witted employer might divine his intention to denounce him to the Holy Office. But Robles added he had not actually seen Pérez de Soto practicing astrology. Nor did this testimony move the Inquisitors to press charges against a man whose services were so useful in the construction of the Cathedral. Instead, they continued to maintain a posture of watchful waiting.

As the months passed further bits of evidence accumulated. A garrulous student, José de la Cruz Benites, one of various translators hired by the bibliophile, decided that he must unbosom himself to the Inquisition officials. He rattled off a series of allegations concerning his former employer, including his possession of banned books, his formulation of remarkably accurate predictions, his casting of horoscopes, and related activities. A number of women also came to unburden consciences to the vigilant Inquisitors, asserting that Pérez de Soto had read their palms and made prognostications. By late 1654 the dossier was bulky with testimony indicating that the injudicious architect was not only guilty of horoscopy and of owning forbidden books, but also of using sorcery to discover stolen property. The moment for action had arrived, the judges decided. On January 12, 1655 they dispatched the familiars of the Holy Office to seize the person of Melchor Pérez de Soto, whether or not he had sought sanctuary in a "church, monastery, or other sacred or privileged place," and to sequestrate all his books and manuscripts.

Well before his arrest the Creole bibliophile must have had intimations of the difficulties into which his ill-advised hobby was leading him for, when the officers came in the evening with summonses to his house, he temporarily evaded detention by entering through a side entrance and locking the front door. But this stratagem merely delayed the event until the following morning when, bringing his own bed and fifty-eight *reales* to pay for his food, he was confined in the jail of the Inquisition.

For many weeks he remained incommunicado and in solitary confinement, interrupted now and then by brief hearings before the judges. Though uninformed of the charges against him he readily guessed their nature and stoutly declared his innocence of any evil intent. He denied being remiss to his Christian obligations, he asserted that, because of his ignorance of Latin, he had hired the translation of his books merely to ascertain their contents—among them were geometrical treatises that, in his profession as architect, he needed to know about—and he alleged that his predictions in no way refuted the doctrine of free will. The judges listened impassively and returned him to his cell with an injunction to make a total recall of his transgressions. This was customary judicial procedure designed to wear down the resistance of the prisoner who was presumed guilty until innocence was established. Justice was slow and the Court's patience was long. In desperation the accused frequently demanded hearings to confess even more than happened in the hope that the judges would relent and close his case. Meanwhile, witness after witness appeared before the Inquisitors, unbeknown to the hapless prisoner, to give testimony against him. One of those who thus added to the record declared that he had been acquainted with Pérez de Soto for thirty years and that he knew him to be dabbling in astrology during the last fifteen of them.

As the weeks of solitary confinement passed into months the accused architect grew profoundly despondent. The separation from his beloved library rendered his lot far more cruel than that of his illiterate fellow captives, and he implored the jail attendant to bring him just one book to divert him from the somber thoughts that oppressed him. Moved by the abject misery of his charge the sympathetic jailor cautiously slipped into his hands a treatise on the duties of a good monarch and his subjects, and later stealthily supplied him with writing materials. For these acts of charity the compassionate turnkey was later tried by the unpitying Inquisition and sentenced to four years of labor in the Hospital de Nuestra Señora de la Concepción.

Sinking ever more deeply into dark depression, Pérez de Soto read and reread this dull guide in his tiny cell until he almost knew it by heart. His ink and paper he used to pen a pathetic epistle to his wife, blaming his enemies for his plight. His mind often reverted to his work on the Cathedral—he had been working out a scheme for transferring the huge bells of the old Cathedral to the lofty belfries of the new when misfortune overtook him—and he wrote a barely decipherable missive instructing a workman on the execution of a constructional detail. Neither communication reached its destination, for the Inquisition authorities intercepted them to add to the bulky proceedings.

Anxiety, frustration, and isolation were rapidly unhinging the prisoner's mind. The only sound of the outside world penetrating into the dark recesses of his cell was the melancholy tolling of the Cathedral bells, and he strove to interpret the meaning of their slow strokes. More and more this distant ringing obsessed him, haunting his distraught spirit, filling him with foreboding as if it were the dread warning so poignantly expressed in the words of Macbeth: "Hear it not, Duncan, for it is a knell that summons thee to heaven, or to hell."

The mental deterioration of Pérez de Soto did not escape the notice of the Inquisitors who relaxed their severity enough to counsel him not to abandon hope but to bow to the Divine Will. This gentle admonition was hardly adequate to the need of their afflicted victim, and his utterances became almost incoherent. The stern judges doubtless believed that considerations of genuine charity decided them to lessen his solitude and relieve his melancholy by allowing him a cellmate. They selected a mestizo fellow prisoner, Diego Cedillo by name, who accordingly moved into the narrow quarters of the now unbalanced book collector.

When the jailer made his rounds the next morning at seven o'clock a sickening sight met his gaze on looking into the cell. Sprawled at the foot of his prison cot lay the battered body of the demented Pérez de Soto, while cowering in a corner was the half-caste, his hands and face spattered with blood and his clothes in tatters. The hastily summoned Inquisitors immediately questioned the trembling cellmate who, in broken phrases, gave his version of the tragedy. After extinguishing the candle the night before, the insane architect had crawled over to the sleeping form of Cedillo and seized him by the throat with the manifest intention of choking him to death. The mestizo awoke and grappled with his assailant in the blackness of the tiny cell. During the fierce scuffle Cedillo's hand encountered a loose stone with which he struck down the maddened Pérez de Soto, killing him with repeated blows. The investigators discovered some discrepancies in Cedillo's account and an autopsy performed upon the dead man did not entirely corroborate his story. Further efforts to determine the exact circumstances of the killing came to an abrupt end, however, when, a few days later, the body of Cedillo was found hanging from a beam of his cell by a rope made of a twisted bedsheet.

Meanwhile, the remains of the ill-fated bibliophile, wrapped in a Carmelite habit, were buried in the Saint Dominic monastery. Only when her husband's effects were brought home did the distracted wife fully sense what had happened. Screaming hysterically, she flung herself upon a bed where a merciful unconsciousness presently enveloped her.

After taking Pérez de Soto into custody the agents of the Holy Office promptly carried off his library for minute inspection by the *correctores*, or censors, of that institution. Confiscation of an accused person's property was a normal formality of judicial procedure and the owner's rights were deemed adequately protected by a written inventory preserved in the legal proceedings. The inquisitional representatives, accordingly, made a hasty list of the books, seemingly in the order that they were found in boxes and trunks, without apparent classification and with abbreviated titles. The exact number remains in doubt owing in part to the carelessness of the compilers, and in part to an unsuccessful effort of Doña Leonor to protect her husband by withholding volumes that she thought incriminating. Her indiscreet remarks in this connection quite nullified her laudable intention, for the Inquisition thus learned of her action and soon placed the missing works with the others in its possession, making a probable total, as already suggested, of 1,663 volumes.

This remarkable collection is much too large and varied for detailed analysis. It included not only an amazing diversity of religious literature, secular nonfiction, and belles-lettres in such different languages as Latin, Italian, French, Flemish, Dutch, and even English, but much in the owner's native Spanish. The prevalence of Italian and Italianate writers and works noted earlier in García Becerril's personal library is here more amply confirmed by the presence of such names as: Dante, Petrarch, Guicciardini, Guarini, Sannazaro, Ariosto, Tasso, and Castiglione in pure literature, and of many others in more technical fields. It is an astonishing miscellany of books assembled by a man of little formal education and modest means, and its existence testifies both to the wide circulation of printed volumes in Old Mexico and to a high level of culture achieved in this outpost of western civilization in the seventeenth century.

Religious literature, currently the most esteemed, claims about one-third of the total, chiefly homiletic writings by Santa Teresa of Ávila, Saint John of the Cross, Luis de Leon, and Luis de Granada, and many others. Perhaps the most unexpected items were those advocating silent prayer for they seem to anticipate the Quietist heresy about to agitate the Catholic world.

A much larger portion of the works falls into the category of secular nonfiction, with many items relating to history, philosophy, architecture, sculpture, music, medicine, mathematics, military science, navigation, astrology, and astronomy, along with numerous treatises on practical arts such as agriculture, mining, horsemanship, carpentry, cookery, and the like. Of history alone there were over one hundred and fifty titles which traced the story of the world from its beginnings to Pérez de Soto's own time. Conspicuous among the works on astronomy were the names of Copernicus and Kepler who were still suspect in the Orthodox Catholic world of which Old Mexico was a part. Indeed, at the mid-point of the seventeenth century when the Baroque age was in full flower, when the neomedieval culture of theology and scholasticism seemed all pervasive, particularly in the overseas possessions of Spain, such an abundance of scientific, mathematical, and technical literature in the library of an artisan with no apparent connection to the intellectual circles of viceregal society is surprising. Almost no field of knowledge evaded his curiosity, and his aggregation of writings provides an impressive sampling of the scientific as well as the esthetic thought of the sixteenth and seventeenth centuries. It makes evident the fact that, beneath the surface of the excessively verbalistic learning of the time, there was a hard substratum of knowledge based on observation and measurement that now and then had outcroppings in New Spain in figures of solid capacity and pragmatic erudition.

Although the third category embracing fiction, poetry, fables, essays, and proverbs claimed only about one-fifth of the collection, it represented the writings that enjoyed most popularity and were most widely read throughout the Hispanic world. They were the books that more frequently passed from hand to hand, particularly in the New World realms of Spain, and hence a few representative titles deserve mention.

If García Becerril in 1620 had been content with only two novels, the famous *Tragi-comedy of Calixto and Melibea* or *La Celestina,* and an inferior pastoral tale, Pérez de Soto owned two *dozen* of these prose narratives, not counting numerous novelettes and short story collections. And some of them hold a surprise for literary historians accustomed to a long-standing article of faith. Cervantes' great masterpiece—which is also absent in this inventory—had allegedly given the *coup de grâce* in 1605 to the protracted vogue of the romances of chivalry. This assumption, enjoying something of the sanctity of dogma, receives a disconcerting jar as the eye roves over this book list of a half century later. Names of fictional heroes, whose exploits had enraptured sixteenth-century readers, bob up unexpectedly. *Amadis of Gaul, Lisuarte of Greece, Amadis of Greece, Don Florisel of Niceae,* in two parts, recount the familiar adventures of legendary knights, curiously impervious to the satire of *Don Quixote.* Present also is the rival dynasty of Palmerin in *Palmerin of Oliva* (in Italian and Castilian), and *Palmerin of England,* and still other tales of this sort have a place in this mid-seventeenth-century library: *Don Belianis of Greece, Knight of the Cross,* and the *History and Military Service of Knight Pilgrim,* the last a pious romance designed to lure readers from the delights of the more mundane species. It is unlikely that Pérez de Soto's taste in this matter was unique, for these old-fashioned entertainments had some of the durability of modern Westerns. The inventory of the Creole architect's books, therefore, supplies an interesting sidelight on the story of chivalric literature after *Don Quixote.*

Still another shopworn form of reading pleasure—and one of even greater longevity—had charmed this Mexican bibliophile. It was the pastoral novel which told about lovesick shepherds and lassies. Of these saccharine tales he had a goodly number, including Sannazaro's epoch-making *Arcadia* (both in Italian and Castilian), Guarini's *Pastor Fido,* and *Diana,* the first and most famous of these falsifications of peasant life in Spain, written by the Portuguese-Spaniard, Jorge Montemayor (1520?-1561). This bestseller helped to inspire Sir Philip Sydney's *Arcadia* and the *Astrée* of Honoré d'Urfé, and it also influenced Cervantes' *Galatea,* and Old Mexico's own Bernardo de Balbuena's *Golden Age in the Groves of Eriphyle,* the latter two works being among Pérez de Soto's treasures.

For the other extreme of the novelistic spectrum—the crassly realistic and satiric tales of roguery—the architect of Mexico City also indulged a taste. The second part of *Guzmán de Alfarache,* whose famous author he had seen, conceivably, on the streets of the capital in his own childhood, stands beside the brutally cynical *History of the Life of the Buscon* by the great Spanish satirist, Francisco de Quevedo. *The Varied Fortunes of Pindaro, the Soldier,* by Gonzalo de Céspedes (1585?-1638), had the added spice of Gothic eeriness in the picaresque adventures related.

Novelettes and short story collections constitute a large miscellany among which is conspicuous the fourteenth century group of fifty moral tales, *Conde Lucanor,* recounted with subtle humor and irony by the grandson of Ferdinand IV of Castile, Juan Manuel, who thus presented a rich vein later tapped by such geniuses as Shakespeare and Cervantes. And similarly plentiful is the didactic literature of fables, proverbs, and aphorisms, often in dialogue form, beginning with Aesop's *Fables* (in Latin, Flemish, and Spanish). Of special interest is the *Book of Live and Witty, Clever and Sententious Sayings* of the great Dutch humanist Erasmus who, by his own admission, owed much to Spain where, however, various of his writings now adorned the *Index of Pro-*

hibited Books. Since García Becerril had submitted his book list to the Inquisition in 1620, the 1623 and 1640 editions of this Index had appeared, each more inclusive and more severe to suspected writers such as "magnus Erasmus."

Poetry had a generous representation in Pérez de Soto's library. The epic is noted in Homer's *Iliad*, Vergil's *Aeneid* (in Latin and Spanish), Dante's *Divine Comedy*, Camoen's *The Lusiads* (in Portuguese and Spanish), Ariosto's *Orlando Furioso*, Tasso's *Jerusalem Liberated*, Ercilla's historical *La Araucana*, and finally Balbuena's enormous *El Bernardo*, much of it written in Mexico. Of lyric verse the Creole architect's inventory almost provides an index from the fifteenth to the seventeenth centuries, including the *Works* of Luis de Góngora (1561-1627), the tutelary deity of Baroque poets and poetasters, particularly in Spanish America.

Among the many historical works present one author deserves a brief comment since his writings are acclaimed for their literary distinction and have a peculiar interest to colonial letters. The Inca Garcilaso de la Vega (1539-1616)—the "first American writer" as he is sometimes called, American in the special sense that he represented a new human species in the New World as the offspring of European and indigenous parents, and dealt particularly with American themes—was the product of a union of a Conquistador and an Incan princess. Born in Cuzco, high in the Andes, he departed for Spain after a childhood spent amidst the alarms of civil strife among the conquering masters. In the Peninsula he passed the rest of his life nostalgically recalling the scenes of his youth and the glories of his imperial ancestors. His *Royal Commentaries of the Incas*, now a classic of colonial literature though written in the mother country, idealized the vanishing civilization of his maternal progenitors. The eloquent simplicity of his style resulted from severe self-discipline in the language of his father gained through rigorous exercise in translation and through the composition of a novelesque account of De Soto's four years wandering in the lower Mississippi valley entitled *The Florida of the Inca*. Both of these artistically written narratives found a place in the admirably selected library of the Mexican Creole.

As a final comment on specific items which appear in Pérez de Soto's inventory, it is of interest to point out a curious coincidence of omission noted in García Becerril's list of 1620. Both collections lack copies of *Don Quixote*, though it is certain that many copies came to Mexico from 1605 on and circulated there. Even more notable is the complete absence in either report of indications of Spanish drama which, in the first half of the seventeenth century and later, was favorite reading fare as well as a popular spectacle throughout the Hispanic world. Odd indeed are these omissions in the personal libraries of two "average" readers of the time.

The existence of this remarkably rounded library in the hands of a relatively humble layman in a region remote from the cultural centers of Europe invites several queries. Where did this Creole of modest means acquire so many volumes? Was he unique in the possession of a collection of books so predominantly secular and nonreligious in nature? What significance is to be deduced from this mid-seventeenth century inventory? Only brief and tentative answers suggest themselves.

It seems reasonably certain that Pérez do Soto purchased his library little by little in local bookshops. Individuals in his circumstances rarely imported, it appears, directly from Peninsular booksellers who, in general, preferred to deal wholesale with colonial merchants. Itinerant peddlers and enterprising persons coming from Spain frequently brought salable volumes in their baggage to help defray the expenses of the voyage, and possibly the Creole bibliophile had acquired items in this manner. The trial proceedings tend to support this theory of local purchase, since one of the witnesses against him, Antonio Calderón, son of the proprietor of the best-established printing and bookshop in the capital, testified that the architect often came to his parent's store where he chatted about his astrological interests. While smuggling of prohibited books was certainly not unknown, it is likely that the Mexican booklover could acquire most of his, including those on his hobby, through legitimate channels.

It is too much to suppose that the arrest of this amateur astrologer revealed the only personal library of such varied works in the entire seventeenth century of Mexico. The earlier, less impressive collection of García Becerril disproves this belief. If one of such modest resources assembled so large and varied an aggregation of books, it is almost certain that wealthier members of the community, laymen as well as clergymen, brought together even richer assortments. Notarial records, published and unpublished, testify to the validity of this assertion, and it is hardly necessary to provide further proof of the inefficacy of earlier legislation against the free circulation of books, the application of which has been greatly misunderstood. The presence of so much creative literature and secular nonfiction on colonial book lists, of which Pérez de Soto's inventory is only one of the more interesting, indicates how little the Inquisition interfered with acquiring and reading works other than those of religious heresy. With the exception of astrological treatises the Holy Office returned in due course the entire collection of Pérez de Soto to his widow. It is clear, therefore, that only a little short of complete freedom of circulation was permitted in the Spanish overseas realms and that the variety and richness of the literary fare enjoyed there far exceeded what was then available to contemporary New Englanders who had to largely content themselves with the Bible and the locally printed *Bay Psalm Book* (1640).[5]

It remains, then, to inquire what became of this particular book collection of mid-century Mexico? Three days after the fateful end of Pérez de Soto in the dungeons of the Inquisition, a careful examination of his library was decreed. Prohibited works and those requiring expurgation, a very small minority, were put aside, and the much larger number of harmless volumes were divided into lots and returned to the widow. Less than two months after her husband's death she received a batch of 524 books, a few days later 416 more, and a third lot of 356 on June 5, 1655. Some 385 titles were withheld for close scrutiny by the Correctors, but six months later 304 of them came back to the deceased architect's domicile. On February 20, 1656, a final group of sixty-three expurgated volumes was delivered to Doña Leonor—actually the total now exceeded the number originally listed in the hasty inventory made by the familiars.

And what became of this remarkable book collection? On December 4, 1655, the impoverished widow begged the Inquisitors to return all permitted works, and especially "a book whose author is Argote de Molina, and the *Efemérides modernas,* because I have a purchaser. And the rest," she added, "I wish to sell as old paper because they seem such a lot and I am in very needy circumstances."

※ VII

THE INQUISITION
AND A PLAY

THE melancholy fate of Pérez de Soto is, unquestionably, a tragic indictment of the Inquisition. Clearly a flagrant miscarriage of justice had precipitated the bookloving architect into an acute manic depression ending in violence and death. The torturing slowness of a due process of law, built on the assumption of guilt until proof of innocence, seems a deliberately malicious procedure calculated to produce outrage and injustice. The methods were undeniably crude and cruel, if not primitive and barbarous, and they fully merit the opprobrium that posterity has so unsparingly heaped upon the tribunal that sanctioned them. Yet critics are unjust who make a sweeping condemnation without allowing the institution a hearing. To be entirely fair the Inquisition must be viewed in its time even more than its place. In that age the presumed guilt of the defendant, the snail-like movement of judicial machinery, its intent to provoke the victim into damaging admissions, the confiscation of property before adjudication, and the resort to physical torture, were legal practices all too common throughout Christendom. In many parts they operated without the restraint that the Holy Office usually exercised, and without the voluminous records that it kept. The surviving documentation is remarkably full and, by a curious irony of historiography, the meticulous detail thus preserved has enabled later generations to single out this particular tribunal for special invective. To the popular mind the Inquisition remains a uniquely sinister and despotic agency which diffused a miasmic pall over the community, darkening individual lives with corroding fear, and shriveling thought to a grisly skeleton of dogma.

This mental image, though with occasional validity, overlooks certain limiting factors. As in most human institutions the degree of severity varied with the character of the administrators and with the existing climate of feeling. Moreover, its power was diminished by jurisdictional and other conflicts with state officials, with business elements fretting at interference with profitable pursuits, and even with the hierarchy of the Church. Quarrels with religious communities on moot matters of doctrine often hampered the undivided sway of the Holy Office and the absolute authority of the Inquisitors. Since viceregal agencies, lay and religious alike, tended to exercise unseparated legislative, executive and judicial powers in performing their functions, each organization was inordinately sensitive about its prerogatives. Paralyzing disputes arising from overlapping jurisdictions were, consequently, almost continuous, and this friction frequently reduced the Spanish system to a vexatious equilibrium. Hence, the Inquisition, representing both Pope and King, often encountered resistance in both lay and ecclesiastical elements of society, and its effectiveness was less complete than commonly believed.

To defend, protect, and maintain "the purity of the Holy Faith and Good Morals" were the repeatedly announced aims of the Holy Office, branches of which Philip II had introduced into Peru and Mexico in 1570 and 1571. Prior to these dates bishops had exercised similar authority in their dioceses much as their predecessors had done in medieval Europe. The religious schisms sundering the Continent, and the determination of Spanish Catholicism to preserve orthodoxy at all costs from the contamination of heresy led to the installation of the Inquisition in outlying parts of the empire. This institution was not a Spanish invention, for it had existed in the Middle Ages and had functioned in Italy since the thirteenth century with little adverse effect on the Renaissance. It was later introduced into Aragon and, when the marriage of Prince Ferdinand of that region and Isabel of Castile established a diarchy in the Spanish Peninsula, it was the one institution common to both kingdoms. With its severity greatly tempered, it passed to the overseas realms of America where the Indian population, clearly recognized as children in the Faith, was specifically excluded from its jurisdiction.

The New World tribunals were staffed by two Inquisitors, or judges, a prosecuting attorney, and varying numbers of *consultores, calificadores,* and *familiares.* The first of these three functionaries were experts who gave advice on technical matters of law and procedure and who often included distinguished members of the viceregal society such as the judges of the Royal Audiencia. The *calificadores* or "qualifiers" were versed in the fine points of theology and their duty was to assay books and ideas for heretical content; hence they acted as censors. The *familiares* performed the pragmatic functions of plainclothesmen, detectives, jail wardens, and informers operating at large in the community. Other employees were constables, accountants, secretaries, lawyers for defense, a physician, jailers, and the like. The court archives were stuffed with wordy records of arrests, confiscations, inventories, transcripts, judicial opinions, and general correspondence. These endless sheaves of repetitive evidence and registers of court decisions that survive offer rich insights into the procedures of a notorious institution, and even more revealing glimpses of Baroque life in Old Mexico.

The emphasis so often placed on the persecution of religious heresy is misleading, for the Inquisition's energies went chiefly into adjudicating crimes and misdemeanors nowadays handled by municipal courts. Offenses of every variety against "good morals" far outnumbered those against "the purity of the Faith." The commonest cases were: bigamy, apparently as usual among women as men; solicitation in the confessional; sexual perversion; blasphemy; perjury; witchcraft; quackery, and superstition in multiple forms; and, finally, the practice of astrology. Prosecution was vigorous and stern edicts carried the authority of laws. Exceptional cases sometimes required instructions from the Supreme Council in Spain, which occasionally was a court of appeal, but generally the local tribunals acted independently, for they commonly confronted problems peculiar to their region. A curious instance appears in an edict of 1620, the year that García Becerril presented his list of books for scrutiny.

Vague reports for a long time had reached the Inquisition concerning the widespread use of a tiny, gray-green, spineless cactus called "peyote" (*Lophophora Williamsii*), possessing remarkable narcotic properties. Back in the middle of the sixteenth century a famous Franciscan missionary and pioneer anthropologist, Friar Bernardino de Sahagún, had noted the intoxicating effect of this plant, and Juan Cárdenas, in his *Primera parte de los secretos maravillosos de las Indias* (First Part of the Marvellous Secrets of the Indies), published in 1591 at Mexico City, had written about hallucinations caused by eating peyote.[1] Knowledge of its use by the Indians was not limited, however, to scientific minds, and the Inquisitors were increasingly aware that other elements of the population were experiencing its peculiar effects. By 1620 the decision to ban it was reached. "Inasmuch as the use of the weed or root called Peyote has been introduced into these Provinces," ran the edict, "for the purpose of detecting thefts, of divining other happenings, and foretelling events, it is an act of superstition and is condemned as opposed to the purity and integrity of our Holy Catholic Faith." The omniscient officers of the Inquisition went on to deny this "weed" some of its demonstrated properties. "This is certain because neither the said weed, nor any other, can possess the virtue, or inherent quality, of producing the effects claimed, nor can any cause the mental images, fantasies, and hallucinations on which the above-stated divinations are based. In these latter are plainly perceived the suggestion and intervention of the Devil, the real author of this vice, who first avails himself of the natural credulity of the Indians and their tendency to idolatry, and later strikes down other persons too little disposed to fear God and of too little faith." Because this abuse was spreading rapidly, the Inquisitors declared that "after consultation and conference with learned and right-minded persons, we order that henceforth no persons of whatever rank or social condition can or may make use of the said weed Peyote, nor of any other kind under any name or appearance for the same or similar purposes, nor shall he make the Indians or any other person take them, with the further warning that disobedience to these decrees shall cause us, in addition to the penalties and condemnations stated, to take action against such disobedient and recalcitrant persons as we would against those suspected of heresy to our Holy Catholic Faith."[2]

Matters of moral turpitude, then, largely preoccupied the Holy Office, while those of purely doctrinal heresy and censorship engaged it more rarely. Though the *calificadores* kept fairly busy checking over newly arrived books and pamphlets, the literature that concerned them was almost exclusively ecclesiastical in character and, as already noted, they seldom hindered the free circulation of secular and fictional works.

The awesome *autos de fe* are usually depicted as occasions when the victims of the Inquisition writhed in the tortures of public incineration while sadistic executioners and cowed masses looked on. Again the common tendency to regard the extreme and the spectacular as typical or, in modern parlance, as newsworthy, has created a distorted impression of reality. The proportion of death sentences was, perhaps, not more than one in a hundred, a ratio far exceeded in contemporary Europe, notably in the days of witchcraft prosecution. The penalties in Mexico were harsh, of course, for everywhere in the seventeenth century brutal punishments publicly administered were the accepted expression of justice, yet a review of the *votos,* or judicial opinions, of the Mexican Inquisitors often reveals unexpected moderation. The judges frequently differed among themselves as to the guilt of the accused, or regarding the proper retribution, and the prosecuting attorney usually abstained from injecting his biased recommendations.[3] Hence it appears, as in every court, justice varied according to personalities and prejudices.

Penalties for the many crimes against "good morals" ranged from penance rendered by marching in public processions, candle in hand and a rope about the neck, or other symbolic indications of guilt, to heavy fines, property confiscations, public whipping, varying periods of banishment from the vicinity or from the realm, and uncompensated service on royal galleys or sailing ships. Death was reserved for the most obstinate heretics, and in especially flagrant cases penalties were compounded. Not long after the establishment of the Holy Office at Mexico City in the late sixteenth century a certain Pedro de Trejo, who included being a poet among his crimes, was condemned not only to public penance and forced service on his Majesty's galleys, but to perpetual renunciation of composing couplets![4] Occasionally the dead received posthumous sentences for offenses subsequently discovered, and punishment was visited upon their effigies or disinterred bones.

After the middle of the seventeenth century, burning at the stake was rare, possibly because the cause of orthodoxy was largely won. The *auto de fe* of 1649, in which 109 persons received sentences of one sort or another, thirteen of whom were put to death, was, apparently, the culminating spectacle of this kind in the viceroyalty of Mexico, though a decade later a smaller one occurred.[5] Among its victims was a mysterious adventurer with illusions of grandeur, an alleged Irishman named Guillén de Lampart, who claimed to be an illegitimate offspring of the king of Spain and aspired to be the Emperor of an independent Mexico. He had, indeed, implicated the Inquisitors, who had imprisoned him, in a fancied conspiracy to detach the viceroyalty from its allegiance, which circumstance may have moved the judges to impose the extreme penalty upon him. During his long years of incarceration— the unhappy Pérez de Soto was briefly a fellow prisoner—Guillén de Lampart had diverted himself by composing in various languages remarkable treatises and literary pieces which survive.[6]

As the century passed its mid-point the routine of the inquisitional tribunal more and more resembled that of a modern police court with petty crimes and misdemeanors filling its docket. Sporadically its censorious activities intensified, and books, pamphlets, and especially plays, continued to receive careful scrutiny, though expurgation and emendation rather than outright prohibition usually resulted from this inspection. It was always expedient to keep a watchful eye on the local theater, which was frequented by the clergy as well as the lay public, for all too often a licentious note crept into the acting of the players, or offensive lines and dubious situations were discovered. But normally the Holy Office limited its interference to the deletion of disapproved passages, after which the play returned to the boards.

The early seventeenth century witnessed the Baroque effulgence of Spain's literary Golden Age, and the most dazzling manifestation of its prolific genius was a popular theater rivaled only by that of England. In the Peninsula a cluster of inspired playwrights burst like rockets in a scintillating display of brilliance and color that drew enthusiastic throngs to the rude playhouses to see and hear the latest comedies from their inexhaustible quills. "In the Castilian drama the stress is on action, on destinies rich in vicissitudes and, at the same time, on the lyrical embellishment of ornate verse," wrote Ortega y Gasset, who likened the prodigious output of the reigning dramatist, Lope de Vega, to painting rather than to sculpture. He declared it "a vast canvas, now luminous, now murky, on which all the figures shine with life and color, noblemen and commoners, archbishops and sea captains, queens and country lasses, a restless, garrulous, extravagant lot, madly swirling about like infusoria in a drop of water . . . ." And the twentieth-century philosopher continues: "Over the varied and intricate pattern of intrigue the poet poured his elaborate volubility, a profusion of glittering metaphors expressed in a vocabulary of darkest shadows alternating with brilliant light, a vocabulary reminiscent of the altar pieces of the same century."[7]

No less enthusiastic were the audiences of the New World capitals and cities who thronged the local *corrales* at the performances of the latest "hit" from Spain. The time lag was slight and, by the turn of the seventeenth century, troupes of Spanish actors entertained the colonial public with recent products of Peninsular dramatists. As early as 1604 Balbuena could metrically declare in his *Grandeur of Mexico City* that:

> entertainments and new comedies every day,
> each with several entr'acts and attractions,
> (give) pleasure, diversion and gaiety.

In the viceregal palace, imitating the luxury of the pleasure-loving court of Philip IV at Madrid, private performances of plays with elaborate costumes and scenery were common features of aristocratic life, while the popular theater offered aspiring Creole writers an opportunity to supply short skits for performance between the acts of the imported comedies. As in Spain these slight pieces served to keep the turbulent audience in check during such interludes.

As the successive decades of the century rolled by the popularity of the theatre remained despite a decline in the quality of plays and actors. Though little is known of the theatrical companies who graced the boards of the Mexican *corrales,* nor are many of the titles of the plays recorded, it appears that, toward the end of the century, the histrionic art in Mexico City had fallen to low estate. In the last ten-year period an Italian traveler, Gemelli Careri, spent a few months there during a remarkable tour of the world. He attended the local playhouse with some regularity and, with equal regularity, he complained to his diary about the inept acting and wretched performances. Under date of April 7, 1698, he wrote: "I went to the theater in the afternoon to see a comedy entitled

La dicha y desdicha del nombre (The Good and Bad Fortune of a Name). It was so badly played that I would more gladly have given the two *reales* it cost me to go in and take a seat not to have seen it. The actors performed badly; there were sixteen of them, American born, for Europeans consider it discreditable to play to the general public." The most charitable of his entries was on July 14, 1698: "Sunday I heard something rare in the theater, that is, a comedy decently played."[8]

Among the literate the Spanish drama evoked enthusiasm in print as well as on the stage, and this public avidly snapped up the collections of plays published in dozen lots called *Partes* and the single plays in pamphlet form known as *sueltas*. Imported from Spain, these publications poured into the bookstores from about 1605 and remained a stock in trade until the end of the colonial period. Whether heard in public or read in private this dramatic literature, like the cinematographic art in the twentieth century, exerted a profound influence on contemporary manners and morals. From the pulpits of the time came ringing denunciations in sermons and exhortations. A pious biography of a saint published in 1633 at Madrid loudly protests that ". . . the reading of books of plays was so general in ladies' drawing rooms and in maidens' chambers that women could only feel sophisticated when they talked about a love affair, an amorous difficulty, the vanquishing of male indifference, or the humble devotion of a swain."[9] Manners, dress, and ways of speaking were subtly modified on both sides of the Atlantic as the three-act plays, in inexpensive editions, attained a universality even greater than that of the romances of chivalry during the previous century. Readers were as absorbed by the shallow intrigues spun by nimble playwrights as their forebears had been by the fantastic adventures of the knights-errant. In Guatemala a chronicler related in shocked tones an incident in which a lady of easy virtue, an actress who had involved two suitors in a murder, impassively read a volume of plays while the men were being executed on the public square. "What I wish to relate so that the readers of these lines may be astonished and learn what women of easy virtue are like is the case of *la Catalina*. They took her to jail and, while they were hanging the two men, she unconcernedly took a seat in a small window facing the square. There she was reading a book of comedies and, when they dropped the body of the first man off the scaffold, she merely glanced up and then resumed reading. When the second man was hung, again she merely looked up and then went on reading her play. Those are the prayers she offered for the men whom she had brought to the gallows!"[10]

Though moralists assailed this diversion with unrelenting vigor this theatrical fare, whether in the form of cold type or live performance, like the earlier fiction of chivalry, never achieved the distinction of a collective ban. Now and then the self-styled custodians of "good morals" forced the withdrawal of a play from the boards and from printed circulation on the grounds of irreverence, disrespect, or downright blasphemy, and these allegations sometimes cloaked other reasons. One such instance occurred in 1682 when the manager of the Mexico City *Coliseo,* a name which had supplanted the plebian *corral de comedias,* was required to omit from the repertory a comedy by the popular Spanish playwright, Juan Pérez de Montalbán entitled *El valor perseguido y traición vengada* (Courage Persecuted, and Treachery Avenged).

Until his death in 1632 the three-act plays of the prolific Lope de Vega, true father of the Spanish theater, dominated the offerings of the stock companies on both sides of the Atlantic. In due course the works of his disciples, together with those of his great successor, Calderón de la Barca (1600-1681), whose theater most perfectly, perhaps, reflected the Baroque spirit, crowded his stagepieces off the boards during much of the remaining colonial period.[11] An uncritical public grew more indiscriminate and, after the first quarter of the seventeenth century, it bestowed a more lasting favor upon the short-lived, spiritual son of the great Lope, Pérez de Montalbán (1602-1638), storyteller and dramatist of a sort.[12] Despite or, perhaps, because of his mediocre talent, his plays still attracted a colonial audience as late as 1805.

This continued popularity is possibly attributable in part to the enduring success of his short stories and miscellaneous essays, notably a collection, *Para Todos* (For Everyone) inspired by the *Decameron* of Boccaccio. It had the good fortune to draw the fire of the remarkably talented satirist, Francisco de Quevedo (1580-1645), who parodied it in his *Perinola* and thus increased its sales in Spain and abroad.[13] An admiring merchant and bookseller in

Lima, Peru, Tomas Gutiérrez de Cisneros by name, purchased a chaplaincy for the young writer, thus delivering him from the grip of economic insecurity.[14]

Montalbán's playwriting began with a comedy *Morir y disimular* (To Die and Dissemble), written when he was seventeen, and during his remaining nineteen years, which were truncated by insanity, he managed to crowd in some fifty-eight plays in a futile effort to equal the prodigious output of his friend and mentor, that "marvel of nature," Lope de Vega. Like the latter he drew his themes from religious, legendary, historical, and adventure literature, and clothed them in ornate and fluent verse. His characterizations were less competent, and his style betrays more clearly a Baroque artificiality, but like his master, he pleased the masses by exploiting familiar ballads and, occasionally, topics of contemporary notoriety. One such work was his play *La monja-alférez* (Nun-Ensign) which utilizes the experience of a strange woman whose last years passed in Old Mexico.[15]

Catalina de Erauso presents a remarkable phenomenon of a masculinized female whose career became legendary. As a young girl she escaped from a nunnery in Spain and, in the garb of a man, fled to the New World in 1603. During the next twenty-one years her adventurous wanderings took her over the west coast of South America, where she gallantly battled Indians and won a commission as *alférez* or ensign. Her sex undetected, she transferred her activities from Chile to the sprawling realm of Peru, and in the mining camps of the Andes and in the underworld of the cities, she became involved in innumerable escapades, which included gambling, courting unsuspecting maidens, street brawls, and duelling. In an affair of honor she allegedly killed her own brother, her identity unbeknown to him. Only when severely wounded on another occasion was her gender revealed and, under the protection of a bishop, she temporarily resumed feminine apparel. Returning to Europe in 1624, she traveled widely and in Italy her celebrity gained her an audience with the Pope and the lavish entertainment of princes, bishops and cardinals. After some years she returned to the New World, in masculine attire and with an incipient mustachio, to spend her last years as a mule driver in packtrains transporting goods between Vera Cruz and Mexico City. On one of these journeys in 1650 a fatal illness reportedly overtook her and, with as much pomp as the circumstances permitted, she was buried on a hillside near the village of Cuitlaxtla.[16] With the theme of the heroine disguised as a man an indispensable part of the stock in trade of the Spanish theater, Montalbán's use of so newsworthy a personage as the "Nun-Ensign" for a play causes no surprise.[17]

His *Courage Persecuted and Treachery Avenged*, whose improprieties merited the unusual distinction of banishment from the Mexican stage in 1682 by the Inquisition, was certainly not his best comedy nor was it even a good play. Indeed, its esthetic defects might justly have entitled it to proscription, but these were not the reasons that moved the Holy Office to so stern a measure. There exists, to be sure, some doubt regarding the authorship of the play, but the evidence points an accusing finger at Pérez de Montalbán as the true begetter. The following summary may suggest its mediocrity.

Act I.

Ramón de Moncada, second son of the Count of Barcelona, returns to Naples flushed with a sea victory over the Turks and eager for the Princess Matilde's love. This daughter of the King of Naples invites the hero to her garden after midnight. Durón, who supplies the comic relief, reminds Ramón of his erstwhile interest in Octavia, daughter of the Duke of Ferrara, and warns of a possible mischance in his rendezvous with the Princess. Count Arnesto, the rejected suitor of Matilde, plots to keep the appointment in place of Ramón and induces the King to detain his rival that night. With Ramón thus held in a game of chess Count Arnesto, mistaken by Matilde in the darkness for Ramón, is admitted and enjoys her favors. The servant Durón, sent by Ramón to watch at Matilde's balcony, falls asleep but awakens to see Arnesto leaving the house. Ramón, arriving later, learns that he has been tricked and, though the Princess from her balcony asks why he fled her arms so abruptly and invites him to return, he believes himself ill-fated and resolves to return to Spain. Durón urges him to go by way of Ferrara and seek Octavia whom he formerly loved.

Act II.

Princess Matilde confesses her dishonor to her father, the King, and demands that her disgrace be avenged. This apparent betrayal and Ramón's subsequent marriage to Octavia angers the King, who seeks Arnesto's aid in bringing Ramón back by guile. Arnesto, fearing discovery of his own guilt, urges that Ramón be compelled to kill Octavia and marry the Princess. Reluctantly the King acquiesces. In an abrupt change of scene Octavia, with forebodings of disaster to her husband, tells Durón of the King's summons to Ramón. Octavia's fears are confirmed by her husband's confession of his projected rendezvous with the Princess and the King's reported command to repair the damaged honor of Matilde by killing Octavia. The latter's devotion to Ramón moves her to sacrifice herself and, as he embraces her, Arnesto arrests him, leaving Octavia fainting in Durón's arms. Arnesto reappears, asking Octavia's favors in return for sparing her life. Her refusal causes the angered Arnesto to tie her to a tree, telling her to die in the knowledge that it was he who dishonored the Princess and that Ramón, though innocent, will be imprisoned. Octavia, about to give birth, is rescued by a farmer, Alberto, who takes her to his cottage.

Act III.

The King of Naples learns that Ramón's insanity has frustrated his scheme to vindicate the Princess' honor. In a mad scene Ramón declares that the truth will out. In another abrupt shift of place Carlos, a farmer lad, pondering over his unknown parentage, comes upon the King lost in the woods on a hunt. Unaware of the King's identity, Carlos recounts the low esteem in which this monarch is held by his subjects and enumerates the qualities that royalty should possess. Octavia, who is the mother of Carlos and is dressed in the garb of a peasant woman, informs the King, likewise ignorant of his identity, of his ill repute and the anger of his people at Arnesto because of the murder of Octavia. Greatly perturbed, the King departs and Carlos learns from Octavia who was his father. Carlos vows to avenge Ramón. From Durón, now a soldier foraging supplies, Octavia learns that her father and the Count of Barcelona are sending troops to liberate Ramón. The King repents accepting Arnesto's advice to kill Octavia and, acquiescing to the demand of Carlos, who has just freed Ramón, his father, he reveals the identity of Arnesto. The latter confesses his crime, whereupon the King orders him to marry the Princess, after which he will be flung to wild beasts. Carlos demands a duel instead, and slays

Arnesto. As the armies close in, all is happily resolved. The Princess becomes a nun, Carlos marries the King's younger daughter, Ramón and Octavia will rule Ferrara with her peasant companions exalted to household servants, and the King will pay the costs of war.[18]

This crude play with its silly plot and unnatural situations exemplifies the Baroque decadence which soon overtook Spanish dramatic genius. Structurally, it is poorly knit, and there is little logic in the ordering of the scenes. Incidents known to the audience are needlessly recapitulated in tiresome monologues of hollow rhetoric, while the unities of time and place receive more than ordinary cavalier treatment. Bad taste obtrudes in the scarcely witty coarseness of Durón, yet the play somehow manages to present a few interesting moments. The tragic dilemma of Ramón when ordered to kill his wife at the King's command and marry the Princess probably recalled the ballad of the Count of Alarcos and the Princess Solisa familiar to the theatergoers of the time. This theme a sixteenth century dramatist, Torres Naharro, had utilized, and it was impressively exploited as late as 1917 by Jacinto Grau, another Spanish playwright, in his *Count Alarcos*.

But what circumstances caused the exceptional penalty of banning in toto *Courage Persecuted and Treachery Avenged* in Mexico City? What were the reasons of the Holy Office for so drastic an action? The answer to these queries is, perhaps, a fruitful means of observing the criteria by which that dreaded institution reached its decisions.

Since this episode occurred in 1682 it is possibly connected with the elevation of Fray Aguiar y Seijas to the archbishopric of Mexico that year. This prelate was of an excessively puritanical cast of mind and, in many respects, the direct antithesis of his famous predecessor earlier in the century, Fray García Guerra. In contrast to the latter, Archbishop Aguiar y Seijas was inclined to attribute the universal state of sinfulness to the general indulgence in the pleasures of the bull ring and the theater. One of his first measures upon assuming his exalted office was to limit, if not eliminate, such public spectacles. His antipathy for the drama extended to the reading of plays as well as to their performance, and he tried to dissuade, somewhat vainly it appears, the local booksellers from keeping in stock the exceedingly popular collections of comedies. His limited knowledge of human nature seems further demonstrated by a naive plan he adopted to induce readers to part with their treasures of dramatic literature in exchange for copies of *Consuelos de pobres* (Consolation of the Poor), a pious tract lauding the virtues of almsgiving, of which he had apparently imported 1,500 copies from Spain. A few devout possessors of printed plays, perhaps fearing the righteousness of the Archbishop, turned over their well-thumbed volumes to the prelate who carefully burned them.[19] But the success of this stratagem was hardly encouraging for no appreciable decline in play-reading or attendance at the local playhouse is recorded.

One Sunday of April in 1682 the Reverend Friar Bartolomé de San Antonio, a Dominican, dropped into the Coliseo of Mexico City and witnessed the first act of a comedy and the *entremés,* or short skit, which followed. Shocked by what he heard he hastily departed from that profane precinct without pausing to ascertain the titles of the plays. Whatever had drawn him to that unholy place of amusement—gentlemen of the cloth frequently found diversion there—he felt obligated to pen a complaint which he promptly presented to the Holy Office the next morning. Specifically, he declared in his *denuncia* that he had heard distorted and profane allusions to the story of Jacob and Esau contained in Genesis 27, and also to Psalms 23 and 31. Obviously, it was his duty to report such sacrilege to the Inquisition.

The Chief Inquisitor lost no time in dispatching a messenger to the manager of the theater to fetch scripts of the offensive comedy and entr'acte. The inquisitional emissary soon brought back the required text which proved to be that of *Courage Persecuted and Treachery Avenged,* authorship attributed to Montalbán, and of *El sacristán* (The Sexton), a skit by Pedro Bezerra. The tribunal promptly passed the manuscripts to the *calificadores,* Fathers Augustín Dorantes and Antonio Núñez de Miranda, the latter a Jesuit.

Three days later the first-named censor, a Dominican, reported his findings. These dramatic pieces, he stated categorically, must not and could not be allowed on the stage or in circulation. He cited examples of the reprehensible material in them, especially the comedy. Blasphemous verses indeed were those of Ramón's overenthusiastic acceptance of Princess Matilde's invitation to visit her after midnight.

> I shall count the minutes of the sun,
> and pray God that, as I desire, it will hasten
> its course, and that night, the cloak of lovers,
> may soon cast its sable shadows.
> And I pray God, as a favor, not to bring out
> the panoply of His bright stars.*

Such a prayer was sacrilegious since it requests God's connivance in the satisfaction of an illicit desire and seeks to make Him an accomplice in a sinful and immoral act.

Similarly condemned was the repeated use of symbolic language and allusions to sacred writings as, for example, Arnesto's aside as he accepted the ardent, if unintentional, invitation of the Princess to enjoy her favors.

> Coming in the disguise of Esau
> I would deceive an Isaac,
> and steal the blessing,
> like Jacob in falling heir.†

The use of the word "blessing" for the intended sin was utter impiety, and especially since it is repeated in the same act. When Ramón finds out that someone else has kept his assignation, he mutters:

> If a man left by the door,
> he doubtless arrived on time,
> and stole the blessing . . . ‡

---

* Ramón: Contarele los minutos
del sol, que en su paralelo
ruego a Dios (como yo quiero)
passe, y que tienda sus lutos
la noche capa de amantes,
y le pido por favor
no saque el aparador
de sus estrellas brillantes.

† Arnesto: Entró con piel de Esau,
enganaría a un Isaac
y hurtando la bendición
qual Jacob al heredar.

‡ Ramón: Si hombre salió por la puerta
sin duda a tiempo llegó
que la *bendición* me hurtó. . . .

The Inquisition's unceasing efforts to eradicate the common evils of sorcery, fortunetelling, faith in omens, astrology, predictions and any disposition to anticipate individual destiny often brought harsh punishment to the guilty, as Pérez de Soto had learned so grievously. Hence, a foreboding speech of the hapless Octavia in Act II was deemed ample justification for a complete ban on *Courage Persecuted and Treachery Avenged*. The offending passage reads:

> The soul never betrays
> and alas! tonight, if I heed
> the melancholy signs and auguries
> in crossing the stream
> that flows through the gorge,
> the horse on which Ramón was riding,
> stumbled on wading through the chill waters,
> and threw him to the ground.
> The nocturnal birds were singing
> amidst the ash trees and beeches
> and, quoth the echo: Don't go!
> for they foretold some great ill.
> The somber crow cawed continuously,
> and its melancholy plaint
> seemed more like weeping than a song.
> Under these and other tidings of evil
> he had hardly reached the Palace
> when almost immediately,
> the King summoned him . . .*

And Ramón's gloomy speech on leaving Octavia to obey the

---

* Octa-   El alma nunca es traydora
   via: Y esta noche, ay tristes señas,
           si los agüeros apoyo
           al pasar aquel arroyo
           que corre entre aquellas peñas.
           Él cavallo tropeçó
           adonde Ramón venía,
           al cortar el agua fría,
           y en la arena le arrojó.
           Aves nocturnas cantavan
           entre los fresnos y hayas,
           diziendo el eco: no vayas,
           que algún gran mal anunciavan.
           La lamentable corneja
           no cessava de cantar

   que más parece llorar
   que canto su triste quexa.
   Con estos y otros agüeros
   apenas llegó a Palacio,
   quando dentro en breve espacio
   le llamó el Rey . . . .

royal summons to repair the damaged virtue of the Princess involved theological definitions. In it he declared:

> I had great good fortune in possessing thee,
> and great misfortune in losing thee.
> If it was grace to win thee,
> it is eternal penance to leave thee.*

"Eternal penance," it is explained, could only be appropriate in case of deprivation of, or separation from, that which is infinite, that is, from God Himself.

As for another speech of Ramón uttered when he fondly embraced Octavia:

> Hug me again and again,
> so that love may order
> that you be indelibly
> printed on my soul
> like a sacred symbol,†

that sentiment simply did not sound well! In conclusion Father Dorante asserted that the author displayed too little delicacy in handling "immoral matters" in the play; in fact, he treated them so persuasively that they could not fail to be detrimental to modesty and good morals.

The second examiner, Father Antonio Núñez de Miranda, contented himself a week later with echoing the objections of his colleague and confirming his judgment. It would be well, indeed, he agreed, to put a stop to such unnatural and pernicious mingling of the reverent and the blasphemous, the sacred and the profane, to which so many, many playwrights were addicted!

Some three weeks later the prosecuting attorney advised the Chief Inquisitor of his acceptance of the findings of the *calificadores,* and he heartily recommended that the play and accompanying skit be prohibited *in toto.* In a marginal note the judge ordered the gathering up of all copies of the offending plays and the pub-

---

* Ramón: Tuve gran suerte en gozarte
            y gran desdicha en perderte,
            si fué gloria el merecerte
            es pena eterna dexarte . . . .
† Ramón: Abráçame muchas vezes
            en fee que en el alma asida
            como caracter sagrado
            me manda amor que te imprima

lication of a corresponding edict forbidding entirely their performance in public or reading in private.[20]

These proceedings required about three months from the date when Father Navarro made his hasty exit from the local theater, but the resulting edict was not immediately posted. Following the customary practice, it was withheld until a sufficient list of books, pamphlets, and other papers meriting expurgation or banning had accumulated. Thus almost a year elapsed after Father Navarro's shocked visit to the Coliseo, it was April 12, 1683, to be exact, before the formal decree against *Courage Persecuted and Treachery Avenged* by the currently popular dramatist, Pérez de Montalbán, was tacked upon the doors of the Cathedral and churches in the cities, towns, and villages of the realm. Meanwhile, the *empresario* of the local theater had dropped the offensive pieces from the extensive repertory of his company of actors.

❧ VIII

A MASCARADA

"TO MAKE of life a drama, and of drama, life" was, in a sense, a fundamental principle of the Baroque age. If this was true in Old Spain, where the tragedy of bloody strife and imperial disintegration was unfolding, it was even more so in New Spain to which the alarms of incessant war in Europe came as distant, muted echoes, and where emotional excitement required the more artificial stimulation of colorful spectacles and histrionic devices. If the mother country was fatally engaged in making of life a tragic drama, its remote and sheltered possessions, dwelling in relative peace and settled order, felt impelled to make of diverting drama a more pulsating way of life.

This isolation of the overseas realms from the turmoil of the Old World presents a contrast which has moved many to picture existence in the former colonies of Spain as tediously dull, monotonous, and drab. There, it is sometimes imagined, the cowed populace passed its days in almost monastic austerity, breathing an atmosphere of fear under the heavy shadow of the Church and the Inquisition, its vitality inhibited save in the devout practices of an intolerant religion. This depressing vision, however, overlooks the inventive resources of an imaginative people and is a false impression of reality. To those whose destiny it was to live divorced from the fratricidal contentions of rising nationalism and sectarian partisanship tormenting Europe, this freedom did not seem so gray nor life so empty as posterity is prone to believe. Indeed, for many, especially in the cities and large towns where much of the

117

populace resided, existence was far from colorless and dreary. If for the majority hard labor, long hours of toil, social indifference, and harsh neglect seemed the law of nature, its severity was mitigated and the heavy routine was broken by feast days and public celebrations so numerous as to make serious inroads on the calendar year. Religious and civic festivals, organized with the pomp, ceremony, and lavish display that the Baroque mind so easily contrived, multiplied in a vain effort to overtake the increasing demand for public spectacles as the seventeenth century progressed. Appropriate occasions for colorful observance seemed to proliferate, and the Mexico of the viceroys experienced no lack of amusements, both public and private.

The temperaments of the Spanish overlords and their wards of whatever racial composition were not so far apart as their social differences. The natural gaiety and love of show were common characteristics of conqueror and conquered, and this similarity made mutual participation in diversions a frequent feature of community life. It was an association, half democratic in spirit, which went far to lessen the tensions of ethnic diversity and caste distinction. The Church, whose influence so clearly permeated every phase of social and cultural existence, did not fail to recognize this general passion for pageantry which it shrewdly utilized to its own advantage by sponsoring processions displaying the richly clothed images and ornate symbols of the Faith with all the pomp, splendor, and wealth at its command. To the many holy days for this kind of observance were added special occasions, such as the canonization of a saint, the arrival of sacred relics, the investiture of bishops, convent festivals for patron saints, and the like. The revered treasures and trophies were then brought forth to dazzle the eyes of the faithful and to convey to their simple minds the great Glory of God and of His Church. Now and then friars and monks of the religious orders solemnly paraded about the streets and public squares to voice their thanks to the Virgin for her favors and to solicit her intercession in times of stress. Especially impressive was the celebration of Corpus Christi, which invariably featured a specially written and lavishly staged morality play. And, much more rarely, occurred an awe-inspiring *auto de fe,* a grave and universal "act of faith."

If these functions appear to confirm the oppressiveness of colonial life, other spectacles, probably outnumbering them, brought joyous excitement and childish delight to the onlookers. Public reaffirmation of allegiance to the crown, births, baptisms, marriages in the royal and viceregal families, oaths of fidelity to the royal standard, news of victories in Europe, the safe arrival of the annual fleets, and many other secular events were occasions for celebration lasting days and weeks. Then gay processions of decorated floats and uniformed figures, with a flourish of trumpets and strains of martial music, wound through the streets festooned with banners and bunting, damask, velvet, and lace hangings, and rugs and tapestries suspended from balconies. All other community activities ceased as every caste and class lined the thoroughfares to enjoy the multicolored spectacle. Similarly, for the emotion and frenzy of war-stricken Europe, they substituted the less sanguinary contests of the bull ring and the cockpit, and found emotional release in romantic and liturgical plays performed at public theaters and temple courtyards. The magnificence and pleasing agitation of these diversions, which appealed to their instinctive *gaieté de coeur,* served to distract the masses from a preoccupation with their ills and thus helped to keep unrest from exploding into violence greater than an occasional riot.

The commonest public spectacle was the *máscara* or *mascarada.* It was, essentially, a parade of persons dressed in varied costumes and wearing peculiar masks, who promenaded about the streets by day or night, on foot, or mounted on horses or other animals; if after dark, they carried lighted torches, giving the city an unaccustomed illumination. They represented historical, mythological, and Biblical personages, gods of primitive religions, astrological planets, allegorical figures of Virtues, Vices, and other abstractions, and almost any bizarre creature, real or imaginary, was a welcome novelty. Impersonations reflected themes which varied from the sublime to the ridiculous, from the refined to the grotesque, and from the exalted to the most satirized. To an illiterate public the *mascarada* was like an animated magazine bringing before their avid eyes a semblance of things real and imagined; it instructed, it diverted, it entertained, and it often expressed their moods, their reverence, and their resentment. Not infrequently these spectacles indulged in satire of such crudeness and vulgarity that they would seem offensive to authorities, but the usual lack of interference from that source reveals a freedom of expression and an absence of censorship hardly suspected in that Baroque society.

The *máscaras* sometimes brought to the vast, unlettered population visual conceptions of characters in well-known novels and books currently enjoyed by the literate minority of the community. On January 24, 1621, at Mexico City, a spectacle of this sort featured a special attraction. Almost entirely composing the masquerade were the familiar figures of heroes of the still-popular romances of chivalry: Amadis of Gaul, Don Belianis of Greece, Palmerin of Oliva, and the Knight of Phoebus. As evident by the presence of these novels in the library of the ill-fated Pérez de Soto, Cervantes' recent burlesquing of the fantastic adventures of these fictional supermen had not yet destroyed their vogue. Perhaps the youthful Pérez de Soto was among the spectators lining the streets when this particular parade was passing and possibly this incarnation of the mythical heroes whetted his appetite to read and acquire copies of these exciting stories. And, likewise, the older García Becerril may have witnessed the same event, though his modest collection of books fails to reflect any influence of this sort.

Immediately following the revue of fictional exemplars of derring-do indicated came the latest and most amusing, the Knight of the Sorrowful Countenance, Don Quixote de la Mancha, whose misadventures for fifteen years now were common knowledge. But only the comic eccentricities of this chivalrous idealist were displayed before the crowds thronging the streets. Behind this most recent paladin of chivalric fiction appeared two odd-looking figures mounted on camels easily recognized as Melia, the Enchantress, and Urganda, the Protectress of medieval knights, here irreverently depicted as a tattered hag. Next in order rode two renowned eunuchs, Ardian and Bucendo, each astride an ungainly ostrich which strutted in awkward fashion before the appreciative onlookers. The climactic feature of this diverting spectacle was a caricature of the rotund Sancho Panza and of Don Quixote's light-of-love, Doña Dulcinea de Toboso, both mounted in comic dignity on patient, decrepit donkeys, whose arrival was the signal for a final, spontaneous burst of laughter from the delighted spectators.[1] The presence of these figures inspired by the novel *Don Quixote* on the streets of Mexico City that historic year of 1621 offers curious testimony to the acceptance of Cervantes' great work in a distant realm so soon after its publication in Spain and indicates the place it already occupied in popular lore.

These *mascaradas* featured the garbs of many nations, and a partiality for that of the Turks still threatening in Europe, was second only to the costumes of Indian tribes nearer home. The impersonation of familiar and exotic types did not, however, exhaust possibilities, for the participants frequently marched in the simulated forms of birds, animals, and imaginary creatures. Variations on these themes were devised by merely inverting these figures, that is, by depicting them upside down, with feet in the air. Rarely missing from these processions were *carros,* or floats, of allegorical or grotesque nature, often with intricate decorative detail.

Spectacles of this sort fell into two more or less distinct categories: a *máscara a lo serio,* in dignified character and *máscara a lo faceto,* composed of ridiculous figures. The two were often combined, but a love of robust humor and crude satire made the second more common. It is hardly surprising that students of the Royal University liked to relieve their ebullience by noisy and sometimes ingenious participation in these activities. Gleefully they flaunted their disrespect of authority by coarse caricatures of persons and by crude buffoonery. Indeed, the *máscaras* provided a convenient outlet for the strong satirical strain in Spanish genius, and in this visible form it was effective in a society predominantly illiterate. The *máscara a lo faceto* was frequently a useful medium of criticism, and it provided opportunities to pillory prominent officials and unpopular dignitaries. A diarist of the time relates that, in the important town of Puebla, a very disrespectful *mascarada* had a float which represented the ruling viceroy and his wife being soundly chastised. As this blatant display of *lèse majesté* rolled through the streets, raucous shouts of approval and foul epithets greeted it from every side. The chronicler piously voices his horror at this scandalous procedure, but he leaves the impression that such overt demonstrations of popular displeasure were not uncommon.[2] Freedom of expression, in the former Spanish possessions, as already stated, was greater than traditionally believed.

The *máscara* was, to a certain extent, a democratic institution in which all castes and classes participated, though usually in separate units. Noble gentlemen delighted to exhibit their equestrian skill and sallied forth, arrayed in polychromatic livery and mounted on magnificent steeds almost concealed in luxurious trappings. Rich merchants and shopkeepers appeared in ornate costumes, and the influential guilds of craftsmen often organized special features. In general these commercial and industrial elements bore the heavy expense of these exhibitions, and they could usually be depended upon to compete with each other in the ingenuity and costliness of their floats. The celebration of the nuptials of the pathetic Charles II lasted for weeks, during which the silversmiths, saddlers, bakers, candlestick-makers and many other guilds vied with each other in the magnificence of successive processions.[3]

The humbler elements of society were also conspicuous in these diversions, and quite often organized elaborate pageants with varied features. The Indians readily shared the enthusiasm of their overlords, drawing inspiration both from European and their own lore. Thomas Gage once again provides curious evidence. "This town (Chiapas)," he reports, "lieth upon a great river, whereunto belong many boats and canoes, wherein those Indians have been taught to act sea fights with great dexterity, and to represent the nymphs of Parnassus, Neptune, Aeolus, and the rest of the heathenish gods and goddesses, so that they are a wonder of their whole nation. They will arm with their boats a siege against the town, fighting against it with such courage till they make it yield, as if they had been trained up all their life to sea fights. . . . They will erect towers and castles made of wood and painted cloth, and from them fight either with boats or one against another with squibs, darts, and many strange fireworks, so manfully that, if in earnest they would perform as well as they do in sport and pastime, the Spaniards and friars might soon repent to have taught them what they have . . ."[4]

Negroes, mulattoes, and other mixed elements paraded in their own *máscaras,* while children occasionally marched in similar manner. Even women took part in these festivities. It is recorded in 1700 that the gentler sex masqueraded in masculine attire, while their mates provided unfailing humor by donning feminine apparel. These functions required little talent and large numbers participated. In February, 1672, over four hundred people, together with many floats, passed through the streets of Mexico City in gala array to celebrate the Fiesta of St. Francis Borgia.[5]

As the century advanced this form of public entertainment occurred more frequently, with ever-increasing lavishness. The expense became a heavy burden as costumes and decorations grew more bizarre and costly, and occasionally the business community resorted to evasive procedures. When the viceroy wished to signalize an event by a customary spectacle of this sort, he rarely evinced a disposition to defray or share the cost. Private individuals, consequently, betrayed a noticeable lack of enthusiasm for such invitations. The news that the Queen had given birth to a Prince reached Mexico City in April, 1658, and the viceroy dutifully summoned one hundred and fifty citizens to remind them tactfully that so auspicious an event called for suitable recognition by her Majesty's subjects. The rich realm of Old Mexico must, of course, celebrate with a splendor proportionate to its wealth, and it was no accident that the viceroy had called in men of acknowledged substance. Many offered rather transparent pleas of poor health, an inability to ride a horse, and similar pretexts, but the king's vicar was adamant, stating firmly that only the payment of a fine, and one proportionate to the deficit incurred, could procure exemption.[6]

This form of public entertainment was not restricted to the celebration of secular events, as already noted, and the impropriety of mingling the ridiculous and the grave in religious festivals troubled no one. Hilarity and reverence were easily reconciled, with little implication of sacrilege. On the whole the *máscaras,* whether *a lo serio* or *a lo faceto,* were a salutory release of emotions and a comparatively innocent diversion. Now and then, they might be the occasion of disorders, particularly when feelings concerning some local or political matter ran high, but this rarely happened. And seldom did accidents or mishaps mar these spectacles. A contemporary diary, however, gravely reports an exception: "a man in Santa Cruz died of a kick which he received from one of the horses in a máscara."[7]

The history of this picturesque custom in the New World goes back to the earliest days of Spanish domination. In 1539, less than two decades after Cortes' conquest, the *máscaras* were so common that licenses for these spectacles were required, presumably because of disturbances associated with them in that unsettled period. But they continued to flourish and enliven the life of a still raw and frontier society. In 1565 the son of the conqueror of Mexico took part in a *máscara* which, with impressive fidelity of detail, simulated the famous entry of his father into the Aztec capital less than a half century before.[8] In the seventeenth century, as already perceived, these spectacles were intimately woven into the pattern of life. It was, indeed, a custom so general and stereotyped that chroniclers seldom bothered to give detailed descriptions despite a common tendency to dwell on the ornamental minutiae of contemporary existence. Of particular interest, therefore, is a lengthy account of a *mascarada* of 1680, contained in a slim volume entitled *Glories of Querétaro*, published that year. The author was a Creole, Carlos de Sigüenza y Góngora, foremost authority of his time on the Indian antiquities of Mexico.[9]

The *Glories of Querétaro* is, in many respects, a typical product of the colonial press. Without newspapers and periodicals to chronicle the happenings of daily life, it was the practice to record in print events deemed important in suitably edifying *relaciones*. Institutions or private individuals usually commissioned these descriptive narratives as a form of self-glorification, hence they were a sort of "vanity literature" whose writers dutifully flattered the paying patron. The style employed was pompous and ornate, the syntax involved, the metaphors strained, and the hyperbole extravagant—a heavy-footed prose that moved ponderously amid a mass of trivia. Now and then glints of pure metal shine amidst the verbal slag, and in this respect the *Glories of Querétaro* assays higher than the average work of its kind. What lifts it above the usual level and gives it a certain documentary importance is the description, among other features, of a *máscara*, peculiarly Baroque in character, in which the Indians were conspicuous.

Querétaro, about thirty leagues northwest of Mexico City, was a pleasant community tucked away in the enclosing hills. From its fertile soil the plow, "with its effective tongue of iron," in the genial phrase of the writer, "coaxed abundant harvests," greatly to the advantage of the white landholders. These favorable circumstances stimulated local pride and even stirred ambition, notably among the clergy, to rival the viceregal capital in the splendor of its public buildings. The fervent cult of the Virgin of Guadalupe, for whom a magnificent structure had been reared near Mexico City, suggested emulation by the construction of a suitable temple in Querétaro to promote this veneration. A successful campaign of soliciting funds brought about the erection of an ornate church formally dedicated in 1680. The varied program of solemn ceremonies and festive events was then duly chronicled in the *Glories of Querétaro.*

The account begins with some curious facts of pre-Cortesian history, moves on to a tactful appreciation of the natural beauty of Querétaro, and then dwells on the singular means by which the devotion of the Virgin of Guadalupe was introduced. With scrupulous care the architectural and sculptural details of the new church are catalogued after which, with barely concealed satisfaction, the author passes on to the more mundane features of the dedication. Such solemn ceremonies as the installation of the Holy Sacrament, the singing of Masses, and the preaching of sermons soon give way to gayer festivities. "Adorned with showy canopies and tapestries," wrote the author, stood a platform at the church entry where, with brilliant costumes and stage settings, a company of actors performed a comedy of Calderón before a large and appreciative audience. "Nothing of all things that are respectable in the comic style was missing" in the performance, the reader is assured, while bullfights, poetic contests, parades, and *máscaras* enlivened successive days, each terminating in noisy and spectacular displays of fireworks. All of this appears, however, a preliminary warming up for the description of the *mascarada,* which affords the writer an opportunity to intercalate data on the Aztec civilization drawn from his formidable erudition. His pages are crowded with a heavy, Latinized diction intermingled with polysyllabic and unpronounceable Nahuatl terms, that hang like shiny baubles on a Christmas tree of Castilian prose. This characteristic Baroque style, turgid, involved, ornate, and ponderous, lends itself better to paraphrase than translation.[10]

His chronicle begins with a grandiose peroration. "If I could present this *máscara* to the ears as it delighted the eyes, I doubt not that I could achieve with my words what the Indians accomplished in it with their adornments. I shall do all that I can, though I know that I shall expose myself to the censure of incredulity," whereupon he launches into his recital.

"At three o'clock in the afternoon the masquerade in four sections started to make its appearance on the city streets. The first part was not especially noteworthy as it consisted of a disorganized band of wild Chichimeca Indians who swarmed about the thoroughfares garbed in the very minimum that decency allows. They had daubed their bodies with clay paints of many hues, and their disheveled hair was made even more unsightly by filthy feathers thrust into it in no particular pattern. Like imaginary satyrs and demoniacal furies they whooped, yelled, and howled, waved clubs, and flourished bows and arrows in such a realistic imitation of their warlike practices, that spectators were quite startled and terrified.

"More enthusiastic applause greeted the second section, a company of infantrymen formed by one hundred and eight youths marching six abreast, each one bedecked in finest Spanish regalia, with bright-colored plumes fluttering from the crest of helmets and multihued ribbons streaming in the breeze from their shoulders. They presented a noble and inspiring appearance, but nothing amazed me quite as much as the superb precision and perfect rhythm with which they marched, with no other practice or training than that acquired in festive parades and on like occasions. Veterans could not have kept their ranks more evenly, or shown greater dexterity in firing and reloading, or manoeuvered their squads more expertly." The Creole author here gives evidence of a growing Mexicanism that would, in time, evolve into nationalism. "This indicates very clearly," he went on, "that these American-born youths are not incapable of discipline should it be necessary to make professional soldiers of them. The rapidity and skill with which the company leader flourished his pike astonished everyone.

"Next came four buglers, mounted on well-trained horses barely visible under scarlet trappings and silver trimmings. The clear, shrill notes of their instruments heralded the approach of the most important section of this brilliant *máscara*. This was the part representing the nobility and lords of the aboriginal aristocracy which, even though it was pagan and heathenish, must be reckoned as majestic and august inasmuch as it held sway over a vast northern empire in the New World. In taking part in these festivities it is quite unthinkable that these Indians should put on tableaux borrowed from an alien culture when they have such an abundance of themes and subjects for pageantry in the lives of their kings and emperors and in the annals of their history. So it was that, on this occasion, they appeared in the ancient garbs of their people as portrayed in their hieroglyphic paintings and as still preserved in tribal memory. All were dressed alike with an amazing array of adornments.

"Leading off was a figure representing the great Conquistador, Don Diego de Tapia, who headed a troop of native monarchs. Behind came the aged Xolotl, first emperor of the Chichimecas in these provinces after the destruction of the Toltecs. Following him were: Nopalton, Tlotzintecuhtli, Quinatzin, otherwise known as Tlaltecatzin, Techotlala, and Ixtlilxochitl, all six of the Chichimeca lineage. Then came two Tepenacs, Tezozomoc and Maxtla who, though tyrants, enjoyed universal rule. The death of the second mentioned and the defeat of his armies brought in the fourth king of the Aztecs, Itzcoatl, and then in succession, Moctecuhzuma Ilhuicamina, Axayacatzin, Tizozic Chalchiuhtonac, Ahiutzotl, Metecuhzuma, Xocoyotzin, Cuitlahuatzin, and the ill-fated, most unfortunate Cuauhtemoc. But the three first Aztec kings were not missing from the *máscara,* that is, Acamapich, Huitzilihuitl, and Chimalpopoca, though they did not achieve the same degree of majesty; nor did the last six kings of Texcoco, namely Netzahualcoyotl, Nezahualpilli, Cacamatzin, Cuicuitzcatl, Coanacotzin, and Ixtlilixochitl, the second of that name who did not win back the control of the empire after the death of Ixtlilxochitl.

"Each monarch bore a crown of turquoises (Xiuhtzolli), the characteristic symbol of authority. Each headpiece presented a complicated arrangement of scintillating jewels of Oriental perfection, tasseled ribbons to hold the hair in place, and shimmering, golden green plumes of the Quetzal bird (Quetzaltlalpilloni). This native royalty was further adorned by featherwork from the same bird (Malacaquetzalli), or the Tlauhquechol (Tlauhuecholtontec), and heron plumes (Aztatzoontli), all alike in exquisite arrangement and beauty. Legbands (Icxipepetlachtli) and bracelets (Icxitecuecuextli, Matzopetzli) decorated ankles and wrists; and exceeding in loveliness all their other garments were the elaborate and costly tilmas, or small cloaks, fastened at the shoulder by a knot and with embroidered hieroglyphic designs (Xiuhtlalpiltilmantli). These the ancient monarchs wore only when seated on a throne . . . But why weary myself cataloguing all these decorative details when it is very likely, since these objects can be properly named only in the elegant tongue of the Aztecs, that those who are unacquainted with the language must inevitably be bored?

"Bringing up the rear of this colorful section was a figure representing the august person of the most valiant Emperor Charles V of Spain and the Holy Roman Empire, whose dominions extended from Germany in the north to the western hemisphere of America. He was arrayed in full armor, burnished black and engraved in gold. Like the Indian monarchs preceding him in the procession, he rode behind airy steeds that pranced with grace and stately rhythm as if fully aware of the sublime majesty of the ruler who held the reins. Indeed, these gallant horses, with the rhythmic swaying of plumes and the even gait of their hooves and the carriage gliding like Apollo's chariot across the heavens, made them seem so like Pegasus that onlookers burst into enthusiastic applause. In short, the elegance and splendor of the trappings harmonized completely with the august majesty of the figure represented.

"Then came the triumphal float, lovelier than the starry firmament and its twinkling constellations. The base, supported by wheels, was six yards long, about half that width, and from the ground it was raised about a yard and a half. On this ample space rested the form of a large ship plowing through imitation waves of silver and bluish white gauze. The sides covering the underparts of the float bore complex designs of involuted spirals, ornate capitals, and decorative emblems, imbuing the whole with an aura of brilliance and splendor. From a large figurehead at the bow of the ship ribbons of scarlet taffeta fell away, intertwined so intricately with the harness traces that they actually seemed to be drawing the conveyance. Above the stern of the simulated vessel rose two exceedingly graceful arches, forming a throne, in the middle of which reposed a large, curved shell, supported from behind by a pair of Persian caryatids. Within it was an image of the Virgin of Guadalupe, and from her canopied throne descended a staircase with silken mats. Further embellishing this lovely ensemble were varicolored taffeta streamers, and a plethora of bouquets of many hues. Like an ambulant springtime, it appeared, dedicated to the immortal Queen of the heavenly paradise, and far exceeding in beauty the Hanging Gardens of Babylon which, in their time, were dedicated to Semiramis. At appropriate intervals stood six graceful angels, symbolizing some of the attributes of the most Holy Virgin. Kneeling on the first step of the throne was a lovely child garbed in the native raiment of the Indians, who thus represented the whole of America, particularly this northern part which, in pagan days, was known as Anahuac. One hand held a heart while the other supported an incensor diffusing perfumes and delicate aromas. All about this triumphal float the Indians were dancing one of the famous, royal *toncontines* of the ancient Mexicans. If their costumes in such ceremonial festivities were lavishly colorful in the days of their monarchs, how much more they would be on so auspicious an occasion as this one!

"This was the fourth and concluding part of the *mascarada* which included several venerable old men who, in chants of marked devotion, intoned praises of the Most Holy Virgin. These were beautifully rendered to the accompaniment of native drums (Tlalpan-Huehuetl) and others beaten by rubber drumsticks (Teponaztli), long, flutelike instruments (Omichicahuztli), timbrels (Ayacaztli), wooden fifes (Cuauhtlapitzalli), and various other instruments typical of the Indians. For hours this magnificent procession wound through the main streets of Querétaro and past the various convents where it paused to recite the versified *loas* which set forth in majestic language the motive of this splendid celebration . . . Night fell at last and once again the brilliant fireworks lit up the skies. . . ."

❧ IX

TOURNAMENTS
OF POETASTERS

THE Baroque passion to make a drama of life exploited art in every form to provide the theatrical spectacles that its spirit craved. Its intensity, exuberance, and extravagance of feeling sought release in bizarre and exaggerated decoration of every aspect of existence: in architecture, in plastic arts, in elegance of dress, in manners, and in public ceremony. All these kinds of expression, however, were, in a sense, scarcely more than scenic effects, even the half-animate pageants and *mascaradas*. Besides settings, drama also demanded articulation in oral and written form. Clearly then, language had an important part to play in externalizing the repressed emotions of the age. Since its use was the privilege of literate and illiterate alike, it was the medium most universally subject to the decorative impulse. Poetry, of course, was its most exalted mode, and the natural music and consonance of Castilian seemed to put this outlet well within the reach of everyone. With form elevated above content, ingenuity, a cheaper commodity, replaced inspiration, and an old institution grew in popularity. This was the *certamen poético,* or poetic tournament which, in the Baroque age, permitted the self-styled elite of Old Mexico to demonstrate an alleged devotion to Euterpe, the muse of lyric verse, by exhibitions of metrical manipulation and verbal gymnastics.

The Renaissance ideal of a gentleman, which required distinction achieved by sword and pen, survived in the seventeenth century, and its difficult fulfillment in the New World was among the major frustrations of transplanted Spaniards. Many of the great writers of Spain, during their career, had served their king as a soldier and had thus helped to form the accepted success pattern. The aspiring Creole, more fortunate than he appreciated, was too remote from the battlefields of Europe to acquire military eminence. Nearer home, to be sure, were opportunities to distinguish himself by repelling hit-and-run attacks of pirates on seaport towns or by suppressing sporadic Indian uprisings on viceregal frontiers. Now and then riots and social upheavals broke out in more settled areas, even within the capital. But to the American-born Spaniard, these disturbances failed to offer occasions for the kind of military valor that brought genuine prestige or fame. Neither buccaneers, rebellious natives, nor riotous masses were foes worthy of a gentleman's steel, and triumphs over them lacked glamor. To the Creole these unpropitious circumstances seemed to close the door of martial renown, leaving open only that of literary distinction.

But even the doorway of letters seemed more than half blocked. Even if the American Spaniard possessed rare talent, as the Mexican dramatist, Ruiz de Alarcón certainly did, he was sure to escape notice unless he transferred his efforts to Spain where, at best, he might expect grudging attention. Until the seventeenth century was well past its mid-point the artistic genius of the Spanish Peninsula was flowering with pyrotechnic brilliance. The names of Cervantes, Góngora, Lope de Vega, Tirso de Molina, and Quevedo, and a host of others echoed so loudly in Europe that quill wielders of the New World could hardly hope to be heard. Plays, novels, and verse poured from the mother country in torrents of printed books, inundating local bookshops and private libraries, even reaching remote mining camps, and this competition could only discourage their endeavors. With the Baroque spirit reaching its culmination in the drama of Calderón (1600-1681), which cast its seductive spell over the remaining colonial period, the would-be writers of the overseas realms felt reduced to abject imitation and artistic inanition. Even when they persisted in creative endeavors, the excessive cost of publication, the chronic scarcity of paper, the requirement of licenses from Spain, and the monopolistic practices of Peninsular printers virtually doomed their works to remain in manuscript.

These obstacles seemed so insuperable as to make literary distinction quite as much out of reach as distinction in arms, yet such were the prestige of letters and the passion to versify in the Hispanic world that few could resist the temptation to sharpen their quills. The tutelary gods of the age were Quevedo, somber and dark in his concettism, and Luis de Góngora, musical, pictorial, and polychromatic in his floridity, called gongorism. These artistic techniques were toys with which to play in an era when the tyranny of kings and the domination of the Church prevented a concern with the great issues of life, and Creole poetasters turned to them eagerly. Such canons of esthetic excellence invited any literate person, with a modest command of the vernacular and a smattering of Latin with which to invent neologisms, to essay his skill in verbal legerdemain, and few failed to accept the opportunity tendered. Industry of this sort required occasions for display, of course, and, since the day of periodicals and "little reviews" had not arrived, public poetic contests provided gratifying showcases. They offered the powerful incentives of a visible audience and, in important tournaments, the possibility of publication in homage volumes.[1]

The origins of these competitions go back to the ancient Greeks, and the revival in later times was a part of the recovery of the classic tradition in Renaissance Europe. Literary academies and societies quickly crossed to the New World to become a familiar feature of cultural life, notably in the seventeenth century. Whether first introduced by the Jesuits or not, these *concursos* were no novelty in Mexico during the closing decades of the sixteenth century. Bernardo de Balbuena could proudly recall that, in a poetic contest held at Mexico City in 1585, he had won a prize against three hundred other contestants. The occasion was the celebration of Corpus Christi, and the laurel was bestowed upon the youth "in the presence of seven bishops assembled there at the time for an ecclesiastical Council." And later that same year he was equally successful in a *certamen* honoring the arrival of a new viceroy.

The lush efflorescence of this custom coincided with the remaining colonial centuries during which it produced the most exuberant growth of Baroque verse. Surviving *relaciones* that record these affairs preserve, probably fortunately, only a fraction of these lyric effusions. Vacuous bombast and extreme artificiality are the prevailing characteristics, and *agudeza,* or cleverness, brought success rather than did true inspiration. These were the qualities that most readily evoked the coveted approbation and proclaimed the winners. To be acclaimed a Poet was to achieve high distinction in the community, and disgruntled losers of these contests occasionally displayed a saltier talent for satirical expression. In 1618, for example, the guild of silversmiths in Mexico City sponsored a poetic tournament intended to signalize the Pope's recent proclamation of the Immaculate Conception, possibly the instigation of as much bad verse as any single theme in Spain's Golden Age. The reluctance of the Dominicans in Mexico to accept this matter of faith precipitated a scandal which rocked the viceregal capital. Members of this order loudly protested the adverse decisions of the judges on their entries in the competition by circulating a series of satirical sonnets and *canciones* which proved far more exciting, if esthetically no more inspired, than the prize-winning poems. The Inquisition was obliged to take a hand in this embarrassing situation and it compiled a record of offensive verses which provide posterity with more entertaining reading than the usual products of colonial *certámenes.*[2]

These functions were an aristocratic pastime, and an event associated with much elegance. Whatever the occasion—reception of a viceroy, an archbishop, or other dignitary, the installation of a university rector, the celebration of a historical incident, or the reiteration of an article of faith—a generous patron invariably underwrote the expense, proud of his role as a collective Maecenas of local poetasters. This philanthropy was often costly, since it included outlays for elaborate decorations, Lucullan repasts, and liberal gratuities as well as valuable prizes, but it was an honor highly esteemed since it bestowed distinction upon gentlemen of wealth otherwise undistinguished. Donors were also titular heads of institutions, ecclesiastical and lay, with ample funds at their disposition.

The patron enlisted the services of experienced functionaries to organize and conduct the tournament in accordance with the best traditions and, if possible, to excel previous performances. These agents were primarily a general secretary, and a panel of respected individuals as judges for the poems submitted. There were other

minor officials but upon the secretary rested the heaviest responsibility, for, as master of ceremonies, he needed to possess gifts of
graceful rhetoric and polite wit as well as administrative talent.
His fundamental task was to devise an *idea,* or symbolic theme,
on which the aspiring members of the local Parnassus might exercise their eager, if meager, genius. This general topic must be
amenable to division into subtopics equivalent to the number of
separate contests contemplated, usually four, each with meters and
strophic forms specifically prescribed. The tournament of 1683,
organized by the University of Mexico to bolster faith once more
in the Immaculate Conception, had the eagle chosen to represent
Mary, and upon its alleged qualities and attributes, fabulous and
otherwise, local wordsmiths fabricated metrical compositions. Each
aspect of the symbolic bird served as a subtopic of an individual
contest and it was suggested by an emblem or allegorical figure
termed *emblema, asunto,* and the like, with verse forms specified
in each case. The collective effusions could then be expected to
result in the maximum glorification of the Virgin.

Hardly less important were the arrangements for processions
and ceremonial functions, for, without the drama of pageantry, the
contests of the muses were incomplete. No effort was spared to
mobilize the very considerable resources of the community in
luxurious raiment, colorful decorations of streets and buildings, and
adornments of man and beast to make the event a gala occasion
for the entire community. A parade marshal prided himself on
bringing out an exhibition of costumes in silk, velvet, and satin,
ornamented with whorls of braid, silver spangles, jewels, and
topped by flowing plumes. Gaily caparisoned horses were an unfailing attraction, mingling with gaudy floats of ingenious symbolism, the whole arranged to endow a familiar spectacle with
desirable variety. The marshal's reward was the coveted privilege
of carrying in the procession the placard of the tournament, an-
nouncing its theme and summoning poets to the lists.

The various units of this column gathered at the marshal's
home, appropriately festooned for the occasion, and took their
place in order of precedence. About midafternoon, after final inspection of uniforms, accoutrements, and details of the floats, the
imposing parade began its slow, measured progress through the
principal streets. Church bells broke into prolonged, rapid, and

discordant clamor, fireworks crackled, and loud reports of mortars strategically placed on corners added to the din. This festive racket delighted the crowds lining the thoroughfares, and intensified their expectancy. Since everyone must revere the Immaculate Conception as a tenet of faith, the procession represented both religious and secular corporations. Friars, monks, and priests marched in their most impressive habiliments, accompanying holy images and sacred insignia, while faculty members of the University in brilliant academic vestments and bearing glittering scepters contributed bright notes to a Baroque symphony of color.

Heralding the approach of the column resounded the shrill trumpets, the rhythmic beats of kettledrums, and martial strains of flageolets, played by gaily uniformed bandsmen. Immediately following on foot and astride horses and mules was a contingent of students in cap and gown, the trappings of their mounts displaying symbols of the scholarly pretensions of the riders. This cavalcade was an overture to the operatic splendor of the lordly gentlemen of the city arrayed in shining livery and mingling with learned doctors of the University in resplendent robes, all riding in stately grace upon restive steeds whose harness glinted in the afternoon sun. This magnificence, contrasting with the more solemn dress of the clergymen, conferred a lofty dignity upon the whole and evoked a feeling of awe in the onlookers.

The climactic feature of the procession was the section that formally announced the poetic tournament and its theme. Leading this group rode the marshal, accompanied by beadles and other University officials, their mounts hardly perceptible under their trappings. Besides a flashing silver mace, and a series of ornate posters with crests, seals, and symbolic devices, this group held aloft an immense *cartel,* or placard, with its grandiose legend. Upon this object the ablest artists had expended their best talent in design, and the effect was dazzling. Surmounted on a staff of solid silver was the *tarja,* a large, filigreed frame of the same metal, which colorfully garbed lackeys kept in balance by holding taut the golden cords strung from its corners. Within it daintily executed lettering set forth its message in excessively rotund diction. Representative of these *carteles* is that of the competition at the University of Mexico in 1683, the involved wording of which is approximately rendered as:

LITERARY PALAESTRA
AND POETIC JOUST
IN WHICH
THE IMPERIAL, PONTIFICAL, AND EVER AUGUST
MEXICAN ATHENS
proposes a design of the triumph of the
MOST HOLY MARY
sketched on a canvas brightened by colors contrived from
a perishable palette, in which
She treads upon the Dragon of Original Sin
at the first Instant of Conception, by summoning the Muses of its Helicon to sing victory
songs celebrating the triumph of the Virgin Birth on
the many-stringed zither of Apollo.
Vergil, the Swan of Mantua, provides the model in verses 71 to 98 in the Third Book of
the Aeneid.[3]

Flanking this dramatic device rode the Secretary and a liveried
retinue of assistants and servants. A company of soldiers formed a
rear guard, their bright uniforms lending a final touch of color to
the procession, and their deftly manipulated pikes providing tacit
reminders of the bearers' function as preservers of public order.

In due course the colorful column arrived outside the spacious
lecture hall of the University where the Rector, the Viceroy, and
other dignitaries were waiting. As the paraders dismounted and
moved into the assembly room, the bells of the city accelerated the
tempo of their dissonance to a fortissimo. An intricate pattern of
decorative detail had transformed the monastic bareness of the
auditorium, and the addition of the ornate emblems and devices
carried in the procession increased its profusion. As the interior
filled with brilliant uniforms and bright costumes, the whole presented a kaleidoscope of color animated by a loud buzzing of conversation and an air of restless excitement.

At last, when a comparative hush fell, the Secretary, with a great
show of dignity, slowly mounted the steps of a pulpit at one side of
the platform. In a clear, precise voice he began his discourse with
high-sounding phrases well studded with Latin quotations. With
ponderous aplomb he described the motives of the tournament and
announced the specific topics and the particular meters and strophic
forms with which contestants should treat them. He also set forth
the rules governing the competition and named the judges who
would decide on the prize winners. A fortnight was allowed for
the final adjudication and the ceremonious awarding of laurels.

Comparatively brief was this introductory rite of the tournament, and the aristocratic audience soon began to disperse, slowly returning to waiting carriages, sedan chairs, and mounts held in readiness by servants and lackies. Many paused to admire at close hand the Baroque splendor of the *cartel* conspicuously affixed at the entrance of the University building. Custom required that the marshal hold a reception at his home and a goodly number of invited guests repaired there to enjoy the rich food and drink lavishly supplied. This gathering of the social elite lasted well into the night. Meanwhile, the less acceptable and more numerous elements of the population, including the students, filled the streets, squares, and *pulquerías*, or bars, where they celebrated the occasion with a boisterousness that permitted little sleep to the more decorous citizens of the neighborhood.

In many a household the days following witnessed intensive activity as aspiring poetasters and wordsmiths laboriously tinkered with tropes, metaphors, and meters in a painful effort to shape them to the prescribed themes. Even if talent had been in greater supply the cramping requirements of the competition gave little play to spontaneity, naturalness, or artistic integrity. The aim was adulation and glorification of the subject matter and it was best achieved by ingenious conceits, by bold juggling of phrases and excessive artifice, together with a pedantic exhibition of classical and scholastic learning. Obscurity was a virtue and a vacuous jumbling of allusions a merit. With the topic in no way disputable, exaggerated panegyrics and bombast were the marks of esthetic excellence.

The frequency of these tournaments had enabled many poetasters to develop techniques for the extraction of acceptable metal from low-grade ores of inventiveness. There were short cuts and easy methods of fitting metrical compositions to specifications against which Secretaries of *certámenes* had to be on guard. They found it expedient to formulate definite laws governing the manufacture of the verbal products submitted to the judges, and they attempted to remove any irritation on the part of contestants by facetious wording. Somewhat typical of this legislation is the following:

I. Prizes must not be limited to a few persons.
   Inasmuch as it is well to restrain covetousness through poetry in persons who, by their profession hardly know what silver is, we decree that two first prizes may not be awarded to one and the

same professor, nor that more than two may be adjudged to anyone else.

II. There must be fitness and propriety in the Glosses.

Inasmuch as it is essential to maintain a proper relation between
the textual verses and the gloss composed upon them, we require
that the words shall be kept in all their proper meanings, and in
the positive sense in which they are employed.

III. There must be no false playing upon words.

Because of the great importance of excluding abuses of Spanish
speech detrimental to good use and poetry in the republic of
letters; we order the elimination, even in humorous passages, of a
false playing on words susceptible of double meaning; only one
meaning may be used, leaving the other implicit in the sound of
the word.

IV. Poets must keep to the highway of their subjects.

Since wandering away from the straight and narrow path of the
subject causes one to fall over verbal cliffs, or lose one's way, we
declare that he who thus loses his bearings also loses prizes.

V. Stolen verses and insincerities of style shall be punished. We
decree exile from Parnassus for those caught on this occasion as
verse pirates or plagiarizers, as manufacturers of empty, pointless
words, of senseless sentences, and of oversubtle and meaningless
metaphors; likewise we ban those who use technical jargon in such
a way as to lack comprehension or reason through misunderstandings that arise from this procedure.

VI. Poems must be submitted in customary form.

We command that poems be submitted signed and sealed, with an
additional copy in a decorated border, on penalty that, in lacking
this adornment, they will not be acceptable in this Parnassus,
inasmuch as we do not concede that poets are too poor to afford
at least a tinted border.

VII. Entries must be submitted on time.

We require the submission of poems to the Secretary of the contest on the specified date. No extension of time will be granted to
anyone, whether major or minor poet.[4]

These rules reveal prevailing practices perhaps more than their
correction, for they did not always apply equally to all contestants.
Literary vanities are among the most susceptible and, in a hierarchy as complex as that of viceregal Mexico, judges of poetic contests often felt it expedient to interpret regulations broadly and
impose them leniently to avoid wounding the pride of highly placed
participants. As a form of insurance against irate reactions of influential contestants a jury of professors, Oidores of the Royal

Audiencia, and other dignitaries of lofty category, lent their support to the appointed referees. As Don Quixote once remarked, "there is no poet who is not arrogant and who does not think that he is the greatest there is," an observation of especial validity in the case of the Creole subjects overseas overly conscious of an inferior status and yearning for recognition. Doubtless of equal pertinence to the tournaments celebrated in the New World centers of culture were the further remarks that the illustrious Knight of the Doleful Countenance addressed to an individual in the throes of contriving verses. "If by chance they are for some literary tournament," he advised, "you should strive to carry off the second prize, for the first is always awarded as a favor to some one of high rank, the second goes to the one who merits first place, and thus the third is, in reality, the second, while the first, by this reckoning, would be third, after the manner of licentiate degrees that are conferred at the universities. But for all that, the first prize carries with it a great distinction."[5]

During the days following the ceremonious announcement of the competition the Secretary received a flood of daintily bordered manuscripts which, in the contest of 1683, totaled more than five hundred metrical compositions. After a preliminary winnowing of the more obvious chaff, he brought these contributions to a meeting of the judges at the home of the patron. This committee attacked the formidable batches of verse, classifying them according to the separate sections into which the *certamen* was divided. A prolonged session doubtless ensued as the judges worked through the welter of strained meters, complicated syntax, and baffling conceits woven into a vast array of ballads, glosses, *décimas,* quintillas, sextets, sonnets, octaves, sapphics, *canciones,* epigrams, and anagrams in Latin as well as Castilian. In making selections they could not ignore the social status of the author, and the application of esthetic criteria was flexible. Despite the Secretary's preliminary sifting, the task was exhausting, and when the committee had finally reached agreement on the prize-winning entries, they gratefully accepted the delicate collation and chilled beverages which the patron had thoughtfully provided. Later, as they rose to leave, their generous host slipped a liberal gratuity into the hands of each, whereupon they departed to their respective homes, doubtless well pleased with their efforts.

The Secretary was a busy man in the time remaining before the public reading of the successful poems. Not only must he supervise the final arrangements for the ceremony, but he must compose a series of brief, witty couplets to recite on bestowing the many awards. Much of the success of the occasion depended upon the deft combination of humor and flattery in these short verses. To amuse the audience and please the vanity of the author required skilful judgment as to the lengths he might go as well as a facile gift of versifying. The Secretary, therefore, devoted much time and thought to this important obligation.

The final, gala event usually occurred about two weeks after the procession proclaiming the tournament. The University auditorium appeared even more brilliantly decorated than before, with draperies of rich cloth, bright bunting, and symbolic insignia veiling its architectural features. The platform, too, seemed more densely crowded, and across its entire width stood a row of large carved chairs; those near the center were surmounted by canopies embroidered with coats-of-arms and other devices, and in front was a massive carved table equipped with writing accessories. The real focus of attention, however, was a large showcase at one side offering a vista of glittering silverware, jewels, and rich fabrics artistically displayed. There were the prizes provided by the patron with ostentatious munificence, among which were trays, vases, salvers, platters, cups and spoons of engraved silver, jewelled snuff-boxes and tobacco containers, scented gloves, and lengths of choice silk, satin, velvet and other fine textiles in brilliant hues arranged with graceful elegance. Only with difficulty did the eyes of the audience stray from these objects, and their gaze quickly returned to them with fascinated wonder.

The assembled public represented the most aristocratic and socially pretentious elements of viceregal society who had come quite as much to be seen at an occasion of such cultural importance as to listen to its tedious proceedings. Some were seated but most remained standing, a perfumed mass in polychromatic splendor of bright attire, plumes, and jewelled swords. A noisy chatter of conversations again pervaded the hall as the assembly awaited the arrival of the viceroy and his retinue without whom the ceremonies could not begin. That lordly official regarded a lack of punctuality as a prerogative of his high office and, to keep in a prolonged state of expectancy so distinguished a gathering, was a satisfying demonstration of personal power. All the more theatrical and regal was his eventual entrance after the long period of suspense.

When a flourish of trumpets at last heralded his approach, a quiver of excitement ran through the audience as its eyes turned toward the portal. From the platform descended a procession of professors, doctors, and others of high degree, in cap and gown, bright hoods, and other regalia; it advanced toward the doorway to welcome the highest magistrate in the land and his gentlemen-in-waiting. As the two columns met much ceremonious bowing and posturing ensued, after which a single line formed with the Viceroy and the Judges of the Royal Audiencia at the head, resplendent in court dress, and in a slow, measured step, it advanced to the platform and took designated seats. As a degree of quiet returned, swelling strains of soft music spread through the auditorium, and the Secretary was observed slowly mounting the pulpit to begin the program.

It was a leisurely age which loved variety and punctilio, and it willingly accepted the varied formalities which preceded the reading of poems and the bestowal of prizes. A pious invocation was *de rigueur,* designed, it would seem, to impress the Deity as well as the aristocratic gathering with its rhetorical flourishes, generous sprinkling of quotations from Latin authors, pedantic allusions, and other literary conventions. Verbal genuflections directed at the viceroy and the royal judges and similar salutations then followed. Congenial to the Baroque spirit was a commingling of this ritualistic solemnity and a mundane humor in public functions of this sort, and the noblest sentiments might rub elbows in democratic fashion with crude satire and witty sallies of dubious propriety. Hence these respectful formalities frequently gave way to comic relief of a graceless nature called *vejámenes.* These were somewhat ludicrous comments which often expressed in jest what jealous rivals were saying of others in private. Oddities of appearance, manners, and conduct attributed to contestants were caricatured in apocryphal anecdotes or verbal sketches little calculated to spare the victim's feelings. The greater his discomfiture the greater the hilarity of the gathering. Usually the object of these mortifying attentions resigned himself to this horseplay, but occasionally sensibilities proved tender and tempers flared. In the light of the prevailing *pundonor,* or brittle code of honor, it is curious that these robust jibes and barbs, so offensively personal, provoked so few reprisals of a physical sort. The Secretary read them to the assembly from a sheaf of notes called *cedulillas* as if they were news items, heightening the effects of the quips by his histrionic gifts.

Few commodities are more perishable than current jokes and few things are more transitory than fashions in wit. In reading these sallies of a by-gone age a modern observer wryly grimaces at their tasteless jocularity and marvels at the tumultuous laughter which, apparently, they evoked from the cultured elite of a Baroque society. An example or two will suffice. The first is from a *vejamen* at the University of San Marcos, in Lima, Peru.

"This *cedulilla* declares that when the gentleman taking the doctor's degree was a school boy, his teacher told him one time to take off his shirt. To this request the lad quickly responded: 'I'm not wearing a shirt today because it is a work day. My mother keeps it in her closet for holidays.'"

A second example from the same source depends for its levity upon the chief stock-in-trade of such mid-nineteenth century North American humorists as "Petroleum V. Nasby" and "Josh Billings," that is, colloquialisms and phonetic spelling of words. Hence its feeble wit (by present standards) which, like that of a pun, can hardly find adequate translation.

"This *cedulilla* is a letter to a certain nun, the object of his affections, and it reads: My dear little shorty: this afternoon I'll cum to see you and I'll take you to where we can eat a *yanqui* of sweet potatoes and jerked beef. As a penalty for not cummin' out yesterday afternoon because you were playin' a game of *chueca* I'm sure goin' to giv you a coupla hard raps and the same number of slaps.
             Your chummy Antuquito, usque ad mortem et infra."[6]

Such drollery often served as the *hors d'oeuvres* of a metrical banquet featured by a surfeit of verbal viands. This act concluded, the Secretary adopted a more unctuous tone as he prepared the public for the feast to follow. In verses of his own composition he lyrically set forth the theme and purpose of the poetic tournament, and followed this overture by a pedantic disquisition in artificial prose on the various symbols around which the competing poetasters had woven their word patterns in the several divisions of the tournament. This discourse did not fail to exhibit the orator's scholastic learning, and his thought hardly emerged from the labyrinthine syntax and the lush foliage of classical allusions and ponderous quotations. However, the listeners knew that the end had come when the Secretary closed with an exhortation to the "Mexican swans to gird the armor of Apollo and go forth to battle the muses." This summons was purely rhetorical, however, for the contestants, having submitted their poems, were already veterans of combats in Parnassus, and the victors were awaiting their laurels. The Secretary then explained the special theme of the first section of the tournament, with its assigned meters, and read the poem adjudged the best. Its proud author then stepped up to receive the designated trophy, and upon delivery the Secretary recited the punning couplets so carefully contrived beforehand. In a similar manner he dealt with second- and third-prize winners, and successively through the several parts into which the competition was divided. Even some entries which failed to receive awards were also read—no doubt to ease the disappointment of a sensitive contestant. These proceedings consumed long hours and their tediousness would hardly seem relieved by the witticisms of the master of ceremonies and the interludes of music. Indeed, so wearisome does it all appear that one wonders whether the viceroy, the noble gentlemen of the Royal Audiencia, and many other dignitaries gracing the occasion by their presence did not often struggle to repress discreet yawns, and whether their thoughts did not wander into more engaging matters. It is easy to imagine that one or another dozed off for a few merciful moments, for the cloying artificiality and exaggerated conceits must have produced a soporific effect beyond the power of the Secretary's pleasantries to overcome entirely.

Despite these apparent defects the poetic tournaments remained the most important events of the cultural and literary life of the New World centers of Hispanic civilization through most of the three colonial centuries. The enduring enthusiasm for this esthetic activity was attributable in part, perhaps, to its dual nature. The satisfaction of the participants, at least the successful ones, was twofold. The aspiring author could have his work read aloud to the most select public of society before whom he might appear in the guise of a Poet, a coveted distinction, and in the *relacion*, or chronicle of the competition published afterward, usually a volume in luxurious format setting forth in prolix fashion the circumstances of the event and reproducing the text of the prize-winning verse, he had almost the sole possibility of seeing his versified lucubrations in the seemingly permanent form of type. There was, then, the double exhilaration of a living audience of contemporaries and the invisible one of posterity. Thus these published records of tournaments became cherished possessions for prominent display in homes and libraries. If most of their contents scarcely deserved embalming in this fashion, they have come down as curious metrical mummies to enliven the excavations of literary archaeologists and to shed light upon the cultural mores of a Baroque antiquity.

For those whom custom obliged to listen patiently during the interminable function the rewards lay, perhaps, in the drama of the spectacle and in the sprightly efforts of the presiding functionary, the Secretary. The humor of his couplets, like that of the *vejámenes,* poorly resists the erosion of time. The chief reliance was on wordplay, in which the Baroque mind developed an extraordinary dexterity. Such legerdemain shares with puns the handicap of being a currency of language rarely convertible into other linguistic coinage, but possibly a single, incomplete example will illustrate well enough the means by which a master of ceremonies sought to excite the risibilities and sustain the interest of an audience. The Secretary of a competition held in Mexico City in 1683 was a well-known scholar who wore spectacles. Exercising a privilege authorized by custom, he had entered a sonnet of his own invention under a pseudonym. The judges, possibly penetrating this disguise without excessive difficulty, had crowned his fourteen-line effort with a first prize. In accepting a silver vase as a fitting tribute to the merit of his brain-child, the recipient, pointing to the glasses he wore, genially declared:

> My sonnet, in its excesses,
> is a most ungraceful monster;
> for, conceived with four eyes,
> it was born with fourteen feet.*

---

* Monstruo de desgracias es
Mi soneto en sus arrojos,
Pues hecho con quatro ojos,
Nació con catorse pies.

SOME CURIOSITIES
OF BAROQUE VERSE

HIGHLY fashionable in the Hispanic world of the seventeenth century was verse writing, a fact the evident addiction to poetic tournaments clearly sustains. An artistic ability of this sort sometimes opened doors to promotion, and the Spanish American Creole, denied higher offices in his own land, eagerly strove for literary distinction as a possible means of breaching the barrier to advancement. Aristocratic prestige, leisure-class dilettantism, and a hunger for material advantage were among other factors which account for the mass production of metrical compositions of all kinds during the Baroque age.

All this outpouring of poesy might have resulted in more creditable art if the overseas subjects of the crown had not succumbed so completely to the literary vices of contemporary Spain. Unhappily, the Baroque retreat from life, with a consequent decline in wit, lightness, irony, and grace of expression, so completely absorbed the Spanish New World that it carried literary abuses to greater extremes. A great poet of Spain, Luis de Góngora (1561-1627), cast so deep a shadow over the artistic expression of the Creole gentry that it extinguished all but the faintest glimmers of light. Much of the early poetry of this bard of Cordoba was strikingly beautiful in clarity and lyric charm but, almost coinciding with Fray García Guerra's arrival at Mexico City, it grew increasingly complex, obscure, and pedantic. The excellence of such highly mannered poems as *Fábula de Polifemo y Galatea* (Fable of

145

Polyphemus and Galatea); and *Soledades* helped to consecrate a cult of the "new poetry" characterized by excessive artificiality, complicated and strained metaphors, invented vocabulary, and syntactical involutions which soon concealed meaning to all but the elect. This involved style paralleled the intricacy already discernible in architectural and sculptural details of Baroque façades and retables. Resembling the euphuism of England, marinism of Italy, and preciosity of France, the new trend in writing, soon referred to as *culteranismo*, or *culto*, or gongorism, descended with blighting effect upon aspiring versifiers of the remote Spanish possessions. A contemporary critic of Góngora had declared that: "Every work, however short, consists of three parts, soul, body, and ornament, that is, subject matter, phrases, and artful expression. . . . Some poets seek only a fanciful exterior, without soul or body."[1] Whatever validity this last statement has with respect to its immediate object, the justice of its application to most writers of verse in Old Mexico is hardly disputable. There, as the poetic competitions have shown, the effort of poetasters to ape the literary habits of the motherland went beyond the models in ridiculous conceits, pomposity, pedantry and other forms of rhetorical flatulence. Destined for a long life in the Hispanic world, this perverse style, with its heavy verbiage and hollow meaning, was still discernible in the writing of the late nineteenth century. An iconoclastic poet of Peru in that period voiced his scorn with characteristic vehemence:

> Thunderous and reverberating Castilian poesy,
> the big drum in the orchestra of Pindar and Homer;
> if hardly dost thou lull souls, surely dost thou deafen ears.

> In the dense foliage of useless words
> grows pallid, the juiceless fruit of thought.
> Oh, speech of Cervantes, thy many-tendrilled vines
> have gigantic leaves and dwarf-like bunches of grapes.*

---

* Atronadora y rimbombante Poesía castellana
Tambor mayor en la orquesta de Píndaro y Homero,
Si poco arrullas a las almas, mucho asordas los oídos.

En el espeso follaje de inútiles vocablos,
Brota, pálida y sin jugo la fruta de la idea.
Oh, verbo de Cervantes, en tu viña empampanada
Son gigantescas las hojas, enanos los racimos
                    —Manuel González Prada. *Exóticas*
                    (Lima, 1948), p. 41.

Least of all, perhaps, did the New World poetasters appreciate, as a recent critic of Castilian letters puts it, ". . . that no one who cared for vigour and integrity of the language could approve of the principles on which Góngora wrote, however much they might admire the results." And they were indifferent to the fact that "he was leading it away from its fertilizing sources in life."[2] The prize-winning verse of the colonial contests amply justifies these various strictures and deserves even severer ones, for their authors did not stop at meaningless jumbles of artificial expressions and numbing Latinisms, but subjected modes of speech and forms of verse to every form of distortion and wordplay that misguided ingenuity could contrive. Few examples, indeed, were more than a fanciful exterior, without soul or substance, and it would seem that the poetic tournament owed its great revival to a disposition to encourage these aberrations. Competing versifiers delighted to make commonplace the most intricate devices of verbal calisthenics and legerdemain, and an attempt to catalogue the resulting oddities would be an undertaking as difficult as unprofitable. But a few specimens may give a more vivid, if depressing, impression of the esthetic wasteland of much colonial poetry and provide an exhibit of literary phenomena of Baroque inspiration.[3] These curious products often defy translation and some can be represented only in the original Spanish.

One of the least objectionable of these metrical diversions was the gloss. Usually the verses of a quatrain taken in order served as the concluding line of four successive *décimas,* or stanzas of ten lines. The gloss, therefore, did not put as much strain on the inspiration of the author as did most other innovations of the time. Indeed, in the hands of a competent craftsman, it was capable of beauty. Many great figures of Spain's Golden Age had cultivated this form successfully, and its appearance in the overseas domains was certainly not the worst form of literary borrowing. To be sure, Cervantes' hero did not entertain a very high regard for this kind of thing. "A friend of mine," observed Don Quixote, "a man of intelligence, is of the opinion that the writing of poetic glosses is a waste of energy, and the reason he gave me was this: that the gloss almost never can come up to the text but very often, or most of the time, goes beyond the meaning and intention of the original lines. And moreover, he added, the rules governing this form of composition are too strict, they do not permit of interrogations or any 'said he,' or 'I will say'; they do not allow verbs to be turned into nouns or the general sense and construction of the passage to be altered, along with other restrictions by which those who write glosses are bound, as your Grace must know."

The gloss which Don Quixote's interlocutor recited to him on the occasion of these sage remarks is here reproduced from the Putnam version of Cervantes' master work. Requirements of English altered the exact rendition of the lines of the quatrain in the concluding verses of the *décimas*.

> *Oh, could my "was" an "is" become,*
> *I'd wait no more for "it shall be";*
> *or could I the future now but see,*
> *and not this present, dour and glum.*
> Gloss
> All things must pass away at last,
> and so, the blessing that was mine,
> fair Fortune's gift, it also pass'd,
> ne'er to return, though I repine;
> my skies are wholly overcast.
> Long hast thou seen me at thy feet,
> O Fortune fickle, Fortune fleet;
> but make me happy once again
> and I'd forget my present pain,
> *could but my "was" and "is" now meet.*
>
> No other pleasure do I crave,
> no other palm or warrior's prize,
> such triumph as befits the brave;
> all that I ask: those happier skies
> to which my memory is a slave.
> Woulds't thou but give this gift to me,
> O Fortune, then perchance I'd see
> this fire of mine—O priceless boon!—
> *I'd wait no more for "it shall be."*
>
> Impossible the thing I ask,
> since Time, once gone, none can recall;
> for to accomplish such a task,
> no power on earth but it is too small.
> No more beneath those skies I'll bask.
> Swift doth he come and swiftly flee,

nor doth return, light-footed he!
and well I know it is not right
to seek to stay Time in his flight;
turn past to present—futile plea!

My life is anxious, filled with gloom;
and living thus 'twixt hope and fear,
is naught but death's familiar doom;
better to lie upon my bier
and seek the door to pain's dark room.
It seemeth me, it would be sweet
to end it now, thus life to cheat;
but living long and living longer,
the fear within grows ever stronger
of that dread "shall be" I must greet.[4]

One of the oldest devices is the acrostic. The Greeks are said
to have made use of such combinations, and in every age and language it appears in almost infinite variety. In the seventeenth century its popularity was possibly greatest in the courtly circles of
Europe and, consequently, in the literate strata of colonial society.
A common form spelled out the name of a person by the initial
letter of a succession of lines, but in Old Mexico the acrostic
makers were rarely content with anything so simple. They strained
their ingenuity to devise novel and complex examples of which
a "royal sonnet acrostic," with the technique of a gloss, is symptomatic. The four-line stanza

> El bronce y buril
> Al valor y el arte
> De tan raro Marte
> Den aplausos mil.

(Let the trumpet and the engraver's tool give applause a thousand-
fold to the courage and art of so rare a martial figure) is spelled
out by the initial letters in four vertical columns of words within
a sonnet.

De a tu
Encumbra
Nítida
Aureada
Penetró
Lanzó al
Antorcha(a su
Cereda al
Sojuzgó al
Otros miden el
Siguiendo
Mil laureles
Al continuo
Leon, le

Diestra
Esmaltes
Trompa
Acción
Zauta) el
Rebelde
Antro
Risco
Orgulloso
Monte
Ayron de
Rozaste en
Turbión de
Mixtingues

Sañoza (que
Liberal
Afana, con
Aplauso
Labaro hacia
Opónese
Rasga
Andaga lo
Empeño
Luego
Audaz flechero
Rudas
Tanto
Esforzado

Excelente
Lucida)
Brunida
Refulgente
Oriente
Zacida
Compelida
Eminente
Inculto
Bramas
Culto
Ramas
Insulto
Llamas[5]

Another *tour de force* of durable fashion in the poetic contests were the so-called "echoes." The final word of each verse repeated the closing syllables of the penultimate word, thus creating the effect of an echo. The predominance of vowel sounds in Castilian made this trick easier to perform than in English in which a similar effect was achieved more often by repeating the last two or three words of a line as:

> A lampe whose beames are ever bright
> And never feares approaching night.
>   Echo   Approaching night.[6]

A quatrain of a prize-winning sonnet in the 1683 competition exemplifies the Castilian phenomenon.

> Si al alto Apolo la sagrada *agrada*
> Piedad Troyana, a que devida *vida*
> Tanta asegure, que eximida *mida*
> Del veloz tiempo en la jornada *nada*.[7]

As one thing leads to another, so bold spirits ventured still more hazardous feats of cerebration. Such was the "double echo," in which the last three words of a verse re-echoed each other as they dwindled in length. Recalling the mystical words pronounced in the Lenten practice of Ash Wednesday, "reverteris, teris, eris, is," a colonial poet, dwelling upon the inevitableness of death—a theme

congenial to the Baroque spirit—wrote a series of quatrains not
entirely devoid of substance. Two of these will reveal the technique
of the "double echo."

> Todo en la vida es mudable
> y en prueba de su inconstancia
> lo que apreciabas constancia
> *invariable—variable—hable.*
> Mira cuan desconocida
> queda, entre humanas memorias
> la aclamación de tus glorias,
> *pues se olvida—vida—ida.*[8]

(All in life is mutable, and in proof of its inconstancy, it may speak
variably about that thou esteemest invariable constancy.
See how the acclaim of thy triumphs remains unrecalled in human
memory, for a life departed is a life forgotten.)

"Difficult poetry, both because of the lofty meter and the arduous
composition, is that in which every word appears with the same
initial letter."[9] This comment which, with equal truth might have
included the adjective "useless" as well as "arduous," accompanies
a series of octaves fashioned in this manner. Yet alliteration on a
large scale was a task of word play often undertaken by colonial
wordsmiths. A half octave of doleful feeling will suffice.

> ¡Cielo! ¿Cómo canciones cantaremos
> con corazones casi consumidos?
> con causa conveniente callaremos,
> congojados, confusos, condolidos . . . .[10]

(Heavens! How will we sing songs with hearts almost consumed?
Afflicted, confused, and grieved, we shall, with appropriate reason,
keep silent . . .)
Separate stanzas shifted in turn to words beginning with A, O, L,
and M respectively to voice variations on the same plaint.

The eleven-syllable line, as the meter of the lofty epic, was especially vulnerable to experimentation by manufacturers of macaronic
verse. One of the bolder ventures was to force the eight lines to
serve the strophic needs of two different verse forms, both of which
treated the same theme independently and could be read separately.
This feat was accomplished by making the first seven of the eleven

syllables of the eight lines form two roundelays or quatrains, while
the full octave formed the second poem. The following example
illustrates this splitting technique. The quatrains appear in ordinary
type, while the remaining syllables of the octave verses are in
italics.

> O Celebre tu gloria *docta Athenas*
> con digna aclamación, *con voces claras*
> la fama por blazón *de aplausos llenos*
> y el tiempo por memoria *de a tus aras.*
> O seráphico Coro! *pues resuenas*
> oy con manera amante *dichas raras,*
> celebra el puro instante *a Delos pura*
> que haze tu edad de oro *mas segura.*[11]

An approximate translation of the internal quatrains is: "Oh, let
thy glory be celebrated with worthy acclaim, with fame as a
heraldic shield, and time as a record! / Oh, the seraphic Chorus
now hails in fond manner the pure instant that forms thy golden
age." The enfolding octave enlarges on the subject of the Immaculate Conception somewhat as follows: "Oh, may this learned
Athens celebrate thy glory / with worthy acclaim and by clear
words, / and, by its full meed of applause may fame / give time
as a record of thy altars. / Oh, seraphic Chorus, since thou singest
/ now in fond manner of rare bliss, / praise to pure Delos the pure
instant / that makes thy golden age more certain."

Still more taxing to ingenuity than the preceding exercises, it
would seem, were the *poesías retrogradas,* or poems with reversible
lines. The Secretary of the 1683 tournament in Mexico City decreed that the theme of the Immaculate Conception demanded the
most difficult and varied efforts of the contestants. As Aeneas had
found refuge and inspiration on the island of Delos in the Aegean
Sea, so the Spanish monarch, Philip III, "had dropped the anchor
of his hope in the safe harbor" of this article of faith which the
aspiring bards of the viceregal capital should celebrate either by
writing ballads or "quatro dezimas retrogradas." "The latter," he
explained to obviate any misunderstanding, "are composed in such
a manner that, by reading from the last line to the first they will
make sense and deal with the same subject as when read in the
natural order."[12] Owing to the greater syntactic flexibility of Castilian this undertaking was not quite so formidable, perhaps, as in

English, but it clearly subordinated content to ingenuity of form.
A ten-line stanza of a poem crowned with the choicest laurel of
the competition will illustrate.

> Assí el Gran Filipo Amante
> a mejor Delos MARÍA
> con devoción rinde pía
> cultos al primer instante;
> no es mucho, si semejante
> de Eneas la Religión
> grande feliz successión
> a su real casa asegura
> Quando más aplaude pura
> en Delos la Concepción.[13]

Following the normal order, this is approximately rendered:
"Just as the great Philip, devoted / to the best refuge, MARY, / wor-
ships with pious devotion / the virginal Conception / so it is not
too much (to believe that), similar / to Aeneas the Faith / will
vouchsafe a great and fortunate succession / to his royal dynasty /
the more the pure Conception / is praised in Delos." Read in re-
verse the same sentiment emerges.

One of the most abject expressions of the cult of the Spanish
poet, Luis de Góngora, were the *centones* which resembled a crazy
quilt of bits and shreds snipped from the poems of the tutelary
bard (occasionally other poets were thus favored). These frag-
ments, to change the figure, were laid end to end in successive
layers like bricks to form a metrical wall. A Mexican critic aptly
described this bizarre product as "a work as difficult as anti-artistic,
in which neither intelligence, imagination, nor sentiment has a
part; it is a labor so mechanically humdrum that it may be compared to the artisan who does inlay work in wood or forms mosaics
of varicolored stones."[14]

The most diverse materials sometimes went into the fabrication
of centos, including scraps of sacred and profane works, of ancient
Greek and Roman poets, proverbs, apothegms, and even snatches
of popular songs. This game was so fascinating that prose compositions and sermons, and even whole books were similarly constructed. It is said that, during the ceremonies in 1701 honoring
the memory of the recently deceased Charles II, last of the House
of Austria on the Spanish throne, Fray Bartolomé Navarro

preached a sermon stitching together patches torn from the writings of such diverse figures as Vergil, Ovid, St. Paul, Horace, Lucan, Machiavelli, St. John, Euripides, Jeremiah, Terence, St. Matthew, and Martial.[15]

Góngora remained, however, the chief inspirer of cento poems of which the often cited 1683 tournament offers numerous examples. Abuses had crept into this practice and the Secretary was explicit in his instructions. "It is indispensable and the express rule," he warned, "that not two or three, nor even one complete verse be taken to form the new poem. For convenience in checking, the folio number and specific poem, from which half-lines or hemistics are taken, must be indicated in the margins before and after each full verse. And elsewhere the edition, with date and place of publication, is to be cited."[16]

A few lines of one of these prefabricated "poems" will suffice as an illustration.

Pan. f. 182	Propicio albor* Oráculo prudente	Son. f. 28
Son. f. 37	El Garzon Phrygio* (quando ya en el puerto)	Can. f. 39
Can. f. 42	con naval pompa* de victoria armado	Can. f. 41
Can. f. 43	Este jardin* (no pisa con pie incierto)	Com. f. 189
Son. f. 13	Oye piadoso* admira reverente:	Can. f. 39

The half lines, separated by an asterisk, have the source and folio number of the first in the left margin, and of the second in the right. The volume used in this instance was the 1654 edition of Góngora's works published at Madrid. Similarly, marriages of half verses continued indefinitely, duly cited, until the diligence of the compiler wearied or until the quota of praises of the theme, in this case, the Immaculate Conception, was complete.[17]

Industry and ingenuity, it is hardly necessary to state, were mistaken for artistic expression, and the perspiration of verbal contortionists had supplanted the inspiration of authentic poets. The inventiveness of puzzle-making, the artful playing of word games, and exhibitions of acrobatic wordplay were the approved ways of deceiving the muses. Especially meritorious was the ability to produce clever puns, rhymed riddles, paranomasias (use of words identical in spelling except for a vowel) and similar artifices. The last-named device is illustrated by an example which, in the eyes of contemporary Spanish Americans, possessed the double virtue of wit and patriotism.

> El Inglés, con frascos frescos
> ebrio, con su baba,—beba,
> y haga de la gula—gala,
> que, con él se trata—treta[18]

(Let the Englishman, in his cups, drink with his drool, and let him display his gluttony, for on him one plays one's tricks.)

Another favorite trick was proof of wit. As verses were made reversible, so letters within words were reversed to spell a different word and thus provide an occasion for ingenious manipulation. If "regal" is spelled backwards, it becomes "lager," while "god" and "top," treated in the same manner, became "dog" and "pot" respectively. In Castilian this technique operates with *odio* (hate) and *oído* (ear, hearing) in the following *quintilla*:

> ¿Cómo ha de pintar un hombre
> la Aurora que nunca vido?
> Y más yo (nadie se asombre)
> que de Aurora sólo el nombre
> me despierta odio al oído.[19]

(How is one to depict the dawn when one has never seen it? And how much harder for me in whose ear (don't be astonished) the mere mention of dawn awakens hatred!)

An intriguing game was to write verses ending in letters which, by giving their alphabet sounds, simulated words.

> Yo soy arriero de R. Q. A.   (recua)
> y de otros arrieros G. F.   (jefe)
> y pues he llegado A. U. Z.   (Auzeta)
> la mala fortuna C. S.   (cese)[20]

which may be rendered: "I'm a muleteer of a packtrain / and the boss of other muleteers, / and since I've come to Auzeta, / my bad luck has ceased."

But the appeal of these artifices palls and the hour has come to close this museum of literary curiosities, though the exhibits observed by no means exhaust the catalogue. These verbal contrivances are, on the whole, more amusing than the windy pomposity of altisonant verse professing to be serious art, and the glimmers of wit they emit are reminders at least that a sense of humor, however perverted, was not entirely absent in an age which, in retrospect, seems so often dominated by a morbid view of life and a preoccupation with death and decay. The more festive notes, however, in most of the surviving verse of the Baroque period are drowned in the deluge of ponderous artificiality, pedantry, and overly ornate diction that flows like a vast verbal lava over the springs of feeling and beauty. Scholasticism and orthodoxy lay heavily upon speculative thought and its expression, and an anachronistic ideology was stifling the free play of ideas and inhibiting every form of controversy. Hence the frustrated imagination and the repressed mental energy of articulate members of society sought release in an ingenious manipulation of verbal symbols and metrical forms which effectively obscured any latent meanings. To *gongorizar,* with an extravagance of Latinisms, neologisms, syntactical subversions, exaggerated metaphors and tropes, classical allusions, chromatic and musical effects, difficult charades, and the like, was to make a safe detour around the intellectual quicksands of Counter Reformation dogmas and absolutes, and these puerile exercises of wit and ingenuity brought literary distinction well within the range of mediocre talent. With vanity thus gratified, few inquisitive minds were tempted to venture into the risky areas of genuine speculation.

This debasement of the creative impulse was, of course, beneficial to neither the mind of the community nor to its literary expression; it even deflected the imagination from the innocuous beauty of nature to a large extent. Little of the charm of the natural setting of the viceregal capital, or of other scenic parts of the vast realm of Old Mexico seeped into contemporary poetry, and almost no lyric verse of authentic merit remains. That gifted talents were not entirely lacking amid the army of versifiers is certain, for an extraordinarily fine poetess, Sister Juana Inés de la Cruz, a nun in the Convent of St. Jerome in Mexico City, wrote poems of enduring excellence during the last half of the seventeenth century, but the few who possessed genius were too often throttled and thwarted by the ineludible tyranny of prevailing esthetic fashions. Succumbing to these oppressive influences the better endowed spirits were constrained to turn from the cultivation of a more worthy literature to the production of such inanities as have passed in review in the preceding pages.

XI

ON THE BOOK
TRADE, 1683

SPAIN had reached the nadir of its political and cultural fortune in the dying years of the seventeenth century. On its troubled throne sat the semi-imbecile Charles II. In 1681 the death of the great dramatist, Calderón de la Barca, rang down the curtain on the Golden Age of Spanish letters and arts, and thus a pall fell upon the peoples of the Hispanic peninsula from which they never emerged completely. But if a sort of nocturnal gloom enshrouded Old Spain in those closing decades, a faint afterglow of the luminous era lit up New Spain. Mexico City, grown more extensive since the days of Fray García Guerra, probably exceeded Madrid itself in physical beauty, and the glittering opulence of its vice-regal court now outshone the tawdriness of the royal palace and the aristocratic circles hovering about the degenerate scion of the Hapsburgs.

Within the Mexican city the broad, central streets still looked as if drawn in straight lines by a ruler, and those with parallel waterways now appeared, especially on market days, even more animated than earlier in the century, with products and flowers. The Jamaica canal now rivaled the Alameda as a place of recreation where old and young of every class and caste floated by in blossom-covered barges, their passengers adding gay songs and guitar-strumming to the lively scene. Humble pedestrians strolled along its banks while the well-to-do sat in carriages, both groups consuming the chocolate, *tamales, atole,* sweetmeats, and other indigestible viands bought from Indian vendors. Now and then a larger barge glided past the muddy margins of the brackish water, its occupants blithely dancing to the melodic rhythms of a stringed orchestra of *mariachi* players.

In the adobe walls lining the streets were variegated stones and pieces of *tezontle,* a porous stone, in the form of hearts, circles, stars, and figured flowers. The low, squat dwellings behind alternated with the more imposing residences which flaunted wide, ornate doorways, and smaller balconies with iron gratings. In every nook and cranny and in every season flamed garden-boxes of orange trees, flowering shrubs, and plants veiling the ugliness of congested living. The unpaved streets were dusty or miry according to circumstances, while the rough cobblestones of other thoroughfares were scarcely more free of dirt or mud. From Chapultepec, west of the city and where the viceroys often preferred to live, a long aqueduct, with its three hundred and sixty-five graceful arches, pointed at the heart of the capital where lay the central square. This open space had grown more unsightly in the course of the century because of "more than two hundred fixed and permanent wooden shops, the majority stocked with large amounts of European and domestic merchandise. The other booths were not so important as they dispensed glassware, crockery, groceries, and foodstuffs. The remainder of the Plaza was covered by Indian stands of reed-grass and *petates,* in which they sell by day and sleep by night. As a result," wrote a contemporary, "one of the best and most spacious squares in the world looks to everyone like an ill-assorted village and a pigsty." The rentals thus provided helped to refill the chronically empty coffers of the municipality.

Contrasting with this crowded ugliness were the ornate buildings facing the square; the Cathedral, still lacking final architectural details, the City Hall, the viceregal Palace, the Inquisition, the Audiencia, the University, the mint, the College of Santo Domingo, and the larger emporiums of wealthy merchants. Elsewhere ecclesiastical establishments had continued to increase since the time of Fray García Guerra, and at varying distances from the center were scattered some seventeen convents for nuns and a greater number of monasteries for monks, and some eighty-nine churches and temples. The city as a whole presented a Baroque sumptuous-

ness, mixed with squalor, hardly rivaled, save for the latter, in contemporary Spain. By moonlight the spires and cupolas gleamed
faintly, casting a ghostly spell over the broken, black masses of the
dwellings in between. On dark nights the lakebound capital lay
under a sable velvet, its somber obscurity scarcely relieved by trembling flickers of lampwicks sputtering beneath images in tiny niches
at domestic doorways.

In 1683 possibly 400,000 souls inhabited Mexico City, which
was then divided into seventeen parishes, five of Spaniards, and the
remaining dozen of Indians and mixtures. Where racial miscegenation had progressed over a century and a half, producing an increasingly complex pattern of pigmented profusion, a total of 72,-
000 passed as of pure European blood. Of these 22,000 were
Spaniards living with their families, and 20,000 more were male
transients. The white female population was reckoned at 30,000.
Permanent Indian residents were estimated at 80,000, with many
more passing in and out of the city continuously. A minority evidently declining in numbers since the days of Fray García but still
conspicuous were the 10,000 or more Negroes and mulattoes,
slave and free, who were domestic servants and petty tradesmen.
Various types of mestizos, or mixed elements comprised the rest of
the inhabitants.[1]

Socially the Creole class was the most powerful, its numbers
and wealth having increased greatly in the course of the century.
The economic depression of the earlier decades had yielded to a
more prosperous period of which the Mexican whites were the
chief beneficiaries. The waning fortunes of the mother country had
enabled many American-born Spaniards to obtain local offices of
government by purchase and other means. If the highest positions
were still out of their reach, the growing economic influence of
this group was making the status of the peninsular Spaniard less
secure and his control less weighty. But this general well-being
was not shared by the proletarian masses who, as their numbers
rose in the city, sank deeper into a morass of misery and alcoholism.
The drinking of pulque, a fermented liquid of the maguey plant,
made drunkenness universal and created fortunes for traffickers in
this beverage. The *pulquerías* were dens of iniquity, and "there is
no quarter, no street, without a public house in which liquor is
sold to the music of guitars, harps, and other instruments, with

rooms in which Negroes, Mulattoes, Mestizos, and many Spaniards meet," wrote a contemporary clergyman.[2] "In the City of Mexico," he went on, "two thousand arrobas of pulque enter every day, and especially on Tuesdays and Saturdays, more than fifteen thousand." Young women were put in charge of these establishments to lure trade, and it was "held for certain that to attract customers these publicans have a provision of persons of both sexes for evil commerce." Moreover, "no royal minister of Justice is allowed to enter the public house to arrest or expel a delinquent." This institution, a fruitful source of corruption, continued to flourish because it brought welcome revenue to an ever-depleted Treasury.

Presiding over the destinies of the sprawling realm in 1683 was the Count of Paredes, the twenty-eighth viceroy, who had held sway for three years amidst a viceregal court perhaps consciously aping the profligacy, luxury, and immorality of the contemporary Versailles of Louis XIV. Though Spain was bankrupt and prostrate, the mines and agriculture of Old Mexico permitted that overseas possession an opulence that even the court of Philip IV in Madrid had scarcely known in its flamboyant period.

A sharply contrasting person and spirit was the newly appointed archbishop (1682-1698), Francisco Aguiar y Seijas, an eccentric clergyman renowned for his puritanical ways, his excessive misogyny, and his extraordinary charities.[3] A twisted Catholic puritan, he had a pathological aversion for women, to whom he imputed all the evils against which the Church inveighed. According to his biographer, he regarded his myopic vision as a special boon since it prevented him from seeing members of the less homely sex. If, through some mischance, a woman crossed his threshold, he promptly ordered the bricks torn up and replaced upon which sacrilegious feet had trod.[4] Lacking entirely, as earlier noted, the taste for worldly pleasures so openly exhibited by his predecessor, Fray García Guerra, he relentlessly campaigned against bullfights, cockfights, gambling, and the theater, and doubtless the fanatic zeal of this mitered bluestocking inspired the Inquisition's renewed energy at this time. Yet his charities were truly munificent, and they even extended to unfortunate elements of despised womanhood. On one occasion he generously supported the efforts of a carpenter and his wife who had taken into their home a demented woman wandering about the streets. So lavish were his benefices that a foreign observer felt that "this ease in finding daily alms is the cause of so many vagrants in Mexico City."[5] Side by side, then, stood the oddly assorted heads of the church-state, each contributing to the indigence of the masses, one by the luxury of a corrupt viceregal court, the other by an exaggerated philanthropy.

Rumors of pirate depredations on both coasts had disturbed the monotony of life in Mexico City from time to time, but in 1683 shudders of alarm shook the capital. News came that in mid-May Vera Cruz had fallen to the dreaded pirate, Lorencillo, whose fierce corsairs sacked the port under the very bastions of the island fortress of San Juan de Ulloa and at a time when the fleet from Spain was hourly expected. In a bold, swift move these buccaneers descended upon the drowsy city, forcing its surprised inhabitants into a parish church. Tightly packed in this narrow space the victims endured for days the horrors of hunger, thirst, heat, and suffocation which must have equalled the torments later experienced in the famous "Black Hole of Calcutta." Children smothered to death and hapless women were dragged out and mercilessly raped, while the invaders threatened to burn the other inmates alive in the building if they did not reveal the hiding places of their wealth. Meanwhile, looting had uncovered a rich haul of silver bars and other treasure awaiting shipment on the incoming fleet. Its imminent approach caused the pirates to hustle their booty and many luckless citizens on board vessels and sail to the nearby Isle of Sacrifices where, without shelter or provisions, they held their victims for high ransoms. Having collected huge sums in this fashion, the buccaneers slipped away almost under the nose of the Spanish ships with the richest plunder ever captured in a port city of the Caribbean.[6]

Another episode which caused tongues to wag furiously that year was the "Case of the Hooded Man." In the midst of the excitement stirred by the sacking of Vera Cruz word reached Mexico City that a mysterious personage known as Antonio Benavides, Marqués de Vicente, was arriving, allegedly as a *visitador,* or royal inspector. The judges of the Audiencia and other viceregal officials, possibly fearing that they would be held responsible for the recent disaster and profiting by the emotional tensions prevailing, chose to regard the newcomer as an imposter. When the latter came to Puebla he was arrested and brought in custody to the capital. Public opinion was sharply divided, some condemning the apparently highhanded imprisonment of the king's representative, and others defending the viceroy's action. The trial of *el Tapado,* or the Hooded Man, as Benavides was called because of the mystery surrounding him, began on June 10, and the population followed its proceedings with eager interest. The effort to wring a confession by judicial torture brought attempted suicide, and feeling ran high during the remainder of 1683.[7] Conservative elements, fearing a threat to their property, believed that the Hooded Man was an agent of the pirates, or that he was bent on inciting revolution in the realm; the more liberal minded espoused his cause and eloquently pleaded for his release. Among these vocal individuals was the remarkable nun-poetess, Sister Juana Inés de la Cruz who, with feminine guile, appealed to the viceroy's clemency by composing a poem on the birthday of his son in which she urged a pardon for *el Tapado.*[8] These efforts, however, were unavailing, for the following year the unfortunate intruder was summarily executed. The enigma of this strange visitor and his mission was never publicly cleared up, and his case long remained a controversial topic of conversation at *tertulias* and social gatherings.

Despite the alarming threats to the security of the realm on the coasts and on the Indian frontiers, cultural life in the capital was vigorous in 1683. It was the year of one of the most elaborate poetic tournaments at the University of Mexico, with its attendant processions, pageantry, oratory, fireworks, and theatrical performances. Plays were written and performed, Sister Juana Inés de la Cruz was composing the best poetry of her time in Castilian, and quantities of books were imported, bought, and read. Indeed, Mexico City was more important than ever as a center of book collections. Religious orders had assembled large libraries, rich in treasures of rare editions and manuscripts. The College of Discalced Carmelites in outlying San Angel, where the famous Spanish novelist, Mateo Alemán, had lived in the days of Fray García Guerra, could boast of ". . . one of the best libraries in America, containing twelve thousand volumes,"[9] and other seminaries and schools were close rivals in this respect. Many collections were semipublic and accessible to interested citizens and scholarly visitors from abroad. Smaller aggregations of books belonged to private individuals, minor officials, lawyers, professors, physicians, merchants, and other laymen who, like Simón García Becerril and

Melchor Pérez de Soto before them, acquired numerous volumes imported regularly through local booksellers, many of which were lighter works of entertainment. In 1683 the rising savant of the University of Mexico, Don Carlos de Sigüenza y Góngora, was busily assembling manuscripts and published materials relating to Indian antiquities, mathematics, astronomy, engineering, history, and philosophy in a collection rated as the finest of the colonial period.

The book-buying public of Old Mexico was so considerable that a surprising number of dealers catered to it. These were usually local printing shops which added large importations to their own products. Probably the most important was that of the Heirs of the Widow of Bernardo Benavides de Calderón. Founded a half century before by a native of Alcalá de Henares in Spain, it had grown rapidly and, in 1683, did much of the local publishing.[10] This success owed much to the business acumen of the widow who assumed management on the death of the founder. Contributing quite as much to the prosperity of the firm, perhaps, was the fact that her six children had all taken orders in the Church, which was an important customer. The eldest son achieved so much distinction by his piety and learning that he was entrusted with high posts, including commissioner of the Inquisition,[11] which possibly accounts for the profitable concession granted to this house for printing and selling primers and catechisms in the realm. One of its annual inventories reveals the large and varied stock on hand in 1683, and this document makes abundantly clear that readers of New Spain could readily enjoy much the same writings as their kinsmen in Old Spain.

Hardly was the Holy Office established in 1571 when the first Inquisitor issued an edict requiring every owner of books to submit a list of them arranged in alphabetical order and with details of title, author, place and date of publication, and the language in which each was printed. While this practice was expected at regular intervals, it was not consistently followed. The advent of a new Inquisitor, a flare-up of heretical rumors, or some other cause occasionally brought renewed enforcement which usually relapsed into extended periods of apathy and indifference. The brief inventory of Simón García Becerril in 1620 preserved in the archive of the Holy Office was, perhaps, the result of censorial activity, momentarily revived. Public booksellers found it expedient to report stock in trade with some regularity, and these documents generally went into the files of the Inquisition without comment. The bookstore of Madame Benavides de Calderón was fairly circumspect in such matters, possibly because of the lucrative concession that her firm enjoyed, and her *memoria de libros* submitted at the end of 1683 rather carefully incorporated the bibliographical data required by the decree of a century before. It thus provides an enlightening glimpse of the varieties of literature carried in stock and presumably in demand. Though invariably listed by short titles— a method to be expected when prolix titles were the fashion— these abbreviations ordinarily permit ready recognition, which is often aided by other bibliographical details present. This inventory lists 276 titles, alphabetically arranged by the author's first name in the awkward practice of the time. Unfortunately it omits the number of copies of each item, thus preventing an analysis of the comparative popularity of individual works, but it provides some revealing insights into the reading preferences and cultural interests of the Mexican public in 1683.[12]

For North Americans the interest of a scrutiny of this booklist of New Spain may be enhanced by a consideration of the literature at the disposal of the New England public that same year. Such a comparison may bring surprises owing to the belief that both the dour Puritans and the inhabitants of Old Mexico shared a deprivation of all light literature, the former presumably by their own choosing, and the latter by the tyranny of the Inquisition. Both communities planted in the North American continent are commonly pictured as spending their slight leisure immersed in prayerbooks and homiletic writings, and eschewing the sensate delights of fiction. An inspection of the booksellers' stock in trade in both regions disproves this misapprehension, and even indicates a curious similarity of taste.

The second half of the seventeenth century had witnessed a rapid expansion of the English colonies, both in population and the area occupied. Massachusetts had prospered mightily and a steady stream of immigration was pouring into it and spreading into its western reaches and neighboring provinces of Rhode Island, Connecticut, and New Hampshire. Its villages and settlements had multiplied, schools were spreading, Harvard College was training many of its clergy, printing presses were functioning, and a brisk book trade was developing with regular importations from England. Boston was clearly the hub of all this commerce and, though hardly comparable to a metropolis like Mexico City, it was becoming a center of cultural activity and refinement. In 1683 it counted some 7,000 inhabitants and was a book market serving 75,000 or more people scattered over New England. Its leading dealer who, like Madame Benavides de Calderón in Old Mexico, had several competitors, was John Usher, son of the founder of the firm whose demise occurred in 1676, "leaving a goodly fortune." A series of invoices extending from 1682 to 1685 indicates that this Boston merchant had imported 3,421 volumes from England, and that the books listed were but a part of his stock. These records show the number of copies of each item, though they supply fewer bibliographical details than the contemporary Mexican inventory.[13]

The titles on both the Mexican inventory and the Boston invoices tend to fall into overlapping categories of religious writings, secular nonfiction, and belles-lettres, with a rough equivalence in the proportions of each. Religion was the dominant thought in both colonial regions, however far apart they were in doctrinal concerns, and approximately half of the items were of this nature. Coincidence of specific titles in the assortments of Protestant and Catholic dealers was, of course, rare, but the common emphasis was on homiletic writings, sermons, and moral disquisitions. The absence of bibliographical information in the Boston lists precludes knowledge of the presses from which the importations came, but presumably they were all from England. The Mexico City inventory, on the other hand, supplies significant and unexpected evidence that many volumes came from printing establishments outside of Spain, notably in the Netherlands and France, particularly Antwerp, Brussels, and Lyon.

Since it was the creative writings that enjoyed most popularity and probably had the widest audience in both regions, it is well, perhaps, to limit comment largely to items of this class. There is added significance in dwelling upon this literature of entertainment owing to a widely held belief that neither the overseas subjects of the Spanish or the English kings could enjoy the pleasures of light reading, the former because of the intolerant despotism of orthodox Catholicism, the latter because of the narrow rigidity of Protestant puritanism. For those still holding these traditional convictions, the records of the bookdealers in Mexico City and Boston that benighted year of 1683 provide revelations. These documents not only proclaim the existence of literary entertainment in both communities, but indicate similarities of taste that are more than vague. The Mexican list, to be sure, displays a richer variety and a more eclectic selection, which situation was to be expected in a more sophisticated society. There the assortment tends to fall into four categories: essays, poetry, drama, and prose fiction.

In both cultures the mark of a gentleman was the mastery of the classics and of history, and works in both fields were in evidence in New England and New Spain. Names of Latin and Greek adorn the book lists of each, but the presence of "Greek Testaments" and "Greek Gramers" in modest quantities on the Boston invoices and their absence on the Mexican inventory suggest a possibly greater concern of Englishmen for that language.[14] In a shipment to Mr. Usher the London dealer had apparently sought to promote by free copies the sales of "Siluanus his Theocritus, Lucian, Isocratis, Essopi Fabula and Plutark" with the notation that ". . . the four books of Siluanus are sent as a present to the Chief Schoolmaster in New England being a New Praxis upon some Greek Authors which is well entertained in our Schooles here and much used." But Latin writings abound on both lists; Vergil, Cicero, Martial, Seneca, and Ovid dot the inventory of Madame Benavides de Calderón, and Cicero, Terence, Horace, and Ovid speck the Boston invoices. The forty-two copies of "Bond's Horrace," and especially the twenty-two of "Farnaby's Ovid," and forty copies of "Ouid de Tristibus" strike the eye on Mr. Usher's lists.

Recalling the universal addiction to verse writing in Old Mexico the small percentage of poetry in stock in 1683 is curious, though hardly startling was the presence of the poetical works of Luis de Góngora whose baneful influence was so unmistakable in the tournament held at the University that year. The demand, it would seem, had shifted from the epic and lyric poetry, so artistically memorable in the sixteenth century, to the banal effusions of pietistic *ramilletes*, or garlands of verse, and to the lure of versified comedies, both of which were important staples in the Mexican book trade.

Dramatic literature is conspicuously absent in the Boston market, but the taste for collections of pious rhymes is warmly shared. Paralleling the Spanish *ramilletes,* sacred and profane, are dozens of copies of the English "Jovial Garland, a collection of all the newest Songs and Sonnets used in Court and Country," "The Crown Garland," "Garland of Delight," "The Royall Arbor of Loyall Poesie . . . Triumph, Elegie, Satyr, Love and Drollerie," and the two copies of the doubtfully moral *Poems on Several Occasions* by the Earl of Rochester. These festive effusions hardly comport with the traditional image of Puritan austerity, and they would seem to cancel out the impression of pious rectitude created by garlands of more proper verse. If now and then copies of Milton's *Paradise Lost* and Robert Wild's *Inter Boreale* appeared on the invoices, the esthetically inferior garlands far outnumbered them, much as the trivial *ramilletes* outweighed the works of Castilian bards in contemporary Mexico.

England and Spain were the two countries of Europe that had a great popular theater in the seventeenth century, but it was only in the overseas domains of the Hispanic empire that the enthusiasm for the drama of the motherland was shared. If the Puritans could only view the stage with a certain horror as one of the more conspicuous works of the Devil, hidebound subjects of orthodox Catholic persuasion in the Spanish realms were quite disposed to be indulgent with that satanic manifestation. As already evident, the *corrales de comedias* of Mexico City were crowded daily, while the printed plays delighted the literate. Since 1605 *Partes,* or collections of a dozen comedies each, had brought the works of playwrights in a continuous stream to the eager audience of the Spanish Indies, and for the printers and dealers this kind of reading matter was a bonanza. Madame Benavides de Calderón's inventory amply supplies confirmatory evidence of this enduring vogue. Despite Archbishop Aguiar y Seijas' currently impassioned zeal to suppress the theater in all its forms, she persisted in having in stock a liberal provision of play collections.

Quite properly as the dramatist who so completely conditioned and reflected the enduring essence of the Baroque spirit and who had become the tutelary genius of Spain's decadence, Pedro Calderón de la Barca, so recently deceased, heads the list, represented by the *Fifth Part, or Collection of Comedies,* published in Madrid in 1677. His shorter-lived disciple, Francisco de Rojas Zorrilla

(1607-1648), whose plays often had a more natural and lifelike quality, is present in a two-volume 1680 edition of his *Several Comedies,* and the works of numerous other dramatists were in stock. Likewise plentiful were collections of one-act plays and skits, often witty and satirical, "by various authors."

If the reading of plays was something of a rage in the seventeenth century Hispanic world, it did not entirely supplant prose fiction in various forms. There was a tendency, generally, to inject didactic elements into it and hence it was less diverting than the sparkling, versified *comedias.* Nevertheless the miscellanies of fables, apothegms, legends, novelettes, and full-length novels had a strong appeal to readers. The early sixteenth century *Silva de Varia Lección* (Miscellany) by Pedro Mexia, a potpourri of articles on history, travel, customs, superstitions, mythology, and related topics still retained an interested following. And popular reading fare were the tales of Pérez de Montalbán, the well-known dramatist, while the Mexican public did not fail to appreciate the more admirable *Exemplary Novels* and the *Don Quixote* of Cervantes.

By 1683 it appears that the enthusiasm for the sixteenth century romances of chivalry, still perceptible in the 1655 book list of Pérez de Soto, had at last expired, but no such extinction had overtaken two other sharply opposed types of novels, the ultrasaccharine pastoral fiction and the picaresque narratives distinguished by their racy pungency and sardonic bitterness. Destined for a long life in the Spanish colonies were the recitals of the amours of moonstruck shepherds and lassies, and here an unexpected similarity of taste in seventeenth century New England is observed. That such bucolic ardors had an appeal to Puritan readers in the chillier north can be deduced from the Boston invoices which record a copy of Sir Philip Sidney's *Arcadia,* and fifteen copies of *Argalus and Pathonia,* a poetical romance of kindred nature by Francis Quarles, whose translations of the Psalms and short devotional poems claimed the esteem of the Pilgrim fathers in soberer moments.

As for the contrasting tales of roguery, their vogue would not reach the English-speaking world until the following century when Spanish models would inspire Fielding, Smollett, and others to produce popular novels. But the Mexican public of 1683 was well accustomed to this reading fare and maintained a steady demand for it. The mid-sixteenth century forerunner and classic of the genre, *Lazarillo de Tormes,* still found a ready sale, though the expurgated version, required a hundred years before by the Inquisition and entitled *Lazarillo de Tormes Castigado* (Lazarillo de Tormes Chastised), was the only one available. Many later narratives of this sort figured in the inventory, notably *The Varied Fortunes of Pindar, the Soldier* by Gonzalo de Céspedes, whose particular fancy for eerie episodes with ghosts rising from tombs to assail guilty mortals faintly anticipates the atmosphere of the tales of Edgar Allen Poe. This Gothic character no doubt explains its inclusion in Pérez de Soto's earlier collection. In Madame Benavides de Calderón's stock there were also brief novels and short stories with mingled touches of realism and satire more or less related to the picaresque theme. Many were sketches of manners that, in the nineteenth century, would receive fuller development and serve to revitalize the Spanish novel. Even the more didactic of these fictional narratives were slightly astringent in their satire if less disposed to echo the heavier cynicism of the true tales of roguery. The sardonic humor, sly wit, and wry pessimism of these stories, also apparent in the short plays and skits so avidly bought and read, made them popular in a world of repressed feeling and wearied by an artificial refinement that substituted shadow for substance. Unconsciously readers were seeking an escape from the prevailing *desengaño* and unreality into a derisively imagined reality, and they took a half-grim delight in those writers who dipped their quills in a corrosive ink of frustration and bitterness.

Most symptomatic of this underlying feeling, perhaps, was the presence of the *Works* of Spain's greatest satirist, Francisco de Quevedo (1580-1645) in the 1683 inventory. The most caustic picaresque tale was his *History of the Life of the Buscón,* written when the author was still in his early twenties. "In the whole literature there can be few books showing such a horror and disgust for life written by a man" so young, observes a critic, and perhaps no one in the Spain of his time saw so clearly the seeds of national decadence that were sprouting. His series of lugubrious visions of the Last Judgment and of Hell contained in his *Sueños* (Dreams) are singularly expressive of the profoundly pessimistic and morbid spirit of the Baroque age.

Quevedo's almost pathological attitude toward existence and his preoccupation with infernal tortures had their counterparts in the Puritan soul of the same century, and the writings of such tormented authors were widely acceptable in both the English- and Spanish-speaking world. A work enjoying the status of a "best seller" in the New England of 1683 was the *Day of Doom* by the Reverend Michael Wigglesworth, whose harrowing depiction of sufferings and punishments in the hereafter must have engendered many a nightmare, but nearly every colonial household counted a copy among its furnishings. The affinity of the transplanted Spaniards and Englishmen in such morbid concerns is patent and, as if to confirm this contention, virtually the only Spanish author represented in the invoice of Mr. Usher, Boston bookseller in the 1680's, was this same dyspeptic Francisco de Quevedo, whose atrabilious *Sueños* were present in two copies dressed in English garb as "Quebedo, Visiones Compl, both parts." Unwittingly this splenetic writer of Catholic Spain was fostering self-hatred and a corroding fear in the hearts of New World Christians widely separated by space, language, and doctrine.

Despite its cursory nature the foregoing survey of the stocks in the leading bookstores of Mexico City and Boston pretty well explodes the traditional theory that the inhabitants of those localities were largely denied the pleasures of light reading in the seventeenth century. The Spanish subjects cowering in the awesome shadow of the Inquisition and the Pilgrim fathers sternly reading their Bibles and reproving any frivolity are both stereotypes that have beclouded the vision of posterity. While it is clear that the literate Mexicans in the more populous New Spain had a richer and more diversified assortment of entertaining books from which to choose, it is equally certain that the English settlers in colder New England could indulge mundane tastes in reading with more freedom and delectation than generally realized. The light and slightly immoral verse and at least eleven different romances which the Boston booksellers found sufficiently salable to keep in stock hardly jibes with the alleged austerity of the Puritans. Indeed, it is instructive to glance at a few of these curious narratives that diverted the reportedly inflexible and ascetic New Englanders.

"Their religious interests and concern with demonology stretched pretty far," remarks an observer, "if these were the reasons leading them to buy three copies of *Venus in the Cloyster, or the Nun in her Smock,* and sixty-six copies of *The History of the Damnable Life and Deserved Death of Dr. John Faustus.* And surely no utilitarian interest in shoemaking caused them to buy twenty-nine copies of *The Pleasant History of the Gentle Art. A Discourse containing Many Matters of Delight, very pleasant to read, set forth with Pictures, and Variety of Wit and Mirth.* And what is one to make of the two copies of *The London Jilt, or the Politick Whore; shewing all the artifices and stratagems which the Ladies of Pleasure make use of, for the intreaging and decoying of men; interwoven with several pleasant stories of the Misses' ingenious performances?* Was it material for sermons, or was it only erotica?"[15] And interesting, too, is the London dealer's notation on an invoice of May 29, 1684: "London Jilt is out of print and not to be had."

Other items at the disposal of New England readers were: *A History of Fortunatus,* about a successful young man; *Pharamond, or the History of France. A Fam'd Romance in Twelve Parts,* translated from the French of La Calprenède; *The Most Famous, Delectable and Pleasant History of Parismus, Prince of Bohemia; the English Rogue comprehending the most eminent Cheats of Both Sexes;* which suggests a latent taste for what readers in Old Mexico were enjoying at the moment; *The Famous History of Valentine and Orson; The Most Pleasant History of Tom a Lincoln;* and *Clelia,* a translation of a ten-volume romance of Mlle. de Scudéry. And what interest did a stern Puritan have in purchasing *Scoggins Jests,* with a foreword declaring that "there is nothing beside the goodness of God that preserves health so much as honest mirth"? Strange fare, indeed, is this for a people so easily outraged by the frivolities of a wicked world! It is refreshing to learn that the stiff-necked dwellers on a "stern and rockbound coast" could unbend in lighter moods even if, as seems quite certain, these softer moments were less frequent, less gay, and less spontaneous than those of their distant neighbors in the sunny vales and broad expanses of Old Mexico.

✠ XII

A BAROQUE POETESS

ONE August day of 1667 in Mexico City an attractive, talented girl, still some months short of her nineteenth birthday, entered the sternly ascetic Order of Discalced Carmelites as a chorister. The convent that received her was the one that had been the dream of those earnest nuns, Sister Inés de la Cruz and Sister Mariana Encarnación when they plied the fickle Archbishop García Guerra so assiduously earlier in the century with sweetmeats and seductive music. Though immediate success had eluded these efforts, it will be recalled, patience was triumphant in 1616, and the new religious community came into being. The young lady who, a half century afterwards, gained admittance to its holy precincts was Doña Juana Inés de Asbaje y Ramírez de Santillana, better known as Sister Juana Inés de la Cruz, already mentioned in these pages and famed as the "last great lyric poet of Spain and the first great poet of America."[1] Also musically gifted, her ecclesiastical name was possibly adopted in veneration of the instrument-playing hostess of Fray García Guerra and cofounder of the Carmelite convent, of which she was now a temporary inmate.

In an age when matrimony and religious reclusion were the sole careers open to respectable females, the act of taking the veil was a commonplace event in Mexican society. In most sisterhoods the discipline was not severe, and within the cloistered walls many comforts and amenities of secular life could be enjoyed, including the services of personal slaves.[2] Indeed, for daughters whose matrimonial prospects were not bright, an immured existence of this sort

172

seemed a desirable alternative, and a young woman whose parents or relatives could provide the requisite dowry was regarded as fortunate. But the case of the adolescent Doña Juana Inés de Asbaje y Ramírez de Santillana seemed exceptional, and strangely obscure the reasons for her decision. Here was a maiden "that was far more beautiful than any nun should be,"[3] the darling of the vice-regal court, and the favorite maid-in-waiting of the vicereine. Her personal attractiveness, her nimble wit in penning verse for any occasion, and her amazing knowledge of books, were all very nearly the talk of the town. In fact, the admiring Viceroy himself, on one occasion, had arranged that a group of the leading professors at the University of Mexico should examine the precocious girl in various branches of learning, and when she emerged triumphant from this ordeal, the learned gentlemen marveled at the erudition and composure of a maiden who hardly seemed more than a child.

Her rise and renown in the courtly circle of the capital had been truly phenomenal. A village lass, born in 1648 in a tiny hamlet called Nepantla, "the land in between," that looked up to the snow-crested volcanoes Popocatepetl and Ixtacihuatl, she had begun to read at the age of three, later devouring the small library of her grandfather. When eight years old she went to Mexico City to live with relatives. Soon this pretty child prodigy caught the eye of the vicereine who brought her to reside amidst the luxury and splendor of the viceregal Palace. In this sophisticated environment the young girl rapidly acquired a maturity that quite belied her years, and in the Court she soon found herself envied for her wit by the women and desired for her physical charms by the men.

Social success of this sort in such aristocratic circles was all the more extraordinary in the light of her illegitimate birth, though this circumstance was, perhaps, undisclosed to anyone save her confessor. Her mother, it was later revealed, had had two separate trios of children by as many men, and neither of these unions the Church had hallowed. It was not an uncommon situation at the time, even in families of some distinction, but it was hardly a genealogical asset for any one of patrician pretensions. That this lowly origin influenced the resolve of Juana Inés de Asbaje y Ramírez de Santillana, who thus bore the surnames of her progenitors, to become a nun is likely but, as the sole explanation of her choice, it is unlikely. Her deep passion for study, her stated "total disinclination to marriage," and the promptings of her zealous confessor, the Jesuit *calificador* of the Inquisition, Antonio Núñez de Miranda, had undoubtedly made a life of reclusion seem attractive to her troubled spirit, and finally moved her to abandon the pomp and glitter of the Palace social whirl, of which she was so conspicuously a part.

That this determination was attended by doubts, misgivings, and inner conflict appears evident in the fact that illness caused her to withdraw from the Carmelite order within three months. The transition from a worldly court to the harsh confinement of a convent proved too abrupt and severe. Early the following year, however, she took her first vows in the Jeronymite community, the milder discipline of which was better suited to the sensitive temperament and scholarly aspirations of the poetess. The remainder of her forty-seven years of life she spent chiefly within the book-lined walls of her cell, to which she retreated as often as her conventual duties permitted. There she pored over her accumulating volumes, attended to an extensive correspondence within and outside of the broad realm of Old Mexico, and wrote the verses so widely known in her time and that have since won enduring fame.

Her poetry is varied in meter and theme, including love lyrics that occasionally border on the erotic, tender Christmas carols, morality plays, allegorical pieces, and even secular three-act comedies like those performed in the public theaters of Spain and Spanish America. Much of this metrical expression abounded in literary conceits and was clothed in the ornate, florid, and obscure style of prevailing Baroque fashion. Unlike most verse of her contemporaries, however, subtle meaning and profound feeling often lay hidden in the intricate foliage of words and clever figures of speech. The most abstruse and inscrutable of her poems, and the only one that she professed to have written with pleasure, bears the title *Primero Sueño* (First Dream). Consisting of 975 verses of seven and eleven syllables' length, it seeks to reveal the subconscious and organic processes of sleep. In this labyrinthian composition of involved syntax and metaphors this strange nun appears to have outdone her master, Luis de Góngora. For one critic it "is a hymn to the awakening of the spirit of investigation or research, and an unsuspected forerunner of the poetry of the eighteenth century Enlightenment"[4]; for others it seems among the most ultra-Baroque manifestations of colonial verse. Yet many of her sonnets and shorter lyric poems have an almost limpid clarity and an exquisite beauty that mark her as the supreme poet of her time in Castilian.

As time passes the appeal of this Creole nun-poetess increases and the circle of her admirers enlarges. It is not merely the esthetic merit of so much of her verse which brings her this homage—though she is often regarded, as already suggested, as among the greatest poets in the speech of Spain—but, perhaps even more, the complex personality refracted in many of her writings. Her more intimate and spontaneous expression offers glimpses so fleeting and elusive of the inner life of an extraordinary woman that they serve to pique the reader's curiosity rather than to satisfy it. In certain lines her intention seems illumined for a bare moment, like a flash of lightning in the night, only to be followed by an obscurity more impenetrable than before. Thus it is that the enigmatic quality of Sister Juana's verses, even more than the technical perfection of the best of them, inspires a veritable cult and wins for her an expanding audience. Through the heavily embroidered veil of the Baroque conventions are discerned the glimmers of a refined spirit in profound conflict, an ambivalent personality of feminine emotion and masculine intellectuality rent and torn by a series of opposing dualisms. Plainly recognizable are the psychological fissures of a distraught nature, but the contributing tensions remain obscure and the causes unfathomable. Yet not so entirely that they fail to intrigue and fascinate the reader. Many verses appear deliberately opaque, as if the poetess feared to divulge what she longed to express and, half revealing, half concealing, they inevitably invite speculation as to their meaning. Hence the temptation to apply modern techniques of evaluation to her utterances becomes well nigh irresistible, and many critics have succumbed with stimulating, if possibly misleading, results.[5]

It is doubtful that any of the inner struggles externalized in Sister Juana's verses arose from a single origin. More likely they were the outward manifestations of a series of subjective discords inextricably confused and irretrievably blended, and any effort to isolate individual elements is largely vain, since it is likely to result in the distortion of oversimplification. Nevertheless, tentative probings in quest of the reality of the personality behind the verbal curtain of literary conceits have yielded some insights, and further ones will, perhaps, bring similar approximations to truth. In this undertaking it is of interest to focus attention on three sonnets which have been called a "tryptic of variations on the same theme."

In these three poems Sister Juana makes use of a device called *encontradas correspondencias,* or triangular antitheses, and of this peculiarity there are occasional echoes in other poems. Most commentators feel that it is merely an ingenious playing with words, the affected wittiness of a comedy, and the sort of dialectics on the subject of love in which the poets of the time delighted to indulge.[6] Yet the reiteration of these *encontradas correspondencias* in three separate sonnets, presumably written on different occasions, together with hints of similar antitheses elsewhere in her writings, suggests that something more than mere cleverness underlies them. These sonnets have English versions which will serve to illustrate the device employed, though inevitably without exact precision:

Who thankless flees me, I with love pursue;
Who loving follows me, I thankless flee:
To him who spurns my love I bend the knee,
His love who seeks me, cold I bid him rue.
    I find as diamond him I yearning woo,
Myself a diamond when he yearns for me;
Who slays my love I would victorious see,
While slaying him who wills me blisses true.
    To favor this one is to lose desire
To crave that one, my virgin pride to tame;
On either hand I face a prospect dire.
    Whatever path I tread, the goal the same:
To be adored by him of whom I tire,
Or else by him who scorns me brought to shame.

Feliciano loves me constantly;
Lisardo hates me, who his name adore.
For the indifferent one my tears will pour;
I have no taste for him who weeps for me.
    To those who tarnish most I give my soul;
The would-be worshippers I but despise.
I scorn the man who would my honor prize,
And favor him who goes away heart-whole.
    If I reproach myself with slighting one,
The other takes offense at my misdeed.
Between the two I finally am undone;
    They vex me with a torment cruel indeed,

the one asking that of which I've none,
the other lacking that for which I plead.

That Fabio does not love me, when I adore him,
Is an unequaled grief, and hurts my will;
But that Sylvio loves me, though I abhor him,
Is no less penance, if a lesser ill.
Such suffering is hardly to be borne,
When toward my ears ever and ever move
Both the vain arrogance of a man I love
And the irksome sighing of a man I scorn.
If Sylvio's surrender wearies me,
I weary Fabio by surrendering;
By one I keenly seek to be approved,
The other courts my approval eagerly.
Active and passive is my suffering:
I grieve in loving, and in being loved.[7]

The possible inspiration of the Latin poet Ausonius and of the great dramatists, Lope de Vega, and Calderón de la Barca, has been pointed out and the differences of treatment analyzed.[8] But, while it is clear that Sister Juana Inés was often influenced by Spanish and other writers, seldom was she content merely to imitate her models. Generally she borrowed only those forms and ideas which enabled her to pour some essence of herself into them by adapting them to her own peculiar need of the moment. As already suggested, the repeated use of these concepts of unrequited love arouses a suspicion that she selected them because they offered a convenient vehicle to externalize some deep-seated and tormenting conflict of a quite different nature. As one critic puts it, there is no doubt that she wrote these sonnets "with her heart in her pen." What, then, was the struggle afflicting her conscious or subconscious mind? Was it, as the words imply, a reflection of an amorous experience presumably before entering the convent? Possibly, but this interpretation seems much too obvious considering the literary conventions of the Baroque age and the complex personality which she clearly possessed. In the lyric poetry of seventeenth century Mexico the use of the language of love could scarcely be taken at face value any more than the name Silvio, Fabio and Feliciano should be considered those of actual persons. Both practices were then standard, of course, and in some of her verses *de encargo* Sister Juana doubtless used these conventions to please those who had solicited such products of her quill. But in the three sonnets cited one senses a deep, inner disquiet, the mental anguish of a difficult choice that gives no peace. Perhaps the key to this dilemma lies in those lines of Sister Juana which read:

> My soul is confusedly divided into two parts,
> One a slave to passion, the other
> measured by reason.
> Inflamed civil war importunately
> afflicts my bosom. Each part
> strives to prevail, and amidst
> such varied storms, both contend-
> ers will perish, and neither
> one will triumph.*

But within both "reason" and "passion" there is abundant room for varied conflicts producing even more bewildering dilemmas such as the triangular antitheses evident in the sonnets quoted.

Returning to these *encontradas correspondencias*, one may express them schematically as: A loves B, but B does not love A; C loves A, but A does not love C. If A is Sister Juana, whom or what do B and C represent? Having discarded the theory of a personal love triangle, one must dismiss the "whom" and endeavor to analyze the "what" that is symbolized in the names Fabio, Silvio, Feliciano, and Lisardo, or the "B" and "C" of the scheme.

In the multiplying criticism of the life and work of the Mexican nun-poetess there is increasing agreement that her intellectual distinction exceeds her eminence as a poet, and that her preoccupation with ideas was greater than with artistic creation.[9] Without minimizing the deeply emotional and feminine nature of Sister Juana, she was basically a rationalist with a passion for knowledge, and the processes of analysis were stronger and more obsessive than any other of her psyche. Her extraordinary gift as a lyric poet was ancillary to her acutely rational mentality, and her supreme aspiration was the freedom of her mind to roam untrammeled and unimpeded through every realm of thought. To read, to study, to experiment ". . . just to see if, by studying, I might grow less ignorant . . ." was the consuming desire of her existence. Since earliest childhood she had experienced this powerful yearning and

---

* En dos partes dividida
tengo el alma en confusión:
una, esclava a la pasión
y otra, a la razón medida

later she had begged her mother to permit her to attend the University of Mexico disguised in male clothing. "What is indeed the truth," she wrote in her famous *Reply to Sister Philotea,* a letter of much autobiographical significance, "and which I do not deny (in the first place because it is well known to everyone, and in the second place because, though it may be to my detriment, Heaven has bestowed upon me the blessing of a very great love of truth), is that, ever since the first glimmer of reason struck me, this inclination to learning has been so urgent and powerful . . ." In her young innocence she had desisted from eating cheese in the belief that such food would make her unpolished and uncouth, hence ". . . the desire to know was stronger in me than the desire to eat, even though the latter is so strong in children . . ."[10] This "inclination" triumphed over every other urge, including the sexual—for marriage she had a "total negation" she had declared—and she candidly confesses that her decision to take the veil—her only other choice— was largely influenced by the relatively freer opportunity it promised for study. The more solitary practices of the Carmelites had induced her, perhaps, to select that Order first. She had thought to escape the tyranny of what almost seemed a vice by dedicating herself as a bride of Christ, but ". . . poor, wretched me! I merely brought myself with me, together with my worst enemy, this inclination!" Instead of extinguishing this passion for reading and cogitation she found that, once subjected to her vows, this thirst for learning ". . . exploded like a charge of powder and what took place in me was *privatio est causa appetitus.*"

In the medieval atmosphere of seventeenth century Mexico where women could not dream of independent lives, where it was axiomatic that they possessed inferior intelligence, and where they were scarcely more than chattels of their fathers, brothers, and husbands, intellectual curiosity in Sister Juana's sex was not only indecorous but sinful. It might, indeed, be the workings of the Evil One and, therefore, imperil one's salvation, as her superiors in the convent more than once assured her. Though there were learned women in history, any emulation of them by a nun was not without an attendant sense of guilt. Sister Juana herself had not escaped this feeling, for she wrote: ". . . I have prayed God to subdue the light of my intelligence, leaving me only enough to keep His law, for anything more (according to some persons) is superfluous in a woman." But, even in these despairing words, one seems to detect in a parenthetical phrase, in which the masculine form is used, a veiled rancor against the man-made world of her time. But her obvious intellectual distinction also aroused the jealousy and antipathy of her companions in the convent, and over the years this hostility developed in her a persecution complex. Her brilliant, inquiring mind seemed always a source of vexation. "If my intelligence is my own," she wrote in one of her poems, "why must I always find it so dull for my ease and so sharp for my hurt?"[11]

This avid curiosity and desire for knowledge, so at odds with her time, place, and sex, seemed only to bring down upon her head the criticism and censure of those about her:

> Why, people, do you persecute me so?
> In what do I offend, when but inclined
> with worldly beauties to adorn my mind,
> and not my mind on beauty to bestow?
>   I value not a treasure trove, nor wealth;
> the greater measure of content I find
> in placing riches only in my mind,
> than setting all my intellect on wealth.
>   And I esteem not beauty, for, when past
> it is the spoils of age's cruelty;
> nor faithless riches carefully amassed.
>   Far better nibble, it seems to me,
> at all life's vanities unto the last
> than to consume my life in vanity.*[12]

And again in one of her ballads she asks bitterly why her fondness for truth must always bring her punishment. "If this fondness I

---

    * ¿En perseguirme, mundo, qué interesas?
¿En qué te ofendo, cuando sólo intento
poner bellezas en mi entendimiento
y no mi entendimiento en las bellezas?
   Yo no estimo tesoros ni riquezas,
y así, siempre me causan más contento
poner riquezas en mi entendimiento
que no mi entendimiento en las riquezas.
   Yo no estimo hermosura que, vencida,
es despojo civil de las edades,
ni riqueza me agrada fementida;
   teniendo por mejor en mis verdades
consumir vanidades de la vida
que consumir la vida en vanidades.

have is licit and even an obligation, why should they chastise me because I do what I must?"

These protests, indicating a sensitiveness to sharp disapproval around her, recur so frequently as to suggest a more disturbed state of mind than would result from eminence in the accepted forms of learning of her time, even after due allowance is made for the fact that such pursuits were deemed unsuitable for a woman, and particularly one bound by vows of perpetual submission. This exaggerated feeling of persecution was possibly generated in part by a growing sense of guilt engendered by the *kind* of knowledge that she was seeking and by the *kind* of methods that she was using to acquire it. In short, her learning might appear more secular than ecclesiastical—"What a pity it is that so rich a mind should so debase itself in the petty matters of this world!"[13] the Bishop of Puebla was to chide her—and her procedures more experimental or scientific in the modern way than scholastic and philosophic. Even more reprehensible than mundane knowledge were the unorthodox means of seeking it. "Experimentation tugged at Sister Juana from earliest childhood," comments a student of her life.[14] Here, then, is the possibility of a conflict, intellectual in origin which, given her environment, profession, and sex, would inevitably be spiritual and emotional as well. This inner discord, with its concomitant overtones of heresy and disobedience, could well produce a brooding conviction of guilt and thus, through anxiety, accentuate a feeling of persecution.

About 1600 began a revolution in the minds of western man which ushered in, as earlier discussed, the Age of Science. Kepler and Galileo had simultaneously formulated the principle that natural laws are to be discovered by measurement, and this radical principle they applied to their work. Where the science of Aristotle and the ancients was content to classify and label, the new science now sought to measure, and the quantitative method involved, as one writer puts it, "a new adjustment at many levels in the hierarchy of the human system." And again, "by the sixteenth century the medieval veil between man and nature had fallen, the individual was setting out to express himself through his faculties."[15]

As the seventeenth century advanced, the individual was more and more challenging authority, empiricism was challenging medieval rationalism, and in this process Mathematics was the new tool, as Descartes was demonstrating.

It was Sister Juana's fate to have her being in this age when, even in Old Mexico, though ever so slightly, the long accepted and sole approach to truth was beginning to be threatened by a new way, a new method. Almost imperceptibly the traditional scholastic and authoritarian concepts of revealed knowledge were yielding to the more sensate procedures of scientific observation and analysis. In the Mexico City of her time there was greater awareness of this intellectual revolution than commonly believed, and the capital had a tiny group of savants who were abreast of contemporary thought, even that of non-Catholic Europe. The comparatively free circulation of nontheological books during the sixteenth and seventeenth centuries,[16] the frequent presence in the viceroyalty of transient men of learning from the Old World, and the personal correspondence of local scholars with thinkers abroad, had all contributed to a more vital mental climate in the New World centers than the contemporary dominance of a medieval Church was thought to permit. A small number of Creole *sabios* were already familiar with the ideas and writings of Erasmus, Copernicus, Kepler, and particularly Descartes, whose philosophies they discussed among themselves in comparative freedom and even cited in their published writings.

Most conspicuous of this intelligentsia of New Spain was Don Carlos de Sigüenza y Góngora. He was a professor of mathematics in the University of Mexico, renowned for his studies of astronomy, archaeology, history and natural philosophy, and also an intimate friend of Sister Juana. Living at the Hospital del Amor de Dios where he served as chaplain, he was a frequent visitor at the Jeronymite convent a few blocks away where the nun-poetess had her cell. It appears that these two intellectually gifted and lonely people enjoyed long discussions together in the locutory of the convent. Sigüenza, a very minor poet, was encouraged in these exercises by Sister Juana, while she in turn received his stimulation and training in scientific disciplines. It is likely that she acquired the mathematical instruments and some of the books said to have furnished her cell as a result of this association. Indeed, the attainments of these two figures working together have moved a discerning critic to comment that they were ". . . the first ones (in Mexico) in whom the modern spirit appears or manifests itself."[17] It was Sigüenza who most often brought visiting savants to her convent, including the great mission-founder of the American Southwest, Father Eusebio Francisco Kino. And it was he who initiated the exceedingly intelligent nun into the new methodology propounded by Descartes, of which there are faint indications in her verse.[18] Doubtless it was he who understood her enthusiasm for, and encouraged her in, the performance of such simple experiments in physics as she mentions in her *Reply to Sister Philotea*. And it was he who shared her love for the dawning Age of Enlightenment of which they both were unconscious precursors in Mexico.

The inherent critical capacity of Sister Juana, coupled with omniverous reading, moved her to welcome a more pragmatic approach to truth. Latent in her mind was a healthy skepticism regarding the effectiveness of purely verbal rationalization, and her eager curiosity was insidiously drawn to experimentation and direct observation. A scrutiny of Sister Juana's verse and prose tends to support the conviction that she felt an instinctive distrust of the scholasticism dominating the intellectual life of viceregal Mexico. Her deeper regard for observation and a more scientific analysis seems apparent when, in the *Reply*, she emphasizes the importance of varied studies and methods in throwing light on speculative learning, particularly theology, and her underlying preference is revealed when she adds: ". . . and when the expositors are like an open hand and the ecclesiastics like a closed fist." Her reactions to the specious learning and rhetorical ratiocination around her, characterized chiefly by polemical disquisitions with ostentatious displays of classical quotations and cloudy verbosity, emerge clearly in the ballad beginning with the pathetic verse "Let us pretend that I am happy." The wordy debates of bookish pedants and charlatans of the so-called intelligentsia filling the air about her with their din move her to exclaim metrically: "Everything is opinions and of such varied counsels that what one proves is black, the other proves is white."* And regarding these doctrinaire pundits she would surely have agreed with Alexander Pope's caustic couplet:

---

* Todo el mundo es opiniones,
de pareceres tan varios,
que lo que el uno, que es negro,
el otro prueba que es blanco.

> The bookful blockhead, ignorantly read,
> with loads of learned lumber in his head.

This universal penchant for splitting hairs in interminable disputes to the neglect of essentials vexes the sound intellect of Sister Juana. "If their soaring rhetoric steeped in false subtleties be not abated, the essential is forgotten in the concern for the accessory."* She seemed to feel that these disputants, to borrow a phrase from Bacon, worked at their endless dialectics ". . . as the spider worketh its web, bringing forth cobwebs of learning, admirable for its fineness of thread and work, but of no substance or profit." The pedantry exhibited in the profusion of Latin and Greek quotations, of classical allusions, and of florid circumlocutions irked the wise nun. "If a trained hand does not prevent the foliage of the tree from becoming too dense, its wild tangle will rob the fruit of its substance."† All this specious erudition moves her to ask: "What silly ambition sweeps us away, forgetful of ourselves? If it is for so short a life, what good is it to know so much?"‡ And in despair she cries: "Oh, if there were only some seminary or school, as there is for knowledge, where they would teach ignorance of such learning!"**

In the *Reply* she comments, with veiled scorn, on the affectation that passed as learning in the excessive number of quotations from authorities: ". . . and I add that their education is perfected (if nonsense is perfection) by having studied a little Philosophy and Theology, and by having a smattering of languages, by which means one may be stupid in numerous subjects and languages be-

---

* Y si el vuelo no le abaten
en sutilezas cebado,
por cuidar de lo curioso
olvida lo necesario.

† Si culta mano no impide
Crecer al árbol copado,
Quita la sustancia al fruto
la locura de los ramos.

‡ Que loca ambición nos lleva
de nosotros oluidados?
Si es para vivir tan poco,
de que sirue saber tanto?

** Oh, si, como hay de saber,
hubiera algún seminario
o escuela donde a ignorar
se enseñaran los trabajos!

cause the mother tongue alone is not room enough for a really big fool." Mindful, likewise, of the self delusion facilitated by the verbalism of scholasticism, Sister Juana believed that everyone should keep within his own mental limitations. If this were so, she tartly exclaims: "How many warped intelligences wandering about there would not be!"

Perhaps the most penetrating stanza of this same ballad is the one in which she puts her finger on the core of true wisdom, the development of sound judgment: "To know how to make varied and subtle discourses is not knowledge; rather, knowledge simply consists of making the soundest choices."*

These and other passages in the writings of Sister Juana reflect a disaffection with the prevailing scholastic methods of thinking in her world and an impatience with an intellectual age which she could not know was passing. She yearned for a newer, freer era of widening horizons, of a differing approach to truth which she did not realize was beginning. But the religious institution, of which she was a part and which was so concerned for her salvation, was wholly identified with the old ways of thinking that did not attract her. Rather, her attachment to the unorthodox kind of thinking became a compulsion against which she struggled constantly, fearful of its implications for her eternal security in its radical departure from ecclesiastical authoritarianism. Her intellectual soul was enamored of this new and scientific approach to truth, but there could be no reciprocation in such a passion for one so closely held in the embrace of medieval tradition as a nun. For her only the concept of knowledge revealed by authority and scholastic methods was proper and permissible. Consequently, she feared this urge to think by unhallowed procedures, and she buried herself deeply in her books in the vain effort to banish such ideas from her mind. Yet this analytical mania obsessed her. "This way of observing everything happened to me and it always happens to me without my having any control in the matter . . . And, continuing on the subject of my cogitations, I must state that this is so constant with me that I do not need any books . . ." When deprived of her reading, as happened for a period, her mind seemed to

---

* No es saber, saber hacer
discursos sutiles vanos;
que el saber consiste sólo
en elegir lo más sano.

accelerate its activity in this manner. "Even though I did not study in books I kept studying everything in God's creation, the individual objects serving me as words and the whole universal scheme as a book. Nothing did I look at and nothing did I hear that I did not speculate on, even the smallest and most material things . . . And so, I repeat, I looked at everything and I wondered about everything . . ." Even in sleep this process operated: ". . . not even in slumber was my mind free of this continuous movement. On the contrary, it seems to operate more freely and unimpeded, bringing out these objects with even greater and more undisturbed clarity than in the daytime."

Thus it appears that Sister Juana found herself not only torn between "reason" and "passion," but also between *two methodologies of reason*. The time-honored dialectics and syllogisms of scholasticism were still entrenched as the accepted means of rationalization in the Church of Christ which held her in its protective arms and to which she was irrevocably bound by vows. This great institution sheltered and loved her, and obedience to its authority and ways was her ineludible obligation. Yet, deep within, she could not reciprocate its love. Instead, she seemed possessed by a way of thinking that threatened to undermine the assumptions on which the Faith rested. On the true object of her affections, the new concept of experimentalism relying on the senses rather than on authority, her benevolent guardian, the Church, severely frowned. Such intellectual exercise might well be inimical to the divine science of theology, and it was potentially, if not actually, heretical. Adherence to such thinking could seriously jeopardize her eternal salvation, which was infinitely precious to her. In her religious play, *The Divine Narcissus,* she wrote: "Behold that what I yearn for I am powerless to enjoy, and in my anxious longing to possess it, I suffer mortal pangs."

In this torturing dilemma Sister Juana, in her long letter to the Bishop of Puebla, sought to rationalize her predilection when she asked how the "Queen of Sciences," that is, Theology, could be understood without knowledge of a series of secular disciplines including Logic, Rhetoric, Physics, Arithmetic, Geometry, Architecture, History, and others. This passage seems a faint echo of the Third Precept of Descartes which reads: ". . . to conduct my thought in such order that, by commencing with objects the simplest and easiest to know, I might ascend little by little and, as it were, step by step, to the knowledge of the more complex, assigning in thought a certain order even to those objects which, in their own nature, do not stand in a relation of antecedence and sequence." But, however cogently she might argue for more pragmatic learning and greater intellectual freedom, the heavy odds of the traditions of her time, place, vocation, and sex were overwhelmingly against her. Inevitably, she fell prey to torturing uncertainty, guilt, and despair, from which she sought release in her more intimate poetry. These inner rendings of her being resulting from the many dualisms of her complex personality became chronic and, in time, made her long for death. In one of her poems appear these words: "I am dying (who will believe it?) at the hands of the thing that I love most, and what is killing me is the love I have for it."* And in a secular play of hers occurs the line: "I am dying for the sake of one who is not dying because of me."

Repeatedly in verse and in prose her guilt complex and torment are revealed by the phrase: "I am my own executioner," which seems a cry of anguish, though "I do not study in order to write, and much less to teach, for that would be unpardonable arrogance in me, but just to see if by studying, I can be less ignorant." In her constricted world with its low, arching dome of heaven, there was no space for her privileged spirit to soar. With deepening despair she knew that such a strange preoccupation with her mind was unseemly in a woman, especially one in religious reclusion; it erected barriers of intercourse with her uncomprehending sisters in the community in which she lived, and their jealousy and envy of her recognized superiority did not grow less. "Let not the head which is the repository of knowledge expect any other crown than that of thorns," she wrote bitterly, for she had known the reprobation of her superiors. Indeed, the chiding letter of the Bishop of Puebla was probably mild and gentle in comparison with the admonitions of her confessor and of the convent sisters. The bishop had reproved her cultivation of "profane letters," by which it was clear

---

* Muero (y quién lo creerá?) a manos
  de la cosa que más quiero
  y el motivo de matarme
  es el amor que le tengo.

that he included her preoccupation with a secular rationalization. He had urged her to confine herself to the exercise of theological scholasticism of which she had given such proof of her skill in her telling critique of the sermon of the celebrated Portuguese Jesuit.

But Sister Juana's mind and heart responded instinctively to a more experimental pragmatism, and she could not bring herself wholly to surrender to the verbal hairsplitting of the intellectual life about her. In many of her poems she used the poetical name "Fabio" as the figure she adored and Silvio, Feliciano and others as the ones she disdained or abhorred. "My will belongs to Fabio, and may Silvio and the world forgive me," are two typical verses. That her preference for "Fabio" stems from its similarity to the Spanish word *sabio,* the wise or learned, is a possibility. Silvio, like other designations, may well refer to the pedants that she could not esteem. But convent-bound in the medieval atmosphere of the ecclesiastical society of Mexico City she could only feel at war with it and with herself. The love and kindliness implicit in the Church's paternalism claimed her gratitude and, of course, her vows compelled obedience to it. Yet the persistent longing for a freer expression of her intuition and for another and more open avenue to truth and to God prevented complete reciprocation and submission in her heart. The sensate experimentalism and scientific methodology of a dawning age beckoned her, while the secular world, which was giving birth to it, was indifferent and unaware of the love of a lonely woman deeply enmeshed in the toils of rigid medievalism. It seemed only to disdain her and, inevitably, Sister Juana's was a blighted love—rejection by the beloved and possession by the unloved—a triangular antithesis. Rarely did she experience even a momentary relief from the incessant conflict within her and, in time, it undermined her health and hastened her death. In this unhappy state of *encontradas correspondencias* she could only externalize her dilemma in verses of obscure symbolism but unmistakable feeling which voiced her suffering repeatedly. In the poignant sonnet, "Who thankless flees me, I with love pursue," the "Who" was, perhaps, experimentalism, a secularized freedom, and a newer age; and in "Who loving follows me, I thankless flee," the "Who" was possibly scholasticism, ecclesiasticism, and medievalism; the first the avenue to salvation by knowledge, the second the avenue to salvation by *faith.*

Who thankless flees me, I with love pursue;
Who loving follows me, I thankless flee;
To him who spurns my love I bend the knee,
His love who seeks me, cold I bid him rue.
    I find as diamond him I yearning woo,
Myself a diamond when he yearns for me:
Who slays my love I would victorious see
While slaying him who wills me blisses true.
    To favor this one is to lose desire,
To crave that one, my virgin pride to tame;
On either hand I face a prospect dire;
    Whatever path I tread, the goal the same;
To be adored by him of whom I tire,
Or else by him who scorns me brought to shame.

As the dawn of April 17, 1695 was casting a wan light over the troubled City of Mexico the wracked and broken spirit of Sister Juana quietly claimed its longed-for release from the prison of her aloneness. "See how death eludes me because I desire it," she had exclaimed in one of her poems, "for even death, when it is in demand," she had added, "will rise in price." Over the long years of her short life she had struggled against the viselike prejudices and incomprehension of her time and place. She had dreamed of a liberation from the shackles of static traditions and stultifying conventions. She had dared to rebuke the men of her society for their double standard of morality and had thus struck a first blow for women's rights.

Which has the greater sin when burned
by the same lawless fever:
She who is amorously deceived,
or he, the sly deceiver?

Or which deserves the sterner blame,
though each will be a sinner:
She who becomes a whore for pay,
Or he who pays to win her?*[19]

---

* Cuál mayor culpa ha tenido
en una pasión errada:
la que cae de rogada,
o el que ruega de caído?

    O cuál es más de culpar
aunque cualquiera mal haga:
la que peca por la paga
o el que paga por pecar?

But more than all else she had struggled for a freedom of thought for all. "There is nothing freer than the human mind," she had proclaimed to a world that could not comprehend these words, or could only hear them as subversive of a God-given truth. Against her the odds were too great and their relentless pressure brought at last a total renunciation of all effort and a complete submission of her intellect. The passionate woman in her capitulated to the devout nun and this surrender left her bereft of life. Physically she survived herself briefly.

To the unhappy nun-poetess during the last four or five years of her existence the world outside must have seemed a projection of her own inner turmoil and affliction. A series of disasters and phenomena were then plaguing the city and its environs, bringing suffering, fear and violence. Heavy rains in 1691 brought successively ruinous floods, crop destruction, famine, and pestilence, while a total eclipse of the sun stirred panic fear. Sullen discontent and mounting tensions erupted into mass riots that nearly toppled Spanish authority in the land. As these sinister events darkened the world without, the storm, so long brewing within Sister Juana Inés, broke.

In 1690 she inadvertently brought to a head the disapproval and hostility of her religious associates slowly gathering over the years. In some way she was induced to write a successful rebuttal of certain views set forth long before in a sermon by a famous Portuguese Jesuit, Father Vieira. Her skill in manipulating the methods of neo-scholasticism evidently pleased the Bishop of Puebla who took it upon himself to publish her paper. At the same time, in the guise of "Sister Philotea," he wrote her a letter chiding her alleged neglect of religious literature and her fondness for profane letters. "You have spent a lot of time studying (secular) philosophers and poets, and now it would seem reasonable to apply yourself to better things and to better books." Clearly, this was a reproof from a superior high in the hierarchy and it could not fail to distress a nun tormented by guilt feelings. Through months of declining health she brooded on a reply to the Bishop's censure. Finally, under date of March 1, 1691, it took form in her famous *Reply* in which, with many autobiographical details and with alternate humility and boldness, she defended herself from the prelate's strictures.

Obscure complications followed this epistolary exchange, chief of which was the withdrawal of her confessor, Father Antonio Núñez de Miranda, who had influenced her decision to enter the convent and had counseled her over the years. Vainly he had urged her to turn from what he considered worldly matters and apply her great talents to things eternal. All her devoted supporters, it seemed to her, were falling away through absence, desertion, or death. And she had never enjoyed the favor of the misogynistic Archbishop Aguiar y Seijas, who had involved her in his frenzied almsgiving. In 1693, as if to remind everyone of her worldliness, a second edition of a volume of her poems, which the vicereine, her friend and patroness, had extracted from her, appeared in Spain, and copies doubtless reached Mexico City soon after. This intended kindness may have hastened her final surrender. On February 8, 1694, using blood from her veins as ink, she indited an abject reaffirmation of her faith and renewed her vows, which she signed: "I, Sister Juana Inés de la Cruz, the worst in the world." She renounced all her possessions, the gifts and trinkets of her admirers, the mathematical and musical instruments that she had so long studied and used, and—the most painful wrench of all—those silent and precious companions of her cell, her beloved books. All were sold and the proceeds given to charity. With this bitter deprivation, she gave herself to excessive acts of penance, self-flagellation, and mortification of the flesh. The coveted death of the body came at last during her tireless ministrations to sisters of her community decimated by a pestilence sweeping the city.

The one kindred spirit that had most nearly understood her, Don Carlos de Sigüenza y Góngora, delivered the funeral oration at her grave. Even his sympathy was denied her in those final, bitter years when his absence on an expedition to Florida, and the preoccupation of public service, private family, and declining health kept him away. The words uttered on the melancholy occasion of her interment are lost but, even more feelingly, they probably echoed sentiments he had expressed in 1680 when both were rising to fame. "There is no pen that can rise to the eminence that hers o'ertops," he had written, and then added, with a sincerity that shines through his pedantic style: "I should like to omit the esteem with which I regard her, the veneration that she has won by her works, in order to make manifest to the world how much, in the encyclopedic nature and universality of her letters, is contained in her genius, so that it may be seen that, in one single person, Mexico enjoys what, in past centuries, the graces have imparted to all the learned women who are the great marvels of history." And he concluded prophetically that the name and fame of "Mother Juana Inés de la Cruz will only end with the world."[20]

❦ XIII

A BAROQUE SCHOLAR

"ON THURSDAY, August 23, 1691, at nine A. M., it was pitch dark, the cocks crowed, and the stars shone, for the sun was in complete eclipse," records a diary. An eerie chill descended with the pall of an unnatural night, bringing superstitious panic upon Mexico City. Amid a pandemonium of shrieking women and children, howling dogs, and braying donkeys the frantic populace fled to the refuge of the Cathedral or the nearest church whose bells clanged a discordant summons for propitiatory prayer. Unnoticed in this frenzied confusion was a solitary, motionless figure who, with strange-looking instruments, surveyed the darkened heavens with a kind of quiet ecstasy. "In the meantime," he wrote soon afterwards, "I stood with my quadrant and telescope viewing the sun, extremely happy and repeatedly thanking God for granting that I might behold what so rarely happens in a given place and about which so few observations are recorded."[1]

These were words of a remarkable scholar of colonial Mexico, Don Carlos de Sigüenza y Góngora, the understanding friend and intellectual companion of Sister Juana Inés de la Cruz. No other incident of his life so well epitomizes the man and his times, for it places in juxtaposition the bold spirit of scientific inquiry which he incarnated and the miasmic atmosphere of ignorance, fear and superstition which he breathed. Intellectual curiosity and independence of mind set him apart from the tradition-bound society of theocratic despotism surrounding him. Yet he remained, nonetheless, an integral part of his milieu and an authentic expression

193

of the Baroque age, for he carefully separated his firm adherence to religious orthodoxy from his speculative attitude toward secular studies. He believed, indeed, that the newer methodology would merely confirm the accepted dogmas of the Faith, and the neo-medievalism of his environment as strongly conditioned him as the Middle Ages did the humanists of the Renaissance. But, even more than the nun-poetess whom he so greatly admired, he symbolized the transition from the extreme orthodoxy of seventeenth century Spanish America to the growing heterodoxy of the eighteenth century.

This Creole scholar liked to boast of his ancestry which, from the times of Isabel and Ferdinand, included men of distinction in arms and letters. His father, Don Carlos de Sigüenza y Benito, a native of Madrid, had been, in his youth, a tutor in the royal household. The Mexican-born son was especially proud that his sire had once instructed the short-lived Prince Baltasar Carlos, upon whom the dynastic hopes of Philip IV and all Spain had vainly rested. Why the father chose to renounce this privileged post and come to the New World is not explained, but the swiftly declining fortunes of the Peninsula doubtless influenced him to join the retinue of the newly appointed viceroy of New Spain, the Marqués of Villena. In 1640, in the same fleet that brought the demented Guillén de Lampart who, presently, would proclaim himself Emperor of Mexico, the elder Sigüenza arrived. If he had hoped to improve his lot materially by emigration to Spain's richest colony, his expectations, like those of so many others, were largely defrauded. It appears that he had to content himself with the modest occupation of a public scribe, though later he became secretary of a viceregal bureau.

Two years after reaching Mexico City he married Doña Dionisia Suárez de Figueroa y Góngora, who hailed from Seville, Spain, and was the daughter of a family of aristocratic pretensions. Her surnames were distinguished in the annals of Spanish literary history, and her eldest son pridefully attached Góngora to his signature to indicate a blood tie with the Cordoban poet. Nine children were the fruit of this union, of whom the Mexican scholar was the second child and the first male. This numerous progeny sorely taxed the meager income of the former instructor of royalty and, in time, his more famous son had to assume responsibility for the family. Whether his brothers and sisters entered the Church, as some did, or acquired mates, all looked to him for economic assistance and counsel.

If Don Carlos, junior, was not so precocious as Sister Juana Inés, his exceptional talents budded early. His experienced father carefully nurtured them, laying a solid foundation for his son's later achievements. For a lad of such promise the Church clearly offered the most distinguished career, and the well-established intellectual distinction of the Jesuits made that Order especially attractive. At the age of fifteen Don Carlos was accepted as a novice and in 1662 he took his first vows. For over seven years he received rigorous training in theology and humanistic studies, but this fruitful period abruptly ended in an episode that seemed to shatter his bright hopes; on the scholar's spirit it left a psychic scar never quite effaced during the remainder of his life.

The proud and impetuous temperament of the young Sigüenza found the Jesuit discipline too severe at times for his independent nature. While his mind enjoyed considerable intellectual latitude, the rigid physical restraints imposed upon his person were galling. A restless impatience with these restrictions finally swept him into a youthful indiscretion which haunted him ever afterward. During his student days at the College of the Holy Spirit in Puebla he yielded to a temptation to elude the vigilance of the prefects and escape from the dormitory to taste the forbidden fruit of nocturnal rambles about the city streets. Discovery of this repeated breach of discipline brought prompt retribution and, on August 15, 1668, he was formally dismissed from the Order. The effect of this disgrace was traumatic, and bitter remorse permanently tinged his nature with a certain melancholy and irascibility. Protesting his repentance, he begged, with tearful earnestness, for reinstatement, but each plea was denied by the implacable Jesuit superiors. In March, 1669, the General of the Order wrote to a Provincial: "Don Carlos de Sigüenza y Góngora also seeks to return to the Company, but I do not grant it to him . . . The cause of the expulsion of this person is so disreputable, as he himself confesses, that he does not deserve this boon . . ." Two years later, a renewed prayer of the contrite youth was refused. "It is not my intention that Don Carlos de Sigüenza shall return to the Company, his case being as you depict it . . ."

Though these rejections seemed definitive the chastened young man never ceased to hope that the Jesuit authorities might relent. Ten years later, in 1677, when his distinction as a professor at the University of Mexico was rising, he again petitioned for reconsideration, trusting, perhaps, that his growing prestige and the passage of time had softened the intransigence of the Jesuit fathers. But another General of the Order, though favorably impressed by Sigüenza's entreaties, was nearly as obdurate. "Don Carlos de Sigüenza y Góngora who, as your Reverence knows, was expelled from the Company, is making a very urgent request for reinstatement on the plea that his salvation would be assured. I am told that he is a person of talent, thirty years old, a professor in the university, and that he can be useful to the Order and that he is most remorseful and repentant. The best that I can do is to absolve him from the impediment of expulsion. I hereby absolve him. Your Reverence will consult with your advisors as to whether it is right to receive him a second time or not. The rest I leave to what comes out of your consultation."[2]

No further progress attended Sigüenza's repeated efforts and the sorrow of his disappointment lay like a shadow on his nature, souring his disposition as the years brought disillusionments and ailments. The zeal displayed throughout his days in intellectual achievement and public service probably arose in some measure from a fervent desire to redeem himself in his own eyes and, conceivably, to bring an awareness to the Jesuit order of the loss sustained in persistently excluding so accomplished a scholar from their ranks. Whether a deathbed reconciliation fulfilled a long-deferred hope still remains uncertain, but the fact that he willed his precious books, manuscripts, maps and instruments to the Company and was interred in a Jesuit chapel points to a final consummation.

Meanwhile, obliged to adapt himself to the painful reality of an apparently irrevocable expulsion, the unhappy Sigüenza was at loose ends in 1668. Clearly, he must make a fresh start in a career outside of his chosen Order. Returning to Mexico City, he resumed theological studies at the University where he began to develop independently the humanistic interests awakened during the years in the Jesuit seminary. Of first importance was mathematics, for which he had a special aptitude. By diligent application, he excelled in this discipline and soon gained recognition as the foremost mathematician in Mexico with a high competence in related sciences.

In 1672 the Chair of Mathematics and Astrology was vacant at the University and Sigüenza decided to compete for it. Two other candidates made a similar decision, one of whom flaunted an academic degree which, he believed, made him solely eligible. Don Carlos, who lacked this accreditation, was unimpressed by his rival's contention, since the University did not grant a bachelor's degree in these particular subjects. Moreover, he tartly reminded the authorities, knowledge of the field was more vital than diplomas; neither of the other aspirants, he declared, had the competence that he possessed who had studied ex-profeso and ". . . was expert in these subjects as is recognized and well known throughout all this Realm because of his two almanacs, one of the preceding year (1671), and the other of the present year which were printed with the approval of Father Julio de San Miguel of the Company of Jesus and of the Holy Office of the Inquisition of New Spain."

These arguments were effective and Don Carlos established his right to enter the competition. The standard practice of selecting faculty members was by a system called *oposiciones*. Each candidate publicly drew texts (*tomar puntos*) from a basic printed authority of the subject matter and, within twenty-four hours, he was obliged to deliver a discourse on the topic thus chosen at random. After the various competitors had each given a rapidly improvised exhibition of erudition, students and degree-holders balloted on the successful contestant, and thus the victor gained the Chair. Elections of this sort were not without fraud, and instances were known when an aspirant had hired a proficient ghost-writer to prepare his lecture for him. Sigüenza professed to suspect a similar intent on the part of the rival who had claimed the sole right to the Chair on the basis of a degree he held, and he demanded that this opponent be placed under the surveillance of two guards during the twenty-four hours allowed for preparing a disquisition. It is indicative, perhaps, of the aggressive and forthright personality of Don Carlos that the University officials acceded to his request. The outcome was a sweeping victory for the blunt young Sigüenza and, on July 20, 1672, he was duly installed as Professor of Mathematics and Astrology.

The University records do not suggest that the Creole scholar was a model occupant of an academic chair, for all too plainly they show frequent petitions for lengthy leaves of absence and for the designation of substitutes to give his lectures. Even more common was his failure to appear in the lecture hall at all, often for weeks at a time. Since university regulations imposed penalties for such derelictions, the fines that Sigüenza paid must have exceeded at times the modest honorarium of one hundred pesos that he received. Immersed in research and, as his reputation grew, in a steady demand for varied public services, routine classroom duties were frequently neglected.

His indifference to these obligations is possibly traceable in part to a lack of regard for the subject of Astrology which, it appears, attracted more students than his beloved mathematics. In an age when that pseudo science retained prestige on both sides of the Atlantic, it is typical of Sigüenza's rugged independence and scientific outlook that he vigorously assailed its false assumptions in his annual almanacs. In a polemic on the nature of comets he gruffly declared: "I also am an Astrologer and I know very well on which foot Astrology limps, and upon what exceedingly weak foundations its structure is reared." And again, in advocating demonstrable evidence in place of the dicta of scholastic authorities—a surprisingly modern attitude in his time—he asked: "What should one infer from them other than that they are all imposed, false, ridiculous, and contemptible, and that astrology is a diabolical invention and, consequently, alien to science, method, principle, and truth? . . ." It is hardly surprising, therefore, that hostile critics saw an inconsistency in this heretical attitude toward a subject that he was paid to teach! But, whatever the causes of his many failures to perform his academic tasks, these omissions sorely troubled his conscience as his last will and testament reveals.

Unlike most of his colleagues on the faculty who were members of religious orders and hence assured of subsistence, Sigüenza had to find means to support himself and assist an assorted family of parents, brothers and sisters, and other dependents. His salary was a nominal fee even when there were no fines to pay and, like many successors in Spanish American universities today, he supplemented his income by varied employments. Over the years these activities brought him titles with various duties and modest emoluments such as: Chief Cosmographer of the Realm; chaplain of the Hospital del Amor de Dios, the most remunerative since it provided living quarters; General Examiner of Gunners; University Accountant; Corrector of the Inquisition, etc., concerning all of which he wryly remarked that they ". . . sound like a lot but are worth very little." He also received remunerated commissions from viceroys for special services of a practical nature and these activities accounted for many absences from his lectures.

When Archbishop Aguiar y Seijas assumed his office in 1682 Sigüenza acquired an influential friend. The comfortable sinecure at the Hospital del Amor de Dios came through this channel which also brought authorization to say mass as a lay priest and thus increase his stipend through fees. As Chief Almoner of the overly generous Archbishop he had onerous obligations which at times he would have been glad to evade. Part of these duties was to distribute one hundred pesos every Monday to the women of the poor whose presence the misogynistic prelate could not abide, and he also gave away large quantities of grain and other cereals at the behest of the philanthropic clergyman.

Sigüenza's gruff spirit and the Archbishop's imperious nature, which contributed to Sister Juan Inés' personal tragedy, occasionally clashed. A contemporary diary reports: "A Controversy: Saturday, October 11th, 1692, Don Carlos de Sigüenza, lay priest, having some differences with the Archbishop, Don Carlos said to the latter that his Illustrious Highness should remember with whom he was talking, whereupon the Archbishop raised the crutch he was using and broke Sigüenza's glasses, bathing his face in blood." Despite these vagaries of temperament the two strong-willed individuals remained close and co-operative friends. Indeed, the veneration of Don Carlos for his assailant increased until, in his mind, the prelate almost acquired the halo of a saint. A clause of the scholar's will reads: "I have in my possession the hat worn by the Most Illustrious and Venerable Don Francisco de Aguiar y Seijas, formerly Archbishop of Mexico. When a number of sick people touched it they recovered from their ailments. Desiring that this practice continue with all veneration, I request that the hat be turned over to Doctor Juan de la Pedrosa and kept in perpetuity in the oratory of Our Father St. Philip Neri."[3] Thus, this Baroque scholar, so modern and clearheaded in many intellectual pursuits, remained the docile child of his age in other respects.

Sigüenza never allowed himself to forget his kinship to the great Luis de Góngora, patron saint of Spanish versifiers in the seventeenth century, and even as a student in the Jesuit seminary he sought to prove worthy of this literary connection. All too plainly his poetic efforts betray a genealogical affiliation, though esthetic degeneracy had set in with this particular descendant. His *Indian Spring,* a fervent hymn to the Virgin of Guadalupe in seventy-nine octaves, faithfully reflects the abuses and excesses of a tired Gongorism. Written while the author was still in his teens and published in 1662, with reprintings in 1668 and 1683, it is more an evidence of a certain precocity than of hereditary genius. His *Evangelical Oriental Planet,* a panegyric of St. Francis Xavier, friend and companion of the founder of the Jesuit order, was printed after Sigüenza's death. This lyric effort was probably composed about the time of his expulsion from the seminary, possibly with the hope of restoring himself to the good graces of the superiors. Never completely satisfied that its artistic merit equaled its lofty subject, he had withheld it from publication. These literary aspirations, which he was reluctant to abandon, were doubtless a topic of many chats with the far more musically gifted Sister Juana Inés in the locutory of her convent. Wisely, he decided to concentrate his energies on scholarly pursuits.

Like the humanists of the Renaissance, no field of investigation was entirely exempt from the workings of his curious mind, but his achievements were most notable in related areas of archaeology and history on one hand, and in mathematics and applied sciences on the other. His studies of the pre-Hispanic civilizations of Mexico which, in time, brought him undisputed authority, he began the year of his dismissal from the Jesuit school. As he mastered the native languages he assembled books, codices, maps, and manuscripts relating to the ancient culture of the aborigines. In the 1670's he acquired a large collection of the papers, notes, and translations which had belonged to Fernando de Alva Ixtlilxochitl, who flourished, it will be recalled, in the days of Archbishop-Viceroy García Guerra. A son of the Indian chronicler, Juan de Alva Cortés, held the family estate in San Juan Teotihuacán, not far from Mexico City, which acquisitive officials sought to wrest from him.

Sigüenza, it appears, had successfully intervened to protect De Alva Cortés from this rapacity of the white masters. In gratitude the Indian owner gave the Creole savant a small plantation and, what was even more appreciated, the precious collection of his father's papers. With these documents and other accessions Sigüenza came to possess the richest library of these materials anywhere, much of which he had intended to will to the Vatican in Rome and to the Escorial in Spain. These data, combined with his own archaeological explorations, particularly in the Toltec pyramids at Teotihuacán, were the substance of monographs of probable importance, most of which unhappily survive in name only. Their existence is chiefly known through occasional references and brief descriptions of contemporaries. His difficulties in getting his findings into print were the perennial ones of scholars lacking private means or philanthropic subsidies to defray the costs of publication. With literacy so low and secular investigations so much less esteemed than theological disquisitions, his studies had little hope of finding their way into the more permanent form of type.

Though Sigüenza tried to give a religious significance to his research as, for example, his ingenuous effort to identify the Aztec Quetzalcoatl with the Apostle St. Thomas in his *Phoenix of the West,* the Church, the most likely Maecenas of such erudite endeavors, was apparently unimpressed by this curious thesis. Other monographs, *The History of the Chichimeca Indians, Mexican Cyclography, Geneaology of the Mexican Monarchs, Calendar of the Months and Feast Days of the Mexicans,* and other similar works, likewise failed to win financial support and presently vanished. In the light of sources used and now lost, these studies probably possessed permanent value and their disappearance is a regrettable loss. Toward the end of his life the author's despondency increased regarding the fate of his findings and this mood moved him to put them generously at the disposition of contemporaries more fortunate in being able to publish their own books. Fathers Florencia and Vetancourt have left comprehensive accounts of phases of Mexican history in which they acknowledge indebtedness to Don Carlos, and the Italian traveler, Gemelli Careri, in his *Giro del Mondo,* devoted an extensive chapter to Aztec hieroglyphics, religion, and culture based on materials, including drawings, supplied by the Mexican Creole. For the most part Sigüenza's only recourse was to slip bits of information on Nahuatl lore into the pages of books of unrelated and ephemeral character which, from time to time, he was commissioned to write.

His historical writings on the period since the Spanish Conquest had a similar fate and most are known by title only. Without doubt, valuable data were embedded in such narratives as *The History of the Mexico City Cathedral; History of the University of Mexico*, concerning which he wrote in his will: "I fondly request the Royal University to accept the affection with which I began to write about its history and greatness but which was called off by the *claustro* for reasons unknown to me"; the *Historical Tribunal*, possibly a history of Mexico; *Theater of the Grandeur of Mexico City; History of the Province of Carolina* (Texas); and various others.

Better fortune attended his contemporary chronicles, written in his later years, which were a kind of rudimentary journalism. The Count of Galve, viceroy from 1688 to 1696, leaned heavily during these critical years upon the counsels of the Creole scholar who became a sort of court chronicler. The Madrid government's support was pitifully weak in the last, inglorious days of the Hapsburg dynasty while both the heart and the frontiers of New Spain presented problems of increasing gravity to the viceregal administration in a series of episodes that Sigüenza recorded. These accounts are often more readable than his learned treatises, though his prose suffered from the involved syntax and pompous rhetoric currently fashionable. He liked to think, however, that his style was simple and natural. In the prologue of the *Occidental Paradise*, the story of a Mexico City convent that he was commissioned to write, he declared: "Regarding the style I employ in this book, it is what I always use, whether I am conversing, writing, or preaching because, perhaps, I could not do otherwise even if I tried . . ." Loftily he condemns gongoristic abuses so universal in his time, seemingly unconscious of his own patent derelictions. Yet he sometimes did approach his self-proclaimed lucidity, and occasionally his accounts of current happenings offer instances of vivid reporting. *The Trophy of Spanish Justice* (1691) relates the adventures of a successful military expedition against the French on Santo Domingo; *An Account of What Happened to the Windward Fleet* (1691) tells of the maritime phase of this undertaking; and the *Flying*

Mercury (1693) recounts the bloodless reconquest of New Mexico. An interesting piece of reportage on the disastrous corn riot of the Indians in Mexico City on June 8, 1692, is contained in a letter intended for publication but unprinted until 1932.[4]

The most charming of these journalistic narratives is a curious account of the misadventures of a Puerto Rican youth during a journey around the world entitled *The Misfortunes of Alonso Ramirez*. Told in the first person, it purports to relate the story of his capture by English pirates who later set him adrift in a small boat which was finally wrecked on the Yucatan coast where he had a Robinson Crusoe-like adventure. Though Sigüenza slows the pace of his recital with pedantic details, he is writing in the picaresque tradition of Spanish literature and with more than his accustomed verve. Indeed, some literary historians like to classify this curious *relación* as a precursor of the Mexican novel.[5]

The more authentic claim of this Baroque scholar to distinction lies in his scientific writings which provide a better index of his intellectual caliber. Here again, however, most of his significant contributions never achieved the semi-permanence of print and hence are known only by hearsay, but the slight number surviving insure him a high place in the annals of the intellectual history of Old Mexico and, indeed, of colonial Spanish America.

Mathematics received his most constant devotion and represented his greatest competence. If his eminence in this discipline derives from its applied rather than theoretical aspects, it is owing probably to the fact that he shared Descartes' belief in the importance of mathematics as a method of search for knowledge and as a tool for the conquest of truth. In this faith he assembled the best collection of treatises and instruments then to be found in the New World, which he ultimately willed to the Jesuits "in gratitude to, and as an adequate compensation for, the good training and good instruction that I received from the reverend fathers during the few years that I lived with them . . ." Though he applied this skill to engineering projects, civilian and military, his most enthusiastic application was to astronomy.

As early as 1670 he observed the phenomena of the heavens, keeping precise records which he was ever eager to exchange with others. He strove continually to make these data as exact as possible, importing the latest instruments available. In his observations of the total eclipse of the sun in 1691 he used a telescope "of four lens which, up to now, is the best that has reached this city. Father Marco Antonio Capus sold it to me for eighty pesos." Thus it is likely that, in solid learning, technical literature, and efficient instruments, he was the best equipped scientist of his time in the Spanish overseas dominions. Through his extensive correspondence with leading men of science, his reputation spread to Europe and Asia. As early as 1680 his distinction had won him appointment as the Royal Cosmographer of the Realm, and it is stated that Louis XIV, with offers of pensions and special honors, sought to lure the Mexican savant to his Court.

A few of the missing works which were the fruit of his diligence are: *A Treatise on the Eclipses of the Sun*, known by title only; *A Treatise on the Sphere*, described merely as consisting of two hundred folio pages; and a polemical pamphlet inspired by the Comet of 1680 and bearing the Baroque caption: *Mathematical Bellerophon Against the Astrological Chimera of Don Martin de la Torre*, etc. It is briefly described as displaying all the subtleties of trigonometry "in the investigations of the movements of comets, either by means of a rectilinear trajection in the hypotheses of Copernicus, or by the conical spheres of the Cartesian vortices." But already by 1690 this paper had disappeared.

Fortunately, a like fate did not overtake an impressive little volume called *Astronomical and Philosophical Libra*, thanks to the generosity of an admiring friend who subsidized a small edition, of which a few copies survive. It is a polemical treatise on the nature of comets that provides the most substantial evidence of the competence and enlightenment of its author. A spirit of modernity pervades its pages which echo the subversive ideas of Gassendi, Descartes, Galileo, Kepler, Copernicus, and other thinkers still suspect in the late seventeenth century. Curiously blending scientific objectivity and emotional subjectivity, it refracts the tensions of the Baroque age as it reveals glimpses of the proud, sensitive, and touchy personality of the Creole scholar.

The "Great Comet of 1680," which so distressed the ignorant and exercised the best minds on both sides of the Atlantic, was first seen in Mexico City on November 15. Everywhere, and particularly there, this strange apparition stirred dread and foreboding of dire calamities and grave misfortunes to come. For Sigüenza it was an exciting event and an auspicious occasion. As the newly appointed Royal Cosmographer of the Realm, he felt it his duty to allay the groundless fears and widespread uneasiness that it caused generally in Mexican society. He therefore brought forth on January 13, 1681, a pamphlet with the resounding title *Philosophical Manifest Against Comets Stripped of their Dominion Over the Timid*. He was well aware that its subject matter was controversial, but he was hardly prepared for the tempest loosed by his well-meant effort to restore public confidence.[6]

In his treatise Don Carlos sharply disagreed with the ominous import that astrologers attributed to these astral manifestations. While freely acknowledging his ignorance of the true significance of these phenomena, he was sure that they should be venerated as the work of a just God. This mild assertion seemed almost subversive in the superstitious atmosphere of New Spain, and it promptly provoked an astringent reply from a Flemish gentleman living in Yucatan, named Martin de la Torre, in a pamphlet entitled: *Christian Manifest in Favor of Comets Maintained in Their Natural Significance*. Basing himself on astrological data, the author asserted that comets were, in fact, warnings from God Himself of coming calamitous events. Sigüenza, whose combative disposition reacted immediately to opposition, quickly retorted with his well-conceived if pompously styled *Mathematical Bellerophon*, previously mentioned, in which he emphasized the superiority of scientific analysis over astrological lore.

Nearer at hand exploded a more startling response to the original pamphlet. It came from the pen of one of his own colleagues in the University of Mexico, a professor of surgery. Bearing the designation *A Cometological Discourse and Account of the New Comet*, etc., it set forth the proposition that this astral apparition was composed of the exhalations of dead bodies and of human perspiration! Contemptuously Don Carlos declared that he would not deign to reply to such arrant nonsense. Still others entered the fray with their theories and one, whose eminence and prestige were too great to ignore, brought forth a stout rebuttal from Sigüenza in the previously cited *Astronomical and Philosophical Libra*.[7]

The person inspiring this supreme effort was a Jesuit from the Austrian Tyrol who happened to arrive from Europe at the height of the polemic en route to the mission frontier of Old Mexico.

Father Eusebio Francisco Kino, as he is known to history, was about the same age as Sigüenza, well educated in various European universities, and highly proficient in mathematics. Of imposing presence, gifted in languages, and widely reputed for his learning, he had declined a proffered professorship at the University of Ingolstadt in order to devote his life to bringing the light of the Gospel to the heathen in a remote and inhospitable region of the globe. The sacrifice of so many talents to so noble a cause was the supreme idealism of the age, and the most distinguished members of the viceregal society eagerly sought out the newcomer, including Don Carlos, who had an additional motive in their common love for mathematics. Moreover, since Father Kino had taken observations of the Comet of 1680 before embarking at Cádiz, an exchange of data would be illuminating. At the home of the Mexican Creole the two savants indulged in long discussions of their mutual interests.[8]

To the sensitive Don Carlos Father Kino seemed a little supercilious and aloof and there was a sort of tacit air of superiority about him; he did not, for instance, display a proper esteem for the Creole's observations. This indifference probably arose, Sigüenza later commented sourly, because the Mexican scholar had not studied at the University of Ingolstadt and the European could not imagine, therefore, that mathematicians might grow "amidst the reeds and cat-tails on the margins of a Mexican pond!" The highly intelligent Creole scholar was peculiarly prone to the feeling of inferiority which his class experienced in the presence of those born in Europe, for he believed that his own gifts and the lofty lineage that he claimed entitled him to equal consideration. Especially galling was the condescending, sometimes disdainful, attitude that Peninsulars assumed toward the American-born, and foreigners from the Continent did not seem to think their learning entitled to any respect at all. "In some parts of Europe," Sigüenza observed caustically, "especially in the north through being more remote, they think that not only the Indian inhabitants of the New World, but those of us who, by chance, were born here of Spanish parentage, either walk on two legs by divine dispensation or that, even using English microscopes, they can hardly discover anything rational in us!" In the case of Father Kino the sensitivity of Don Carlos was possibly exacerbated by the fact that his guest was a member in high standing of the religious Order from which he himself had been summarily ejected and to which he was repeatedly denied reinstatement.

Father Kino's stay in Mexico City, where he was preparing himself for the mission field, had not been long when rumors reached the Creole professor that this visitor was about to publish a work on the recent comet refuting Sigüenza's contentions. Friends of the Mexican scholar repeatedly warned him that the eminent Jesuit, so recently in contact with German scientists, would be a formidable antagonist in the debate. Father Kino himself gave no hint of these intentions and Don Carlos, confident of the soundness of his stand, allegedly awaited developments with composure. At last one evening, as the missionary was about to depart for Sinaloa to begin his work, he paid the Mexican ex-Jesuit a farewell call in his lodgings. In the course of the conversation the visitor casually handed his host a copy of a treatise *Astronomical Exposition,* just off the press. His manner was patronizing, or so thought the hypersensitive Creole scientist, as he suggested that the latter might peruse with profit this book that he had written, for it might give the worthy Mexican-Spaniard something to think about. Don Carlos interpreted these words as a challenge to an intellectual duel and the *Astronomical and Philosophical Libra* was his answer!

The fact that Father Kino did not anywhere mention Sigüenza by name did not lessen the conviction of the thin-skinned Creole that the statements were aimed at him. When he read, for example, that comets were really dire omens and harbingers of evil and that the opposite opinion was contrary to what all mortals were aware, the high, the low, the noble and plebian, the learned and unlearned, Don Carlos was certain to whom this comment alluded. "No one knows better where the shoe pinches than he who wears it and, since I assert that I am the object of his invective, everyone may believe that, without question, it was I." Since the rational view of these natural phenomena was held by no one, according to Father Kino, the implication was that Sigüenza was nothing! And when the Jesuit missionary concluded that the ominous portent of comets was evident to all ". . . unless there be some *trabajosos juicios* (dull wits) who cannot perceive it," the Mexican professor exploded: "Those who understand the Castilian language well know that, in telling someone that he is a 'trabajoso juicio,' it is the same as calling him crazy. Since this is the case, as it undoubtedly is, long life to the Reverend Father for the exceedingly rare praise with which he honors me!"

In this fashion the Mexican scholar vents his choler in the opening chapter, after which he settles down to a methodical discussion of the problem, setting forth a geometrical analysis of the movements of comets, their paralaxes, refractions, etc., accompanied by carefully executed diagrams. The offended Creole scientist struggles to keep his exposition on the dispassionate plane of reason but, despite himself, throughout the text mica-like glints of sarcasm and resentment shine amid the solid substance of his discourse, and he is unable to resist here and there a sardonic thrust at his opponent.

No attempt will be made to follow this very technical discussion. It is enough, perhaps, to point out its underlying significance in the intellectual history of colonial Mexico. The great struggle between the authoritarianism of neo-scholasticism and the empiricism of experimentalism, hardly initiated in the days of Fray García Guerra, but which so troubled the brilliant mind of Sister Juana Inés, had now reached a break in the work of her friend and intellectual companion. Less shackled by sex and religious vows than the poetess, Don Carlos had succeeded in divorcing secular concerns from the tradition of authority, thus enabling his thoughts to soar unhampered in such matters. Though a lay priest, he had no solemn pledge of submission to monastic superiors to respect, and he was freer to separate his rationalism in natural philosophy from the immutable dogma of theology than the convent-bound nun. This fact suggests a curious paradox in the lives of these two superior individuals; if Sister Juana Inés' secret sorrow was the impossibility of escaping into a world of wider horizons, Sigüenza's private grief was the impossibility of returning to the strict rule of a religious community.

What emerges perhaps most clearly from a reading of the *Astronomical and Philosophical Libra* is the heterodoxy of its author in the pursuit of truth in nature. His radical disposition is apparent in a bluntly expressed disrespect for authority in learning, in his belief in methodical doubt, in his conviction of the necessity of demonstration, and in his reliance on mathematics as a means of measuring natural phenomena. The direct influence of Descartes is obvious in the occasional references to that philosopher by name and the citations of his works. The Mexican thinker is disposed to strip away the long-standing prejudices still inhibiting his contemporaries in Europe as well as in Old Mexico. For the moment timeworn superstitions and shallow delusions assume material form in the person of the ungrateful and haughty Father Kino, the very embodiment of the spiritual ideal of his culture and the image of his own lost hope. With unconcealed venom the Creole ex-Jesuit assails the dogmatic utterances of his opponent on the significance of comets and he decisively disposes of the validity of authority in such matters. ". . . I hereby point out that neither his Reverence, nor any other mathematician, even if he is Ptolemy himself, can set up dogmas in these sciences, because authority has no place in them at all, but only proof and demonstration. . . ." Here, plainly, is the modern spirit lighting up the darkness of neomedieval thought. The problems and doubts that the spectacle of nature presents to mankind, he went on, could never be resolved by merely searching through old texts to find out what the ancient authorities of classical learning had said on the subject. "What would I say to satisfy one who affirmed," he exclaimed, "that, in a subject open to discussion, it is necessary to accept what others say when clearly no one, with a mind and reasoning power, is ever guided by authorities if these authorities lack congruity . . ." "And would it be wise," he asks, promptly adding that it would be unwise, "to assert in these times that the heavens are solid and unchangeable just because most ancient authors state that they are? That the moon is eclipsed by the shadow of the earth and that all comets are semilunary merely because these authorities so advise? Would it be creditable to the intelligence to accept the teachings of others without looking into the premises on which their ideas are based? . . ." This kind of skepticism was rare in the Baroque world of seventeenth century Mexico, and it was a little subversive in a culture in which Theology, as the "Queen of Sciences," still reigned supreme.

This unequivocal flouting of the sacrosanct principle of authority, which most contemporaries did not dare to challenge, foreshadowed an intellectual scuffle destined to enliven the academic halls of Old Mexico and of Spanish America nearly two generations later, namely, the dethronement of Aristotle as the high priest of knowledge. As early as 1681 Sigüenza had proclaimed his heresy. ". . . even Aristotle, the avowed Prince of Philosophers who, for so many centuries, has been accepted with veneration and respect, does not deserve credence . . . when his judgments are opposed to truth and reason. . . ." Here, indeed, was a sharp break with the past and an utterance that the Jesuits, by whom he so longed to be accepted, would hardly have condoned. Indeed, soon after the death of Don Carlos the members of that intellectually advanced Order were reminded that they must teach Aristotelian philosophy only, and that they must eschew the "erroneous propositions of Cartesian thought."[9]

Such, then, was the bold thinking which the sensitive and highly intelligent Mexican savant revealed in his carefully reasoned rebuttal of Father Kino's assertions and insinuations. Every page of the *Astronomical and Philosophical Libra* discloses a logical and erudite, if somewhat atrabilious, mind well versed in the ideas of thinkers such as Conrad Confalonier, Athanasius Kircher, Pico della Mirandola, Juan Caramuel, Kepler, Gassendi, Oldenburg, Descartes, and many others cited in the text and in the footnotes. It is plain that this isolated and lonely worker was more than dimly aware of the currents of scientific thought flowing more strongly in contemporary Europe and that he was in the ranks of those exalted spirits who strove to slip the bandage of ignorance and superstition from the darkened eyes of his fellowmen. In the closing pages of this small but impressive treatise its author effectively demolishes the astrological misapprehensions of Martin de la Torre and records his own observations of the controversial comet from January 3 to January 20, 1681.

Ten years elapsed before this remarkable little volume found its way into print, though the necessary license was obtained at once. This delay doubtless stemmed from the inability of the impecunious author to defray the cost of publication of so technical a work for so limited a readership, and it owed its final appearance to the generosity of an admiring friend. Sigüenza was immensely proud of this effort and upon especially distinguished visitors passing through Mexico City he was wont to bestow a copy. When the famed Italian traveler, Gemelli Careri, dropped into the Creole scholar's quarters at the Hospital del Amor de Dios, he departed with the *Astronomical and Philosophical Libra* along with much other data that the learned professor supplied for the forthcoming book about his tour of the world. Whether Father Kino ever took any particular notice of the treatise which his own work had called forth does not appear. Explorations and mission-building in the northwestern provinces of Old Mexico absorbed his energies and interests and no indications are available that he renewed acquaintance with the oversensitive Creole on the one or two widely spaced visits that he subsequently made to the viceregal capital.

The closing years of Sigüenza's life coincided with those of the seventeenth century and of the Hapsburg dynasty on the Spanish throne, and the cancerous ills of the Empire had their counterparts in the body of the Mexican humanist. Marked physical decline was already visible in 1694, and it accelerated in the years following. He suffered intensely from stones in the kidney and ". . . . one in the bladder the size of a large pigeon's egg according to the statement of the surgeons who have felt it." Walking, even a short distance, was difficult and painful. As the specter of death loomed, beloved relatives and associates succumbed to it, accentuating the grief and despondency of the dying scholar. The year 1695 deprived him of a favorite brother, and about the same time he sustained an equally poignant loss in the final release of the tormented mind and spirit of Sister Juana Inés. As he delivered a funeral oration at her grave, an acute realization of his own desolate aloneness fell upon him. In succession his aged father, ex-tutor of the long-dead Prince Baltasar Carlos, the viceroy, Count of Galve, and the Archbishop Aguiar y Seijas, his most influential patrons, passed away. The prelate's decease probably ended Don Carlos' remunerative employment as Chief Almoner and, along with his health, his economic circumstances deteriorated, though the demands of numerous relatives remained unceasing. Abruptly the office of University Accountant with its perquisites was taken from him, and his status of professor emeritus had come only after vexatious delays owing to his less than faithful performance of its duties. In this near penury he accepted the post of Corrector for the Inquisition and to the tedious scrutiny of suspected books he devoted his waning vigor—a task singularly uncongenial to his enlightened spirit and a misapplication of his talents.

His last year was clouded by an episode that hastened his end, for it touched a most sensitive part—his integrity as a scientist.

Back in 1693, at the urgent request of the Count of Galve, he had made his longest journey and undertaken his most momentous mission. French intrusions in the Gulf of Mexico, which threatened the coast of Texas, Louisiana, and Florida, had frightened Spanish authorities into a belated effort to occupy effectively that part of the Gulf region. Among other measures they sent an expedition to reconnoiter and map the promising bay of Pensacola. Leaving his quiet, comfortable study he embarked on his only sea voyage and explored and charted that Florida inlet.[10] A recommendation for immediate occupation by the Spaniards only met procrastination owing to the grave uncertainties of an expiring dynasty and the feeble resources of the empire until French aggression brought tardy action. In 1698 Andrés de Arriola, an officer famed for his voyage to and from the Philippine Islands in record time, reluctantly accepted a commission to plant a settlement at Pensacola Bay. When a French vessel made its appearance at its mouth Arriola scuttled back to Vera Cruz and the Mexican capital and brought a highly critical report of the locality, challenging the accuracy of Sigüenza's earlier survey.

The ailing scholar reacted sharply to these aspersions with more than his customary acerbity, promptly accusing the returned officer of deserting his post and falsifying the findings of 1693. The offended Arriola then demanded that the viceroy—no longer Sigüenza's loyal friend, Count of Galve—require the scholar to go back to Pensacola with him and prove his contentions by a new survey. The fact that Don Carlos was obviously too ill to travel did not deter Arriola from insisting, and Viceroy Moctezuma felt constrained to oblige Sigüenza to comply or give a satisfactory explanation.

Mustering his failing strength the Creole professor drew up a masterful reply, bringing into play the dialectical skill and biting sarcasm that had left their marks on opponents in other polemics. With analytical precision he broke Arriola's statement into its component parts which, one by one, he battered with merciless cogency and unassailable logic. "I am not one who has to unsay what he has once said," he proudly declared. If the viceroy insisted on a journey to Pensacola, he was ready to comply despite his precarious health and crippled state, but he would impose his own conditions. If his body was frail, his spirit was as stout and pugnacious as ever. So confident was he of the correctness of his earlier report that he would wager his dearest possession, his library, on the favorable outcome of a new survey. This collection "is the best of its kind in the realm" and, "together with his mathematical instruments, telescopes, pendulum clocks and valuable paintings, the total is appraised at more than three thousand pesos," and this he would bet "against an equivalent sum posted by Arriola . . ." on the rightness of his earlier findings. But, he stipulated, the viceroy must send them on separate ships to the Florida coast, otherwise there would be no lack of occasions, he stated grimly, "either for him to throw me into the sea or for me to throw him."[11]

This second voyage by Sigüenza never occurred, partly because his health rendered it impracticable, but more probably, because he had effectively refuted his opponent's allegations. The incident did not fail, however, to deepen his despondency, and it had called forth his last revealing communication. In a measure it was the counterpart of Sister Juana Inés' remarkable *Reply,* for both documents symbolize a crisis in the lives of the writers. Both are answers to criticism of their activities; both contain intimate personal data; both are a defense against imputations on the use of their intellects; both are carefully meditated and subjective records; and both herald the disintegration and decease of their authors. While Sister Juana Inés' *Reply* is clearly more moving and significant, the exceptional character and unique personality of both ill-starred individuals are poignantly etched in the phrases of their lengthy depositions. For the nun the pace of death was slower; for the scholar it was speedier. A little more than a year after signing his rejoinder his troubled spirit and tormented body found rest. August 22, 1700 brought liberation.

In character and attainments this Baroque scholar resembled the humanists of the Renaissance whose curious, encyclopedic minds laid the foundations of modern science and learning. Like them he confronted the task of keeping in balance the increasing independence of the human spirit and the unquestioned authority of the Church. His rugged mind, methodical doubt, and sturdy pragmatism in secular matters were exceptional in the Baroque time and place in which he lived. In religious dogma and pious faith he remained ever submissive and devout, accepting implicitly ecclesiastical authority and the validity of the tenets of orthodox Catholicism. This dichotomy of his mental life is nowhere more apparent than in his last will and testament prepared in the final weeks of his existence. There, in curious juxtaposition, is the testimony of his unquestioning and naive acceptance of miracles and of things supernatural, and there also he proclaims his unswerving devotion to the luminous spirit of scientific investigation and to the enlightened service of mankind. One testamentary clause attests to the thoroughly modern attitude that infused his being and epitomizes a lifelong dedication.

"Inasmuch as the physicians and surgeons attending me in my long and painful illness relating to the urine have been unable to determine whether it is due to gallstones or the bladder and, since there is apparently no known remedy for the exceedingly severe pain and torment that I am enduring, it is my desire that whoever may have a similar disease may regain health or, at least, obtain some relief through learning the cause of this ailment. Without this knowledge or experience no relief can be found, nor any medicine applied which will reach it. Therefore, since my body must return to the clay from which it came, I request, in the name of God, that, so soon as life has departed from me, my body shall be opened by any physicians or surgeons desiring to do so, and that the right kidney, the bladder, the small end of which is to deprive me of life, and the arrangement of the organisms shall all be examined carefully. I request that whatever deductions are made shall be revealed to other physicians and surgeons so that they may have data to guide them in administering to other sufferers. I ask in God's name that this be done for the common good, and I command my heir not to interfere, for it matters little that this be done to a body which, within a few days, must be corruption and decay."

An executor of the will reported: "His command was carried out, and, after opening him, they found a stone the size of a peach-stone in the right kidney where he had said that he felt pain."[12] Thus, in an age when among his class human remains were deemed sacred and dissection was still counted a desecration, this consecrated savant of seventeenth century Mexico demonstrated, in his last act, a desire to seek truth and to serve mankind even beyond the boundary of life. His spirit clearly foreshadowed the end of the Age of the Baroque and the beginning of the Age of Reason in Hispanic America.

❧ XIV

A SUMMING UP

IN THE seamless fabric of time the year 1700 seems to mark a visible conjunction of two centenary epochs of changing events and shifting patterns in the history of the western world. The civil, religious, and dynastic wars of the Baroque age that had so long wracked Europe were evolving into struggles of colonial and commercial rivals. The emerging national states of the early seventeenth century had acquired, or had occupied more effectively, overseas possessions which transformed these political entities into competing empires. The chief contenders were Portugal, Spain, Holland, France, and England, but by 1700 the period of active growth of the first three was past, leaving the last two to lock horns in the eighteenth century like titans in a contest for supremacy on the high seas, in North America, and in India, as well as in continental Europe. And thus the era of "world wars" was ushered in, transferring the parochial strife of nationalistic peoples from a regional stage on the western fringe of the Eurasian land-mass to a global theater.

An inadvertent catalytic agent of this development was Spain, owing to the inglorious end in 1700 of nearly two centuries of Hapsburg rule through the death of the childless Charles II. The magnitude of the Spanish empire still gave the Peninsula an impressive semblance of might and, in the age of absolute monarchs who reckoned territories as personal possessions, the extinction of a royal line exposed a rich estate to the cupidity of claimants of all shades of legitimacy. Such pretensions, however, were increasingly encumbered by grave considerations of a "balance of power," and, whoever the successful contestant might be, the award of this grand prize would inevitably create an inequilibrium in the international affairs of Europe. When the dying Charles II changed his will in favor of Philip of Anjou, grandson of Louis XIV, the "Grand Monarch," the preponderance of power clearly lay in Bourbon hands. A coalition led by Great Britain challenged this French hegemony in the War of Spanish Succession, and from 1702 to 1713 military campaigns on a larger scale than ever before devastated the Continent, including Spain, and this conflagration spread to North America in the so-called Queen Anne's War. With the Bourbon heir finally confirmed on the Spanish throne as Philip V, Spain had entered a new era.

Old Mexico could not remain untouched by these events and a few inhabitants were dimly conscious that the year 1700 signified a crossing into an epoch of disruptive consequences. Up to then the belief persisted that New Spain was far removed from the ideological conflicts and bloody strife rending Europe, which had scarcely known seven years of peace in an entire century. It almost seemed as if Mexico was reserved by God for a more perfect realization of His plan which was a static, peaceful order, and for this fulfillment the mother country had, in part at least, bled itself white despite liberal transfusions from the silver veins of the New World. Sheltered and remote the broad realm of Old Mexico hardly comprehended the inevitability of change and the futility of Spain's ideal.

But to many officials entrusted with the direction of its affairs the advancing decades had brought a slow awareness of the delusion engendered by a fancied isolation. Even before Fray García Guerra arrived in 1608, jealous rivals of Spain had encroached upon its imperial preserve in America. Bold adventurers of England, France, and Holland had seized neglected islands of the Caribbean, and even portions of the mainland. During the rule of the Archbishop-Viceroy Dutch activities in this island-strewn sea seriously threatened the approaches to the treasure-yielding realm. In the course of the century this nibbling at the edges of empire grew more aggressive and seriously disturbed Spanish authorities. The important islands of Barbados, the Bahamas, and Jamaica fell like plums into the English lap, and the strategic entrepôt at the isthmus of Panama suffered brutal destruction by the piratical Morgan. Hardly less ominous were the French gains in the West Indies: Martinique, Guadeloupe, Guiana, and the western end of Santo Domingo, the island on which the Spaniards had planted their first settlements and which would become the richest overseas possession of France in the eighteenth century.

Menacing as these losses were to viceregal Mexico, the silver mines of its northern regions still seemed immune to attack, and the re-enforced convoys of treasure fleets generally managed to elude the enemies lodged in the islands. But the closing decades of the century brought alarming indications that remoteness no longer guaranteed the security of this mineral wealth. Far to the north on the mainland the English settlements in Virginia and New England were expanding until, in 1688, their populations numbered three hundred thousand. Bold representatives were pushing southward from the Carolinas and presently they would carve out a region from the vacant, vaguely delimited spaces of Spanish Florida and name it Georgia. So imperfect was the geographical knowledge of the Spaniards concerning this general area that the fancied proximity to the northern mines of these intrusions caused deep anxiety.

But far more corroding was the fear inspired by French activities. The settlers of New France in the "northern mystery," though less numerous than the English, were more widely dispersed in regions along the St. Lawrence river, Lake Superior, and the Ohio river. During Colbert's rule they had increased three hundred per cent in a score of years. In 1682 Sieur de la Salle had paddled down the Mississippi and claimed its great basin for France, naming it Louisiana in honor of the king. Two years later he led an ill-fated expedition of four vessels and three hundred colonists to the Gulf of Mexico to plant a settlement at the mouth of the great river as a base of operations against the northern frontier of New Spain. Miscalculations landed him on the bleak coast of Texas where disaster ended his enterprise. But the news of this undertaking startled Spanish officialdom from a troubled somnolence, and frantically they dispatched expedition after expedition to seek out the rumored colony and pre-empt any desirable ports on the neglected northern Gulf coast. As a scientific observer and map-maker, Sigüenza y Góngora, it will be remembered, had shared in these efforts, visiting Pensacola and Mobile bays, and entering the mouth of the Mississippi.

The Treaty of Ryswick in 1697 brought a truce to the intermittent warfare of Spain and France which merely freed the latter country for more aggressive acts against Spanish possessions in America. Soon Iberville was on his way to occupy Louisiana and link it with New France, thus driving a formidable wedge between Spanish Florida and the silver region of Mexico. The intent of France was unmistakable. "La grande affaire est la decouverte des mines," ran the orders of the French leader,[1] and Mexican authorities shuddered at the implications of this intrusion. The splendid isolation, which had so long facilitated a static order and Baroque brilliance in New Spain, was ending.

If relatively few within Mexico were fully aware of these external developments, many more were acutely conscious of internal events which filled them with a strange, *fin de siècle* uneasiness as if all things were coming to a close. In 1691 heavy rains brought flash-floods that hurled masses of water through parched ravines, destroying homes, barns, mills, and cattle of Spaniards and Indians alike. Even churches, shrines, and convents were swept away as the torrents charged through villages and hamlets. The downpour caused the canals of the capital to overflow and Lake Texcoco, its great expanse nearly dry normally, was soon capable of floating ships of heavy burden, while the causeways leading across it to the city became impassable; packtrains could not bring supplies to relieve the starving inhabitants. Adobe houses disintegrated in the excessive moisture and formed mounds of viscous mud which slithered into the watery streets and squares, leaving wretched occupants without shelter, food or fire. In the surrounding country the cloudbursts transformed fields into a water-logged morass, which ruined crops completely. When at last the rains diminished, a blight, spreading with the rapidity of a conflagration, attacked the wheat and corn in outlying districts and, for long months, famine and deprivation stalked the land.

Dread phenomena of Nature, such as had attended Fray García Guerra's demise earlier in the century and seemingly had ushered in the Baroque era, now repeated themselves as if to herald the approaching end of that age. The superstitious masses interpreted an eclipse of the sun as a dark indication of divine displeasure which spawned hysterical fears slow to dissipate. It was the same phenomenon that Sigüenza y Góngora had observed with his telescope and which he pronounced "not only a total eclipse but one of the greatest that the world has ever seen." In this atmosphere of wretchedness, misery, and panic all the hidden resentments, the gnawing injustices, and repressed hatreds came to the surface and a sullen mood of restiveness pervaded the city. The apprehension of the privileged minority turned to fright as rumors of impending riots and public disturbances hardened into facts. On June 8, 1692 mounting tension exploded into mob violence which burned the viceregal palace and other important buildings and made a bloody shambles of the cluttered square in front of the Cathedral. The viceroy luckily escaped from the frenzy of the rioters, but the complete overthrow of the Spanish government was barely averted. For long months a nervous expectancy of further uprisings agitated the entire realm.

Hardly did this state of alarm subside when a pestilence of high mortality swept through the viceregal community, exacting a heavy toll from every caste and class. Even when the force of the plague was spent death, with remorseless insistence, continued to select its victims among the illustrious and powerful, including the viceroy, and the Archbishop. These somber happenings accentuated the Baroque concern with dissolution and decay and, in the hearts of the inhabitants, the conviction strengthened that the end of the age, indeed of the world itself, was imminent.

If the eighteenth century was to witness the beginnings of a breakdown of the orthodoxy so carefully imposed by Spain on its overseas possessions, the seventeenth century had placed an almost ineffaceable seal upon the character and personality of embryonic nations. The fluidity of the earlier age of conquest and settlement had given way to the rigidity of a fixed pattern after Spain's expansive effort ground to a virtual halt in 1600. The mounting repression of the Counter Reformation had slowed movement and facilitated the consolidation of a neomedieval civilization and culture. Circumstances were propitious to this development in Old Mexico and they produced perhaps its most complete manifestation. An accelerated fusion of varied human elements favored an intricate hierarchy of class and caste, and this ethnic diversity tended toward a social immobility that left the dominant whites unchallenged in a permanent position of privilege. It thus created a societal design nearly immune to the erosion of time and modernity. Economically these heterogeneous constituents formed a proletarian mass largely deprived of the fruits of its toil. If the *encomienda*, a semi-feudal system of lord and serf, or master and slave, implanted in the sixteenth century, was breaking down in the Baroque age, already replacing it was a harsher system of debt peonage, destined to linger on into twentieth century Mexico and plunge that nation into the anarchy and chaos of social revolution.

Inherent in the colonial order was an arbitrary, monolithic state headed by a vice-sovereign with nearly absolute authority who functioned essentially as an overseer of the enormous estate of its absentee owner, the king of Spain. The royal master wished to derive the maximum income from his property but, as a Christian monarch, his attitude was usually paternalistic and he believed that he was benefiting his subjects by often enlightened decrees. Vast distances and slow communications nullified most of these good intentions, and his Majesty's representatives often were little less than unrestrained despots. Exercising judicial, executive, and even lawgiving powers, they were unassailable and omnipotent; their will took on the semblance of statutes and their persons an aura of infallibility. Surrounded by an obsequious bureaucracy they were accessible only through a fawning adulation or the influence of favorites. Few viceroys and governors of the seventeenth century were men of more than mediocre talent and character who could hardly help but feel transformed into demigods by such unlimited authority. This haughty importance, so gratifying to vanity, fostered a tradition of personalism and dictatorship fated to haunt the political life of the later republic.

The same period witnessed the planting of the seeds of *caciquismo*, or political boss rule in local communities, an evil which flourished in all its malignity when the right of suffrage under republican institutions provided the illusion of popular sovereignty. The provincial *corregidores* and *alcaldes mayores* were district magistrates who often usurped absolute authority within their jurisdiction. Enjoying unchallenged sway, they easily enriched themselves through a monopolistic sale of salt, seeds, tools, and other necessities to the defenseless Indian peasantry. And these corrupt agents of government were seldom averse to accommodating aristocratic families of the locality by abusing their prerogatives to coerce the wretched peons into wageless service to them and by suppressing any latent restlessness of the exploited. Thus a pattern of petty despotism and personal rule in local government hardened and became virtually immune to the subsequent attrition of political experience.

Clearly evident in the seventeenth century was the consolidation of the power and wealth of the Church. Theoretically subordinate to the State, its influence was felt in every aspect of secular life. In many ways it acquired a predominance in human affairs rivaling that of the medieval Church in Europe, and this tradition it was slow to relinquish. Its dual task of converting the native population and preventing backsliding among the faithful was sufficient warrant to justify the accumulation of material wealth and the constant enlargement of the staff of clergymen. Well before the close of the sixteenth century its immense holdings of land identified its interests with those of the landed aristocracy, and its equalitarian ardor soon cooled. The leisurely life of many churchmen made an ecclesiastical career attractive, and monasteries, convents, and churches rapidly multiplied to accommodate the increasing numbers of the religious community. Vast resources of treasure and real estate, permanently retained by a system of mortmain, soon transformed the Church, particularly the various Orders, into the chief fiscal agencies of the realm. Fiduciary activities such as moneylending, mortgages, leases, rentals and the like, were highly lucrative and, as an important supplier of capital, it exercised a powerful influence on the colonial economy. This abundant wealth and an easy command of artisan and manual labor enabled the Church to transform cities and hamlets, especially in the core region of Mexico, into an immense museum of Baroque architecture and art which remains a patrimony of the modern nation. These rich resources, coupled with an unquestioned spiritual authority, bestowed upon the institution a tremendous weight in every phase of social, cultural, intellectual, and even political life of the people with lasting effects. Through its secular arm, the Inquisition, it brooked no criticism or dissidence in public opinion while it exerted severe restraint upon private behavior. Thus the Church acquired a position, particularly in the seventeenth century, that became almost impregnable and highly resistant to the corrosive effects of modern secularism.

An agrarian capitalism was the underlying economic ideology of this neomedieval, semifeudal order, the prosperity of which rested mainly on the ownership of land and its products. Hence of paramount importance to the ruling groups was the absolute possession of these productive means and the despotic control of the peasantry. A system of latifundia readily solidified, and this concept of social organization involving large estates owned by a select few, and a vast proletariat, provided a pattern which endured into the twentieth century. The Baroque age witnessed an oppressive development of this order owing to the relatively limited amount of arable soil, the inefficient methods of cultivation, the deteriorating effects of sheep-raising and pastoral pursuits, and the insatiable acquisitiveness of landholders who generally preferred to live in the cities. European invaders had early taken up the best tracts which their descendants expanded, often by absorbing the communal lands of Indian villages. This procedure reduced the aboriginal owners to a condition of debt peonage, and in one fell swoop, increased acreage and a labor supply for the white masters. It was a method which achieved its fullest efficiency under the Díaz regime of the late nineteenth century.

The rewards of proprietorship were psychological as well as material. Extensive holdings of land brought a coveted social prestige and, for elevation into a seigneurial position, an enormous estate was often a valid substitute for a lofty lineage of aristocratic distinction. Many an adventurer was thus able to overcome the handicaps of an undistinguished origin and bequeath an honored name to his family. Patrician pride quite as much as economic advantage contributed to the perpetuation of hereditary ownership through the institution of *mayorazgos,* or primogeniture, which flourished well into the republican period. In the course of the seventeenth century the Creole class became predominantly the landholders, and they tended to adopt a less paternal attitude toward their Indian serfs than the Spanish Peninsulars whom they supplanted. The ultimate abolition of the controversial *encomienda* had thus brought no improvement to the unenviable lot of the Indians, and the persistence of *latifundismo,* with all its evils, was guaranteed by the tradition of mortmain preserved by the Church and of primogeniture retained by the aristocracy. Much later this rigid order would expire belatedly in the fury of social revolution.

With slight modification, then, a neomedieval civilization sank deep roots into the Mexican soil during the seventeenth century. The privileged minorities of the State, Church, and landed proprietors, aided and abetted by a small but influential group of merchants and entrepreneurs chiefly engaged in the extractive industries, collaborated to preserve a fixed and constant order in a world of accelerating change. The long decades of this middle century saw the solidification of Hispanic culture in its most orthodox form in a semifeudal society of class and caste based on a system of latifundia directed by an absolute State and an even more arbitrary Church. The aim of this civilization was immobility, spiritual, intellectual, cultural, social, political, and economic. In this static order inspiration, imagination, and ingenuity could have free play only within the accessory and not the formal or essential aspects of life and reality. The repressed vitality of a heterogeneous but enormously creative people was consequently denied a fruitful outlet and was forced to expend itself for the most part in dramatic trivia and excessive ornamentation—a heritage of the Baroque age still not wholly extinguished.

This formative era of Old Mexico did not, of course, begin with the Spanish Archbishop-Viceroy, Fray García Guerra, nor did it expire with the intellectually curious Sigüenza y Góngora, but these two figures symbolize, in a measure, important stages in its evolution. The Baroque period, which they represent, clearly does not offer the abundant external history of the days of the Conquistadors nor that of the times that immediately preceded the War of Independence, yet it was not wholly static. Behind its heavily embroidered veil there was movement, for the Baroque spirit sought to reconcile a bold modernism in form with an extreme oldness in content. This effort, which evaded issues and avoided the concrete, resulted in some changes of an inner nature during the century that suggest a vague polarity in the contrasting times and personalities of Fray García and Don Carlos de Sigüenza.

The earlier figure epitomizes the neomedieval ideal of the Spanish Counter Reformation with its fusion of ecclesiastical and secular authority, its theological learning, and its reliance on verbalism in the quest of truth, and Fray García seemed a nearly perfect embodiment of this spirit. If at that moment the resolute endeavor of Spain to preserve orthodoxy in religion and thought in Old Mexico from the schismatic differences of contemporary Europe seemed successful, considerable seepage of ideas regarded as subversive had occurred when Sigüenza y Góngora began his studies. Just as the weakening monarchy of the Peninsula could not prevent foreign encroachment on its New World territories, so it was unable to prevent the encroachment of foreign ideas there. Doctrinal rigidity, backed by Inquisitorial censorship, may have kept them to a mere trickle, but it did not exclude them altogether; and, if the colonial mentality seemed parched, it did not cause newer concepts to evaporate entirely. Receptive minds such as that of Sigüenza y Góngora were quietly initiating a shift from the semantic ambiguities of scholasticism as a means of explaining everything to the more precise language of mathematics as a means of explaining natural phenomena. Where Fray García was single-minded in his approach to all problems, Don Carlos discriminated between those relating to things eternal, which he left to traditional rationalization, and those temporal, to which he applied the new methodology of observation and measurement. Where Fray García did not question the authority of Aristotle in secular disciplines Don Carlos, two generations or more ahead of his time in Mexico, was vigorously anti-Aristotelian. He and, to a lesser degree, his contemporary, Sister Juana Inés de la Cruz, were precursors of the Enlightenment that presently reached their *patria*.

In less abstruse matters the interval between Fray García and Don Carlos was likewise a transition. The Archbishop-Viceroy, a Peninsular Spaniard, came to Mexico City with the absolute power of a proconsul to administer the affairs of a federated kingdom of an empire consciously aping the ancient Roman system. For the provincial subjects, and especially the Creoles, the boon of imperial citizenship was enough, and they acknowledged the distant grandeur of the Hapsburgs with pride and awe. As the decades passed this attitude remained outwardly unchanged, but inwardly the Creoles had grown restive, and their antagonism increased toward the Europe-born Spaniards who continued to occupy the highest offices. These American-bred whites had risen in numbers and, through interlocking family interests that gave them a certain cohesion, their power was consolidating. The fact that the declining fortunes of the mother country and its perennial bankruptcy enabled the Creoles to acquire many minor offices by purchase served only to sharpen their resentment at an exclusion still main-

tained by the crown from the major offices. Since common griev-
ances suffered often unite more closely than common blessings
shared, the Creoles thought of themselves more and more as Mexican Americans and sought compensatory pride in their homeland.
Though the feeling was not without conflicts and insecurity arising out of the friction of races and a morbid sense of cultural
inferiority, an embryonic nationalism was emerging. By 1700 the
Spanish Americans were obtaining a firm grip on the affairs and
management of their country.

This nascent Mexicanism crops out occasionally in Sigüenza's
writings as in his frequent allusions to "mi Patria," his reference
to the supercilious indifference of Europeans, and his claims of
Mexican equality with the Old World in artistic and even intellectual potentialities. All this was no more, probably, than a manifestation of regionalistic loyalty characteristic of Hispanic peoples
everywhere, and it is doubtful if Sigüenza's conception of his
"Patria" extended much beyond his own class or far beyond the
bounds of the populous vicinity of Mexico City.

To him, as to those of his social milieu, his conceptions were in-
separably associated with things Spanish. Yet it is significant that,
perhaps more than anyone of his time, he also included in this
national consciousness the aboriginal heritage of his land. His lifelong dedication to the Indian antiquities bears witness to this fact.
Great Spanish scholars such as Sahagún and Torquemada had
earlier given their lives to these studies, but in the Mexican Creole's
work one senses a greater identification with this ancient lore.
From the age of twenty-three he collected books, codices, maps, and
paintings relating to pre-Hispanic native life until he had assembled the richest assortment of archaeological and historical materials on the Aztec civilization then in existence. Mastering various
Mexican languages, he compiled scholarly monographs, practically
none of which survive. "If there were someone in New Spain who
would pay the cost of printing. . . . there is no doubt that I would
bring forth several works, in the composition of which I have
been stimulated by the great love I have for my country . . ." he
wrote, and mournfully added, ". . . these and other data require
large volumes, and so they will probably die with me (for I shall
never be able to publish them because of my great poverty)."[2]
Another incident reveals a certain Creole boldness in the face

of Spanish authority as well as the scholar's disposition to count
the indigenous culture as a component of his Mexicanism. A new
viceroy, Marqués de la Laguna, came from Spain in 1680 and, as
was customary, elaborate arrangements were made for his ceremonious entry into the capital. An important feature was invariably
an Arch of Triumph with appropriate allegorical decorations and
emblematic designs. Nearly always in these devices the organizers
made use of myths and legends of Greek and Roman antiquity
shaped to please the vanity of the vice-sovereign. Sigüenza y Góngora was commissioned on this occasion to select the topics and
execute the designs, and he chose to break rather sharply with
tradition. Ignoring the standard models of ancient classics, he represented pictorially and with suitable inscriptions the Aztec gods
and emperors, each of whom embodied a virtue or trait deemed
desirable in rulers. In his *Theater of the Political Virtues Apper-
taining to a Prince as Noted in the Ancient Monarchs of the Mexican Empire,* a volume commemorative of the occasion and written
in the turgid, indigestible prose of Baroque scholarship, Sigüenza
sets forth in much detail the remarkable character and accomplish-
ments of the aboriginal kings scorned and despised by the Spaniards.[3] As European Christians could find inspiration in the pagan
culture of Greeks and Romans so, this Creole scholar seems to
imply, Mexican Christians could derive similar understanding from
an American past, and with warmth and enthusiasm he exalts the
qualities and achievements of the heathen magistrates of his native
land. In all this one senses that, in a subtle fashion, the highly intelligent Sigüenza wished to remind a proud Peninsular that the
realm over which he had come to preside was no mere adjunct of
the Spanish empire but a land with a rich heritage of its own.
And it is likely that, in praising the integrity and political acumen
of the pre-Hispanic rulers of Mexico, he artfully sought to in-
struct the new appointee of the king of Spain in matters of states-
manship and right government for his Creole *patria.*

In this intention, so carefully veiled in Baroque fashion by a
welter of detail and heavy verbalism, is evident a dawning Mexicanism which the more articulate Spanish American expressed on
more than one occasion. In his description of the *mascarada* at
Querétaro, it will be remembered, he had seized the opportunity to
expatiate on the virtues of the rulers of pre-Cortesian Mexico and

also on the military potentialities displayed by his countrymen in that parade. Open expression of such sentiments marked an advance in national consciousness, for it is doubtful that in the times of Fray García Guerra even the most discontented Creole would have had either the appreciation of the Indian past or the effrontery to draw upon it for an allegorical theme to honor the accession of the king's vicar in the realm. Indeed, to have held up the pagan chieftains of the Aztec barbarians as models for instruction and emulation of the haughty conquerors would have seemed scarcely less than *lèse majesté*. In the closing decades of the century, however, the Creole class was conscious of its growing strength and cohesion and increasingly disposed to assert itself, though still with discreet restraint. Moreover, in the course of the century the complex and involuted pattern of the transplanted Spanish Baroque had absorbed elements of indigenous history and feeling as well as Indian motifs in art and architecture, thus imbuing sentiment and artistic expression with a hybrid character distinct from that of Spain and, in a measure, unique. As ethnic fusion had advanced in the progressive mixing of the races, an amalgamation in the sphere of esthetics and psychology had paralleled it.

During the decades that followed the seventeenth century little change appears in the Baroque spirit save, perhaps, its tendency to intensify a predilection for exaggeration, extravagance, hyperbole, and superlatives which sometimes carried artistic and literary expression to even more grotesque extremes. These manifestations were, perhaps, the products of the sustained repression of an inner vitality which was about to explode. The prolonged crisis in the "eternal order of theology" had built up tensions that orthodoxy and tradition could not contain much longer. The long incubation of expanding pressures was to release the revolutionary ideologies of eighteenth century rationalism and nineteenth century republicanism. Yet when they came and violent as the resulting convulsions were, they failed to shatter completely the Baroque matrix which the long years of Spanish domination had tempered to a granitic hardness. Its indelible imprint remained etched upon the personality and civilization of Spanish America everywhere. Indeed, to sum it all up, so pronounced is this peculiar legacy today that it has moved a discerning critic and distinguished citizen of that area to comment recently: "The Baroque was one of the most

profoundly rooted elements of tradition in our culture. In spite of
nearly two centuries of encyclopedism and modern criticism, we
Hispanic Americans have not yet fully emerged from its labyrinth.
It still heavily influences our esthetic sensibility and many complex
aspects of our collective psychology."*

* "Sin embargo (lo Barroco) fué uno de los elementos más prolongada-
mente arraigado en la tradición de nuestra cultura. A pesar de casi dos
siglos de enciclopedismo y de crítica moderna, los hispanoamericanos no nos
evadimos enteramente aun del laberinto barroco. Pesa en nuestra sensibilidad
estética y en muchas formas complicadas de psicología colectiva." Mariano
Picón Salas. *De la conquista a la independencia. Tres siglos de historia cultural hispanoamericana* (Mexico City, 1944; 3rd Ed., 1958), p. 107.

NOTES

1. Cf. José A. Calderón Quijano, *Historia de las fortificaciones en Nueva España* (Seville, 1953), pp. 15 ff.
2. Juan Diez de la Calle, *Noticias sacras i reales (1657-1659), Manuscritos de América* 3023 (Madrid, Biblioteca Nacional).
3. Cf. A. P. Newton (ed.), *Thomas Gage, The English American. A New Survey of the West Indies, 1648* (London, Guatemala City, 1946), chap. 5.
4. These details and most of the account of Fray García Guerra given in this chapter are derived from Mateo Alemán, *Sucesos de D. Frai García Gera Arçobispo de Mejico . . .* (Mexico, 1613). Critical edition of Alice H. Bushee. Reprinted in *Revue hispanique*, 25 (New York, Paris, 1911), pp. 1-99.
5. Francisco Sosa, *El episcopado mexicano. Biografía de los Excelentísimos Señores arzobispos desde la Época Colonial hasta nuestros días* (Mexico City, 1939; earlier ed. Mexico City, 1877)
6. "Letter of Don Carlos de Sigüenza y Góngora to Admiral Andrés de Pez Recounting the Incidents of the Corn Riot in Mexico City, June 8, 1692," Appendix B of Irving A. Leonard, *Don Carlos de Sigüenza, A Mexican Savant of the Seventeenth Century* (Berkeley, University of California Publications in History, vol. 18, 1929). The original text from a contemporary copy in the Bancroft Library of the University of California, Berkeley, appears in a critical, annotated edition by Irving A. Leonard. *Alboroto y motín de los indios de México del 8 de Junio de 1692* (Mexico City: Museo Nacional, 1932), and in more abbreviated form in Manuel Romero de Terreros (ed.), *Carlos de Sigüenza y Góngora. Relaciones históricas* (Mexico City: Biblioteca del estudiante universitario, 13, 1940).

7. Newton, *op. cit.*, p. 90.

8. Cf. Artemio de Valle-Arizpe, *El Palacio Nacional de México* (Mexico City, 1936), chap. iii, *passim*. Sosa, *op. cit.*, appendix, quotes this anecdote taken from *Reformas de los descalzos de Nra Señora de Primitiva Observancia*, vol. 1, chap. xxvi.

9. Andrés Cavo, *Los Tres Siglos de México durante el Gobierno Español hasta la Entrada del Ejército Trigarante* . . . (Mexico City, 1836-1838), 4 vols., entry of June 10, 1611.

10. *Ibid.*, entry of December 25, 1611.

11. Sosa, *op. cit.*, pp. 87 ff., gives detailed description of funeral obsequies.

12. Vicente Riva Palacio, *México através de los Siglos* (Barcelona, 1888-89), 5 vols., vol. II, p. 561.

CHAPTER II

1. Americo Castro, *The Structure of Spanish History* (Princeton University Press, 1954), p. 191.

2. G. R. G. Conway (ed.), *Friar Francisco Naranjo and the Old University of Mexico* (Mexico City, 1939), pp. 37-38.

3. This discussion is indebted to Ernest Nagel in chapter 8 of *Chapters in Western Civilization* (New York: Columbia University Press, 1954).

4. Darnell H. Roaten and Federico Sánchez y Escribano, *Wölfflin's Principles in Spanish Drama, 1500-1700* (New York: Hispanic Institute in the United States, 1952), pp. 7-12.

5. Cf. Guillermo Díaz-Plaja, *Historia de la literatura española* (Barcelona, 1953), 2 vols., vol. I, pp. 220-23.

6. Roaten and Sánchez y Escribano, *op. cit.*, p. 168, n. 2.

7. Pál Kelemen, *Baroque and Rococo in Latin America* (New York, 1951), p. 14.

8. *Ibid.*, p. 22.

9. A stimulating discussion of the Baroque in Colonial Spanish America, to which this description owes much, is found in Mariano Picón Salas, *De la Conquista a la Independencia. Tres Siglos de Historia Cultural Hispanoamericana* (Mexico City, 1944), chaps. v, vi.

10. Carl J. Friedrich, *The Age of the Baroque, 1610-1660* (New York, 1952), chap. v.

11. Brooks Adams, *Law of Civilization and Decay* (New York, 1955), chap. x.

12. Friedrich, *loc. cit.*

CHAPTER III

1. Salvador de Madariaga, *The Fall of the Spanish American Empire* (London, 1947), pp. 3-4.
2. Cf. Pedro Henríquez Ureña, "Observaciones sobre el español en América," *Revista de filología española*, 18 (Madrid, 1931), pp. 122 ff.
3. Madariaga, *op. cit.*, chap. x, *passim*.
4. Bernal Díaz del Castillo, *The Discovery and Conquest of Mexico, 1517-1521*, Introduction by Irving A. Leonard (New York, 1956), p. 267.
5. Alberto M. Carreño (ed.), *Gonzalo Gómez de Cervantes. La vida económica y social de Nueva España al finalizar el siglo XVI* (Mexico City, 1944), p. 124.
6. Irving A. Leonard, *Don Carlos de Sigüenza y Góngora, A Mexican Savant of the Seventeenth Century* (Berkeley, 1929), p. 240.
7. A. P. Newton (ed.), *Thomas Gage. The English American. A New Survey of the West Indies, 1648* (London and Guatemala City, 1946). A newer edition is: *Thomas Gage's Travels in the New World*, edited by Eric S. Thompson (Norman: Univ. of Oklahoma Press, 1958).
8. Newton, *op. cit.*, p. 42.
9. Jorge Juan and Antonio de Ulloa, *Noticias secretas de América* (Madrid, 1918), Part II, chap. viii.
10. Newton, *op. cit.*, p. 84.
11. José Antonio Saco, *Historia de la esclavitud de la raza africana en el Nuevo Mundo* (Barcelona, 1879), p. 62. New edition (Havana, 1932), 2 vols.
12. Hubert Herring, *A History of Latin America* (New York, 1955), p. 101.
13. Saco, *op. cit.*, p. 130.
14. *Ibid.*, p. 164.
15. Newton, *op. cit.*, pp. 119, 164-65.
16. Irene Diggs, "Color in Colonial Spanish America," *Journal of Negro History*, 2 (1953), pp. 405-27.
17. Cf. Hensley C. Woodbridge, "Glossary of names used in colonial Latin America for crosses among Indians, Negroes, and Whites," *Journal of the Washington Academy of Sciences*, 38, no. 11 (Nov. 15, 1948), pp. 353-62.

CHAPTER IV

1. Cf. Woodrow Borah, *New Spain's Century of Depression*. Ibero-

Americana series, 25 (Berkeley: Univ. of California Press, 1951), *passim*.

2. Chapter xiii of *Repertorio de los tiempos* quoted in Francisco de la Maza. *Enrico Martínez, cosmógrafo e impresor de Nueva España* (Mexico City: Sociedad Mexicana de Geografía y Estadística, 1943).

3. Gerald Brenan, *The Literature of the Spanish People* (New York-Cambridge, 1951), p. 173.

4. Printed in Dorothy Schons, *Notes from Spanish Archives*. Book I (Ann Arbor, Mich., 1946), p. 17.

5. Francisco Rodríguez Marín, *Documentos referentes a Mateo Alemán y a sus deudos más cercanos* (1546-1607) (Madrid, 1933), pp. 52-53.

6. *Ibid.*, p. 52, note; Francisco Rodríguez Marín. *Discursos leídos ante la Real Academia Española* ... (Seville, 1907), p. 37.

7. Cf. Irving A. Leonard, "Mateo Alemán in Mexico: a Document," *Hispanic Review*, 17, no. 4 (1949), pp. 316-27.

8. Rodríguez Marín, *Documentos* ... , pp. 54-55; José Gestoso y Pérez, *Nuevos datos para ilustrar las biografías del maestro Juan de Malara y de Mateo Alemán* (Seville, 1896), pp. 16-22.

9. Printed in Leonard, *op. cit.*, pp. 327-30.

10. José Toribio Medina, *La Imprenta en México* (1539-1821) (Santiago de Chile, 1907-1912: 8 vols.), vol. 2, p. 43.

11. Brenan, *op. cit.*, p. 171.

12. Antonio Castro Leal, *Juan Ruiz de Alarcón, su vida y su obra* (Mexico City, 1943), p. 29; Dorothy Schons, "The Mexican background of Alarcón," *Publications of the Modern Language Association*, 57 (1942), pp. 89-104.

13. Cf. Francisco Pérez Salazar, "Dos nuevos documentos sobre D. Juan Ruiz de Alarcón," *Revista de Literatura Mexicana*, 1, No. 1 (1940), pp. 154-65.

14. Francisco de Icaza, *Sucesos reales que parecen imaginados de Gutierre de Cetina, Juan de la Cueva, y Mateo Alemán* (Madrid, 1919), pp. 253-63.

15. William A. Kincaid, "Life and Works of Luis Belmonte Bermúdez (1587-1650?)," *Revue hispanique*, 74 (1928), pp. 1-260.

16. Cf. Alfonso Méndez Plancarte, *Poetas novohispanos*. Biblioteca del estudiante universitario, 33 (Mexico City, 1942), pp. xxx-xxxi.

17. Cf. Emilio Carilla, *El Gongorismo en América* (Buenos Aires, 1946), chaps. ii, iii, iv, for a general discussion.

18. Pedro Henríquez Ureña as quoted in Méndez Plancarte, *op. cit.*, p. xxxiv.

19. Cf. John Van Horne, *Bernardo de Balbuena. Biografía y Crítica* (Guadalajara, 1940), *passim*. Also José Rojas Garcidueñas, *Bernardo de Balbuena: La vida y obra* (Mexico City, 1958), pp. 139-72.

20. De la Maza, *op. cit., passim*.

CHAPTER V

1. A. P. Newton (ed.), *Thomas Gage. The English American. A New Survey of the West Indies, 1648* (London and Guatemala City, 1946), p. 62.

2. Antonio Vázquez de Espinosa, *Nueva España en el Siglo XVII* (Mexico City, 1944), pp. 117 ff.

3. Artemio de Valle Arizpe, *Calle vieja y calle nueva* (Mexico City, 1949), p. 25; Fernando Cepeda y Fernando Alonso Carillo, *Relación universal legítima y verdadera del sitio en que está fundada la muy noble, insigne, y leal Ciudad de México . . . lagunas, ríos, montes que la ciñen y rodean, calzadas que la dividen y azequías que la atraviesan . . .* (Mexico City, 1637), *passim*.

4. Trent Elwood Sanford, *The Story of Architecture in Mexico* (New York, 1947), p. 180.

5. Details for this description are derived from various sources, including A. P. Newton, *op. cit.*; Vázquez de Espinosa, *op. cit.*; Valle-Arizpe, *op. cit.*; Luis González Obregón, *The Streets of Mexico*, trans. by B. C. Wagner (San Francisco, 1937); Bernardo de Balbuena, *La Grandeza Mexicana*, Edición y pról. de Francisco Monterde, Biblioteca del estudiante universitario, 23 (Mexico City, 1941; also 1954).

6. Marcelino Menéndez y Pelayo, quoted in Alfonso Méndez Plancarte, *Poetas novohispanos. Primer siglo, 1521-1621.* Biblioteca del estudiante universitario, 33 (Mexico City, 1942), p. xli.

7. Translation of Thomas Walsh in *Hispanic Anthology: Poems Translated from Spanish by English and North American Poets* (New York, London, 1920). Regarding Miguel Guevara and the famous sonnet, see Alberto M. Carreño, *No me mueve mi Dios para quererle. Consideraciones nuevas sobre un viejo tema* (Mexico City, 1942), *passim*; Victor Adib, "Fray Miguel de Guevara y el soneto a Cristo crucificado," *Ábside*, 13, no. 3 (1949), pp. 311-26.

8. This inventory is reproduced in Irving A. Leonard, "One Man's Library, Mexico City, 1620," *Estudios Hispánicos*, Homenaje a Archer M. Huntington (Wellesley, Mass., 1952), pp. 327-34.

9. Francisco Javier Sánchez Cantón, *La Librería de Juan de Herrera* (Madrid, 1941).

10. This author's work "en todo idioma," as well as the novels and *Labyrinth of Love* of Boccaccio are listed in the *Índice último de los libros prohibidos y mandados expurgar para todos los reynos y señoríos* . . . (Madrid, 1790).

11. Irving A. Leonard, "Un envío de libros para Concepción de Chile, 1620," *El Bibliófilo Chileno* (Santiago de Chile), vol. 2 (1948), pp. 1-7.

12. Robert Stevenson, "The Distinguished Maestro of New Spain: Juan Gutiérrez de Padilla," *Hispanic American Historical Review*, 35 (1955), pp. 363-73.

13. James D. Hart, *The Popular Book. A History of America's Literary Taste* (New York, 1950), p. 4.

CHAPTER VI

1. The original inspiration of this chapter came from a pamphlet by the Marqués de San Francisco (Manuel Romero de Terreros y Vinent) entitled *Un Bibliófilo en el Santo Oficio* (Mexico City: Librería de Pedro Robredo, 1920). While in Mexico City in 1932 I had a typescript made of the "Inventario de los libros que se hallaron a Melchor Pérez de Soto, vecino desta Ciudad, y obrero mayor de la Santa Iglesia Catedral della, los cuales se metieron en la Cámara del Secreto deste Santo Oficio (1655)," (Archivo General de la Nación. *Inquisición*, tomo 440), a manuscript of 107 folio pages, with the intention of making a detailed analysis of a colonial book list of such exceptional interest. (Professor Julio Jiménez Rueda published it in 1947 without commentary in *Documentos para la historia de la cultura en México*, Mexico City, as one of a series of publications under the auspices of the Archivo General and the Universidad Nacional Autónoma de México.) As other matters intervened I finally turned the typescript over to my student Donald G. Castanien, who made the projected analysis a doctoral dissertation under my direction. This thesis is now available in microfilm at the Library of the University of Michigan. Dr. Castanien published a summary of it as an article entitled "The Mexican Inquisition Censors a Private Library," in the *Hispanic American Historical Review*, 34 (1954), pp. 374-92, and the account in this chapter is indebted to both of these works.

2. Juan José de Eguiara y Egurén, *Prólogos a la Biblioteca Mexicana*, Ed. de Agustín Millares Carlo (Mexico City, 1944), p. 121.

3. Cf. Julio Jiménez Rueda, *Herejías y supersticiones en la Nueva España. Los Heterodoxos en México* (Mexico City, 1946), *passim*.

4. *Ibid.*, pp. 214-25.

5. James D. Hart, *The Popular Book. A History of America's Literary Taste* (New York, 1950), p. 9.

CHAPTER VII

1. R. E. Schultes, "The Appeal of Peyote (*Lophophora Williamsii*) as a Medicine," *American Anthropologist*, 40 (1938), pp. 698-715; R. E. Schultes, "Peyote, an American Indian Heritage from Mexico," *El Mexico antiguo* (Tacubaya, 1938), 5, nos. 5-6; W. LaBarre, *The Peyote Cult* (New Haven, 1938).

2. *Ramo de Inquisición*, tomo 289, Archivo General de la Nación, Mexico City. Original text and translation in Irving A. Leonard, "Peyote and the Mexican Inquisition, 1620," *American Anthropologist*, 44, no. 2 (1942), pp. 324-26.

3. *Libro primero de votos de la Inquisición de México, 1573-1600*. Introducción de Edmundo O'Gorman. Archivo General de la Nación (Mexico City, 1949), *passim*.

4. Francisco Pérez Salazar, "Las obras y desventuras de Pedro de Trejo, *Revista de literatura mexicana*, 1, no. 1 (1940), p. 124; Julio Jiménez Rueda, "Poesías sagradas y profanas de Pedro de Trejo," *Boletín del Archivo General de la Nación* (Mexico City), 15 (1944), pp. 209-312.

5. Charles Henry Lea, *The Inquisition in the Spanish Dependencies* (New York, 1908), chap. 6.

6. Luis González Obregón, *D. Guillén de Lampart. La Inquisición y la Independencia en el siglo XVII* (Mexico City, 1908), pp. 73-235; Gabriel Méndez Plancarte, "Don Guillén de Lampart y su Regio salterio," *Ábside*, 12, no. 2 (1948), pp. 125-92; no. 3 (1948), pp. 287-372.

7. José Ortega y Gasset, "Notes on the Novel," in *The Dehumanization of Art, and Other Writings on Art and Culture*, Anchor Book A72 (Garden City, N. Y., 1956), p. 67.

8. Juan Francisco Gemelli Carreri, *Viaje a la Nueva España* (Mexico City, 1927), pp. 101, 179.

9. Joseph de Buendía, *Vida del . . . P. Francisco del Castillo, S. J.*, (Madrid, 1693), fol. 444.

10. Antonio de Molina, *Antigua Guatemala* (Guatemala City, 1943), pp. 28-30.

11. Everett W. Hesse, "Calderon's Popularity in the Spanish Indies," *Hispanic Review*, 23, no. 1 (1955), pp. 12-27. A very useful compendium of the colonial theater is José J. Arrom, *El teatro de Hispanoamérica en la Época Colonial* (La Habana, 1956).

12. George W. Bacon, "The Life and Dramatic Works of D. Juan Pérez de Montalbán (1602-1638)," *Revue Hispanique,* 26 (1912), pp. 1-474.

13. An account of this controversy is given in *ibid.,* pp. 24-51.

14. Irving A. Leonard, "Pérez de Montalbán, Tomás Gutiérrez and Two Book Lists," *Hispanic Review,* 12, no. 4 (1944), p. 278.

15. Text of this play is available in James Fitzmaurice-Kelly, *The Nun Ensign* (London, 1908).

16. Joaquín María Ferrer, *Historia de la Monja Alférez, Doña Catalina de Erauso, escrita por ella misma e ilustrada con notas y documentos* (Paris, 1829), pp. 113-19.

17. C. Bravo-Villasante, *La Mujer vestida de hombre en el teatro español. Siglos XVI-XVII* (Madrid, 1955), *passim.*

18. The copy of the play used is a photostat from the University of California (Berkeley, *Osuna,* tomo colecticio 132, folios 273-90v.)

19. Dorothy Schons, "Some Obscure Points in the Life of Sor Juana Inés de la Cruz," *Modern Philology,* 24, no. 2 (1926), p. 153.

20. These proceedings are preserved in manuscript at the Archivo General de la Nación, Mexico City, *Ramo de la Inquisición,* tomo 667, no. 14, fojas 233-36, with the title: "Autos en raçon de Vna Comedia Titulada El Valor perseguido y traicion Vengada del Dor Juan Perez de Montalban y el entremes Titulado del Sacristan. Su Autor Pedro Bezerra." Cf. Irving A. Leonard. "Montalbán's El Valor Perseguido, and the Mexican Inquisition, 1682," *Hispanic Review,* 11 (1943), pp. 47-56.

CHAPTER VIII

1. Luis González Obregón, *México Viejo* (Paris, Mexico City, 1900), p. 254.

2. Antonio de Robles, "Diario de sucesos notables," *Documentos para la historia de México,* Series 1, vol. II and III (Mexico City, 1853), vol. II, p. 31.

3. Robles, *op. cit.,* vol. III, pp. 60-61; Irving A. Leonard, *Don Carlos de Sigüenza y Góngora, A Mexican Savant of the Seventeenth Century* (Berkeley, 1929), p. 219.

4. A. P. Newton (ed.), *Thomas Gage, The English-American. A New Survey of the West Indies, 1648* (London and Guatemala City, (1946), p. 165.

5. Gregorio Martín de Guijo, "Diario de Sucesos notables," *Documentos para la historia de México,* 1 series (Mexico City, 1853),

vol. I, p. 224; Robles, *op. cit.*, vol. III, pp. 289, 290; vol. II, p. 123.

6. Guijo, *op. cit.*, vol. I, p. 395-96.

7. Robles, *op. cit.*, vol. II, p. 224.

8. González Obregón, *op. cit.*, p. 252. A compilation of notices referring to *máscaras,* largely taken from the Robles and Guijo diaries, is given in Vicente Riva Palacio, *México através de los siglos* (Barcelona, 1888-1889), 5 vols, vol. II, pp. 722-23.

9. *Glorias de Querétaro en la Nueva Congregación Eclesiástica de María Santíssima de Guadalupe . . .* (Mexico City, 1680). Reprinted by Ediciones Cimatario, (Querétaro, 1945).

10. The text is available on pp. 47-51 of the 1680 edition, and pp. 50-54 of the 1945 reprinting. It also appears, with notes on Aztec terms, in Irving A. Leonard, "A Mexican *Máscara* of the Seventeenth Century," *Revista de estudios hispánicos*, II, no. 2 (1929), p. 163-67.

CHAPTER IX

1. The description of the formalities of a poetic tournament (*certamen*) given in this chapter is a composite one derived from notes compiled from many contemporary printed accounts of these competitions occurring during the seventeenth and early eighteenth century in Mexico City, Lima, Bogotá, and other centers of Colonial Spanish America. While basically all such functions were conducted in the manner set forth, differences of detail were present, of course, in most of them from time to time and from place to place. With the Baroque preoccupation with the elaboration of form, diversity in an artistic activity of this sort is clearly to be expected. In many years of investigation of the cultural and literary history of colonial Hispanic America I have not come across any systematic effort to describe the practice of a custom as complete in detail as the one here undertaken. While the data presented are drawn from many contemporary descriptions, usually quite brief, it should be acknowledged that a large measure of reliance was placed on the record of these two tournaments held in Mexico City in 1682 and 1683 contained in the *Triunfo Parténico* of Carlos de Sigüenza y Góngora, published in that city in 1683 and reprinted there in 1945 in the Biblioteca Mexicana de Libros Raros y Curiosos (Ediciones Xochitl), with a prologue by José Rojas Garcidueñas. Of incidental interest is Francisco Pérez Salazar, "Los concursos literarios en Nueva España," *Revista de literatura mexicana,* 1, no. 2 (1940), pp. 290-306.

2. "El certamen de los plateros en 1618 y las coplas satíricas que de él se derivaron," *Boletín del Archivo General de la Nación* (Mexico City), 16, No. 3 (1945), pp. 343-84.

3. Carlos de Sigüenza y Góngora, *Triunfo Parténico* (Mexico, 1945), p. 137.

4. These regulations are taken from Pedro de Peralta Barnuevo, *El Cielo en el Parnaso, cartel del certamen que . . . la Real Universidad de San Marcos de Lima . . .* (Lima, 1736), no pagination. They are reproduced in José Toribio Medina, *La imprenta en Lima* (Santiago de Chile, 1904), 4 vols., vol. II, pp. 386-87.

5. Part II, chap. 18. Quoted from the Putnam translation with the permission of the Viking Press, Inc., New York.

6. Luis Antonio Eguigurén, *El paseo triunfal y el vejamen del graduando,* Biblioteca del cuarto centenario de la fundación del la Universidad Major de San Marcos (Lima, 1949).

CHAPTER X

1. Juan Martínez de Jáuregui, *Discurso poético* (Madrid, 1624).

2. Gerald Brenan, *The Literature of the Spanish People* (New York, Cambridge, 1951), p. 252.

3. Irving A. Leonard, "Some Curiosities of Spanish Colonial Poetry," *Hispania,* 15, no. 1 (1932), pp. 39-54.

4. Part II, chap. 18. Quoted from the Putnam translation with the permission of the Viking Press, Inc., New York.

5. Reprinted in José Toribio Medina, *La Imprenta en Lima* (Santiago de Chile, 1904), 4 vols., vol. III, pp. 463-64.

6. From "The Sea Nymphes Dittie," in R. Warwick Bond, *The Complete Works of John Lyly* (Oxford, 1902), 3 vols., vol. I, p. 443.

7. Carlos de Sigüenza y Góngora, *Triunfo parténico* (Mexico City, 1945), p. 216.

8. Ricardo Palma, *Flor de academias* (Lima, 1899), p. 289.

9. Quoted in Medina, *op. cit.,* vol. II, p. 503.

10. *Ibid., loc. cit.*

11. Sigüenza y Góngora, *op. cit.,* p. 230.

12. *Ibid.,* p. 206.

13. *Ibid.,* p. 213.

14. Francisco Pimentel, *Historia crítica de la literatura y de las ciencias en México* (Mexico City, 1885), p. 140.

15. Vicente Riva Palacio, *México através de los siglos* (Barcelona, 1888-89), 5 vols., vol. II, pp. 751-52.

16. Sigüenza y Góngora, *op. cit.,* p. 216.

17. *Ibid.,* p. 219; Irving A. Leonard, "Some Góngora Centones in Mexico," *Hispania,* 12, No. 6 (1929), pp. 568-69.

18. Ricardo Palma, *op. cit.*, acta décima cuarta.
19. *Ibid.*, acta décima sexta.
20. *Ibid.*, p. 258.

CHAPTER XI

1. These details are drawn from the description by Leonel Waffer entitled "La Ciudad de México en 1678," in Artemio de Valle-Arizpe, *Historia de la Ciudad de México según los relatos de sus cronistas* (Mexico City, 1939), pp. 453-57. Also useful was the Fer map of 1715 reproduced in Luis González Obregón, *México Viejo* (Paris, Mexico City, 1900), opposite p. 579. A key to the streets and buildings indicated on the Fer map is given in the appendix of the same work.

2. Agustín de Vetancourt, quoted in Salvador de Madariaga, *The Fall of the Spanish American Empire* (London, 1947), p. 53.

3. Francisco Sosa, *El episcopado mexicano* (Mexico City, 1877), p. 150.

4. Joseph de Lezamis, *Vida del Apóstol Santiago el Mayor* (Mexico City, 1699). This work contains a prefatory biography of Aguiar y Seijas, without pagination.

5. Francesco Gemelli Careri, *Giro del mondo parte sesta* (Naples, 1721), p. 150. There are good modern Spanish translations of this interesting account.

6. Vicente Riva Palacio, *México através de los siglos* (Barcelona, 1888-89), 5 vols., vol. II, chap. xv.

7. *Loc. cit.*

8. Ezequiel A. Chávez, *Ensayo de psicología de Sor Juana Inés de la Cruz* (Barcelona, 1931), p. 452.

9. Gemelli Careri, quoted in Valle-Arizpe, *op. cit.*, p. 377.

10. Cf. José Toribio Medina, *La imprenta en Mexico, 1539-1821* (Santiago de Chile, 1907-1912), 8 vols., vol. I, p. cxxviii; Francisco Pérez Salazar, "Dos familias de impresores mexicanos del siglo XVII," *Memorias de la sociedad científica Antonio Alzate* (Mexico City), 43 (1925), pp. 447 ff.

11. Sigüenza y Góngora gives a highly laudatory account of this individual in the fragment of his *Piedad heroyca de don Fernando Cortés* in Francisco Pérez Salazar (ed), *Carlos de Sigüenza y Góngora. Obras* (Mexico City: Sociedad de Bibliófilos Mexicanos, 1928), pp. 331-40.

12. This inventory is in the Archivo General de la Nación, Mexico City, *Ramo de la Inquisición*, tomo 661, fol. 40-47v, and is reproduced in Irving A. Leonard, "On the Mexican Book Trade, 1683," *Hispanic American Historical Review*, 27, no. 3 (1947), pp. 419-35.

This document, which I discovered and photographed in 1940, is not included in the interesting collection of similar book lists assembled by Edmundo O'Gorman and published as "Bibliotecas y librerías coloniales, 1585-1694," in *Boletín del Archivo General de la Nación* (Mexico City), X, no. 4 (dated 1939, but published subsequently), pp. 663-1006. Document XD of this collection is a 1655 *memoria* (1,126 titles) of the bookshop of the Viuda de Bernardo Calderón, as is Document XVI (1,239 titles), a *memoria* of the year 1660.

13. These and the following details relating to the Boston book trade are gleaned from Thomas G. Wright, *Literary Culture in Early New England, 1620-1730* (New Haven, 1920), and Samuel E. Morison, *The Puritan Pronaos. Intellectual Life of New England in the Seventeenth Century* (New York University Press, 1936).

14. Tom B. Jones, "The Classics in Colonial Hispanic America," *Transactions of the American Philological Association*, 70 (1939), pp. 37-45.

15. James D. Hart, *The Popular Book. A History of America's Taste* (New York, 1950), p. 16. Quoted with permission of the Oxford University Press, Inc., New York.

CHAPTER XII

1. Arturo Torres-Ríoseco, *New World Literature, Tradition, and Revolt in Latin America* (Berkeley, 1949), p. 40. There are numerous biographical studies of the nun-poetess; perhaps the best to date is Anita Arroyo, *Razón y pasión de Sor Juana Inés de la Cruz* (Mexico City, 1952).

2. Interesting data on life in colonial convents are given in Josefina Muriel, *Conventos de monjas en la Nueva España* (Mexico City, 1946).

3. Frederick B. Luquiens, "Spanish American Literature," *Yale Review Quarterly*, XVII, no. 3 (1928).

4. Francisco López Cámara, "El cartesianismo en Sor Juana y Sigüenza y Góngora," *Filosofía y letras* (Mexico City), no. 39 (1950).

5. Particularly interesting in this connection are: Ezequiel Chávez, *Ensayo de Psicología de Sor Juana Inés de la Cruz* (Barcelona, 1931); and Ludwig Pfandl, *Die zehnte Muse von Mexico Juana Ines de la Cruz. Ihr Leben, Ihre Dichtung. Ihre Psyche.* (Muenchen, 1946).

6. Julio Jiménez Rueda, *Sor Juana Inés de la Cruz en su época (1651-1951)* (Mexico City, 1951), p. 76.

7. Original text of the sonnets:

Al que ingrato me deja, busco amante;

al que amante me sigue, dejo ingrata;
constante adoro a quien mi amor maltrata;
maltrato a quien mi amor busca constante.
Al que trato de amor hallo diamante;
y soy diamante al que de amor me trata;
triunfante quiero ver al que me mata
y mato a quien me quiere ver triunfante.
Si a éste pago, padece mi deseo:
si ruego a aquél, mi pundonor enojo:
de entrambos modos infeliz me veo.
Pero yo por mejor partido escojo
de quien no quiero ser violento empleo,
que de quien no me quiere, vil despojo.

. . . .

Feliciano me adora y le aborrezco;
Lisardo me aborrece y yo le adoro;
por quien no me apetece ingrato, lloro
y al que me llora tierno, no apetezco:
a quien más me desdora, el alma ofrezco;
a quien me ofrece víctimas, desdoro;
desprecio al que enriquece mi decoro
y al que le hace desprecios enriquezco;
si con mi ofensa al uno reconvengo,
me reconviene el otro a mí ofendido
y al padecer de todos modos vengo;
pues ambos atormentan mi sentido:
aquéste con pedir lo que no tengo
y aquél con no tener lo que le pido.

. . . .

Que no me quiera Fabio al verse amado
es dolor sin igual, en mi sentido;
mas que me quiera Silvio aborrecido
es menor mal, mas no menor enfado.
¿Que sufrimiento no estará cansado,
si siempre le resuenan al oído,
tras la vana arrogancia de un querido,
el cansado gemir de un desdeñado?
Si de Silvio me cansa el rendimiento,
a Fabio canso con estar rendida:
si de este busco el agradecimiento,
por activa y pasiva es mi tormento,
pues padezco en querer y ser querida.

. . . .

Translation of the first sonnet is by Pauline Cook in *The Pathless Grove* (Prairie City, Ill.: Decher Press, 1951), and is quoted with her permission; the second by S. G. Morley in Torres-Ríoseco, *op. cit.*, p. 218, and is quoted by permission of the University of California Press; and the third by Peter H. Goldsmith in Thomas Walsh, *Hispanic Anthology: Poems Translated from the Spanish by English and North American Poets* (New York, London, 1920).
These sonnets and other poems cited in this discussion are available

in Alfonso Méndez Plancarte, *Obras Completas de Sor Juana Inés de la Cruz* (Mexico City, 1951-57), 4 vols., vol. I, Lírica Personal. Edición, prólogo y notas de . . . Poems are indexed by the first verse.

8. *Obras completas*, vol. i, p. 531; and especially Carlos González Echegaray, "Sor Juana y Frey Lope," *Boletín de la Biblioteca Menéndez y Pelayo*, 24 (1948), pp. 281-89.

9. Pfandl, *op. cit., passim;* Arroyo, *op. cit., passim;* José María de Cossío, "Observaciones sobre la vida y la obra de Sor Juana Inés de la Cruz," *Boletín de la Real Academia Espanola* (Madrid), 32 (1952), pp. 27-47; *see also* Jose María Pemán, "Sinceridad y artificio en la poesía de Sor Juana Inés de la Cruz," *ibid.,* pp. 55-72.

10. The text of this *Respuesta* is in vol. IV of the *Obras completas*.

11. *Obras completas*, vol. I, p. 6, verses 57-60.

12. Translated by Pauline Cook, *op. cit.,* p. 25, and quoted with her permission.

13. The text of this letter of the Bishop of Puebla, Manuel Fernández de Santa Cruz to Sor Juana Inés is reproduced in *Sor Juana Inés de la Cruz. Carta Atenagórica. Respuesta a Sor Filotea.* Edición, prologo, y notas de E. Abreu Gómez. Clásicos Mexicanos (Mexico City, 1934), pp. 46-48.

14. Cossío, *op. cit.,* p. 36.

15. Lancelot Law Whyte, *The Next Development in Man* (New York, 1950), pp. 106, 107.

16. Cf. Irving A. Leonard, *Books of the Brave* (Cambridge: Harvard Press 1949), *passim.* Regarding works in Sister Juana's library, see E. Abreu Gómez, *Sor Juana Inés de la Cruz. Bibliografía y Biblioteca.* Monografías Bibliográficas Mexicanas, 29 (Mexico City, 1934), *passim.*

17. López Cámara, *op. cit.,* p. 129.

18. *Ibid.,* pp. 122-23. Sigüenza cites Descartes in his *Libra astronómica y filosófica* (Mexico City, 1690).

19. Translation of Robert Graves, in *Encounter,* no. 3 (December, 1953), and quoted with his permission.

20. Carlos de Sigüenza y Góngora, *Teatro de virtudes políticas,* in Francisco Pérez Salazar, *Obras de Carlos de Sigüenza y Góngora* (Mexico City, 1928), p. 38.

CHAPTER XIII

1. This and numerous other quotations in this chapter are from the long letter of Sigüenza y Góngora addressed to Admiral Andrés de

Pez in Madrid. It was entitled *Alboroto y motín de los Indios de México del 8 de Junio de 1692,* a contemporary copy of which is preserved in the Bancroft Library of the University of California (Berkeley). A translation appears as Appendix B of Irving A. Leonard, *Don Carlos de Sigüenza y Góngora, A Mexican Savant of the Seventeenth Century* (Berkeley, 1929). From this copy an annotated edition by Irving A. Leonard was made in 1932 and published by the National Museum, Mexico City. In 1940 (again in 1954) it was reprinted in shortened form in Manuel Romero de Terreros (ed), *Carlos de Sigüenza y Góngora. Relaciones históricas.* Biblioteca del estudiante universitario, 13 (Mexico City). On the life of this Creole scholar the biography of Leonard cited above still remains the fullest treatment. A shorter life is that of José Rojas Garcidueñas, *Don Carlos de Sigüenza y Góngora, erudito barroco.* Vidas Mexicanas 23 (Mexico City, 1945). Sigüenza's verse is available in *Carlos de Sigüenza y Góngora. Poemas.* Recopilados por Irving A. Leonard. Estudio preliminar de E. Abreu Gómez. Biblioteca de Historia Hispanoamericana (Madrid, 1931).

2. Cf. Edmundo O'Gorman, "Datos sobre D. Carlos de Sigüenza y Góngora, 1669-1677," *Boletín del Archivo General de la Nación de Mexico,* 15, No. 4 (1944), pp. 593-612, and E. J. Burrus, "Sigüenza y Góngora's efforts for readmission into the Jesuit Order," *Hispanic American Historical Review,* 33 (1953), p. 387.

3. This interesting will of Sigüenza is printed in Francisco Pérez Salazar, *Biografía de D. Carlos de Sigüenza y Góngora, seguida de varios documentos inéditos* (Mexico City, 1928), pp. 161-92.

4. *The Trophy of Spanish Justice* and the account of the Windward Fleet are reprinted in Pérez Salazar (ed.), *Obras de Carlos de Sigüenza y Góngora.* The *Mercurio Volante* or *Flying Mercury* was published by the Quivira Society in facsimile with a translation and introduction by Irving A. Leonard, *The Mercurio Volante of Sigüenza y Góngora. An Account of the First Expedition of Don Diego de Vargas into New Mexico in 1692* (Los Angeles, 1932). Regarding the corn riot of the Indians, see note 1.

5. The text of *Infortunios de Alonso Ramírez* is available in vol. 20 of the *Colección de libros raros y curiosos que tratan de América* (Madrid, 1902), and in Manuel Romero de Terreros, *Relaciones Históricas de Carlos de Sigüenza y Góngora* (Mexico City, 1940, 1954).

6. This exceedingly rare pamphlet is reprinted in modernized form in *Universidad de Mexico,* 11, No. 11 (1957), pp. 17-19.

7. There is no modern edition of this important treatise. The text here used was a photostatic copy in the Bancroft Library of the University of California (Berkeley), from an original preserved in the John Crerar Library of Chicago, Ill.

8. Concerning Father Kino, see Herbert Eugene Bolton, *Rim of Christendom* (New York, 1936).

9. Gerard Decorme, S. J., *La obra de los jesuitas mexicanos, durante la Época Colonial, 1572-1767* (Mexico City), vol. 1, p. 231.

10. For a full account, see Irving A. Leonard, *The Spanish Approach to Pensacola, 1689-1693*, Quivira Society Publications, vol. 9 (Albuquerque, 1939).

11. This letter, dated May 9, 1699, is printed in Pérez Salazar, *Biografía, . . .*, pp. 119-60. A detailed account of the Pensacola project as a whole is given in William E. Dunn, *Spanish and French Rivalry in the Gulf Region of the United States, 1678-1702, University of Texas Bulletin, No. 1705* (Austin, 1917), and of Arriola's part in Irving A. Leonard, "Don Andrés de Arriola and the Occupation of Pensacola Bay," in *New Spain and the Anglo-American West*, Historical Contributions Presented to Herbert Eugene Bolton (Los Angeles, 1932), 2 vols., vol. 1, pp. 81-106.

12. Antonio de Robles, "Diario de sucesos notables," *Documentos para la historia de México*, Series 1, vols. II and III (Mexico City, 1853), vol. III, p. 262.

CHAPTER XIV

1. Pierre Margry, *Decouvertes et etablissements des Français dans l'ouest et dans le sud de l'Amerique Septentrionale, 1614-1756* (Paris, 1879-1888), 6 vols., vol. IV., p. 351.

2. Carlos de Sigüenza y Góngora, *Parayso Occidental* (Mexico City, 1684), prologue.

3. *Teatro de virtudes politicas que constituye un principe: Advertidas en los monarcas antiguos del Mexicano Imperio . . .* (Mexico City, 1680), reprinted in Francisco Pérez Salazar, *Obras de Carlos de Sigüenza y Góngora con una biografía* (Mexico City, 1928), p. 1-148. See also Francisco López Cámara, "La Conciencia criolla en Sor Juana y Sigüenza," *Historia mexicana*, 6 (1957), no. 3, pp. 350-73. Hermenegildo Corbató, "La emergencia de la idea de nacionalidad en el México colonial," *Revista Iberoamericana*, 6 (1943), pp. 377-92.

A BRIEF BIBLIOGRAPHY

Alemán, Mateo. *Sucesos de D. Frai Garcia Gera Arcobispo de Mejico* . . . Critical edition of Alice H. Bushee, *Revue hispanique* (New York-Paris, 1911), vol. 25, pp. 1-99.

Andrade, Vicente de Paula. *Ensayo bibliográfico mexicano del siglo XVII* (Mexico City, 1899).

Arróm, José J. *El teatro de Hispanoamérica en la Época Colonial* (Havana, 1956).

Arroyo, Anita. *Razón y pasión de Sor Juana Inés de la Cruz* (Mexico City, 1952).

Balbuena, Bernardo de. *La grandeza mexicana*. Biblioteca del Estudiante Universitario, 23 (Mexico City, 1954).

Bancroft, Hubert Howe. *History of Mexico* (San Francisco, 1883-88), 6 vols.

Bolton, Herbert Eugene. *Rim of Christendom* (New York, 1936).

Borah, Woodrow. *New Spain's Century of Depression*. Ibero-Americana series, 25 (Berkeley, 1951).

Carilla, Emilio. *El gongorismo en América* (Buenos Aires, 1946).

Carreño, Alberto (ed.). *Gonzalo Gómez de Cervantes. La vida económica y social de Nueva España al finalizar el siglo XVI* (Mexico City, 1944).

Cavo, Andrés. *Los tres siglos de México durante el gobierno español* . . . (Mexico City, 1936-38), 4 vols.

Cepeda, Fernando, y Carrillo, Fernando Alonso. *Relación universal legítima y verdadera del sitio en que está fundada la muy noble, insigne, y leal Ciudad de México* . . . (Mexico City, 1637).

Chávez, Ezequiel A. *Ensayo de psicología de Sor Juana Inés de la Cruz* (Barcelona, 1931).

Conway, G. R. G. (ed.). *Friar Francisco Naranjo and the Old University of Mexico* (Mexico City, 1939).

Cuevas, Mariano, S. J. *Historia de la Iglesia en México* (Tlalpam, D. F., Mexico, 1921-24), 3 vols.

245

Diggs, Irene. "Color in Colonial Spanish America," *Journal of Negro History*, 2 (1953), pp. 405-27.

Friedrich, Carl J. *The Age of the Baroque, 1610-1660* (New York, 1952).

García, Genaro (ed.). *Documentos inéditos o muy raros para la historia de México* (Mexico City, 1905-11) 35 vols.

Gemelli Careri, Juan Francisco. *Viaje a la Nueva España* (Mexico City, 1927).

González Obregón, Luis. *The Streets of Mexico*. Translated by B. C. Wagner (San Francisco, 1937).

———. *D. Guillén de Lampart. La Inquisición y la independencia en el siglo XVII* (Mexico City, 1908).

———.*México Viejo* (Paris, Mexico City, 1900).

Guijo, Gregorio Martín de. *Diario de sucesos notables*. Documentos para la historia de México (Mexico City, 1853).

Jiménez Rueda, Julio. *Herejías y supersticiones en la Nueva España. Los heterodoxos en México* (Mexico City, 1946).

Kelemen, Pál. *Baroque and Rococo in Latin America* (New York, 1951).

Lea, Charles Henry. *The Inquisition in the Spanish Dependencies* (New York, 1908).

Leonard, Irving A. *Don Carlos de Sigüenza y Góngora, A Mexican Savant of the Seventeenth Century* (Berkeley, 1929).

———. *Alboroto y Motín de los indios de México del 8 de junio de 1692* (Mexico City, 1932).

———. *The Spanish Approach to Pensacola, 1689-1693*. Quivira Society Publications, vol. 9 (Albuquerque, 1939).

Madariaga, Salvador de. *The Fall of the Spanish American Empire* (London, 1947).

Marroqui, J. M. *La Ciudad de México* (Mexico City, 1900-1903: 3 vols.).

Maza, Francisco de la. *Enrico Martínez, cosmógrafo e impresor de Nueva España* (Mexico City, 1943).

Medina, Baltasar de. *Crónica de la Santa Provincia de San Diego* (Mexico City, 1682).

Medina, José Toribio. *La Imprenta en México (1539-1821)* (Santiago de Chile, 1907-1912), 8 vols.

Méndez Plancarte, Alfonso. *Poetas novohispanos. Primer siglo 1521-1621*. Biblioteca del Estudiante Universitario, 33 (Mexico City, 1942).

Méndez Plancarte, Alfonso, and Alberto G. Salcedo. *Obras completas de Sor Juana Inés de la Cruz* (Mexico City, 1951-57), 4 vols.

Morison, Samuel E. *The Puritan Pronaos. Intellectual Life in New England in the Seventeenth Century* (New York, 1936).

Muriel, Josefina. *Conventos de monjas en la Nueva España* (Mexico City, 1946).

Newton, A. P. (ed.). *Thomas Gage. The English American. A New Survey of the West Indies, 1648* (London, Guatemala City, 1946).

Pérez Salazar, Francisco (ed.). *Obras de Don Carlos de Sigüenza y Góngora* (Mexico City, 1928).

———. *Biografía de D. Carlos de Sigüenza y Góngora, seguida de varios documentos inéditos* (Mexico City, 1928).

Picón-Salas, Mariano. *A Cultural History of Spanish America: From Conquest to Independence.* Translated by Irving A. Leonard. (Berkeley, 1962, paperback edition, 1963).

Pimentel, Francisco. *Historia crítica de la literatura y de las ciencias en México* (Mexico City, 1885).

Rangel, Nicolás (ed.). *Cristóbal de la Plaza y Jaén. Crónica de la Real y Pontificia Universidad de México* . . . (Mexico City, 1931), 2 vols.

———. *Historia del toreo en México: Época Colonial, 1529-1821* (Mexico City, 1924).

Riva Palacio, Vicente. *México através de los siglos* (Barcelona, 1888-89), 5 vols.

Rivera, Juan Antonio. *Diario curioso de México.* Documentos para la Historia de México, series 1, vol. 7 (Mexico City, 1854).

Rivera Cambas, Manuel. *Los gobernantes de México* (Mexico City, 1872-1873), 2 vols.

Robles, Antonio de. *Diario de sucesos notables.* Documentos para la historia de México, series 1, vols. 2, 3 (Mexico City, 1853).

Rojas Garcidueñas, José. *Don Carlos de Sigüenza y Góngora, Erudito barroco.* Vidas mexicanas 23 (Mexico City, 1945).

———. *Bernardo de Balbuena: La vida y la obra* (Mexico City, 1958).

Romero de Terreros, Manuel. *Carlos de Sigüenza y Góngora. Relaciones históricas.* Biblioteca del Estudiante Universitario 13 (Mexico City, 1957).

Schons, Dorothy. *Notes from Spanish Archives.* Book I (Ann Arbor, Michigan, 1946).

———. *Book Censorship in New Spain* (Austin, Texas, 1949).

Sigüenza y Góngora, Carlos de. *Glorias de Querétaro en la nueva congregación eclesiástica de María Santísima de Guadalupe* (Mexico City, 1680; 1945).

————. *Triunfo parténico* (Mexico City, 1683; 1945).

————. *Teatro de virtudes políticas* . . . (Mexico City, 1680; 1928).

————. *Poemas*. Recopilado por Irving A. Leonard. Estudio preliminar de E. Abreu Gómez (Madrid, 1931).

————. *The Mercurio Volante*. Facsimile. Translation, Introduction, and Notes by Irving A. Leonard. Quivira Society Publications, vol. 2 (Los Angeles, 1932).

————. *Parayso occidental* (Mexico City, 1684).

————. *Libra astronómica y philosóphica* (Mexico City, 1690).

Sosa, Francisco. *El episcopado mexicano. Biografías de los excelentísimos señores arzobispos desde la Época Colonial hasta nuestros días* (Mexico City, 1939).

Valle-Arizpe, Artemio. *El Palacio Nacional de México* (Mexico City, 1936).

————. *Historia de la Ciudad de México según los relatos de sus cronistas* (Mexico City, 1939).

————. *Calle Vieja y Calle Nueva* (Mexico City, 1949).

Vázquez de Espinosa, Antonio. *Nueva España en el siglo XVII* (Mexico City, 1944).

Vetancourt, Augustín de. *Teatro mexicano* (Mexico City, 1698; 1870-1871), 4 vols.

Wright, Thomas G. *Literary Culture in Early New England, 1620-1730* (New Haven, 1920).

INDEX

This index does not include the documentary references which are assembled on pages 229-44. Except in certain proper names, including titles of books, the definite and indefinite articles, whether in Spanish or English, are disregarded in alphabetizing subject matter.

Ann Arbor Paperbacks

MW00756002

THE DARKNESS IS COMING,
AND I DON'T KNOW IF I CAN STOP IT...
OR IF I WILL SURVIVE IT.

Book Four

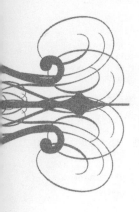 

sweep

Cate Tiernan

DARK MAGICK

speak

An Imprint of Penguin Group (USA) Inc.

All quoted materials in this work were created by the author.
Any resemblance to existing works is accidental.

Dark Magick

SPEAK
Published by the Penguin Group
Penguin Young Readers Group, 345 Hudson Street, New York, New York 10014, U.S.A.
Penguin Group (Canada), 90 Eglinton Avenue East, Suite 700, Toronto, Ontario, Canada M4P 2Y3
(a division of Pearson Penguin Canada Inc.)
Penguin Books Ltd, 80 Strand, London WC2R 0RL, England
Penguin Ireland, 25 St Stephen's Green, Dublin 2, Ireland (a division of Penguin Books Ltd)
Penguin Group (Australia), 250 Camberwell Road, Camberwell, Victoria 3124, Australia
(a division of Pearson Australia Group Pty Ltd)
Penguin Books India Pvt Ltd, 11 Community Centre, Panchsheel Park, New Delhi - 110 017, India
Penguin Group (NZ), 67 Apollo Drive, Mairangi Bay, Auckland 1311, New Zealand
(a division of Pearson New Zealand Ltd)
Penguin Books (South Africa) (Pty) Ltd, 24 Sturdee Avenue, Rosebank, Johannesburg 2196, South Africa

Registered Offices: Penguin Books Ltd, 80 Strand, London WC2R 0RL, England

Published by Puffin Books, a division of Penguin Young Readers Group, 2001
This edition published by Speak, an imprint of Penguin Group (USA), Inc, 2007

1 3 5 7 9 10 8 6 4 2

Copyright © 2001 17th Street Productions, an Alloy company,
and Gabrielle Charbonnet
All rights reserved

Produced by 17th Street Productions,
an Alloy company
151 West 26th Street
New York, NY 10001

17th Street Productions and associated logos
are trademarks and/or registered trademarks of Alloy, Inc.

Speak ISBN 978-0-14-240989-3

Printed in the United States of America

Except in the United States of America, this book is sold subject to the condition that
it shall not, by way of trade or otherwise, be lent, re-sold, hired out, or otherwise
circulated without the publisher's prior consent in any form of binding or cover
other than that in which it is published and without a similar condition
including this condition being imposed on the subsequent purchaser.

The publisher does not have any control over and does not assume any
responsibility for author or third-party Web sites or their content.

For my mùirn beatha dàn

1

Falling

November 1999

The council pronounced me not guilty of killing Linden. The vote of the seven elders of the Great Clans was not unanimous, though. The Vikroth representative and the Wyndenkell, my mother's own clanswoman, voted against me.

I had almost hoped they would condemn me, for then at least my life's path would be certain. And in a way, I was guilty, was I not? I filled Linden's head with my talk of vengeance, and opened his mind to the idea of calling on the darkness. If I had not actually killed my brother, then I knew he had found his way to his death along a path I had shown him.

When I was found innocent, I felt lost. I knew only that I would spend the rest of my life atoning for Linden's death.

—Giomanach

Snowflakes mixed with sleet whipped at my cheeks. I stumbled through the snow, supporting my boyfriend Cal's weight against me, my feet growing leaden and icy in my clogs. Cal stumbled, and I braced myself. In the moonlight I peered up at his face, alarmed by how white he looked, how beaten, how ill. I trudged through the dark woods, feeling like every step away from the cliff took an hour.

The cliff. In my mind, I saw Hunter Niall falling backward, his arms windmilling as he went over the edge. Bile rose in my throat, and I swallowed convulsively. Yes, Cal was a mess, but Hunter was probably dead. Dead! And Cal and I had killed him. I drew in a shuddering breath as Cal swayed against me.

Together we stumbled through the woods, accompanied only by the malevolent hiss of the sleet in the black branches around us. Where was Cal's house?

"Are we headed the right way?" I asked Cal. The freezing wind snatched the words from my throat.

Cal blinked. One eye was swollen shut and already purple. His beautiful mouth was bloody, and his lower lip was split.

"Never mind," I said, looking ahead. "I think this is it."

By the time Cal's house was in view, we were both soaked through and frozen. Anxiously I scanned the circular driveway for Selene Belltower's car, but Cal's mother was still out. Not good. I needed help.

"Tired," Cal said fuzzily as I helped him up the steps. Somehow we made it through the front door, but once inside, there was no way I could get him up to his attic room.

"There." Cal gestured with a hand swollen from punching Hunter. Feeling unbearably weary, I lurched through the parlor doors and helped Cal collapse on the blue sofa. He toppled over, curling to fit on the cushions.

He was shaking with cold, his face shocked and pale.

"Cal," I said, "we need to call 911. About Hunter. Maybe they can find him. It might not be too late."

Cal's face crinkled in a grotesque approximation of a laugh. His split lip oozed blood, and his cheek was mottled with angry bruises. "It's too late," he croaked, his teeth chattering. "I'm positive." He nodded toward the fireplace, his eyes shut. "Fire."

Was it too late for Hunter? A tiny part of me almost hoped it was—if Hunter was dead, then we couldn't help him, and I didn't even have to try.

But was he? A sob rose in my throat. Was he?

Okay, I thought, trying to calm down. Okay. Break down the situation. Make a plan. I knelt and clumsily piled newspaper and kindling on the grate. I chose three large logs and arranged them on top.

I didn't see any matches, so, closing my eyes, I tried to summon fire with my mind. But my magickal powers felt almost nonexistent. In fact, just trying to call on them made my head ache sharply. After nearly seventeen years of living without magick, to find myself bereft of it now was terrifying. I opened my eyes and looked wildly around. Finally I saw an Aim 'n' Flame on the mantel, and I grabbed it and popped its trigger.

The paper and kindling caught. I swayed toward the flames, feeling their healing warmth, then I glanced at Cal again. He looked wretched.

"Cal?" I helped him sit up enough to tug him out of his leather jacket, taking care not to scrape his wrists, which were raw and blistered where Hunter had tried to bind them with a strange magickal chain. I pulled off Cal's wet boots. Then I covered him up with a patchwork velvet throw that was draped artistically over one end of the couch. He squeezed my fingers and tried to smile at me.

"Be right back," I said, and hurried to the kitchen. I felt horribly alone as I waited for water to boil. I ran upstairs and rummaged through the first bathroom I found for bandages, then went back down and fixed a pot of herb tea. A pale face with accusing green eyes seemed to form in the steam that rose from the top of the teapot. Hunter, oh, God, Hunter.

Hunter had tried to kill Cal, I reminded myself. He might have tried to kill me, too. Still, it was Hunter who had gone over the edge of the cliff into the Hudson River, the river filled with ice chunks as big as his head. It was Hunter who had probably been swept away by the current and Hunter whose body would be found tomorrow. Or not. I clamped my lips together to keep from sobbing as I hurried back to Cal.

Slowly I got Cal to drink a whole mug of goldenseal-and-ginger tea. His color looked better when he had finished it. I gently swabbed his wrists with a damp cloth, then wrapped them with a roll of gauze I had found, but the skin was blistered, and I knew it must hurt incredibly.

After the tea Cal lay down again and slept, his breathing uneven. Should I have given him Tylenol? Should I hunt around for witch-type medicine? In the short while I had known Cal, he had been the strong one in our relationship. I had counted on him. Now he was counting on me, and I didn't know if I was ready.

The mantel clock above my head struck three slow chimes. I stared at it. Three o'clock in the morning! I set my mug down on the coffee table. I was supposed to be home by one. And I didn't even have my car—Cal had picked me up. He was clearly in no shape to drive. Selene wasn't back yet. Dammit! I said to myself. Think, think.

I could call my dad and have him come get me. Very unappealing option.

It was too late to call the only taxi service in Widow's Vale, which was in essence Ed Jinkins in his old Cutlass Supreme hanging out at the commuter station.

I could take Cal's car.

Five minutes later I let myself out of the house carefully. Cal was still asleep. I had taken the keys from his jacket, then written a note of explanation and tucked it in his jeans pocket, hoping he would understand. I stopped dead when I saw Hunter's gray sedan sitting in the driveway like an accusation. Crap! What to do about his car?

There was nothing I could do. Hunter had the keys. And he was gone. I couldn't push the car anywhere by myself and anyway, that seemed so—methodical somehow. So planned.

My head spun. What should I do? Waves of exhaustion flowed over me, almost making me weep. But I had to accept the fact that I couldn't do anything about this. Cal or Selene would have to deal with Hunter's car. Trembling, I climbed into Cal's gold Explorer, turned on the brights, and headed for home.

Cal had used spells on me tonight, spells of binding so I couldn't move. Why? So I wouldn't interfere in his battle with Hunter? So I wouldn't be hurt? Or because he didn't trust me? Well, if he hadn't trusted me before, he knew better now. I clamped my teeth together on a semihysterical giggle. It wasn't every girl who would throw a Wiccan ceremonial dagger into the neck of her boyfriend's enemy.

Hunter had tried to kill Cal, had bound his hands with spelled silver chain that had started to sizzle against Cal's flesh as soon as it touched him. That was when I'd hurled the athame at him and sent him over the cliff's edge. And probably killed him. Killed him.

I shuddered as I turned onto my street. *Had* we actually killed him? Did Hunter have a chance? Maybe the wound in his neck wasn't as horrific as it had seemed. Maybe, when he went over the cliff, he had landed on a ledge. Maybe he was found by a park ranger or someone like that.

Maybe.

I let the Explorer drift to a halt around the corner from my house. As I pocketed the keys, I noticed all the birthday gifts Cal had given me earlier, piled up on the backseat. Well, almost all. The beautiful athame was gone—Hunter had taken it over the cliff with him. With a sense of unreality I gathered up the other gifts and then ran home down the shoveled and salted walks. I let myself in silently, feeling with my senses. Again my magick was like a single match being held in a storm wind instead of the powerful wave I was used to feeling. I couldn't detect much of anything.

To my relief, my parents didn't stir as I went past their bedroom door. In my own room I sat for a moment on the edge of my bed, collecting my strength. After the nightmarish events of tonight my bedroom looked babyish, as if it belonged to a stranger. The pink-and-white-striped walls, flowered border, and frilly curtains had never been me, anyway. Mom had picked everything out and redone the room for me as a surprise while I was at camp, six years ago.

I threw off my clammy clothes and sighed with relief as I

pulled on sweats. Then I went downstairs and dialed 911.

"What is the nature of the emergency?" a crisp voice asked.

"I saw someone fall into the Hudson," I said quickly, speaking through a tissue like they did in old movies. "About two miles up from the North Bridge." This was an estimate, based on where I thought Cal's house was. "Someone fell in. He may need help." I hung up quickly, hoping I hadn't stayed on the phone long enough for the call to be traced. How did that work? Did I have to stay on for a minute? Thirty seconds? Oh, Jesus. If they tracked me down I would confess everything. I couldn't live with this burden on my soul.

My mind was racing with everything that had happened: my wonderful, romantic birthday with Cal; almost making love but then backing out; all my gifts; the magick we shared; my birth mother's athame, which I had shown Cal tonight and was now clutching like a security blanket; then the battle with Hunter, the horror as he fell. And now it was too late, Cal said. But was it? I had to try one last thing.

I put on my wet coat, went outside, and walked around the side of my house in the darkness. Holding my birth mother's athame, I leaned close to a windowsill. There, glowing faintly beneath the knife's power, shimmered a sigil. Sky Eventide and Hunter had surrounded my house with the charms; I still didn't know why. But I hoped this would work.

Once more closing my eyes, I held the athame over the sigil. I concentrated, feeling like I was about to pass out. Sky, I thought, swallowing. Sky.

I hated Sky Eventide. Everything about her filled me with loathing and distrust, just as Hunter did, though for some reason Hunter upset me more. But she was his ally, and she was the person who should be told about him. I sent my thought out toward the purplish snow clouds. Sky. Hunter is in the river, by Cal's house. Go get him. He needs your help.

What am I doing? I thought, beyond weariness. I can't even light a match. I can't feel my family sleeping inside my house. My magick is gone. But still I stood there in the cold darkness, my eyes closed, my hand turning to a frozen claw around the knife handle. Hunter is in the river. Go get him. Go get Hunter. Hunter is in the river.

Tears came without warning, shockingly warm against my chilled cheeks. Gasping, I stumbled back inside and hung up my coat. Then I slowly mounted the steps, one by one, and was dimly surprised when I made it to the top. I hid my mother's athame under my mattress and crawled into bed. My kitten, Dagda, stretched sleepily, then moved up to coil himself next to my neck. I curled one hand around him. Huddled under my comforter, I shook with cold and wept until the first blades of sunlight pierced the childish, ruffled curtains at my window.

2

Guilty

November 1999

Uncle Beck, Aunt Shelagh, and Cousin Athan held a small celebration for me back at the house, after the trial. But my heart was full of pain.

I sat at the kitchen table. Aunt Shelagh and Alwyn were swooping around, arranging food on plates. Then Uncle Beck came in. He told me that I'd been cleared of the blame and I must let it go.

"How can I?" I asked. It was I who'd first tried to use dark magick to find our parents. Though Linden had acted alone in calling on the dark spectre that killed him, he wouldn't have had the idea if I hadn't put it into his head.

Then Alwyn spoke up. She said I was wrong, that Linden had always liked the dark side. She said he liked the power, and that he'd thought making herb mixtures was beneath him. Her halo of corkscrew curls, fiery red like our Mum's, seemed to quiver as she spoke.

"What are you on about?" I asked her. "Linden never mentioned any of this to me."

She said Linden had believed I wouldn't understand. He'd told her he wanted to be the most powerful witch anyone had ever seen. Her words were like needles in my heart.

Uncle Beck asked why she hadn't told us sooner, and she said she had. I saw her jut her chin in that obstinate way she has. And Aunt Shelagh thought about it, and said, "You know, she did. She did tell me. I thought she was telling stories."

Alwyn said no one had believed her because she was just a kid. Then she left the room, while Uncle Beck, Aunt Shelagh, and I sat in the kitchen and weighed our guilt.

—Giomanach

I woke up on my seventeenth birthday feeling like someone had put me in a blender and set it to chop. Sleepily I blinked and checked my clock. Nine. Dawn had come at six, so I had gotten a big three hours' sleep. Great. And then I thought—is Hunter dead? Did I kill him? My stomach roiled, and I wanted to cry.

Under the covers, I felt a small warm body creeping cautiously along my side. When Dagda poked his little gray head out from under the covers, I stroked his ears.

"Hi, little guy," I said softly. I sat up just as the door to my room opened.

"Morning, Birthday Girl!" my mom said brightly. She

crossed my room and pushed aside the curtains, filling my room with brittle sunlight.

"Morning," I said, trying to sound normal. A vision of my mom finding out about Hunter made me shudder. It would destroy her.

She sat on my bed and kissed my forehead, as if I was seven instead of seventeen. Then she peered at me. "Do you feel all right?" She pressed the back of her hand against my forehead. "Hmmm. No fever. But your eyes look a bit red and puffy."

"I'm okay. Just tired," I mumbled. Time to change the subject. I had a sudden thought. "Is today really my actual birthday?" I asked.

Mom stroked my hair back from my face with a gentle hand. "Of course it is. Morgan, you've seen your birth certificate," she reminded me.

"Oh, right." Until a few weeks ago I had always believed I was a Rowlands, like the rest of my family. But when I met Cal and began exploring Wicca, it became clear that I had magickal powers and that I was a blood witch, from a long line of blood witches—witches from one of the Seven Great Clans of Wicca. That's how I'd found out I was adopted. Since then it had been pretty much of an emotional roller-coaster ride here at home. But I loved my parents, Sean and Mary Grace Rowlands, and my sister, Mary K., who was their biological daughter. And they loved me. And they were trying to come to terms with my Wiccan heritage, my legacy. As was I.

"Now, since today is your birthday, you can do what you want, more or less," Mom said, absently tickling Dagda's batlike gray ears. "Do you want to have a big breakfast and we'll go to a later mass? Or we can go to church now and then do something special for lunch?"

I don't want to go to church at all, I thought. Lately my relationship with church had seemed like a battle of wills as I struggled to integrate Wicca into my life. I also couldn't face the idea of sitting through a Catholic mass and then having lunch with my family after what had happened the night before. "Um, is it all right if I just sleep in today?" I asked. "I am feeling a little under the weather, actually. You guys do church and lunch without me."

Mom's lips thinned, but after a moment she nodded. "All right," she said. "If that's what you want." She stood up. "Do you want us to bring you back something for lunch?"

The idea of food repulsed me. "Oh, no thanks," I said, trying to sound casual. "I'll just find something in the fridge. Thanks, anyway, though."

"Okay," Mom said, touching my forehead again. "Tonight Eileen and Paula are coming over, and we'll do dinner and cake and presents. Sound good?"

"Great," I said, and Mom closed the door behind her. I sank back on my pillow. I felt as if I had a split personality. On the one hand, I was Morgan Rowlands, good daughter, honor roll student, math whiz, observant Catholic. On the other hand, I was a witch, by heritage and inclination.

I stretched, feeling the ache in my muscles. The events of the night before hovered over my head like a storm cloud. What had I done? How had I come to this? If only I knew for sure whether or not Hunter was dead ...

I waited until I heard the front door close behind my

family. Then I got up and began pulling on my clothes. I knew what I had to do next.

I drove my car to the back road that ran behind Cal's house and parked. Then I crunched across the snow to the cliff's rocky edge. Carefully I stretched out on my stomach and peered over. If I saw Hunter's body, I would have to climb down there, I warned myself. If he was alive, I would go for help. If he was dead . . . I wasn't sure what I would do.

Later I would go up to Cal's house and see how he was, but first I needed to do this, to look for Hunter. Had Sky gotten my message? Had 911 responded?

The ground around this area was churned and muddy, evidence of the horrific battle Hunter and Cal had fought. It was awful to think about it, to remember how helpless I had been under Cal's binding spell. Why had he done that to me?

I leaned over farther to try to see beneath a rocky ledge. The icy Hudson swept beneath me, clean and deadly. Sharp rocks jutted up from the riverbed. If Hunter had hit them, if he'd been in the water any length of time, he was surely dead. The thought made my stomach clench up again. In my mind I pictured Hunter falling in slow motion over the edge, his neck streaming blood, an expression of surprise on his face. . . .

"Looking for something?"

I turned quickly, already scrambling to my feet as I recognized the English-accented voice. Sky Eventide.

She stood fifteen feet away, hands in her pockets. Her pale face, whitish blond hair, and black eyes seemed etched against the painful blue of the sky.

"What are you doing here?" I said.

"I was about to ask the same thing," she said, stepping toward me. She was taller than me and as thin. Her black leather jacket didn't look warm enough for the cold.

I said nothing, and she went on, a razor's edge in her voice. "Hunter didn't come home last night. I felt his presence here. But now I don't feel it at all."

She hasn't found Hunter. Hunter's dead. Oh, Goddess, I thought.

"What happened here?" she went on, her face like stone in the cold, bright sun. "The ground looks like it was plowed. There's blood everywhere." She stepped closer to me, fierce and cold, like a Viking. "Tell me what you know about it."

"I don't know anything," I said, too loudly. *Hunter's dead.*

"You're lying. You're a lying Woodbane, just like Cal and Selene," Sky said bitterly, spitting out the words as if she were saying, You're filth, you're garbage.

The world shifted around me, became slightly unreal. There was snow beneath my feet, water below the cliff, trees behind Sky, but it was like a stage set.

"Cal and Selene aren't Woodbane," I said. My mouth was dry.

Sky tossed her head. "Of course they are," she said. "And you're just like them. You'll stop at nothing to keep your power."

"That's not true," I snapped.

"Last night Hunter was on his way to Cal's place, on council business. He was going to confront Cal. I think you were there, too, since you're Cal's little lapdog. Now tell me what happened." Her voice rang out like steel, actually hurting my ears, and I felt the strength of her personality pressing on me. I wanted to spill out everything I knew. All of a sudden I realized she was putting a spell on me. A flash of rage seared through me. How dare she?

I straightened up and deliberately walled off my mind.

Sky's eyes flickered. "You don't know what you're doing," she said, her words chipping away at me. "That makes you dangerous. I'll be watching you. And so will the council."

She whirled and disappeared into the woods, her short, sunlight-colored hair riffling in the breeze.

The woods were silent after she left. No birds chirped, no leaves stirred, the wind itself died. After several minutes I went back to my car and drove it up to Cal's house. Hunter's car was no longer there. I climbed the stone steps and rang the doorbell, feeling a fresh wash of fear as I wondered what I might find, what might have happened to Cal since I left.

Selene opened the door. She was wearing an apron, and the faint scent of herbs clung to her. There was a wealth of warmth and concern in her golden eyes as she reached out and hugged me to her. She had never hugged me before, and I closed my eyes, enjoying the lovely feeling of comfort and relief she offered.

Then Selene withdrew and looked deeply into my face. "I heard about last night. Morgan, you saved my son's life," she said, her voice low and melodious. "Thank you." She looped her arm through mine and drew me inside, shutting out the rest of the world. We walked down the hallway to the large, sunny kitchen at the back of the house.

"How is Cal?" I managed.

"He's better," she said. "Thanks to you. I came home and

found him in the parlor, and he managed to tell me most of what happened. I've been doing some healing work with him."

"I didn't know what to do," I said helplessly. "He fell asleep, and I had to get home. I have his car at my house," I added inanely.

Selene nodded. "We'll come get it later," she said, and I dug in my pocket and gave her the keys. She took them and pushed open the kitchen door.

I sniffed the air. "What's that?" I asked.

Now I noticed that the kitchen was ablaze with light, sound, color, scent. I paused in the doorway, trying to separate out the different stimuli. Selene walked over to the stove to stir something, and I realized she had a small, three-legged cast-iron cauldron bubbling on the burner of her range. The odd thing was how normal it looked somehow.

She caught my glance and said, "Usually I do all this outside. But this autumn has been so awful, weatherwise." She stirred slowly with a long wooden spoon, then leaned over and inhaled, the steam making her face flush slightly.

"What are you making?" I asked, moving closer.

"This is a vision potion," she explained. "When ingested by a knowledgeable witch, it aids with scrying and divination."

"Like a hallucinogen?" I asked, a little shocked. Images of LSD and mushrooms and people freaking out flashed through my mind.

Selene laughed. "No. It's just an aid, to make it easier to find your visions. I only make it every four or five years or so. I don't use it that often, and a little goes a long way."

On the gleaming granite counter I saw labeled vials and small jars and, at one end, a stack of homemade candles.

"Did you do all this?" I asked.

Selene nodded and brushed her dark hair away from her face. "I always go through a flurry of activity around this time of year. Samhain is over, Yule hasn't begun—I suppose I just itch for something to do. Years ago I started making many of my own tinctures and essential oils and infusions—they're always fresher and better than what you can buy in the store. Have you ever made candles?"

"No."

Selene looked around the kitchen, at the bustle and clutter, and said, "Things you make, cook, sew, decorate—those are all expressions of the power and homages to the Goddess." Busily she stirred the cauldron, deasil, and then tasted a tiny bit on the end of her spoon.

At any other time I would have found this impromptu lesson fascinating, but at the moment I was too keyed up to focus on it. "Will Cal be okay?" I blurted out.

"Yes," Selene said. She looked directly at me. "Do you want to talk about Hunter?"

That was all it took, and suddenly I was crying silently, my shoulders shaking, my face burning. In a moment she was beside me, holding me. A tissue appeared, and I took it.

"Selene," I said shakily, "I think he's dead."

"Shhh," she said soothingly. "Poor darling. Sit down. Let me give you some tea."

Tea? I thought wildly. I think I *killed* someone, and you're offering me *tea*?

But it was witch tea, and within seconds of my first sip I felt my emotions calm slightly, enough to get myself under control. Selene sat across the table from me, looking into my eyes.

"Hunter tried to kill Cal," she said intently. "He might

have tried to kill you, too. Anyone standing there would have done what you did. You saw a friend in danger, and you acted. No one could blame you for that."

"I didn't mean to hurt Hunter," I said, my voice wavering.

"Of course you didn't," she agreed. "You just wanted to stop him. There was no way to predict what would happen. Listen to me, my dear. If you hadn't done what you did, if you hadn't been so quick thinking and loyal, then it would be Cal now in the river, and I would be mourning him and possibly you, too. Hunter came here looking for trouble. He was on our property. He was out for blood. You and Cal both acted in self-defense."

Slowly I drank my tea. The way Selene put it, it sounded reasonable, even inevitable. "Do you—do you think we should go to the police?" I asked.

Selene cocked her head to one side, considering. "No," she said after a moment. "The difficulty is that there were no other witnesses. And that knife wound in Hunter's neck would be hard to explain as self-defense, even though you and I both know that's the truth of it."

A fresh wave of dread washed over me. She was right. To the police, it would probably look like murder.

I remembered something else. "And his car," I said. "Did you move it?"

Selene nodded. "I spelled it to start and drove it to an abandoned barn just outside of town. It sounds premeditated, I know, but it seemed the prudent thing to do." She reached out and covered my hand with her own. "I know it's hard. I know you feel that your life will never be the same. But you must try to let it go, my dear."

I swallowed miserably. "I feel so guilty," I said.

"Let me tell you about Hunter," she said, and her voice was suddenly almost harsh. I shivered.

"I've heard reports about him," Selene went on. "By all accounts he was a loose cannon, someone who could not be trusted. Even the council had their doubts about him, thought he had gone too far, too many times. He's been obsessed with Woodbanes all his life, and in the last few years this obsession had taken a deadly turn." She seemed quite serious, and I nodded.

A thought occurred to me. "Then why was he going after Cal?" I asked. "You guys don't know what clan you are, right? I heard Hunter call Cal Woodbane—did he think Cal . . . wait—" I shook my head, confused. Cal had told me that he and Hunter probably had the same father. And Sky had said Cal was Woodbane like his father. Which made both Cal and Hunter half Woodbane? I couldn't keep all this straight.

"Who knows what he thought?" said Selene. "He was clearly crazy. I mean, this is someone who killed his own brother."

My eyebrows knitted. I vaguely remembered Cal throwing that accusation at Hunter last night. "What do you mean?"

Selene shook her head, then started as her cauldron hissed and spat on the stove, almost boiling over. She hurried over to adjust the flame. For the next few minutes she was very busy, and I hesitated to interrupt her.

"Do you think I could see Cal?" I asked finally.

She looked back at me regretfully. "I'm sorry, Morgan, but I gave him a drink to make him sleep. He probably won't wake up until tonight."

"Oh." I stood up and retrieved my coat, unwilling to pursue the story about Hunter if Selene didn't want to tell me. I felt a thousand times better than I had, but I knew instinctively the pain and guilt would return.

"Thank you for coming," Selene said, straining a steaming mixture over the sink. "And remember, what you did last night was the right thing. Believe that."

I nodded awkwardly.

"Please call me if you want to talk," Selene added as I headed for the door. "Anytime."

"Thank you," I said. I pushed through the door and headed home.

3

Dread

April 2000

Scrying doesn't always mean you see a picture—it can be more like receiving impressions. I use my lueg, my scrying stone. It's a big, thick chunk of obsidian, almost four inches at its widest and tapering to a point. It was my father's. I found it under my pillow the morning he and Mum disappeared.

Luegs are more reliable than either fire or water. Fire may show you pasts and possible futures, but it's hard to work with. There's an old Wiccan saying that goes: Fire is a fragile lover, court her well, neglect her not; her faith is like a misty smoke, her anger is destructive hot. Water is easier to use but very misleading. Once I heard Mum say that water is the Wiccan whore, spilling her secrets to any, lying to most, trusting few.

Last night I took my lueg and went down to the kill that flows at the edge of my uncle's property. This was where we swam in the summer, where Linden and I caught minnows, where Alwyn used to pick gooseberries.

I sat at the water's edge and scryed, looking deep into my obsidian, weaving spells of vision.

After a long, long time, the rock's face cleared, and in its depths I saw my mother. It was my mother of all those years ago, right before she disappeared. I remember the day clearly. An eight-year-old me ran up to where she knelt in the garden, pulling weeds. She looked up, saw me, and her face lit, as if I was the sun. Giomanach, she said, and looked at me with love, the sunlight glinting off her bright hair. Seeing her in the lueg, I was almost crushed with longing and a childish need to see her, have her hold me.

When the stone went blank, I held it in my hand, then crumpled over and cried on the bank of the kill.

—Giomanach

My birthday dinner was like a movie. I felt like I was watching myself through a window, smiling, talking to people, opening presents. I was glad to see Aunt Eileen and her girlfriend, Paula Steen, again—and Mom and Mary K. had worked hard to make everything special. It would have been a great birthday, except for the horrific images that kept crashing into my brain. Hunter and Cal grappling in the churned, bloody snow. Myself, sinking to my knees under Cal's binding spell, then me looking down at the athame in my hand and looking up to see Hunter. Hunter, rivulets of blood on his neck, going over the edge of the cliff. "Hey, are you all right?" Mary K. asked me as I stood by the window, gazing out into the darkness. "You seem kind of out of it."

"Just tired," I told her. I added quickly, "But I'm having a great time. Thanks, Mary K."

"We aim to please." She flashed me a grin.

Finally Aunt Eileen and Paula left, and I went upstairs and called Cal. His voice sounded weak and scratchy.

"I'm okay," he said. "Are you okay?"

"Yes," I said. "Physically."

"I know." He sighed. "I can't believe it. I didn't mean for him to go over the edge. I just wanted to stop him." He laughed dryly, a croaking sound. "Helluva seventeenth birthday. I'm sorry, Morgan."

"It wasn't your fault," I said. "He came after you."

"I didn't want him to hurt you."

"But why did you put binding spells on me?" I asked.

"I was afraid. I didn't want you to jump into the middle of it and get hurt," Cal said.

"I wanted to help you. I hated being frozen like that. It was awful."

"I'm so sorry, Morgan," Cal breathed. "Everything was happening so fast, and I thought I was acting for the best."

"Don't ever do that to me again."

"I won't, I promise. I'm sorry."

"Okay. I called 911 when I got home," I admitted softly. "And I sent Sky an anonymous witch message, telling her where to look for Hunter."

Cal was silent for a minute. Then he said, "You did the right thing. I'm glad you did."

"It didn't help, though. I saw Sky at the river this morning. She said Hunter didn't come home last night. She was sure I knew something about it."

"What did you tell her?"

"That I didn't know what she was talking about. She said she didn't feel Hunter's presence or something like that. And she called me a lying Woodbane."

"That bitch," Cal said angrily.

"Could she find out about what happened somehow? Using magick?"

"No," said Cal. "My mom put warding spells around the whole place to block anyone from scrying and seeing what happened. Don't worry."

"I am worried," I insisted. A bubble of panic was rising in my throat again. "This is horrible. I can't stand it."

"Morgan! Try to calm down," said Cal. "It will all be okay, you'll see. I won't let anything happen to you. The only thing is, I'm afraid Sky is going to be a problem. Hunter was her cousin, and she's not going to let this rest. Tomorrow we'll spell your house and your car with wards of protection. But still—be on your guard."

"Okay." Dread settled more heavily on my shoulders as I hung up. Wherever this is going, I thought, there's no way it can end well. No way at all.

On Monday morning I got up early and grabbed the morning paper before anyone else could see it. Widow's Vale doesn't have its own daily paper, just a twice-monthly publication that's mostly pickup articles from other papers. I quickly paged through the *Albany Times Union* to see if there was any mention of a body being fished out of the Hudson. There wasn't. I gnawed my lip. What did that mean? Had his body not been found yet? Or was it just that we weren't close enough to Albany for them to cover the story?

I drove with Mary K. to school and parked outside the building, feeling like I had aged five years over the weekend.

As I turned off the engine, Bakker Blackburn, Mary K.'s boyfriend, trotted up to meet her. "Hey, babe," he said, nuzzling her neck.

Mary K. giggled and pushed him away. He took her book bag from her, and they went off to meet their friends.

Robbie Gurevitch, one of my best friends and a member of my coven, strolled up to my car. A group of freshman girls stared admiringly at him as he passed them, and I saw him blush. Being gorgeous was new to him—until I'd given him a healing potion a month ago, he'd had horrible acne. But the potion had cleared up his skin and even erased the scars.

"Are you going to fix your car?" he asked me.

I looked at my broken headlight and smashed nose and sighed. A few days ago I'd thought someone was following me, and I had skidded on a patch of ice and crunched my beloved behemoth of a car, fondly known as Das Boot, into a ditch. At the time it had seemed utterly terrifying, but since the events of Saturday night, it felt more in perspective.

"Yep," I said, scanning the area for Cal. That morning I'd noticed the Explorer was gone from my block, but I didn't know if he'd be back at school today.

"I'm guessing it'll cost at least five hundred bucks," Robbie said.

We walked toward the old, redbrick former courthouse that was now Widow's Vale High. I was striving for normalcy, trying to be old reliable Morgan. "I wanted to ask you—did you go to Bree's coven's circle on Saturday?" Bree

Warren had been my other best friend since childhood—
my closest friend—until we fought over Cal. Now she
hated me. And I . . . I didn't know what I felt about her. I was
furious at her. I didn't trust her. I missed her fiercely.

"I did go." Robbie held the door open for me. "It was
small and kind of lame. But that English witch, Sky Eventide,
the one who leads their circles . . ." He whistled. "She had
power coming off her in waves."

"I know Sky," I said stiffly. "I met her at Cal's. What did
you guys do? Did Sky mention me or Cal?"

He looked at me. "No. We just did a circle. It was interesting because Sky does it slightly differently than Cal. Why
would she mention you or Cal?"

"Different how?" I pressed, ignoring his question. "You
guys didn't, um, do anything scary, did you? Like call on spirits or anything?"

Robbie stopped walking. "No. It was just a circle, Morgan.
I think we can safely say that Bree and Raven are not having
their souls sucked out by the devil."

I gave him an exasperated look. "Wiccans don't believe in
the devil," I reminded him. "I just want to make sure that
Bree isn't getting into anything dangerous or bad." *Like I did.*

We walked to the basement stairs, where our coven,
Cirrus, usually hung out in the morning. Ethan Sharp was
already there, doing his English homework. Jenna Ruiz sat
across from him, reading, her fair, straight hair falling like a curtain across her cheek. They both looked up and greeted us.

"Bad?" Robbie repeated. "No. Sky didn't strike me as bad.
Powerful, yes. Sexy—absolutely." He grinned.

"Who's this?" Jenna asked.

"Sky Eventide," Robbie reported. "She's the blood witch

that Bree and Raven have in their new coven. Oh, guess their coven's name." He laughed. "Kithic. It means 'left-handed' in Gaelic. Raven picked out that name from something she read, without knowing what it meant."

The rest of us smiled. After our fight, Bree had split off from Cirrus to start her own coven with Raven. To me it seemed both of them were just playing at being Wiccan, doing it to look cool, to get back at me for winning Cal, or just to do something different. Widow's Vale is a small town, and there aren't that many entertainment opportunities.

Or maybe I was selling them short. Maybe they were really sincere in their commitment. I sighed and rubbed my forehead, feeling like I didn't know anything anymore.

In homeroom people were already planning their Thanksgiving holidays, which would start at noon on Wednesday. It would be a relief not to have to go to school for a few days. I've always been an A student (well, mostly), but it was getting harder and harder to keep my mind on schoolwork when so many more compelling things were taking up my time and energy. Nowadays I just flashed through my physics and trig homework and did the bare minimum in other classes so I would have more time to study spells, plan my future magickal herb garden, and read about Wicca. Not only that, but just reading the Book of Shadows written by my birth mother, which I'd found in Selene's library over a week ago, was like a college course in itself. I was stretched very thin these days.

In homeroom I opened my book *Essential Oils and Their Charms* under my desk and started reading. In the spring I would try to make some of my own, the way Selene did.

When Bree came into class, I couldn't help looking up.

Her face was as familiar as my own, but nowadays she had another layer to her, a layer that didn't include me. She wore mostly black, like Raven did, and although she hadn't adopted any of Raven's gothy piercings or tattoos, I wondered if it was just a matter of time.

Bree had always been the beautiful one, the one boys flocked around, the life of the party. I had been the plain friend that people put up with because Bree loved me and was my best friend, but then Cal had come between us. Bree had even lied and told me they'd slept together. We'd quit speaking, and then Cal and I started going out.

After being like conjoined twins for eleven years, I'd found the last few Breeless weeks bizarre and uncomfortable. She still didn't know I was adopted, that I was a blood witch. She didn't know about what had happened with Hunter. At one time she had been the only person in the world I might have told.

I couldn't resist looking at her face, her eyes the color of coffee. For just a second she met my gaze, and I was startled by the mix of emotions there. We both looked away at the same time. Did she miss me? Did she hate me? What was she doing with Sky?

The bell rang, and we all stood. Bree's dark, shiny hair disappeared through the doorway, and I followed her. When she turned the corner to go to her first class, I was seized by a spontaneous desire to talk to her.

"Bree."

She turned, and when she saw it was me, she looked surprised.

"Listen—I know that Sky is leading your coven," I found myself saying.

"So?" No one looked imperious like Bree looked imperious.

"I just—it's just that Sky is dangerous," I said quickly. "She's dangerous, and you shouldn't hang out with her."

Her perfect eyebrows rose. "Do tell," she drawled.

"She has this whole dark agenda; she's caught up in this whole program that I bet she hasn't told you about. She's— she's evil, she's bad, and dangerous." I realized in despair that I sounded melodramatic and muddled.

"Really." Bree shook her head, looking like she was trying not to laugh. "You are too much, Morgan. It's like you get off on lying, raining on people's parades."

"Look, I heard you and Raven last week in the bathroom," I admitted. "You were talking about how Sky was teaching you about the dark side. That's dangerous! And I heard you saying you gave Sky some of my hair! What was that about? Is she putting spells on me?"

Bree's eyes narrowed. "You mean you were spying on me?" she exclaimed. "You're pathetic! And you have no idea what you're talking about. Cal is filling your head with ridiculous crap, and you're just sucking it up! He could be the devil himself, and you wouldn't care because he's the only boy who ever asked you out!"

Before I realized what was happening, my hand had shot out and smacked Bree hard across the face. Her head snapped sideways, and within seconds the pink outline of my palm appeared on her cheek. I gasped and stared at her as her face twisted into anger.

"You bitch!" she snarled.

Out of lifelong habit, I started to feel remorseful, and then I thought, Screw that. I took a deep breath and called on my own anger, narrowing my eyes. "You're the bitch," I snapped. "You can't stand the fact that I'm not your puppet anymore, that I'm not your charity case, your permanent audience. You're jealous of *me* for once, and it's eating you up. I have a fantastic boyfriend, I have more magickal power than you'll ever dream about, and you can't stand it. Finally I'm better than you. I'm amazed your head doesn't explode!"

Bree gaped at me, her eyes wide, her mouth open. "What are you talking about?" she practically shrieked. "You were never my audience! You make it sound like I was using you! This is what I'm talking about! Cal is brainwashing you!"

"Actually, Bree," I said coldly, "you'd be amazed at how little we talk about you. In fact, your name hardly comes up."

With that, I swept off, my teeth clenched so tight, I could feel them grinding together. I didn't think I'd ever had the last word in an argument with Bree before. But the thought didn't make me feel any better. Why had I talked to her? I had just made everything worse.

4

Haven

May 2000

I remember it rained the day Mum and Dad disappeared. When I woke up that morning they were already gone. I had no idea what was going on. Uncle Beck called late that day, and I told him I couldn't find Dad, or Mum either. Beck called around, to get a neighbor to stay overnight with us until he could get there, and he couldn't find anyone still around. In the end, I was in charge all that long day and night, and the three of us—me, Linden, and Alwyn—stayed in our house alone, not knowing what was happening to us, to our world.

Now I know that twenty-three other people besides my parents either died or disappeared that night. Years later, when I went back, I tried asking around. All I got were cautious mumbles about a dark wave, a cloud of fury and destruction.

I've heard rumors of a dark wave destroying a Wyndenkell

coven in Scotland. I'm on my way there. Goddess, give me strength.

—Giomanach

After my fight with Bree, I was so upset that I couldn't concentrate on anything. My math teacher had to call my name three times before I responded, and then I answered his question incorrectly—which almost never happened to me under normal circumstances. During lunch period I sneaked off to Cirrus's hangout spot to be by myself. I scarfed down my sandwich and a Diet Coke, then meditated for half an hour. Finally I felt calm enough to deal with the rest of my day.

I slogged through my afternoon classes. When the last bell rang, I went to my locker, then followed the crush of students outside. The snow was turning rapidly to slush, and the sun flowed down with an Indian-summerish warmth. After weeks of freezing weather, it felt wonderful. I raised my face to the sun, hoping it would help heal the pain I carried inside, the guilt over what I'd done to Hunter, the terror of being found out.

"I'm getting a ride home with Bakker, okay?" Mary K. bounced up to me as I took out my car keys, her cheeks flushed pink, her eyes clear and shining.

I looked at her. "Are you going home, or . . ." Don't go anywhere with him alone, I thought. I didn't trust Bakker—not since I'd caught him pinning Mary K. down on her bed and practically forcing himself on her two weeks earlier. I couldn't believe she'd forgiven him.

"We're going to get a latte first, then home," she said, her eyes daring me to say something.

"All right. Well, see you later," I said lamely. I watched her climb into Bakker's car and knew that if he hurt her, I would have no problem doing to him what I had done to Hunter. And in Bakker's case I wouldn't feel guilty.

"Whoa. I'm glad you're not looking at me like that," said Robbie, loping up to me. I shook my head.

"Yeah, just watch your step." I tried to sound light and teasing.

"Is Cal sick? I didn't see him all day," said Robbie. He smiled absentmindedly at a sophomore who was sending flirtatious looks his way.

"Morgan?" he prompted.

"Oh! Um, yes, Cal is sick," I said. I felt a sudden jangle of nerves. Robbie was a close friend, and I had told him about being adopted and a blood witch. He knew more about me than Bree did now. But I could never tell him about all that had happened on Saturday night. It was too horrible to share, even with him. "I'm going to call him right now— maybe go see him."

Robbie nodded. "I'm on my way to Bree's. Who knows, today might be the day I go for it." He wiggled his eyebrows suggestively, and I smiled. Robbie had recently admitted to me that he was totally in love with Bree and had been for years. I hoped she wouldn't break his heart the way she did with most of the guys she got involved with.

"Good luck," I said. He walked off, and I dumped my backpack in Das Boot and headed back to the pay phone in the school lunchroom.

Cal answered after four rings. His voice sounded better than it had the night before.

"Hi," I said, comforted just to talk to him.

"I knew it was you," he said, sounding glad.

"Of course you did," I said. "You're a witch."

"Where are you?"

"School. Can I come see you? I just really need to talk to you."

Groaning, he said, "I would love that. But some people just came in from Europe, and I've got to meet with them."

"Selene's been having people over a lot lately, it seems."

Cal paused, and when he spoke, his voice had a slightly different tone to it. "Yeah, she has. She's kind of been working on a big project, and it's starting to come together. I'll tell you about it later."

"Okay. How are your wrists?"

"They look pretty bad. But they'll be okay. I really wish I could see you," Cal said.

"Me too." I lowered my voice. "I *really* need to talk to you. About what happened."

"I know," he said quietly. "I know, Morgan."

In the background on Cal's end I heard voices, and Cal covered his mouthpiece and responded to them. When he came back on, I said, "I won't keep you. Call me later if you can, okay?"

"I will," he said. Then he hung up. I hung up, too, feeling sad and lonely without him.

I walked through the hall and out the door, got in Das Boot, and drove to Red Kill, to Practical Magick.

*   *   *

The brass bells over the door jingled as I pushed my way in. Practical Magick was a store that sold Wiccan books and supplies. Although I hadn't realized it until now, it was also becoming the place I went to when I didn't want to go anywhere else. I loved being there, and I always felt better when I left. It was like a Wiccan neighborhood bar.

At the end of the room the checkout desk was empty, and I figured Alyce and David must be busy restocking.

I began reading book titles, dreaming of the day I would have enough money to buy whatever books and supplies I wanted. I would buy this whole store out, I decided. That would be so much more fun than being a relatively poor high school junior who was about to wipe out her whole savings to pay for a crumpled headlight.

"Hi, there," came a soft voice, and I looked up to see the round, motherly figure of Alyce, my favorite clerk. As my eyes met hers, she stood still. Her brows drew together in a concerned look. "What's the matter?"

My heart thudded against my ribs. Does she know? I wondered frantically. Can she tell just by looking at me?

"What do you mean?" I asked. "I'm fine. Just a little stressed. You know, school, family stuff." I shut my mouth abruptly, feeling like I was babbling.

Alyce held my gaze for a moment, her eyes probing mine. "All right. If you want to talk about it, I'm here," she said at last.

She bustled over to the checkout counter and began to stack some papers. Her gray hair was piled untidily on top of her head, and she wore her usual loose, flowing clothes. She moved with precision and confidence: a woman at ease with herself, her witchhood, her power. I admired her, and it broke my heart to think how horrified she would be if she knew what I had done. How had this happened? How had this become my life?

I can't lose this, I thought. Practical Magick was my haven. I couldn't let the poison of Hunter's horrible death seep out and taint my relationships with this place, with Alyce. I couldn't bear it.

"I can't wait for spring," I said, trying to get my mind back on track. It wasn't even Thanksgiving yet. "I want to get started on my garden." I walked up the book aisle to the back of the store and leaned against a stool by the counter.

"So do I," Alyce agreed. "I'm already dying to be outside, digging in the dirt again. It's always a struggle for me to remember the positive aspects of winter."

I looked around at the other people in the store. A young man with multiple earrings in his left ear came up and bought incense and white candles. I tentatively sent out my senses to see if I could tell if he was a witch or not, but I couldn't pick up on anything unusual.

"Morgan, good to see you again."

I turned to see David stepping through the faded orange curtain that separated the small back room from the rest of the store. A faint scent of incense wafted in with him. Like Alyce, David was also a blood witch. Recently he'd told me that he was from the Burnhide clan. I felt honored to have gained his confidence—and terrified of losing it again if he ever found out what I'd done, that I'd killed someone.

"Hi," I said. "How are you?"

"I'm all right." He held a sheaf of invoices in his hand and looked distracted. "Alyce, did the latest batch of essential oils come? The bill is here."

She shook her head. "I have a feeling the shipment is lost somewhere," she said as another person checked out. This woman was buying a Wiccan periodical called *Crafting Our Lives*. I picked up on faint magickal vibrations as she passed me and was once again naively amazed that real witches existed.

I wandered around the store, fascinated as always by the candles, incense, small mirrors the shop contained. Slowly the place emptied, then new people came in. It was a busy afternoon.

Gradually the sunlight faded from the high windows, and I began to think about heading home. Alyce came up as I was running my fingers around the rim of a carved marble bowl. The stone was cool and smooth, like river stones. The stones Hunter had probably hit when he fell hadn't been smooth. They had been jagged, deadly.

"Marble is always thirteen degrees cooler than the air around it," Alyce said at my side, making me jump.

"Really? Why?"

"It's the property of the stone," she said, straightening some scarves that customers had rumpled. "Everything has its own properties."

I thought about the chunks of crystal and other stones I had found in the box containing my mother's tools. It seemed like ages ago—but it had actually been less than a week.

"I found Maeve's tools," I said, surprising myself. I hadn't planned to mention it. But I felt the need to confide *something* in Alyce, to make her feel I wasn't shutting her out.

Alyce's blue eyes widened, and she stopped what she was doing to look at me. She knew Maeve's story; it had been she who'd told me of my birth mother's awful death here in America.

"Belwicket's tools?" she asked unbelievingly. Belwicket had been the name of Maeve's coven in Ireland. When it was destroyed by a mysterious, dark force, Maeve and her lover, Angus, had fled to America. Where I'd been born—and they had died.

"I scryed," I told Alyce. "In fire. I had a vision that told me the tools were in Meshomah Falls."

"Where Maeve died," Alyce remembered.

"Yes."

"How wonderful for you," Alyce said. "Everyone thought those tools were lost forever. I'm sure Maeve would have been so happy for her daughter to have them."

I nodded. "I'm really glad about it. They're a link to her, to her clan, her family."

"Have you used them yet?" she asked.

"Um—I tried the athame," I admitted. Technically, since I was uninitiated, I wasn't supposed to do unsupervised magick or use magickal tools or even write in Cirrus's Book of Shadows. I waited for Alyce to chide me.

But she didn't. Instead she said briskly, "I think you should bind the tools to you."

I blinked. "What do you mean?"

"Wait a minute." Alyce hurried off and soon came back with a thick, ancient-looking book. Its cover was dark green and tattered, with stains mottling its fabric. She leaned the book on a shelf and flipped through pages soft and crumbling with age.

"Here we go." She pulled a quaint pair of half-moon glasses from her sweater pocket and perched them on her nose. "Let me copy this down for you." Then, just like the women at my church exchange recipes and knitting patterns, Alyce copied down an age-old Wiccan spell that would bind my mother's tools to me.

"It will be almost as if you're part of them and they are part of you," Alyce explained as I folded the paper and put it in my inside coat pocket. "It will make them more effective for you and also less effective for anyone else who tries to use them. I really think you should do this right away." Her gaze, usually so mild, seemed quite piercing as she examined me over the rims of her glasses.

"Um, okay, I will," I said. "But why?"

Alyce paused for a moment, as if considering what to say. "Intuition," she said finally, shrugging and giving me a smile. "I feel it's important."

"Well, all right," I said. "I'll try to do it tonight."

"The sooner the better," she advised. Then the bells over the door rang as a customer came in. I hastily said good-bye to Alyce and David and went out to Das Boot. I flipped on my one headlight, blasted the heater, and headed for home.

5

Bound

June 2000

Two covens in Scotland were wiped out: one in 1974 and one in 1985. The first was in the north, the second, toward the southeast. Now the trail is leading into northern England, so I am making plans to go. I have to <u>know</u>. This started out being about my parents. Now it's a much bigger picture.

I've heard that the council is seeking new members. I've put my name in. If I were a council member, I would have access to things that are usually not publicized. It seems the fastest way to have my questions answered. When I come back from the north, I'll learn of their decision.

I applied to become a Seeker. With a name like mine, it seems almost inevitable.

—Giomanach

Mary K. breezed in halfway through dinner. Her cheeks were pink. There was also something wrong with her shirt. I gazed in puzzlement at the two flaps of the hem. They didn't meet—the shirt was incorrectly buttoned. My eyes narrowed as I thought about what that meant.

"Where have you been?" Mom asked. "I was worried."

"I called and let Dad know I'd be late," my sister said, sitting down at the table. Seated, her telltale shirt wasn't so obvious. "What's that?" she asked, sniffing the serving platter.

"Corned beef. I made it in the Crock-Pot," Mom said.

Dad had glanced up at the sound of his name, pulled back to reality for a moment. He's a research-and-development guy for IBM, and sometimes he seems more comfortable in *virtual* reality.

"Hmmm," said Mary K. disapprovingly. She picked out some carrots, cabbage, and onions and conspicuously left the meat. Lately she'd been on a major vegetarian kick.

"It's delicious," I said brightly, just to needle her. Mary K. sent me a look.

"So I think Eileen and Paula have decided on the York Street house, in Jasper," my mom said.

"Cool," I said. "Jasper's only about twenty minutes away, right?" My aunt and her girlfriend had decided to move in together and had been house hunting with my mom, a real estate agent.

"Right," Mom said. "An easy drive from here."

"Good." I stood up and carried my plate to the kitchen, already anxious for my family to be asleep. I had work to do.

The spell for binding tools to oneself was complicated but not difficult, and it didn't involve any tools or ingredients that I didn't have. I knew I would need to work undisturbed, and I didn't want to do it outside. The attic seemed like a good place.

At last I heard my parents turn in and my sister brush her teeth noisily in the bathroom we shared. She poked her head into my room to say good night and found me hunched over a book discussing the differences between practicing Wicca on your own and within a coven. It was really interesting. There were benefits—and drawbacks—to both ways.

"Night," said Mary K., yawning.

I looked at her. "Next time you're late, you might want to make sure your shirt is buttoned right," I said mildly.

She looked down at herself, horrified. "Oh, man," she breathed.

"Just . . . be careful." I wanted to say more but forced myself to stop there.

"Yeah, yeah, I will." She went into her room.

Twenty minutes later, sensing that everyone was asleep, I tiptoed up the attic stairs with Maeve's tools, the spell Alyce had written out for me, and four white candles.

I swept one area clean of dust and set the four candles in a large square. Inside the square I drew a circle with white chalk. Then I entered the circle, closed it, and set Maeve's tools on one of my old sweatshirts. Theoretically, it would be full of my personal vibrations.

I meditated for a while, trying to release my anguish over Hunter, trying to sink into the magick, feeling it unfold before me, gradually revealing its secrets. Then I gathered Maeve's tools: her robe, her wand, her four element cups, her athame, and things I wasn't sure were tools but that I'd found in the same box: a feather, a silver chain with a claddagh charm on it, several chunks of crystal, and five stones, each one different.

I read the ritual chant.

"Goddess Mother, Protectress of Magick and Life, hear my song. As it was in my clan, so shall it be with me and in my family to come. These tools I offer in service to you and in worship of the glory of nature. With them I shall honor life, do no harm, and bless all that is good and right. Shine your light on these tools that I may use them in pure intent and in sure purpose."

I laid my hands on them, feeling their power and sending mine into them.

The same way it had happened in the past, a song in Gaelic came to my lips. I let it slip quietly into the darkness.

> "An di allaigh an di aigh
> An di allaigh an di ne ullah
> An di ullah be nith rah
> Cair di na ulla nith rah
> Cair feal ti theo nith rah
> An di allaigh an di aigh."

Quietly I sang the ancient words again and again, feeling a warm coil of energy circling me. When I had sung this before, it had drawn down an immense amount of power—I'd felt like a goddess myself. Tonight it was quieter, more focused, and the power flowed around and through me like water, going down my hands into the tools until I couldn't tell where the tools left off and I began. I couldn't feel my knees where I was kneeling, and giddily I wondered if I was levitating. Suddenly I realized that I was no longer singing and that the warm, rich power had leached away, leaving me breathing hard and flushed, sweat trickling down my back.

I looked down. Were the tools bound to me now? Had I done it correctly? I had followed the instructions. I had felt the power. There was nothing else on the paper Alyce had given me. Blinking, feeling suddenly incredibly tired, I gathered everything up, blew out the candles, and crept downstairs. Moving silently, I unscrewed the cover for the HVAC vent in the hallway outside my room and put my tools, except the athame, back into my never-fail hiding place.

Back in my room, I changed into my pajamas and brushed my teeth. I unbraided my hair and brushed it a few times, too tired to give it any real attention. Finally, with relief, I got into bed with Maeve's Book of Shadows and opened it to my bookmark. Out of habit I held my mother's athame, with its carved initials, in my hand.

I started to read, sometimes pointing the athame to the words on the page, as if it would help me decipher some of the Gaelic terms.

In this entry Maeve was describing a spell to strengthen her scrying. She mentioned that something seemed to be blocking her vision: "It's as if the power lines are clouded and dark. Ma and I have both scryed and scryed, and all we get is the same thing over and over: bad news coming. What that means, I don't know. A delegation is here from Liathach, in northern Scotland. They, like us, are Woodbanes who have renounced evil. Maybe with their help we can figure out what's going on."

I felt a chill. *Bad news coming.* Was it the mysterious dark force that had destroyed Belwicket, Maeve's coven? No, it couldn't be, I realized; that hadn't happened until 1982. This entry had been written in 1981, nearly a year earlier. I tapped the athame against the page and read on.

"I have met a witch."

The words floated across the page, written in light within the regular entry. I blinked and they were gone, and I stared at Maeve's angular handwriting, wondering what I had seen. I focused, staring hard at the page, willing the words, the writing to appear again. Nothing.

I took the athame, passing it slowly over the blue ink. Splashes, pinpricks of light, coalescing into words. "I have met a witch."

I drew in my breath, staring at the page. The words appeared beneath the athame. When I drew it away, they faded. I passed the knife over the book again. "Among the group from Liathach, there is a man. There is something about him. Goddess, he draws me to him."

Oh my God. I looked up, glanced around my room to make sure I was awake and not dreaming. My clock was ticking, Dagda was squirming next to my leg, the wind was blowing against my windows. This was all real. Another layer of my birth mother's history was being revealed: she had written secret entries in her Book of Shadows.

Quickly I flipped to the very beginning of the book, which Maeve had started when she was first initiated at fourteen. Holding the athame close to each page, I scanned the writing, seeing if other hidden messages were revealed. Page after page I ran the knife down each line of writing, each spell, each song or poem. Nothing. Nothing for many, many pages. Then, in 1980, when Maeve was eighteen, hidden words started appearing. I began reading, my earlier fatigue forgotten.

At first the entries were things Maeve had simply wanted to keep hidden from her mother: the fact that she and a girl-friend were smoking cigarettes; about how Angus kept pressuring her to go "all the way" and she was thinking about it; even sarcastic, teasing remarks or observations about people in the village, her relatives, other members of the coven.

But as time went on, Maeve also wrote down spells, spells that were different from the others. A lot of what Maeve and Mackenna and Belwicket had done was practical stuff: healing potions, lucky talismans, spells to make the crops perform. These new spells of Maeve's were things like how to communicate with and call wild birds. How to put your mind into an animal's. How to join your mind to another person's. Not practical, perhaps. But powerful and fascinating.

I went back to the passage I had found a few minutes ago. Slowly, word by word, I read the glowing letters. Each entry was surrounded by runes of concealment and symbols I didn't recognize. I memorized what they looked like so I could research them later.

Painstakingly, I picked out the message.

"Ciaran came to tea. He and Angus are circling each other like dogs. Ciaran is a friend, a good friend, and I won't have Angus put him down."

Angus Bramson had been my birth father. Ciaran must be the Scottish witch Maeve had just met. Previous entries had detailed Maeve and Angus's courtship—they'd known each other practically forever. When Belwicket had been destroyed, Maeve and Angus had fled together and settled in

America. Two years later I had been born, though I don't think they ever married. Maeve had once written about her sadness that Angus wasn't her *mùirn beatha dàn*—her preordained life partner, her soul mate, the person who was meant for her.

I believed Cal was mine. I'd never felt so close to anyone before—except Bree.

"Today I showed Ciaran the headlands by the Windy Cliffs. It's a beautiful spot, wild and untamed, and he seemed just as wild and untamed as the nature surrounding him. He's so different from the lads around here. He seems older than twenty-two, and he's traveled a bit and seen the world. It makes me ache with envy."

Oh, God, I thought. Maeve, what are you getting into?

I soon found out.

"I cannot help myself. Ciaran is everything a man should be. I love Angus, yes, but he's like a brother to me—I've known him all my life. Ciaran wants the things I want, finds the same things interesting and boring and funny. I could spend days just talking to him, doing nothing else. And then there's his magick—his power. It's breathtaking. He knows so much I don't know, no one around here knows. He's teaching me. And the way he makes me feel . . .

"Goddess! I've never wanted to touch anyone so much."

My throat had tightened and my back muscles had tensed. I rested the book on my knees, trying to analyze why this revelation shook me so much.

Is love ever simple? I wondered. I thought about Mary K. and Bakker, boy most likely to be a parolee by the time he was twenty; Bree, who went out with one loser after another; Matt, who had cheated on Jenna with Raven. . . . It was completely discouraging. Then I thought about Cal, and my spirits rose again. Whatever troubles we had, at least they were external to our love for each other.

I blinked and realized my eyelids were gritty and heavy. It was very late, and I had to go to school tomorrow. One more quick passage.

"I have kissed Ciaran, and it was like sunlight coming through a window. Goddess, thank you for bringing him to me. I think he is the one."

Wincing, I hid the book and the athame under my mattress. I didn't want to know. Angus was my birth father, the one who had stayed by her, who had died with her. And she had loved someone else! She'd betrayed Angus! How could she be so cruel, my mother?

I felt betrayed, too, somehow, and knowing that I was perhaps being unfair to Maeve didn't help. I turned off my light, plumped my pillow up properly, and went to sleep.

6

Knowledge

I'm going to have these scars forever. Every time I look at my wrists, I feel rage all over again. Mom has been putting salves on them, but they ache constantly, and the skin will never be the same.

Thank the Goddess Giomanach won't bother us anymore.

—Sgàth

"If you hum that song one more time, I may have to kick you out of the car," I informed my sister the next morning.

Mary K. opened the lid of her mug and took a swig of coffee. "My, we're grumpy today."

"It's natural to be grumpy in the morning." I polished off the last of my Diet Coke and tossed the empty can into a plastic bag I kept for recyclables.

"Tornadoes are natural, but they're not a *good* thing."

I snorted, but secretly I enjoyed the bickering. It felt so . . . normal.

Normal. Nothing would ever be normal again. Not after what Cal and I had done.

There'd been no mention of a body in the river in this morning's paper, either. Maybe he'd sunk to the bottom, I thought. Or snagged on a submerged rock or log. I pictured him in the icy water, his pale hair floating around his face like seaweed, his hands swaying limply in the current. . . . A sudden rush of nausea almost made me retch.

Mary K. didn't notice. She looked through the windshield at the thin layer of clouds blotting out the morning sun. "I'll be glad when vacation starts."

I forced a smile. "You and me both."

I turned onto our school's street and found that all my usual parking spaces were taken. "Why don't you get out here," I suggested, "and I'll go park across the street."

"Okay. Later." Mary K. clambered out of Das Boot and hurried to her group of friends, her breath coming out in wisps. Today it was cold again, with a biting wind.

Across the street was another small parking lot, in back of an abandoned real estate office. Large sycamores surrounded the lot, looking like peeling skeletons, and several shaggy cypresses made it feel sheltered and private—which was why the stoners usually hung out there when the weather was warmer. No one else was around as I maneuvered Das Boot into a space. Wednesday, after school let out at noon, I had an appointment to take it to Unser's Auto Repair to have the headlight repaired.

"Morgan." The melodious voice made me jump. I whirled to see Selene Belltower sitting in her car three spaces away, her window rolled down.

"Selene!" I walked over to her. "What are you doing here? Is Cal okay?"

"He's much better," Selene assured me. "In fact, he's on his way to school right now. But I wanted to talk to you. Can you get in the car for a moment, please?"

I opened the door, flattered by her attention. In so many ways, she was the witch I hoped someday to be: powerful, the leader of a coven, vastly knowledgeable.

I glanced at my watch as I sank into the passenger seat. It was covered with soft brown leather, heated, and amazingly comfortable. Even so, I hoped Selene could sum up what she had to say in four minutes or less since that was when the last bell would ring.

"Cal told me you found Belwicket's tools," she said, looking excited.

"Yes," I said.

She smiled and shook her head. "What an amazing discovery. How did you find them?"

"I saw Maeve in a vision," I said. "She told me where to find them."

Selene's eyebrows rose. "Goodness. You had a vision?"

"Yes. I mean, I was scrying," I admitted, flushing. I didn't know for sure, but I had a feeling scrying was another thing I wasn't supposed to do as an uninitiated witch. "And I saw Maeve and where the tools might be."

"What were you scrying with? Water?"

"Fire."

She sat back, surprised, as if I had just come up with an impossibly high prime number.

"Fire! You were scrying with fire?"

I nodded, self-conscious but pleased at her astonishment. "I like fire," I said. "It ... speaks to me."

There was a moment of silence, and I started to feel uneasy. I had been bending the rules and following my own path with Wicca practically from the beginning.

"Not many witches scry with fire," Selene told me.

"Why not? It works so well."

"It doesn't for most people," Selene replied. "It's very capricious. It takes a lot of power to scry with fire." I felt her gaze on me and didn't know what to say.

"Where are Maeve's tools now?" Selene asked. I was relieved that she didn't sound angry or disapproving. It felt very intimate in the car, very private, as though what we said here would always be secret.

"They're hidden," I said reassuringly.

"Good," said Selene. "I'm sure you know how very powerful those tools are. I'm glad you're being careful with them. And I just wanted to offer my services, my guidance, and my experience in helping you learn to use them."

I nodded. "Thank you."

"And I would hope, because of our close relationship and your relationship with Cal, that you might want me to see the tools, test them, share my power with them. I'm very strong, and the tools are very strong, and it could be a very exciting thing to put our strengths together."

Just then a familiar gold Explorer rolled into the parking lot. I saw Cal's profile through his smoked window, and my heart leaped. He glanced toward us, pausing for a moment before pulling into a spot and turning off the engine. Eagerly I rolled down my window, and as I did, I heard the morning bell ring.

"Hi!" I said.

He came closer and leaned on the door, looking through the open window. "Hi," he said. His injured wrists were covered by his coat sleeves. "Mom? What are you doing here?"

"I just couldn't wait to talk to Morgan about Belwicket's tools," Selene said with a laugh.

"Oh," said Cal. I was puzzled by the flat tone in his voice. He sounded almost annoyed.

"Um, I feel like I should tell you," I said hesitantly. "I, uh, I bound the tools to me. I don't think they'll work too well for anyone else."

Cal and Selene both stared at me as if I had suddenly announced I was really a man.

"What?" said Selene, her eyes wide.

"I bound the tools to me," I said, wondering if I had acted too hastily. But Alyce had seemed so certain.

"What do you mean, you bound the tools to you?" Cal asked carefully.

I swallowed. I felt suddenly like a kid called in front of the principal. "I did a spell and bound the tools to me, sending my vibrations through them. They're part of me now."

"Whoa. How come?" Cal said.

"Well," I said, "you know, to make it harder for others to use them. And to increase my power when I use them."

"Heavens," said Selene. "Who told you how to do that?"

I opened my mouth to say, "Alyce," but instead, to my surprise, what came out was, "I read about it."

"Hmmm," she said thoughtfully. "Well, there are ways to unbind tools."

"Oh," I said, feeling uncertain. Why would she want me to unbind them?

"I would love to show you some hands-on ways to use them." Selene smiled. "You can't get everything from books."

"No," I agreed. I still felt uncertain and indefinably uneasy. "Well, I'd better get going."

"All right," said Selene. "Congratulations again on finding the tools. I'm so proud of you."

Her words warmed me, and I got out of the car feeling better.

I looked at Cal. "You coming?"

"Yeah," he said. He hesitated as if he were about to say something else, then seemed to change his mind, calling merely, "Talk to you later, Mom."

"Right," she said, and the window rolled up.

Cal set off for school. His strides were so long that I practically had to run to keep up. When I glanced at his profile, I could see that his jaw was set. "What's wrong?" I asked breathlessly. "Are you upset about something?"

He glanced at me. "No," he said. "Just don't want to be late."

But I didn't need my witch senses to see that he was lying. Was he angry at me because I'd bound the tools to me and now no one else could use them?

Or was he angry with Selene? It had almost seemed like he was. But why?

My day went downhill from there. While I was changing classes at fourth period, I accidentally walked in on Matt Adler and Raven Meltzer making out in an empty chem lab. When our eyes met, Matt looked like he wanted to vaporize himself, and Raven looked even more smug than usual. Ugh, I thought. Then it occurred to me that I could never judge anyone again about anything because what I had done was so terrible, so unnatural. And as soon as I thought that, I went into the girls' bathroom and cried.

At lunchtime Cal and I sat with Cirrus at our usual table. The group was quiet today. Robbie was tight-faced, and I wondered how it had gone at Bree's house yesterday. Probably not well since Bree was across the lunchroom sitting on Chip Newton's lap and laughing. Great.

Jenna was even paler than usual. When Cal asked her where Matt was, she said, "I wouldn't know. We broke up last night." She shrugged, and that was that. I was surprised and impressed by how calm she seemed. She was stronger than she looked.

Ethan Sharp and Sharon Goodfine were sitting next to each other. After months of flirting, they were looking into each other's eyes as if they'd finally realized the other was a real person and not just a clever simulation. Sharon shared her bagel with him. It was the only cheerful thing that happened.

Somehow I slogged through the afternoon. I kept thinking about Selene teaching me to use Maeve's tools. One minute I would want to do it, and the next minute I would remember Alyce's warning and decide to keep them to myself. I couldn't make up my mind.

When the final bell rang, I gathered up my things with relief. Only half a day tomorrow, thank the Goddess, and then a four-day weekend. I walked outside, looking for Mary K.

"Hey," said my sister, coming up. "Cold enough for you?"

We glanced up at the striated clouds that scudded slowly across the sky.

"Yeah," I said, hitching up my backpack. "Come on. I'm parked over in the side lot."

Just as I turned, Cal came up. "Hey, Mary K.," he said. Then he ducked his head and spoke only to me. "Is it okay if I come over this afternoon?" There was an unspoken message—we had tons to talk about—and I nodded at once.

"I'll meet you there."

He touched my cheek briefly, smiled at Mary K., then walked beside us to his own car. My sister raised an eyebrow at me, and I shot her a glance.

Once we were in Das Boot and I was cranking the engine, Mary K. said, "So, have you done it yet?"

I almost punched the gas, which would have slammed us right into a tree.

"Good God, Mary K.!" I cried, staring at her.

She giggled, then tried to look defiant. "Well? You've been going out a month, and he's gorgeous, and you can tell *he's* not a virgin. You're my sister. If I don't ask you, who can I ask?"

"Ask about what?" I said irritably, backing out.

"About sex," she said.

I rested my head for a second against the steering wheel. "Mary K., this may surprise you, but you're only fourteen years old. You're a high school freshman. Don't you think you're too young to worry about this?"

As soon as the words were out of my mouth, I wished I could take them back. I sounded just like my mom. I wasn't surprised when my sister's face closed.

"I'm sorry," I said. "You just . . . took me by surprise. Give me a second." I tried to think quickly and drive at the same time. "Sex." I blew out my breath. "No, I haven't done it yet."

Mary K. looked surprised.

I sighed. "Yes, Cal wants to. And I want to. But it hasn't seemed exactly right yet. I mean, I love Cal. He makes me feel unbelievable. And he's totally sexy and all that." My cheeks heated. "But still, it's only been a month, and there's a lot of other stuff going on, and it just . . . hasn't seemed right." I frowned at her pointedly. "And I think it's really important to wait until it *is* exactly right, and you're totally comfortable and sure and crazy in love. Otherwise it's no good." Said the incredibly experienced Morgan Rowlands.

Mary K. looked at me. "What if the other person *is* sure and you just want to trust them?"

Note to self: Do a castration spell on Bakker Blackburn. I breathed in, turned onto our street, and saw Cal in back of us. I pulled into our driveway and turned off the engine but stayed in the car. Cal parked and walked up to the house, waiting for us on the porch.

"I think you know enough to be sure for yourself," I said quietly. "You're not an idiot. You know how you feel. Some people date for years before they're both ready to have sex." Where was I getting this stuff? Years of reading teen magazines?

"The important thing," I went on, "is that you make your own decisions and don't give in to pressure. I told Cal I wasn't ready, and he was majorly disappointed." I lowered my voice as if he could hear us from twenty feet away, outside the car. "I mean, *majorly*. But he accepted my decision and is waiting until I'm ready."

Mary K. looked at her lap.

"However, if for some reason you think it might happen,

for God's sake use nine kinds of birth control and check out his health and be careful and don't get hurt. Okay?"

My sister blushed and nodded. On the porch I saw Cal shifting his feet in the cold.

"Do you want me to send Cal home so we can talk some more?" Please say no.

"No, that's okay," said Mary K. "I think I get it."

"Okay. I'm always here. I mean, if you can't ask your sister, who can you ask?"

She grinned, and we hugged each other. Then we hurried inside. Twenty minutes later Mary K. was doing her homework upstairs and Cal and I were drinking hot tea in the kitchen. And I hoped my sister had taken my words to heart.

7
Self

July 2000

The council called me to London upon my return from the North. I spent three days answering questions about everything from the causes of the Clan wars to the medicinal properties of mugwort. I wrote essays analyzing past decisions of the elders. I performed spells and rituals.

And then they turned me down. Not because my power is weak or my knowledge scanty, nor yet because I am too young, but because they distrust my motives. They think I am after vengeance for Linden, for my parents.

But that's not it, not anymore. I spoke to Athar about it last night. She's the only one who truly understands, I think.

"You aren't after vengeance. You're after redemption," she told me, and her black eyes measured me. "But, Giomanach, I'm not sure which is the more dangerous quest."

She's a deep one, my cousin Athar. I don't know when she grew to be so wise.

I won't give up. I will write to the council again today. I'll make them understand.

—Giomanach

Our kitchen was about one-sixth the size of Cal's kitchen, and instead of granite counters and custom country French cabinets, we had worn Formica and cabinets from about 1983. But our kitchen felt homier.

I rested my legs over Cal's knees under the table and we leaned toward each other, talking. The idea that maybe someday we would have our very own house, just us two, made me shiver. I looked up at Cal's smooth tan skin, his perfect nose, his strong eyebrows, and sighed. We needed to talk about Hunter.

"I'm really shaken up," I said quietly.

"I know. I am, too. I never thought it would come to that." He gave a dry laugh. "Actually, I thought we would just beat each other up a bit, and the whole thing would blow over. But when Hunter pulled out the *braigh*—"

"The silver chain he was using?"

Cal shuddered. "Yes," he said, his voice rough. "It was spelled. Once it was on me, I was powerless."

"Cal, I just can't believe what happened," I said, my eyes filling with tears. I brushed them away with one hand. "I can't think about anything else. And why hasn't anyone found the body yet? What are we going to do when they do find it? I swear, every time the phone rings, I think it's going to be the police, asking me to come down to the station and answer some questions." A tear overflowed and ran down my cheek. "I just can't get over this."

"I'm so sorry." Cal pushed his chair closer to mine and put his arms around me. "I wish we were at my house," he said quietly. "I just want to hold you without worrying about your folks coming in."

I nodded, sniffling. "What are we going to do?"

"There's nothing we can do, Morgan," Cal said, kissing my temple. "It was horrible, and I've cursed myself a thousand times for involving you in it. But it happened, and we can't take it back. And never forget that we acted in self-defense. Hunter was trying to kill me. You were trying to protect me. What else could we have done?"

I shook my head.

"I've never been through anything like this before," Cal said softly against my hair. "It's the worst thing in my life. But you know what? I'm glad I'm going through it with you. I mean, I'm sorry you were involved. I wish to the Goddess that you weren't. But since we were in it together, I'm so glad I have you." He shook his head. "This isn't making sense. I'm just trying to say that in an awful way, this has made me feel closer to you."

I looked up into his eyes. "Yeah, I know what you mean."

We stayed like that, sitting at the table, our arms around each other, until my shoulder blades began to ache from the angle and I reluctantly pulled away. I had to change the subject.

"Your mom seemed really excited about my tools," I said, taking a sip of my tea.

Cal pushed his hands through his raggedy dark hair. "Yeah. She's like a little kid—she wants to get her hands on every new thing. Especially something like Belwicket's tools."

"Is there something special about Belwicket in particular?"

Cal shrugged, looking thoughtful. He sipped his tea and said, "I guess just the mystery of it—how it was destroyed, and how old the coven was and how powerful. It's a blessing the tools weren't lost. Oh, and they were Woodbane," he added as an afterthought.

"Does it matter that they were Woodbane since Belwicket had renounced evil?"

"I don't know," said Cal. "Probably not. I think it probably matters more what you *do* with your magick."

I breathed in the steam from my tea. "Maybe I bound the tools to me without thinking it through too well," I said. "What would happen if another witch tried to use them now?"

Cal shrugged. "It's not predictable. Another witch might subvert the tools' power in an unexpected way. Actually, it's pretty unusual for someone to bind a coven's tools only to themselves." He looked up and met my glance.

"I just felt they were mine," I said lamely. "Mine, my birth mother's, her mother's. I wanted them to be all mine."

Nodding, Cal patted my leg, across his knee. "I'd probably do the same thing if they were mine," he said, and I adored him for his support.

"And then Mom would kill me," he added, laughing. I laughed, too.

"Your mom said I was an unusually powerful witch, this morning in the car," I said. "So witches have different strengths of power? In one of my Wiccan history books it talks about some witches being more powerful than others. Does that mean that they just know more, or does it mean something about their innate power?"

"Both," Cal said. He put his feet on either side of mine under the table. "It's like regular education. How accomplished you are depends on how intelligent you are as well as how much education you have. Of course, blood witches are always going to be more powerful than humans. But even among blood witches there's definitely a range. If you're naturally a weak witch, then you can study and practice all you want and your powers will be only so-so. If you're a naturally powerful witch, yet don't know anything about Wicca, you can't do much, either. It's the combination that matters."

"Well, how strong is your mother, for example?" I asked. "On a scale of one to ten?"

Laughing, Cal leaned across and kissed my cheek. "Careful. Your math genes are showing."

I grinned.

"Let's see," he mused. He rubbed his chin, and I saw a flash of bandage on his wrist. My heart ached for the pain he had gone through. "My mother, on a scale of one to ten. Let's make it a scale of one to a hundred. And a weak witch without much training would be about a twelve."

I nodded, putting this mythical person on the scale.

"And then someone like, oh, Mereden the Wise or Denys Haraldson would be up in the nineties."

I nodded, recognizing the names Mereden and Denys from my Wiccan history books. They had been powerful witches, role models, educators, enlighteners. Mereden had been burned at the stake back in 1517. Denys had died in 1942 in a London bomb blitz.

"My mom is about an eighty or an eighty-five on that scale," Cal said.

My eyes widened. "Wow. That's way up there."

"Yep. She's no one to mess with," Cal said wryly.

"Where are you? Where am I?"

"It's harder to tell," Cal said. He glanced at his watch. "You know, it'll be dark soon, and I'd really like to put some spells on your house and car while Sky's still in town."

"Okay," I agreed, standing up. "But you really can't say where we are on the Cal scale of witch power? Which reminds me: is it Calvin or just Cal?"

He laughed and brought his mug over to the sink. From upstairs we heard Mary K. blasting her latest favorite CD. "It's Calhoun," he said as we walked into the living room.

"Calhoun," I said, trying it out. I liked it. "Answer my question, Calhoun."

"Let me think," said Cal, putting on his coat. "It's hard to be objective about myself—but I think I'm about a sixty-two. I mean, I'm young; my powers will likely increase as I get older. I'm from good lines, I'm a good student, but I'm not a shooting star. I'm not going to take the Wiccan world by storm. So I'd give myself about a sixty-two."

I laughed and hugged him through his coat. He put his arms around me and stroked my hair down my back. "But you," he said quietly, "you are something different."

"What, like a twenty?" I said.

"Goddess, no," he said.

"Thirty-five? Forty?" I made my eyes look big and hopeful. It made me happy to tease and joke with Cal. It was so easy to love him, to be myself, and to like who I was with him.

He smiled slowly, making me catch my breath at his

beauty. "No, sweetie," he said gently. "I think you're more like a ninety. Ninety-five."

Startled, I stared at him, then realized he was joking. "Oh, very funny," I said, laughing. I pulled away and put on my own coat. "We can't *all* be magickal wonders. We can't *all* be—"

"You're a shooting star," he said. His face was serious, even grave. "You *are* a magickal wonder. A prodigy. You could take the Wiccan world by storm."

I gaped, trying to make sense of his words. "What are you talking about?"

"It's why I've been trying to get you to go slowly, not rush things," he said. "You have a tornado inside you, but you have to learn to control it. Like with Maeve's tools. I wish you'd let my mother guide you. I'm worried that you might be getting into something over your head because you're not seeing the big picture."

"I don't know what you mean," I said uncertainly.

He smiled again, his mood lightening, and dropped a kiss on my lips. "Oh, it's no big deal," he said with teasing sarcasm. "It's just, you know, you have a power that comes along every couple of generations. Don't worry about it."

Despite my confusion, Cal really wouldn't talk about it anymore. Outside, he concentrated on spelling Das Boot and my house with runes and spells of protection, and once that was done, he went home. And I was left with too many questions.

That night after dinner my parents took Mary K. to her friend Jaycee's violin recital. Once they were gone, I locked all the doors, feeling melodramatic. Then I went upstairs, took out Maeve's tools, and went into my room.

Sitting on my floor, I examined the tools again. They felt natural in my hands, comfortable, an extension of myself. I wondered what Cal had meant about not seeing the big picture. To me, the big picture was: these had been my grandmother's tools, then my mother's; now they were mine. Any other big picture was secondary to that.

Still, I was sure Selene could teach me a lot about them. It was a compelling idea. I wondered again why Alyce had urged me to bind them to myself so quickly.

I was halfway through making a circle before I realized what I was doing. With surprise, I looked up to find a piece of chalk in my hand and my circle half drawn. My mother's green silk robe, embroidered with magickal symbols, stars, and runes, was draped over my clothes. A candle burned in the fire cup, incense was in the air cup, and the other two cups held earth and water. Cal's silver pentacle was warm at my throat. I hadn't taken it off since he'd given it to me.

The tools wanted me to use them. They wanted to come alive again after languishing, unused and hidden, for so long. I felt their promise of power. Working quickly, I finished casting my circle. Then, holding the athame, I blessed the Goddess and the God and invoked them.

Now what?

Scrying.

I looked into the candle flame, concentrating and relaxing at the same time. I felt my muscles ease, my breathing slow, my thoughts drift free. Words came to my mind, and I spoke them aloud.

"I sense magick growing and swelling.
I visit knowledge in its dwelling.
For me alone these tools endure,
To make my magick strong and sure."

Then I thought, I am ready to see, and then . . . things started happening.

I saw rows of ancient books and knew these were texts I needed to study. I knew I had years of circles ahead of me, years of observing and celebrating the cycles. I saw myself, bent and sobbing, and understood that the road would not be easy. Exhilarated, I said, "I'm ready to see more."

Abruptly my vision changed. I saw an older me leaning over a cauldron, and I looked like a children's cartoon of a witch, with long, stringy hair, bad skin, sunken cheeks, hands like claws. It was so horrible, I almost giggled nervously. That other me was conjuring, surrounded by sharp-edged, dripping wet stone, as if I stood in a cave by a sea. Outside, lightning flashed and cracked into the cave, shining on the walls, and my face was contorted with the effort of working magick. The cave was glowing with power, that other Morgan was giddy with power, and the whole scene felt awful, bizarre, frightening, yet somehow seductive.

I swallowed hard and blinked several times, trying to bring myself out of it. I couldn't get enough air and was dimly aware that I was gaping like a fish, trying to get more oxygen to my brain. When I blinked again, I saw sunlight and another, older Morgan walking through a field of wheat, like one of those corny shampoo commercials. I was pregnant. There was no dramatic power around me, no ecstatic conjuring or anything—just peace and quiet and calm.

Now I was breathing quickly, and every time my eyes closed, I alternated between the two images, the two Morgans. I became aware of a deep-seated pain in my chest and throat, and I started to feel panicky and out of control.

I want to get out of this, I thought. I want to get out. Let me *out!*

Somehow I managed to wrench my gaze away from the candle flame, and then I was leaning over, gasping on my carpet, feeling dizzy and sick. I was flooded with sensation, with memories and visions I couldn't interpret or even see clearly, and suddenly I knew that I was about to vomit. I staggered to my feet, breaking my circle, and lurched drunkenly to the bathroom. I yanked off my robe, slid across the tiled wall until I hovered over the toilet, and then I threw up, almost crying with misery.

I don't know how long I was in there, but it was a long while, and finally I started to cry, aching, deep sobs. I sat there till the sobs subsided, then shakily got to my feet, flushed the toilet, and crept to the sink. Splashing my face with cold water helped, and I brushed my teeth and washed my face again and changed into my pajamas. I felt weak and hollow, as if I had the flu.

Back in my room, Dagda sat in the middle of the broken circle, gazing meditatively at the candle. "Hi, boy," I whispered, then cupped my hand and blew out the candle. My hands trembling, I dismantled everything, storing the tools in their metal box, folding my mother's robe, which seemed alive, crackling with energy. The very air in my room felt charged and unhealthy. I flung open a window, welcoming the twenty-five-degree chill.

I vacuumed up my circle and hid the toolbox again, spelling the HVAC vent with runes of secrecy. Soon after that, the front door opened and I heard my parents' voices. The phone rang at the same moment. I sprang over to the hall extension and said breathlessly, "Hi. I'm glad you called."

"Are you okay?" Cal said. "I suddenly got a weird feeling about you."

He would not be thrilled to hear about my using my mother's tools in a circle. Lack of experience, lack of knowledge, lack of supervision. And so on.

"I'm okay," I said, trying to slow my breathing. I did feel much better, though still a bit shaky. "I just—missed you."

"I miss you, too," he said quietly. "I wish I could be there with you at night."

A cool breeze from my room gave me a quick shiver. "That would be wonderful," I said.

"Well, it's late," he said. "Sleep tight. Think of me when you're lying there."

I felt his voice in the pit of my stomach, and my hand tightened on the phone.

"I will," I whispered as Mary K. started coming upstairs loudly.

"Good night, my love."

"Good night."

8

Symbols

September 2000

I'm in Ireland. I went to the town of Ballynigel, where the Belwicket coven once was. It was wiped out around Imbolc in 1982, along with most of the town. So far it's the only Woodbane coven I've found that the dark wave has destroyed. But everyone knows Belwicket renounced evil back in the 1800s and had kept to the council's laws since the laws were first written. Did that have something to do with it? When I stood there and saw the bits of riven earth and charred stones that are all that's left, it made my heart ache.

Tonight I am meeting with Jeremy Mertwick, from the second ring of the council. I have written them a letter every week, appealing their decision. I still hope to make them see reason. I am strong and sure, and my pain has made me older than they know.

—Giomanach

"C'mon, last day before break," Mary K. coaxed, standing over my bed. She waved a warm Toaster Strudel under my nose. I sat up, patted Dagda, and then staggered unhappily to the shower.

"Five minutes," Mary K. called in warning. Then I heard her say, "Come on, little guy. Auntie Mary K. will feed you."

Her voice faded as the hot spray needled down my skin, making me feel semihuman.

Downstairs, my sister handed me a Diet Coke. "Robbie called. His car won't start. We need to pick him up on the way."

We headed out and detoured over to Robbie's house. He was waiting out front, leaning against his red Volkswagen.

"Battery dead again?" I greeted him as he climbed into Das Boot's backseat.

He nodded glumly. "Again." We drove on in companionable morning silence.

At school Mary K. was met as usual by Bakker.

"Young love," Robbie said dryly, watching them nuzzle.

"Ugh," I said, turning off the engine.

"Thanks for the ride," Robbie said. Something in his voice made me turn and look at him.

"So I kissed Bree on Monday," he said.

I sat back, taking my hand off the door handle. I had been so wrapped up in my own misery that I had forgotten to check in with Robbie about Bree. "Wow," I said, examining his face. "I wondered what had happened. I, um, I saw her yesterday with Chip."

Robbie nodded, scanning the school grounds through the car window. He said nothing, and I prompted him: "So?"

He shrugged, his broad shoulders moving inside his army surplus parka. He gave a short laugh. "She let me kiss her. It blew my mind. She just laughed and seemed into it, and I thought, All *right*. And then I came up for air and said that I loved her." He stopped.

"And?" I practically screeched.

"She wasn't into *that*. Dropped me like a stone. Practically pushed me out the door." He rubbed his forehead, as if he had a headache. Silently I offered him my soda, and he finished it off and wiped his mouth with the back of his hand.

"Hmmm," I said. I didn't trust Bree anymore. Before, she might have done the same thing to Robbie, but now I couldn't help wondering how her involvement in Kithic had affected her actions.

"Yeah. Hmmm."

"But the making out worked?" I asked.

"Worked fabulously. Hot, hot, hot." He couldn't help grinning at the memory.

"Okay, I don't need to know," I said quickly.

I took a minute to think. Was Bree capable of using Robbie for some dark purpose, or was she just toying with him in her usual way? I didn't know. I decided to take a chance.

"Well, my advice to you is," I said, "just make out with her. Don't talk to her about your feelings. Not yet, anyway."

He frowned. Outside the car, we saw Cal crunching toward us through the leftover snow, his breath puffing like a dragon's. As usual, my heart lurched when I saw him.

"Hey, I *love* her. I don't want to use her like that."

"No. My point is, let *her* use *you* like that."

"Like a boy toy?" He sounded outraged, but I saw a fleeting interest cross his face.

"Like someone who knocks her off her feet," I pointed out. "Someone who gives her something she can't get from Chip Newton or anyone else."

Robbie stared at me. "You are *ruthless*." I heard admiration in his voice.

"I want you to be happy," I said firmly.

"I think, deep down, you want *her* to be happy, too," Robbie said, unfolding his long frame from the backseat. "Hey, Cal," he said, before I could respond to his remark.

Cal leaned into the open door. "Getting out anytime soon?"

I looked at him. "How about you get in, we take off, and just keep driving until we run out of gas?" I checked my gauge. "Got a full tank." I was only half joking.

When I glanced up, I was startled by the look in his eyes. "Don't tempt me," he said, his voice rough. For a long moment I hung there, suspended in time, pinned by the fierce look of desire and longing. I remembered how it had felt, making out on his bed, touching each other, and I shuddered.

"Hey, Cal," said Ethan from the sidewalk, waving at us as he went into the building.

Cal sighed. "Guess we better go in."

I nodded, not trusting myself to speak.

Cal and I joined the other Cirrus members at the top of the basement stairs.

"Talk about brutal weather," said Jenna as we walked up. She hugged her Nordic sweater closely around her, looking ethereal. I wondered how her asthma was lately and if I could use my tools to help her breathing.

"It's not even officially winter yet. This is the third-coldest autumn on record," Sharon complained, and snuggled closer to Ethan, who looked pleased. Hiding a smile, I sank down on a step, and Cal sat next to me and twined his hand through mine.

"Oh, this is cozy," said Raven's voice. Her dark head appeared over the staircase, followed by another dark head: Matt's. He sat down on a step, the picture of guilt, and she stood there smiling down at us, the Wicked Witch of the Northeast.

"Hi, Raven," said Cal, and she looked him up and down with her shining black eyes.

"Hello, Cal," she drawled. "Having a coven meeting?" She didn't bother lowering her voice, and some students walking past glanced up, startled. And this was Bree's new best friend.

"How's *your* coven going?" I heard myself ask. "Everything okay with Sky?"

Raven's eyes focused on me. Her silver nose ring glinted, her full lips were painted a rich purple, and I was struck by her presence: she was bizarre and luxurious, silly and compelling at the same time.

"Don't talk about Sky," Raven said. "She's a better witch than you'll ever be. You have no idea what you're up against." She stroked two fingers along Matt's smooth cheek, making him flinch, and walked off.

"Well, that was fun," said Robbie when she was gone.

"Matt, why don't you just join Kithic?" Jenna said abruptly, her jaw tight.

Matt frowned, not raising his eyes. "I don't want to," he mumbled.

"Okay, we only have a minute," said Cal, getting down to business. "We have a circle coming up this Saturday, our first in two weeks, and I have an assignment for you."

"I'm sorry, Cal, I won't be here," said Sharon.

"That's okay," he said. "I know you have plans with your family. Do these exercises on your own, and tell us about it the next time we see you. Now, one of the basic platforms of Wicca is self-knowledge. One of my teachers once said, 'Know yourself, and you know the universe,' and that may have been overstating it a bit, but not entirely."

Jenna and Sharon nodded, and I saw Ethan gently massaging Sharon's shoulder.

"I want you to work on self-imaging," Cal went on. "You're going to find your personal correspondences, your own . . . what's the word? I guess *helpers* or *connectors* sort of comes close. They're the things that speak to you, that feel like you, that awaken something in you. Objects or symbols that strengthen your connection to your own magick."

"Not following you here," said Robbie.

"Sorry—let me give you some examples. Things like stones, the four elements, flowers, animals, herbs, seasons, foods," said Cal, ticking them off on his fingers. "My stone is a tigereye. I often use it in my rituals. My element is fire. My metal is gold. My personal rune is—a secret. My season is autumn. My sign is Gemini. My cloth is linen."

"And your car of choice is Ford," Robbie said, and Cal laughed.

"Right. No, seriously. Think especially about elements, stars, stones, seasons, and plants. Define yourselves, but don't limit yourselves. Don't force anything. If nothing speaks to you, don't worry about it. Just move on to something else. But explore your connection to earthly things and to unearthly things." Cal looked around at us. "Any questions?"

"This is so cool," said Sharon.

"I already know your correspondences," Ethan told her. "Your metal is gold, your stone is a diamond, your season is the post-Christmas sale season . . . ouch!" he said as Sharon clipped him smartly on the head. He laughed and raised his hands to defend himself.

"Very funny!" said Sharon, trying not to smile. "And your element is *dirt,* and your metal is *lead,* and your plant is *marijuana!*"

"I don't smoke anymore!" Ethan protested.

We were all laughing, and I felt almost lighthearted in a way that I hadn't since Hunter—

The first bell rang, and suddenly the halls were filled with students swarming to their homerooms. We gathered our various belongings and went our separate ways. And I wondered how much longer I could take this inner darkness.

After the school bell rang at noon, I waited for Cal and Mary K. by the east entrance. It was snowing again. Footsteps sounded behind me, and I turned to see Raven and Bree heading toward the double doors. Bree's face hardened when she saw me.

"So, what are you guys doing for Thanksgiving?" I blinked in surprise as the words left my mouth. Two pairs of dark eyes locked in on me as if I were glowing like a neon light.

"Um, well, gee," Raven said. "I guess I'm celebrating a day

of wonder and thankfulness in the arms of my loving family. How about you?"

Since I knew her loving family consisted of a mother who had too many boyfriends and an older brother who was away in the army, I guessed she didn't have plans.

I shrugged. "Family. Turkey. A pumpkin pie gone wrong. Keeping my cat off the dining room table."

"You have a cat?" Bree asked, unable to help herself. She had a major weakness for cats.

I nodded. "A gray kitten. He's incredibly adorable. Totally bad. Bad and adorable."

"This is delightful"—Raven sighed as Bree opened her mouth to speak—"but we really must be going. We have things to do, people to see."

"Sky?" I asked.

"None of your business," Raven said with a smirk.

Bree was silent as they thumped down the stairs in their matching heavy boots.

A second later Mary K. ran up to say she was going to Jaycee's and Mom had said it was okay, and then Cal came up and asked if I could come over and of course I wanted to. I called Unser's Auto Shop and canceled Das Boot's repair appointment. Then I followed Cal to his house, where we could be alone.

Cal's room was wonderful. It ran the whole length and breadth of the big house since it was the attic. Six dormer windows made cozy nooks, bookcases lined the walls, and he had his own fireplace and an outside staircase leading down to the back patio. His bed was wide and romantic-looking, with white bed linens and a gauzy mosquito net looped out of the way. The dark wooden desk where he did his home-work had rows of cream-colored candles lining its edge. I had never been in here without envying him this magickal space.

"Want some tea?" he asked, gesturing to the electric ket-tle. I nodded, and we didn't speak, enjoying the silence and safety of his room.

Two minutes later Cal put a cup of tea into my hand, and I adjusted its temperature and took a sip. "Mmm."

Cal turned away and stood looking out the window. "Morgan," he said. "Forgive me."

"For what?" I asked, raising my eyebrows.

"I lied to you," he said quietly, and my heart clutched in panic.

"Oh?" I marveled at how calm my voice sounded.

"About my clan." The words had almost no sound.

My heart skipped a beat, and I stared at him. He turned to me, his beautiful golden eyes holding promises of love, of passion, of a shared future. And yet his words . . .

He took a sip of tea. The pale light from the window outlined the planes of his cheekbones, the line of his jaw. I waited, and he came close to me, so that his shirt was almost brushing mine and I could see the fine texture of his skin.

Cal turned toward the window again and pushed his fingers through his hair, holding it back from his left temple. I caught a glimpse of a birthmark there, beneath the hair. I reached up and traced its outline with my fingers. It was a dark red athame, just like the one I had under my arm. The mark of the Woodbane clan.

"Hunter was right," Cal went on, his voice low. "I am Woodbane. And I've always known it."

I needed to sit down. I had been so upset when I first found out about my heritage, and Cal had said it wasn't so terrible. Now I saw why. I put down my tea and walked across the room to the futon couch. I sank onto it, and he came to kneel at my side.

"My father was Woodbane, and so is my mother," he said, looking more uncomfortable than I'd ever seen him. "They're not the Belwicket kind of Woodbanes, where everyone renounces evil and swears to do good." He shrugged, not looking at me. "There's another kind of Woodbane, who practices magick traditionally, I mean traditionally for their clan. For Woodbanes that means not being so picky about how you get your knowledge and why you use your power. Traditional Woodbanes don't subscribe to the council's edict that witches never interfere with humans. They figure, humans interfere with us, we all live in the same world, not two separate universes, so they're going to use their powers to take care of problems they might have with humans, or to protect themselves, or to get what they need. . . ."

I was unable to take my eyes off his face.

"After my dad married my mother, I think they started to go different ways, magickally," Cal continued. "Mom has always been very powerful and ambitious, and I think my father disagreed with some of the things she was doing."

"Like what?" I asked, a little shocked.

He waved an impatient hand. "You know, taking too many risks. Anyway, then my dad met Fiona, his second wife. Fiona was a Wyndenkell. I don't know if he wanted a Wyndenkell alliance or he just loved her more. But either way, he left my mother."

I was finally getting some answers. "But if Hunter was right and your father was also *his* father, then wasn't he half Woodbane himself?" This sounded like some awful soap opera. *The Young and the Wiccan.*

"That's the thing," said Cal. "Of course he was. So it made no sense for him to persecute Woodbanes. But he seemed to have a thing about them, like Mom said. An obsession. I wondered if he blamed my father—our father—for what happened to his parents and their coven, for some reason, and so decided to get all Woodbanes. Who knows? He was unhinged."

"So you're Woodbane," I said, still trying to take it all in.

"Yes," he admitted.

"Why didn't you tell me before? I was *hysterical* about being Woodbane."

"I know," he said, sighing. "I should have. But Belwicket was a different kind of Woodbane, a completely good Woodbane, above reproach. I wasn't sure you would understand my family's heritage. I mean, it isn't like they're all evil. They don't worship demons or anything like that. It's just—they do what they want to do. They don't always follow rules."

"Why are you telling me now?"

At last he looked at me, and I felt the pull of his gaze. "Because I love you. I trust you. I don't want any secrets to come between us. And—"

The door to his room suddenly flew open. I jumped about a foot in the air. Selene stood there, dressed beautifully in a dark gold sweater and tweed pants.

Cal stood with swift grace. "What the hell are you doing?"

I had never heard anyone speak to their mother this way, and I flinched.

"What are *you* doing?" she countered. "I felt—what are you talking about?"

"None of your business," he said, and Selene's eyes flashed with surprise.

"We discussed this," she said in a low voice.

"Mom, you need to leave," Cal said flatly. I was embarrassed and confused and also worried: no way did I want to get in between these two if they were fighting.

"How—how did you know he was telling me anything?" I ventured.

"I felt it," Selene said. "I felt him say Woodbane."

This was really interesting. Creepy, but interesting.

"Yes, you're Woodbane," I said, standing up. "I'm Woodbane, too. Is there a reason I shouldn't know your clan?"

"Mom, I trust Morgan, and you need to trust me," Cal said thinly. "Now, will you get back to your work and leave us alone, or do I have to spell the door?"

My lips curved into an involuntary smile, and a second later the tension on Selene's face broke. She breathed out. "Very nice. Threaten your mother," she said tartly.

"Hey, I'll make it so you'll *never* find your way up here again," Cal said, his hands on his hips. He was smiling now, but I felt he wasn't entirely joking. I thought of Selene walking in on us when we were rolling around on Cal's bed and secretly decided maybe spelling the door wouldn't be such a bad idea.

"Forgive me," Selene said at last. "I'm sorry. It's just—Woodbanes have a terrible reputation. We're used to guarding our privacy fiercely. For a moment I forgot who Cal was talking to—and how extraordinary and trustworthy you are. I'm sorry."

"It's okay," I said, and Selene turned around and left. Quickly Cal stepped to the door and snapped the lock behind her, then traced several sigils and runes around the frame of the door with his fingers, muttering something.

"Okay," he said. "That will keep her out." He sounded smug, and I smiled.

"Are you sure?"

The answering look he gave me took my breath away. When he held out his hand, I went to him immediately, and next we tumbled onto his wide bed, the white comforter billowing cozily beneath us. For a long time we kissed and held each other, and I knew that I felt even closer to him than before. Each time we were alone together, we went a little further, and today I needed to feel close to him, needed to be comforted by his touch. Restlessly I pushed my hands under his shirt, against his smooth skin.

I never wore a bra, having a distinct lack of need, and when his hands slipped under my shirt and unerringly found their way to my breasts, I almost cried out. One part of my mind hoped the spell on his door was really foolproof; the other part of my mind turned to tapioca.

I pulled him tightly to me, feeling his desire, hearing his breathing quicken in my ear, amazed at how much I loved him.

This time it was Cal who gradually slowed, who eased the fierceness of his kisses, who calmed his breathing and so made me calm mine. Apparently today would not be the day, either. I was both relieved and disappointed.

After our breathing had more or less returned to normal, he stroked my hair away from my face and said, "I have something to show you."

"Huh?" I said. But he was rolling off the bed, straightening his clothing.

Then he held out his hand to me. "Come," he said, and I followed him without question.

9

Secrets

It's odd to be the son of a famous witch. Everyone watches you, from the time you can walk and talk—watches you for signs of genius or of mediocrity. You're never offstage.

Mom raised me as she saw fit. She has plans for me, my future. I've never really discussed them with her, only listened to her tell me about them. Until recently, it never crossed my mind to disagree. It's flattering to have someone prepare you for greatness, sure of your ability to pull it off.

Yet since my love came into my life, I feel differently. She questions things, she stands up for herself. She's so naive but so strong, too. She makes me want things I've never wanted before.

I remember back in California—I was sixteen. Mom had started a coven. It was the usual smoke and mirrors—Mom using her circle's powers as sort of an energy boost so she wouldn't have to deplete her own—but then to our surprise she unearthed a very strong witch, a woman about twenty-five or so, who had no idea of her bloodlines. During circles she blew us away. So Mom asked me to get close to her. I did—it was surprisingly easy. Then Mom extinguished her during the Rite of Dubh Síol. It upset me, even though I'd known that it might happen.

It won't come to that this time. I'll make sure.

—Sgàth

As Cal led me down his outside steps to the back patio, the last flakes of falling snow brushed my face and landed on my hair. I held tightly to the iron rail; the metal stairs were slick with snow and ice.

Cal offered me his hand at the bottom of the stair. I crunched onto the snow, and he began to lead me across the stone patio. We were both cold; our coats had been in the downstairs foyer, and we hadn't gotten them.

I realized we were heading toward the pool. "Oh, God, you can't be thinking about going skinny-dipping!" I said, only half joking.

Cal laughed, throwing back his head as he led me past the big pool. "No. It's covered for the winter, underneath that snow. Of course, if you're willing ..."

"I'm not," I said quickly. I had been the lone holdout from a group swim at our coven's second meeting.

He laughed again, and then we were at the little building that served as the pool house. Built to look like a miniature version of the big house, its stone walls were covered with clinging ivy, brown in winter.

Cal opened a door, and we stepped into one of the small

dressing rooms. It was decorated luxuriously, with gold hooks, spare terry-cloth robes, and full-length mirrors.

"What are we doing here?" I looked at my pale self in the mirror and made a face.

"Patience," Cal teased, and opened another door that led to a bathroom, complete with shower stall and a rack of fluffy white towels. Now I was really confused.

From his pocket Cal took a key ring, selected a key, and opened a small, locked closet. The door swung open to reveal shallow shelves with toiletries and cleaning supplies.

Cal stood back and gently swept his hands around the door frame, and I saw the faint glimmer of sigils tracing its perimeter. He muttered some words that I couldn't understand, and then the shelves swung backward to reveal an opening about five feet high and maybe two feet wide. There was another room behind it.

I raised my eyebrows at Cal. "You guys have a thing for hidden rooms," I said, thinking of his mother's concealed library in the main house.

Cal grinned. "Of course. We're witches," he said, and ducked through the door. I followed, stepping through, then straightening cautiously on the other side.

Cal stood there, expectant. "Help me light candles," he said, "so you can see better."

I glanced around, my magesight immediately adjusting to the darkness, and found myself in a very small room, perhaps seven feet by seven feet. There was one tiny, leaded-glass window set high up on the wall, beneath the unexpectedly high ceiling.

Cal started lighting candles. I was about to say it wasn't necessary, I could see fine, but then I realized he wanted to create an effect. I looked around, and my gaze landed on the burnt wick of a thick cream-colored pillar candle. I need fire, I thought, then blinked as the wick burst into flame.

It mesmerized me, and I leaned, timelost, into the wavering, triangular bloom of flame swaying seductively about the wick. I saw the wick shrivel and curl as the intense heat made the fibers contract and blacken, heard the roar of the victorious fire as it consumed the wick and surged upward in ecstasy. I felt the softening of the wax below as it sighed and acquiesced, melting and flowing into liquid.

My eyes shining, I glanced up to see Cal staring at me almost in alarm. I swallowed, wondering if I had made one of those Wiccan faux pas I was so good at.

"The fire," I murmured lamely in explanation. "It's pretty."

"Light another one," he said, and I turned to the next candle and thought about fire, and an unseen spark of life jumped from me to the wick, where it burst into a bloom of light. He didn't have to encourage me to do more. One by one, I lit the candles that lined the walls, covered the tiny bookcase, dripped out of wine bottles, and guttered on top of plates thick with old wax.

The room was now glowing, the hundreds of small flames lighting our skin, our hair, our eyes. In the middle of the floor was a single futon covered with a thin, soft, oriental rug. I sat on it, clasped my arms around my knees, and looked around me. Cal sat next to me.

"So this is your secret clubhouse?" I asked, and he chuckled and put his arm around me.

"Something like that," he agreed. "This is my sanctuary."

Now that I wasn't lighting candles, I had the time to be awestruck by my surroundings. Every square inch of wall and ceiling was painted with magickal symbols, only some of which I recognized. My brows came together as I tried to make out runes and marks of power.

My mathematician's brain started ticking: Cal and Selene had moved here right before school started—the beginning of September. It was almost the end of November now: that left not quite three months. I turned to look at him.

"How did you do all this in three months?"

He gave a short laugh. "Three months? I did this in three weeks, before school started. Lots of late nights."

"What do you do in here?"

He smiled down at me. "Make magick," he said.

"What about your room?"

"The main house is full of my mother's vibrations, not to mention those of her coven members. My room is fine for most things; it's no problem for us to have circles there. But for my stuff alone, sensitive spells, spells needing a lot of energy, I come here." He looked around, and I wondered if he was remembering all the warm late-summer nights he had been in here, painting, making magick, making the walls vibrate with his energy. Bowls of charred incense littered the floor and the bookshelves, and the books of magick lined up behind them were dark and faded, looking immeasurably old. In one corner was an altar, made of a polished chunk of marble as big as a suitcase. It was draped with a purple velvet cloth and held candles, bowls of incense, Cal's athame, a vase of spidery hothouse orchids, and a Celtic cross.

"This is what I wanted to show you," he said quietly, his arm warm across my back. "I've never shown this to anyone, although my mother knows it's here. I would never let any of the other Cirrus members see this room. It's too private."

My eyes swept across the dense writing, picking out a rune here and there. I had no idea how long we had been sitting there, but I became aware that I was sweating. The room was so small that just the heat of the candles was starting to make it too warm. It occurred to me that the candles were burning oxygen, and Practical Morgan looked for a vent. I couldn't see one, but that didn't mean anything. The room was so chaotic that it was hard to focus on any one thing.

I realized in surprise that I wouldn't be comfortable making magick in this room. To me it was starting to seem claustrophobic, jangling, as if all my nerves were being subtly irritated. I noticed that my breath was coming faster.

"You're my soul mate," Cal whispered. "Only you could handle being here. Someday we'll make magick here, together. We'll surprise everybody."

I didn't know what to think of that. I was starting to feel distinctly ill at ease.

"I think I'd better get home," I said, gathering my feet beneath me. "I don't want to be late."

I knew it sounded lame, and I could sense Cal's slight withdrawal. I felt guilty for not sharing his enthusiasm. But I really needed to get out of there.

"Of course," Cal said, standing and helping me to my feet. One by one he blew out the candles, and I could hear the minuscule droplets of searing wax splatting against the walls. One candle at a time, the room grew darker, and although I could see perfectly, when the room was dark, it felt unbearable, its weight pressing in on me.

Abruptly, not waiting for Cal, I stepped back through the small door, ducking so I wouldn't whack my head. I didn't stop till I was outside in the blessedly frigid air. I breathed in and out several times, feeling my head clear, seeing my breath puff out like smoke.

Cal followed me a moment later, pulling the pool-house door closed behind him.

"Thank you for showing it to me," I said, sounding stiff and polite.

He led me back to the house. My nerves felt raw as I collected my coat from the front foyer. Outside again, Cal walked me to my car.

"Thanks for coming over," he said, leaning in through the car window.

I was chilled in the frosted air, and my breath puffed out as I remembered the things we had done in his bedroom and the sharp contrast with how I had felt in the pool house.

"I'll talk to you later," I said, tilting my head up to kiss him. Then I was pulling out, my one headlight sweeping across a world seemingly made of ice.

10

Undercurrents

October 2000

I came home from Ireland this week for Alwyn's initiation. It's hard to believe she's fourteen: she seems both younger, with her knobby knees and tall, coltish prettiness, and somehow also older—the wisdom in her eyes, life's pain etched on her face.

I brought her a russet silk robe from Connemara. She plans to embroider stars and moons around its neck and hem. Uncle Beck has carved her a beautiful wand and pounded in bits of malachite and bloodstone along the handle. I think she'll be pleased when she sees it.

I know my parents would want to be here if they could, as they would have wanted to see my initiation and Linden's. I'm not sure if they're still alive. I can't sense them.

Last year I met Dad's first wife and his other son at one of the big coven meetings in Scotland. They seemed very Woodbane:

cold and hateful toward me. I had wondered if perhaps Dad still kept in touch with Selene—she's very beautiful, very magnetic. But his name seemed to set off a storm within them, which is not unreasonable, after all.

I must go—Alwyn needs help in figuring the positions of the stars on Saturday night.

—Giomanach

That night, after the house was quiet, I lay in bed, thinking. I had been disturbed by Cal's secret room. It had been so intense, so strange. I didn't really like to think about what Cal had done to make the room have those kinds of vibrations, vibrations I could only begin to identify.

And now I knew that Cal was Woodbane. So Hunter had been speaking the truth when he told me that. I understood why Cal and Selene would want to hide it—as Selene said, Woodbanes have a bad reputation in the Wiccan community. But it bothered me that Cal had lied to me. And I couldn't help remembering how he had said that he and Selene were "traditional" Woodbanes. What exactly did that mean?

Sighing, I made a conscious effort to set aside thoughts about my day and immerse myself in Maeve's BOS. Almost every entry in this section was overwritten with an encoded one, and painstakingly I made my way through several days' worth. I already knew that my birth mother had met a witch from Scotland named Ciaran and had fallen in love with him. It was horrible to read about, knowing the whole story of her and Angus. So far it didn't seem like she had slept with Ciaran—but still, the feelings she had for him must have broken Angus's heart. Yet Maeve and Angus had ended up together. And they'd had me.

At last I hid the book and the athame under my mattress. It was the night before Thanksgiving. Hunter's face rose once more before my eyes, and I shuddered. It would be hard, this year, to give thanks.

Downstairs the next morning the kitchen was a crazed flurry: a turkey on the counter, boiling cranberries spitting deep pink flecks of lavalike sauce, Dad—entrusted with only the simplest tasks—busily polishing silver at the kitchen table. Mary K. was wiping the good china, my mother was bustling about, flinging salad, hunting for the packages of rolls, and wondering out loud where she had put her mother's best tablecloth. It was like every other Thanksgiving, comforting and familiar, yet this year I felt something lacking.

I managed to slip outside without anyone noticing. The backyard was serene, a glittering world of icicles and snow, every surface blanketed, every color muted and bleached. What an odd, cold autumn it had been. Kneeling beneath the black oak, I made my own Thanksgiving offering, which I had planned almost a week ago, before the nightmarish events of the weekend. First I sprinkled birdseed on the snow, seeing how the smaller seeds pelted their way through the snow's crust but the large sunflower nuts rested on top. I hung a pinecone smeared with peanut butter from a branch. Then I put an acorn squash, a handful of oats, and a small group of pinecones at the base of the tree.

I closed my eyes and concentrated. Then I quietly recited the Wiccan Rede, which I had learned by heart. I was about to go inside to tell Mom that for some reason, she had left the bags of rolls in the hall closet, when my senses prickled. My eyes popped open, and I looked around.

Our yard is bordered on two sides with woods, a small parklike area that hadn't been developed yet. I saw nothing, but my senses told me someone was near, someone was watching. Using my magesight, I peered into the woods, trying to see beyond the trees.

I feel you. You are there, I thought with certainty, and then I blinked as a flash of darkness and pale, sun-colored hair whirled and disappeared from sight.

Hunter! Adrenaline flowed into my veins and I stood, taking a step toward the woods. Then I realized with a sick pang that it couldn't be him. He was dead, and Cal and I had killed him. It must have been Sky, with that hair. It was Sky, hiding in the woods outside my house, spying on me.

Walking backward, scanning the area around me intently, I moved toward the house and stumbled up the back steps. Sky thought I had killed her cousin. Sky thought Cal was evil and so was I. Sky was planning to hurt me. I slipped into the steamy, fragrant kitchen, soundlessly muttering a spell of protection.

"Morgan!" my mom exclaimed, making me jump. "There you are! I thought you were still in the shower. Have you seen the rolls?"

"Uh—they're in the hall closet," I mumbled, then I picked up a silver-polishing cloth, sat down next to my dad, and went to work.

Thanksgiving was the usual: dry turkey; excellent cranberry sauce; salty stuffing; a pumpkin pie that was an odd, pale shade but tasted great; soft, store-bought rolls; everyone talking over each other.

Aunt Eileen brought Paula. Aunt Margaret, Mom and Eileen's older sister, had finally broken down and started speaking to Aunt Eileen again, so she and her family joined us. She spent most of the evening silently but obviously stewing over the fact that her baby sister was going to roast in hell because she was gay. Uncle Michael, Margaret's husband, was jovial and good-natured with everyone; my four little cousins were bored and only wanted to watch TV; and Mary K. kept making faces at me behind our cousins' backs and giggling.

All par for the course, I guessed.

By nine o'clock people started trickling homeward. Sighing, Mary K. plunked down in front of the TV with a slice of pie. I went upstairs to my room, and I heard Mom and Dad turn in early and then the click of the TV turning on in their room.

I turned off my bedroom light, then crept to the window and looked out. Was Sky still out there, haunting me? I tried to cast out my senses, but all I got was my own family, their peaceful patterns in the house. Using my magesight, I looked deeply past the first line of trees and saw nothing unusual. Unless Sky had shape-shifted into that small owl on the third pine from the left, everything was normal.

Why had she been there? What was she planning? My heart felt heavy with dread, thinking about it. I turned my light back on, pulled down my shades, and twitched my curtains into place.

I hadn't talked to Cal all day, and I both wanted to and didn't want to. I longed for him, yet whenever I thought of his secret room, I felt unsettled.

I climbed into bed and took out one of my Wiccan books. I was working my way through about five Wiccan-related books at one time, reading a bit each day. This one was an English history of Wicca, and it was dry going sometimes. It was amazing that this writer had managed to suck the excitement out of the subject, but often he had, and only a determination to learn everything about everything Wiccan kept me going.

I made myself read the history for half an hour, then spent another hour memorizing the correspondences and values of crystals and stones. It was something I could spend years doing, but at least I was making a start.

Finally, my eyes heavy, I had earned the reward of reading Maeve's BOS.

The first section I read described a fight she'd had with her mother. It sounded awful, and it reminded me of the fights I'd had with my parents after I'd found out I was adopted.

Then I found another hidden passage. "September 1981. Oh, Goddess," I read. "Why have you done this? By meeting Ciaran, I have broken a heart that's true. And now my own heart is broken, too.

"Ciaran and I joined our hearts and souls the other night, on the headland under the moonlight. He told me about the depth of his love for me . . . and then I found out about the depth of his deception, too. Goddess, it's true he loves me more than anything, and I feel in my heart he's my soul mate, my one life love, my second half. We bound ourselves to each other.

"Then he told me another truth. He is already wed, to a girl back in Liathach, and has got two children with her."

Oh, no, I thought, reading it. Oh, Maeve, Maeve.

"Married! I couldn't believe it. He's twenty-two and has been married four years already. They have a four-year-old boy and a three-year-old girl. He told me he'd been forced to marry the girl to unite their two covens, which had been at war. He says he cares for her, but not the way he loves me, and should I give him the word, he would leave her tomorrow, break up his marriage, to be with me.

"But he will never be mine. I would never ask a man to desert his woman and children for me! Nor can I believe that he would even offer. Thank the Goddess, I kept a few of my wits and did not do anything that might see me with my own child by him!

"For this I broke Angus's heart, went against my ma and da, and almost changed the course of my life."

I rested the BOS on my comforter. Maeve's anguished words glowed beneath the blade of the athame, and I felt her pain almost as keenly as if it were my own. It was my own, in a way. It was part of my history; it had changed my future and my life.

I turned the page. "I have sent him away," I read. "He will go back to Liathach, to his wife, who is the daughter of their high priestess. Goddess, he was sickened with pain when I sent him away. If I willed it, he would stay. But after a night of talk we saw no clear path: this is the only way. And despite my fury at his betrayal, my heart tonight is weeping blood. I will never love another the way I love Ciaran. With him I could have drunk the world; without him I will be dosing runny-nosed children and curing sheep my whole life. If it were not a sin, I would wish that I were dead."

Oh, God, I thought. I pictured Cal and me being split apart and missed him with a sudden urgency. I looked at the clock. Too late to call. It would have to wait till morning.

I hid the athame and the Book of Shadows, which lately was seeming like a Book of Sorrows, turned out the light, and went to sleep.

My last thought before drifting off was something about Sky, but in the morning I couldn't remember what it was.

On Friday morning I was blessedly alone in the house. I showered and dressed, then ate leftover stuffing for breakfast. My parents had gone to see some old friends of my mom's who were in town for the weekend. Bakker had already picked up Mary K. He had looked less than enthusiastic about Mary K.'s plan to hit the mall for some early Christmas shopping.

After they left, I made an effort to sort through my troubled thoughts. Okay, number one: Hunter. Number two: Cal's secret room. Number three: The fact that Cal lied to me about his Woodbane heritage. Number four: Selene being upset that Cal had told me about their being Woodbane. Number five: Everything Maeve had gone through with Ciaran and my father. Number six: Sky spying on my house yesterday.

When the phone rang, I knew it was Cal.

"Hi," I said.

"Hi." His voice was like a balm, and I wondered why I hadn't wanted to talk to him earlier. "How was your Thanksgiving?"

"Pretty standard," I said. "Except I made an offering to the Goddess."

"We did, too," he said. "We had a circle with about fifteen people, and we did Thanksgiving-type stuff, witch style."

"That sounds nice. Was this your mom's coven?"

"No," said Cal, and I picked up an odd new tone in his voice. "These are some of the same people who have been coming and going for the last couple of weeks. People from all over. They're Woodbane, too."

"Wow, they're all over the place," I exclaimed, and he laughed. "You can't shake a stick around here without hitting a Woodbane," I added, enjoying his amusement.

"Not in my house, at least," Cal agreed. "Which is why I'm calling, actually. Besides just wanting to hear your voice. There are people here who really want to meet you."

"What?"

"These Woodbanes. Kidding aside, pure Woodbanes are few and far between," said Cal. "Often when they find out about others, they look them up, get together with them, exchange stories and spells and recipes and clan lore. Stuff like that."

I realized I was hesitating. "So they want to meet me because I'm Woodbane?"

"Yes. Because you're a very, very powerful pureblood Woodbane," Cal coaxed. "They're dying to meet the untrained, uninitiated Woodbane who can light candles with her eyes and help ease asthma and throw witch fire at people. And who has the Belwicket tools, besides."

Run, witch, run.

"What?" asked Cal. "Did you say something?"

"No," I murmured. My heart kicked up a beat, and I started breathing as if I had just run up a flight of stairs.

What was wrong? Glancing around the kitchen, everything looked fine, the same. But a huge, crashing wave of fear had slammed into me and was now engulfing me and making me shake.

"I feel odd," I said faintly, looking around the room.

"What?" said Cal.

"I feel odd," I said, more strongly. Actually, I felt like I was losing my mind.

"Morgan?" Cal sounded concerned. "Are you all right? Is someone there? Should I come over?"

Yes. No. I don't know. "I think I just need to, um, splash water on my face. Listen, can I call you back later?"

"Morgan, these people really want to meet you," he said urgently.

As he spoke, I was sucked under the swell of fear, so that I wanted to crawl under the kitchen table and curl into a ball. Ask him for help, a voice said. Ask Cal to come over. And another voice said, No, don't. That would be a mistake. Hang up the phone. And run.

Cal, I need you, I need you, don't listen to me.

Now I *was* under the kitchen table. "I have to go," I forced out. "I'll call you later." I was shaking, cold, flooded with so much adrenaline that I could hardly think.

"Morgan! Wait!" said Cal. "These people—"

"Love you," I whispered. "Bye." My trembling thumb clicked the off button, and the phone disconnected. I waited a second and hit talk, then put the phone on the floor. If anyone tried to call now, they'd get a busy signal.

"Oh my God," I muttered, huddled under the table. "What's wrong with me?" I crouched there for a moment, feeling like a freak. Trying to concentrate, I slowly took several deep breaths. For a minute I stayed there, just breathing.

Slowly I began to feel better. I crawled out from under the table, my knees covered with crumbs. Dagda gazed owlishly down at me from his perch on the counter.

"Please do not tell anyone about this," I said to him, standing up. By now I felt almost back to normal physically, though still panicky. Once more I glanced around, saw nothing different, wondered if Sky was putting a spell on me, if someone was *doing* something.

"Dagda," I said shakily, stroking his ears, "your mother is losing her mind." The next thing I knew, I was putting on my coat, grabbing my car keys, and heading outside. I ran.

11

Link

I've been studying formally since I was four. I was initiated at fourteen. I've taken part in some of the most powerful, dangerous, ancient rites there are. Yet it's very difficult for me to kindle fire with my mind. But Morgan . . .

Mom wants her desperately. (So do I, but for slightly different reasons.) We're ready for her. Our people have been gathering for weeks now. Edwitha of Cair Dal is staying nearby. Thomas from Belting. Alicia Woodwind from Tarth Benga. It's a Woodbane convention, and the house is so full of vibrations and rivulets of magick that it's hard to sleep at night. I've never felt anything like this before. It's incredible.

The war machine is starting to churn. And my Morgan will be the flamethrower.

—Sgàth

Outside of Practical Magick, I parked Das Boot and climbed out, not seeing the Closed sign until I was pushing on the door. Closed! Of course—it was the day after Thanksgiving. Lots of stores were closed. Hot tears sprang to my eyes, and I furiously blinked them back. In childish anger I kicked the front door. "Ow!" I gasped as pain shot through my toes.

Dammit. Where could I go? I felt weird; I needed to be around people. For a moment I considered going to Cal's, but another strange rush of fear and nausea swept over me, and gasping, I leaned my head against Practical Magick's door.

A muffled sound from within made me peer inside the store. It was dark, but I saw a dim light on in the back, and then the shadow moving toward me metamorphosed into David, jingling his keys. I almost cried with relief.

David opened the front door and let me in. He locked the door behind me, and we stood for a moment, looking at each other in the dimness.

"I feel odd," I whispered earnestly, as if this would explain my presence.

David regarded me intently, then began to lead me to the small room behind the orange curtain. "I'm glad to see you," he said. "Let me get you a cup of tea."

Tea sounded fabulous, and I was so, so glad I was there. I felt safe, secure.

David pushed aside the curtain and stepped into the back room. I followed him, saying, "Thanks for let—"

Hunter Niall was sitting there, at the small round table.

I screamed and clapped my hands over my mouth, feeling like my eyes were going to pop out of my head.

He looked startled to see me, too, and we both whirled to stare at David, who was watching us with a glint of amusement in his hooded eyes. "Morgan, you've met Hunter, haven't you? Hunter Niall, this is Morgan Rowlands. Maybe you two should shake hands."

"You're not dead," I gasped unnecessarily, and then my knees felt weak, just like in mystery novels, and I pulled out a battered metal chair and sank onto it. I couldn't take my eyes off Hunter. He wasn't dead! He was very much alive, though even paler than usual and still bearing scrapes and bruises on his hands and face. I couldn't help looking at his neck, and seeing me, he hooked a finger in his wool scarf and pulled it down enough for me to see the ugly, unhealed wound that I had made by throwing the athame at him.

David was pouring me a steaming mug of tea. "I don't understand," I moaned.

"You understand parts of it," David corrected me. He pulled up another chair and sat down, the three of us clustered around a small, rickety table with a round plywood top. "But you haven't quite got the big picture."

It was all I could do not to groan. I had been hearing about the big picture since I'd first discovered Wicca. I felt I would never be clued in.

I felt a prickle of fear. I disliked and distrusted Hunter. I'd grown to trust David, but now I thought of how he used to disturb me. Could I trust anyone? Was anyone on my side? I looked from one to the other: David, with his fine, short, silver hair and measuring brown eyes; Hunter, his golden hair so like Sky's but with green eyes where hers were black.

"You're wondering what's going on," said David. It was a massive understatement.

"I'm afraid," I said in a shaking voice. "I don't know what to believe."

As soon as I started speaking, it was as if a sand bagged levee had finally collapsed. My words poured out in a torrent. "I thought Hunter was dead. And . . . I thought I could trust *you*. Everything is upsetting me. I don't know who I am or what I'm doing." Do not cry, I told myself fiercely. Don't you *dare* cry.

"I'm sorry, Morgan," said David. "I know this is very hard for you. I wish it could be easier, but this is the path you're on, and you have to walk it. My path was much easier."

"Why aren't you dead?" I asked Hunter.

"Sorry to disappoint you," he said. His voice was raspier than before. "Luckily my cousin Sky is an athletic girl. She found me and pulled me out of the river."

So Sky had gotten my message. I swallowed. "I never meant to—hurt you that badly," I said. "I just wanted to stop what you were doing. You were killing Cal!"

"I was doing my *job*," Hunter said, his eyes flaring into heat. "I was fighting in self-defense. There was no way Cal would go to the council without my putting a *braigh* on him."

"You were killing him!" I said again.

"He was trying to kill me!" Hunter said. "And then *you* tried to kill me!"

"I did not! I was trying to stop you!"

David held up his hands. "Hold it. This is going nowhere. You two are both afraid, and being afraid makes you angry, and being angry makes you lash out."

"Thank you, Dr. Laura," I said snippily.

"I'm not afraid of *her*," Hunter said, like a six-year-old, and I wanted to kick him under the table. Now that I knew he was actually alive, I remembered just how unpleasant he was.

"Yes, you are," David said, looking at Hunter. "You're afraid of her potential, of her possible alliances, of her power and the lack of knowledge she has concerning that power. She threw an athame into your neck, and you don't know if she'd do it again."

David turned to me. "And you're afraid that Hunter knows something you don't, that he might hurt you or someone you love, that he might be telling the truth."

He was right. I gulped my tea, my face burning with anger and shame.

"Well, you're both right," said David, drinking from his mug. "You both have valid reasons to fear each other. But you need to get past it. I believe things are going to be very tough around here very soon, and you two need to be united to face them."

"What are you *talking* about?" I asked.

"What would it take for you to trust Hunter?" David asked. "To trust me?"

My mouth opened, then shut again. I thought about it. Then I said, "Everything I know—almost everything—seems to be secondhand knowledge. People *tell* me things. I ask questions, and people answer or don't answer. I've read different books that tell me different things about Wicca, about Woodbanes, about magick."

David looked thoughtful. "What do you trust?"

In a conversation I'd had once with Alyce, she'd said that in the end, I really had to trust myself. My inner knowledge. Things that just *were*.

"I trust *me*. Most of the time," I added, not wanting to sound arrogant.

"Okay." David sat back, putting his fingertips together. "So you need firsthand information. Well, how do you suggest getting it?"

On my birthday Cal and I had meditated together, joining our minds. Standing, I walked around the table, next to Hunter. I saw the tightening of his muscles, his wariness, his readiness for battle if that was what I offered.

Setting my jaw, focusing my thoughts, I slowly reached out my hand toward Hunter's face. He looked at it guardedly. When I was almost touching him, pale blue sparks leaped from my fingers to his cheek. We all jumped, but I didn't break the contact, and finally I felt his flesh beneath my curled fingertips.

In the street a couple of weeks ago I had brushed past him, and it had been overwhelming: a huge release of emotions so powerful that I had felt ill. It was something like that now, but not as gut-wrenching. I closed my eyes and focused my energy on connecting with Hunter. My senses reached out to touch his, and at first his mind recoiled from me. I waited, barely breathing, and gradually I felt his defenses weaken. His mind opened slightly to let me in.

If he chose to turn on me, I was cooked. Connected like this, I could sense how vulnerable we were to each other. But still I pressed on, feeling Hunter's suspicion, his resistance, and then very slowly his surprise, his acquiescence, his decision to let me in further.

Our thoughts were joined. He saw me and what I knew of my past, and I saw him.

Gìomanach. His name was Gìomanach. I heard it in Gaelic and English at the same time. His name meant Hunter. He really was a member of the High Council. He was a Seeker, and he'd been charged to investigate Cal and Selene for possible misuse of magick.

I almost pulled back in pain, but I stayed with Hunter, feeling him searching my mind, examining my motives, weighing my innocence, my connection to Cal. I felt him wonder if Cal and I had been lovers and was embarrassed when he was relieved that we hadn't.

Our breathing was slight and shallow, noiseless in the deep silence of the little room. This connection was deeper still than the one I had forged with Cal. This was bone deep, soul deep, and we seemed to sift through layer upon layer of connection, and suddenly I found myself in the middle of a sunny, grassy field, sitting cross-legged on the ground, with Hunter by my side.

This was nice, and I smiled, felt the sun heat warm my face and hair. Insects buzzed around us, and there was the fresh, sweet smell of clover.

I looked at Hunter, and he at me, and we needed no words. I saw his childhood, saw him with his cousin Athar, who I knew as Sky, felt the agony of his parents' leaving. The depth of his anguish over his brother's death was almost unbearable, though I saw that he had been tried and found not guilty. This was something about which Cal didn't know the truth.

Hunter saw my normal life, the shock of finding out I was a blood witch, the growing sweetness of my love for Cal, the disturbing feelings I'd had about his secret room. I couldn't hide my concern about Mary K. and Bakker, my love for my family, my sorrow over the sadness of my birth mother's life and her unsolved death.

Gradually I realized it was time to go, and I stood up in

the field, feeling the grass brush against my bare legs. Hunter and I didn't smile as we said good-bye. We had achieved a new level of trust. He knew I hadn't meant to kill him and that I wasn't part of any larger, darker plan. In Hunter, I had seen pain, anger, even vengefulness, all surrounded by a layer of caution and mistrust—but still, I hadn't seen what I had looked for. I hadn't seen evil.

When I came out of it, I felt light-headed, and David's hand guided me back to my chair. Shyly I glanced up to meet Hunter's eyes.

He looked back at me, seeming as shaken as I was.

"That was interesting," said David, breaking the silence. "Morgan, I didn't know you knew how to join with Hunter's mind, but I suppose I shouldn't be surprised. What did you learn?"

I cleared my throat. "I saw that Hunter wasn't—bad or anything."

Hunter was looking at David. "She ought not to be able to do that," he said in a low voice. "Only witches with years of training—she got right inside my mind—"

David patted his hand. "I know," he said ruefully.

I leaned across the table toward Hunter. "Well, if you're not evil," I said briskly, "why have you and Sky been stalking me? I saw you two in my yard a week ago. You left sigils all over the place. What were they for?"

Hunter twitched in surprise. "They're protection spells," he said.

Just then the back door, a door I had barely noticed, opened. Its short curtain swung in, and a blast of cold air swirled into the room.

"You!" Sky snapped, staring at me from the doorway. She

looked quickly at Hunter, as if to make sure I hadn't been trying to kill him in the last twenty minutes. "What is she doing here?" she demanded of David.

"Just visiting," David said with a smile.

Her black eyes narrowed. "You shouldn't be here," she snarled. "You almost killed him!"

"You made me think I *had* killed him!" I snapped back. "You knew what had happened, you knew he was alive, yet you let me think he was dead. I've been sick about it!"

She made a disbelieving face. "Not sick enough."

"What were you doing at my house yesterday? Why were you spying on me?"

"Spying? Don't flatter yourself," she said, flinging down her black backpack. "I've had more important things to do."

My eyes widened. "Liar! I saw you yesterday!"

"No, that was me," Hunter put in, and Sky and I both turned to stare at him.

He shrugged. "Keeping tabs."

His arrogance was infuriating. He might not be evil, but he was still a horrible person.

"How dare you—" I began, but Sky interrupted me.

"Of course he's keeping tabs on you!" she snapped. "He's on the council, and you tried to kill him! If another witch hadn't seen what you'd done and sent me a message to go get Hunter, he would have died!"

I exploded, leaping to my feet. "What other witch? *I* was the one who sent you the message that night! *I* was the one who told you to go get him! And I called 911, too!"

"Don't be ridiculous," Sky said. "You couldn't have sent that message. You're nowhere near strong enough."

"Oh, yes, she is," Hunter said mournfully, leaning his chin on his hand. "She just flushed out my brain. I have no secrets anymore."

Sky gaped at him as if he'd been speaking in tongues. He took careful sips of his tea, not looking at her. "What are you talking about?" Sky asked.

"She did *tàth meanma*," Hunter said, his accent thickening with the Gaelic words. A shiver went down my spine, and I knew instinctively he'd referred to what we had done, the thing I thought of as the "Wiccan mind meld."

Sky was taken aback. "But she can't do that." She stared at me, and I felt like an animal in a zoo. Abruptly I sat down again.

"You're Athar," I said, remembering. "Athar means Sky. Cousin Athar."

No one had much to say to that.

"She's not in league with Cal and Selene," Hunter offered finally. I got angry again.

"*Cal* and *Selene* aren't in league with Cal and Selene, either!" I said. "For your info, Cal and I have done . . . *tàth menama*—"

"*Meanma*," Hunter corrected.

"Whatever. And he wasn't evil, either!"

"Did he lead it or did you?" Hunter asked.

Nonplussed, I thought back. "He did."

"Did you go as deep as with me?" he pressed. "Did you see childhood and future, wake and sleep?"

"I'm not sure," I admitted, trying to think.

"You need to be sure," David told me, almost impatiently.

I looked at all three of them. They seemed to be waiting for my response, and I had nothing to give them. I loved Cal, and he loved me. It was ridiculous to think he might be evil.

A picture of the little room in the pool house suddenly rose in front of my mind's eye. I pushed it angrily away. My mind seized on something else.

"I heard Bree and Raven talking about how you were teaching them about the dark side," I accused Sky.

"Of course I was," she countered, black eyes flashing. "So they could recognize it and fight it! It seems someone should have been teaching you the same thing!"

I stood again, overwhelmed with anger. "Thanks for the tea," I told David. "I'm glad you're not dead," I growled at Hunter. Then I stalked out the back door.

As I stomped down the alley and back to my car, my brain pounded with possibilities. Hunter wasn't dead! It was a huge relief, and waves of thankfulness washed over me. And he wasn't evil! Just—misguided. Unfortunately, Sky was still a total bitch and leading Bree and Raven and the rest of Kithic into what seemed to me to be a gray area.

But first things first. Hunter was alive!

12

The Bigger Picture

October 2000

Alwyn's initiation went well. I was so proud of her, giving her answers in her clear, high voice. She will grow up Wyndenkell and, we hope, marry within Vinneag, Uncle Beck's coven.

For one moment, as Uncle Beck pressed his athame to her eye and commanded her to step forward, I wondered if her life would be better had she not been born a witch. She would be just a fourteen-year-old girl, giggling with her friends, getting a crush on a boy. As it is, she's spent the last six years memorizing the history of the clans, tables of correspondences, rituals, and rites; going to spell-making classes; studying astronomy, astrology, herbs, and a thousand other things along with her regular schoolwork. She's missed school functions and friends' birthdays. And she lost her parents when she was only four.

Is it better for her this way? Would Linden still be alive if he hadn't been a witch? I know our lives would have held less pain if we had been born just human.

But it's pointless to consider. One cannot escape one's destiny— if you hide from it, it will find you. If you deny it, it will kill you. A witch I was born, and my family, too, and witches we'll always be, and give thanks for it.

—Giomanach

When I got home, I found a note saying that Cal had stopped by while I was gone. I ran upstairs, brought the phone into my room, and called Cal's house. He answered right away.

"Morgan! Where have you been? Are you okay?"

"I'm fine," I said, the familiar feeling of warmth coming over me at the sound of his voice. "I don't know what was wrong with me this morning. I just felt so weird."

"I was worried about you. Where did you go?"

"To Practical Magick. And you'll never guess who I saw there."

There was silence on Cal's end, and I felt his sudden alertness. "Who?"

"Hunter Niall," I announced. I pictured Cal's eyes widening, his face showing astonishment. I smiled, wishing I could see him.

"What do you mean?" Cal asked.

"I mean he's alive," I said. "I saw him."

"Where has he been all this time?" Cal asked, sounding almost offended.

"Actually, I didn't ask," I said. "I guess he's been with Sky. She found him that night and brought him home."

"So he wasn't dead," Cal repeated. "He went over that cliff with an athame in his neck, and he wasn't dead."

"No. Aren't you thrilled?" I said. "The weight of this has been so awful. I couldn't believe I had done something so terrible."

"Even though he was killing me," Cal said flatly. "Putting a *braigh* on me. Trying to take me to the council so they could turn me inside out." I heard the bitterness in his voice.

"No, of course not," I said, taken aback. "I'm glad I stopped him from doing that. We *won* that battle. I don't regret that at all. But I thought I had killed someone, and it was going to be a shadow over my life forever. I'm really, really glad that it won't."

"It's like you've forgotten that he was trying to kill me," Cal said, his tone sharpening. "Do you remember what my wrists looked like afterward? Like hamburger. I'm going to have scars for the rest of my life."

"I know, I know," I said. "I'm sorry. He was—more than wrong. I'm glad I stopped him. But I'm also glad I didn't *kill* him."

"Did you talk to him?"

"Yes." I was getting so weirded out by how Cal sounded that I decided not to tell him about the *tàth menima— mamena*—whatever. "I also saw his charming cousin, Sky, and we got into an argument. As usual."

Cal laughed without humor, then was quiet. What was he thinking? I felt the need to meld with his mind again, to feel his inner self. But I wanted to lead it myself this time.

That was a disturbing thought. *Did* I have doubts about Cal?

"What are you thinking about?" he asked softly.

"That I want to see you soon," I said. I felt guilty at the partial truth.

"I wanted to see you today," he said. "I asked you, and you said no, and then you went to Practical Magick. You weren't even home when I came by to see if you were all right."

"I'm really sorry," I said. "I just—this morning I felt so strange. I think I was having a panic attack. I wasn't thinking clearly and just wanted to get out of here. But I'm sorry—I didn't mean to blow you off."

"There were people here who wanted to meet you," he said, sounding slightly mollified.

All the hairs on the back of my neck stood up. "I'm sorry," I said again. "I just wasn't up to it today."

He sighed, and I pictured him running a hand through his thick, dark hair. "I've got to do a bunch of stuff tonight, but we've got a circle tomorrow at Ethan's house. So I'll see you there, if not during the day."

"Okay," I said. "Give me a call if you can get away."

"All right. I missed you today. And I'm worried about Hunter. I think he's psycho, and I was relieved when I thought he couldn't hurt either of us anymore."

I felt a sudden twinge of alarm. I hadn't even considered that. I'd have to talk to Hunter and make sure he didn't try to go after Cal again. We'd have to find a way to straighten out all these—misunderstandings or whatever they were—without violence.

"I have to go. I'll see you soon." Cal made a kissing noise into the phone and hung up.

I sat on my bed, musing. When I talked to Cal, I hated the

whole idea of Hunter. But today, when Hunter and I were doing the *tàth* thing, he'd seemed okay.

I sighed. I felt like a weather vane, blowing this way and that, depending on the wind.

After dinner Mary K. and I were in the kitchen, cleaning up. Doing mundane things like working in the kitchen felt a little surreal after my conversation with Cal.

For the hundredth time I thought, Hunter is alive! I was so happy. Not that the world necessarily needed Hunter in it, but now I didn't have his death on my conscience. He was alive, and it felt like a thousand days of sunshine, which was bizarre, considering how I couldn't stand him.

"Any plans for tonight?" I asked Mary K.

"Bakker's picking me up," she answered. "We're going to Jaycee's." She made a face. "Can't you talk to Mom and Dad, Morgan? They still say that I can't go out on dates by myself, I mean, just me and Bakker. We always have to be with other people if it's at night."

"Hmmm," I said, thinking that it was probably a good idea.

"And my curfew! Ten o'clock! Bakker doesn't have to be home till midnight."

"Bakker's almost seventeen," I pointed out. "You're fourteen."

Her brows drew together, and she dropped a handful of silverware into the dishwasher with an angry crash.

"You hate Bakker," she grumbled. "You're not going to help."

Too right, I thought, but I said, "I just don't trust him after he tried to hurt you. I mean, he held my sister down and made her cry. I can't forget that."

"He's changed," Mary K. insisted.

I didn't say anything. After I'd scraped the last plate, I went up to my room. Twenty minutes later I picked up on Bakker's vibrations, and then the doorbell rang. I sighed, wishing I could protect Mary K. from afar.

Up in my room, I studied my book on the properties of different incenses, essential oils, and brews that one can make from them. After an hour I turned to Maeve's Book of Shadows once more, dreading what I would find out and yet compelled to keep reading. It was so full of sadness right now, of anguish over Ciaran. Even though he had concealed his marriage and proved ready to desert his wife and children, she still felt he was her *mùirn beatha dàn*. It was hard for me to understand how she could still love him after learning all that. It reminded me of Mary K. and Bakker. If someone had held me down and almost raped me, I knew there was no way I would ever forgive him or take him back.

Who's there? I looked up, my senses telling me that another person's energy was nearby. I scanned the house quickly. I did that so often and was so familiar with my family's patterns that it took only a second to know that my parents were in the living room, Mary K. was gone, and a stranger was in the yard. I flicked off my bedroom light and looked out my window.

I peered down into the darkest shadows behind the rhododendron bushes beneath my window, and my magesight picked out a glint of short, moonlight-colored hair. Hunter.

I ran downstairs and through the kitchen, grabbing my coat off the hook by the door. Boldly I crunched through the snow across the backyard, then down the side, where my bedroom window was. If I hadn't been looking for him, if I didn't have magesight, I never would have seen Hunter blending with the night's shadows, pressed against our house. Once again I got a strong physical sensation from his presence—an uncomfortable, heightened awareness, as if my system was being flooded with caffeine over and over.

Hands on hips, I said, "What the hell are you doing here?"

"Can you see in the dark?" he asked conversationally.

"Yes, of course. Can't every witch?"

"No," he said, stepping away from the house, dusting off his gloves. "Not every witch has magesight. No uninitiated witch does, except you, I suppose. And not even every full-blood witch has it. It does seem to run strongly in Woodbanes."

"Then you must have it," I said. "Since you're half Woodbane."

"Yes, I do," he said, ignoring the challenge in my voice. "In me it developed when I was about fifteen. I thought it had to do with puberty, like getting a beard."

"What are you doing here?"

"Redrawing the protection sigils on your house," he said, as if he was saying, Just neatening up these bushes. "I see Cal laid his own on top of them."

"He was protecting me from you," I said pointedly. "Who are *you* protecting me from?"

His grin was a flash of light in the darkness. "Him."

"You're not planning to try to bind him again, are you?" I asked. "To put the *braigh* on him? Because you know I won't let you hurt him."

"No fear, I'm not trying that again," Hunter said. He touched his neck gingerly. "I'm just watching—for now, anyway. Until I get proof of what he's up to. Which I will."

"This is great," I said, disgusted. "I'm tired of both of you. Why don't you two leave me out of whatever big picture you're playing out?"

"I wish I could, Morgan," said Hunter, sounding sober. "But I'm afraid you're part of the picture, whether you want to be or not."

"But why?" I cried, fed up.

"Because of who you are," he said. "Maeve was from Belwicket."

"So?" I rubbed my arms up and down my shoulders, feeling chilled.

"Belwicket was destroyed by a dark wave, people said, right?"

"Yes," I said. "In Maeve's Book of Shadows, she said a dark wave came and wiped out her coven. It killed people and destroyed buildings. My dad went to look at the town. He said there's hardly anything left."

"There isn't," said Hunter. "I've been there. The thing is, Belwicket wasn't the only coven destroyed by this so-called dark wave. I've found evidence of at least eight others, in Scotland, England, Ireland, and Wales. And those are only the ones where it was obvious. This—force, whatever it is—could be responsible for much more damage, on a smaller scale."

"But what is it?" I whispered.

"I don't know," Hunter said, snapping a small branch in frustration. "I've been studying it for two years now, and I still don't know what the hell I'm dealing with. An evil force of some kind. It destroyed my parents' coven and made my parents go into hiding. I haven't seen them in almost eleven years."

"Are they still alive?"

"I don't know." He shrugged. "No one knows. My uncle said they went into hiding to protect me, my brother, my sister. No one's seen them since."

The parallels were clear. "My birth parents went into hiding, here in America," I said. "But they were killed two years later."

Hunter nodded. "I know. I'm sorry. But they're not the only ones who have died. I've counted over a hundred and forty-five deaths in the eight covens I know about."

"And no one knows what it is," I stated.

"Not yet." His frustration was palpable. "But I'll find out. I'll chase it till I know."

For a long minute we stood there, not speaking, each lost in our thoughts.

"What happened with Linden?" I asked.

Hunter flinched as if I'd struck him. "He was also trying to solve the mystery of our parents' disappearance," he said in a low voice. "But he called up a force from the other side, and it killed him."

"I don't understand," I said. A chill breeze riffled my hair, and I shivered. Should I ask Hunter in? Maybe we could hang in the kitchen or family room. It would be warm there.

"You know, a dark spirit," Hunter said. "An evil force. I'm guessing the dark wave is either an incredibly powerful force like that or a group of many of them, banded together."

This was too much for me to take in. "You mean, like a dead person?" My voice squeaked. "A ghost?"

"No. Something that's never been alive."

I shivered again and wrapped my arms around myself. Before I knew it, Hunter was rubbing my back and arms, trying to warm me up. I glanced up at his face in the moonlight, at his carved cheekbones, the green glitter of his eyes. He was beautiful, as beautiful as Cal in his own way.

This is who hurt Cal, I reminded myself. He put a *braigh* on Cal and hurt him.

I stepped away, no longer wanting to ask him inside. "What will you do with this dark force when you find it?" I asked.

"I won't be able to do anything to it," he said. "What I hope to do is to stop the people who keep calling it into existence."

I stared at him. He held my gaze; I saw him glance at my mouth.

"And then," he said quietly, "maybe then people who have been hurt by this, like you, like me . . . will be able to get on with their lives."

His words fell like quiet leaves onto the snow as I stood, trapped by his eyes. My chest hurt, as if I had too much emotion inside, and to let it all out was unthinkable: I wouldn't know where to begin.

Frozen, I watched Hunter lean closer to me, and then his hand was on my chin, and it was cold, like ice, and he tilted up my face. Oh, Goddess, I thought. He's going to kiss me. Our eyes were locked on each other, and again I felt that connection with him, with his mind, his soul. A small spot of heat at my throat reminded me that I wore Cal's silver pentacle on a cord around my neck. I blinked and heard a car drive up and realized what we were doing, and I stepped back and pushed against him with my hands.

"Stop that!" I said, and he looked at me with an unfathomable expression.

"I didn't mean to," he said.

A car door opened, then slammed shut, then opened, and Mary K.'s voice said, "Bakker!" Her tone was shrill, alarmed.

Before the door slammed shut again, I was running across the yard to find Mary K., with Hunter right behind me.

Bakker had parked in front of our house. Inside the dark car I caught glimpses of arms and legs and the auburn flash of my sister's hair. I yanked the car door open, spilling Mary K. on her back into the snow, her legs up on the car seat.

Hunter reached down to help Mary K. up. Tear tracks were already frosting on my sister's face, and one of her jacket's buttons had been ripped. She was starting to cry and hiccup at the same time. "M-m-morgan," she stammered.

I leaned into the car to glare at Bakker.

"You stupid bastard," I said in a low, mean voice. I felt cold with rage. If I'd had an athame right then, I would have stabbed him.

"Stay out of it," he said, sounding upset. He had scratch marks on one cheek. "Mary K.!" he called, shifting in his seat as if he would get out. "Come back—we need to talk."

"If you ever look at, touch, talk to, or stand next to my sister again," I said very softly, "I'll make you sorry you were ever born." I didn't feel at all afraid or panicky: I wanted him to get out of the car and come after me so I could rip him apart.

His face turned red with anger. "You don't scare me with all that witch crap," he spat.

An evil smile snaked across my face. "Oh, but I should," I whispered, and watched the color drain from his cheeks. I narrowed my eyes at him for a second, then drew out of the car and slammed the door shut.

Hunter was watching us from a few feet away. Mary K. was holding his arm, and now she blinked up at him, saying, "I know you."

"I'm Hunter," he said as Bakker peeled away, burning rubber.

"Come on, Mary K.," I said, taking her arm and leading her toward the house. I didn't want to look at Hunter—I was still trying to process that almost kiss.

"Are you okay?" I asked, hugging Mary K. to my side as we went up the steps.

"Yes," she said shakily. "Just get me upstairs."

"Will do."

"I'll see you later, Morgan," said Hunter. I didn't reply.

13

The Circle

Giomanach is alive. Back from the dead. Dammit! Having the council's dog breathing down our necks could ruin everything. I need to take care of him. It's my responsibility.

I'll put the braigh on him, around his neck, and he can see how it feels.

—Sgàth

The next day Mary K. came into the family room as I was researching correspondences on the computer. There were dozens of Wiccan sites online, and I loved cruising from one to another.

"Morgan?"

"Yeah? Hey." I turned to look at her. Head hanging down, she looked uncharacteristically drawn and defenseless. I stopped what I was doing and pulled her into a tight hug.

"Why did he do it?" she whispered, her tears making my cheeks wet. "He says he loves me. Why does he try to hurt me?"

A rage began to boil in me. Was there some kind of spell I could do to Bakker that would teach him a lesson?

"I don't know," I told her. "He can't take no for an answer. Somehow he doesn't mind hurting you."

"He *does* mind," Mary K. cried. "He doesn't want to hurt me. But he always does."

"If he can't control himself, he needs help," I said slowly and carefully. "He needs to be in therapy. He's going to end up killing someone someday, a girlfriend or a wife." I pulled away and looked my sister in the eyes. "And Mary K.? That person will not be you. Understand?"

She looked at me helplessly, her eyes awash with tears. I shook her shoulders gently, once, twice, until she nodded.

"It won't be me," she said.

"It's over this time," I said. "Right?"

"Right," she said, but her eyes slid away, and I swore to myself.

"Do you want to tell Mom and Dad about him, or should I?" I said briskly.

"Oh, uh . . ."

"I'll tell them," I said, setting off to find them. In my opinion, keeping this a secret only made it more likely it would happen again. If my folks knew, Mary K. would have a harder time forgiving Bakker and going back to him again.

My parents did not take it well. They were angry with me for not telling them sooner, furious with Mary K. for continuing to see Bakker after the first time, and almost murder-ous in their rage toward Bakker, which cheered me up. In the end there was a big group hug, complete with tears and sobbing.

Half an hour later I paced off a small plot in the backyard, where my parents had agreed I could have a garden. The ground was too hard to dig, but I hammered in stakes and string to show where next spring's herbs would be. Then I sat on the snowy ground and tried to meditate for a while, clearing my mind and sending good thoughts into the earth below me, thanking it for being receptive to my garden. Feeling refreshed, I went back inside to look for a spell to put on Bakker.

Technically, of course, I wasn't supposed to do spells. I wasn't initiated, and I'd been a student for barely a couple of months. So I wasn't *committed* to spelling Bakker. But if the necessity arose ...

Once more we had turkey sandwiches for dinner. I was approaching my saturation point with turkey and was glad to see the carcass was almost bare.

"Any plans for tonight?" my mom asked me.

"Cal's going to pick me up," I said. "Then we're going to Ethan's." Mom nodded, and I could almost see her weighing my boyfriend against Mary K.'s. On the one hand, Cal was Wiccan. On the other hand, he had never hurt me.

By the time Cal rang our doorbell, I had dressed in faded gray cords and the purple batik blouse he had given me for my birthday. I'd French braided my hair to the nape of my neck, then let the rest hang down. In the mirror I looked excited, pink-cheeked, almost pretty: a vastly different crea-ture than the Morgan I had been two months ago and a different Morgan than just two days ago. Now I knew I wasn't a murderer. I knew I wasn't guilty. I could breathe again, and enjoy life, without Hunter's death hanging over me.

"Hi!" I greeted Cal, shuffling into my coat. I said good-bye to my parents, and we walked down the salt-strewn pathway to the Explorer. In the dark car he leaned over and kissed me, and I welcomed his familiar touch, the faint scent of incense that clung to his jacket, the warmth of his skin.

"How's Mary K.?"

"So-so." I rocked my hand back and forth. I'd told him the gist of what had happened last night, omitting the Hunter part. "I've decided to fix it so that every time Bakker speaks, a toad or snake will slither from his mouth."

Cal laughed and turned onto the main street that would take us to Ethan's. "You are one bloodthirsty woman," he said. Then he flicked me a serious glance. "No spells, okay? Or at least, please talk to me about them first."

"I'll try," I said with exaggerated virtue, and he laughed again.

He parked in back of Robbie's red Beetle outside Ethan's house and turned to me again. "I haven't seen you in days, it feels like." He looped his hand around my neck and pulled me closer for a breathless kiss.

"Just one day," I answered, kissing him back.

"I wanted to ask you—what did you think about my seòmar?"

"What's a shomar?"

"Seòmar," Cal corrected my pronunciation. "It's a private place, usually used by one witch alone, to work magick. Different from a place where you meet with others."

"Does every witch have one?" I asked.

"No. Quit evading the question. What did you think of *mine*?"

"Well, I found it sort of disturbing," I said. I didn't want to hurt his feelings, but I couldn't lie, either. "After a while I wanted to get out of there."

He nodded, then opened the car door and got out. We walked up the pavement to Ethan's small, split-level brick rambler. "That's natural," he said, not sounding offended. "I'm the only one who's worked there, and I've done some intense stuff. I'm not surprised it seemed a little uncomfortable." He sounded relieved. "You'll get used to it pretty fast."

He rang the doorbell while I wondered if I even wanted to get used to it.

"Hey, man," said Ethan. "Come on in."

This was the first time I'd been to Ethan's house: before we were coven mates, we'd never socialized in or out of school. Now I saw that his house was modest but tidy, the furniture worn but cared for. Suddenly two small apricot bundles skittered around the corner from the hall, barking wildly, and I backed up a little.

Jenna laughed from the couch. "Here, pup dogs," she called. The two doglets ran toward her, panting happily, and Jenna gave them each a tortilla chip. She'd obviously been here before and knew Ethan's dogs. Another surprise.

"I never figured you for Pomeranians," Cal told Ethan with a straight face.

"They're my mom's," Ethan said, scooping one under each arm and carrying them back down the hall.

Robbie came out of the kitchen, munching a chip. Matt arrived last, and we went downstairs to the basement, which had been finished to be a large family room.

"Is Sharon still out of town?" I asked, helping Ethan push back furniture.

"Yeah. In Philly," he said. He pushed one of his straggly ringlets out of his eyes.

Once the furniture was out of the way, Cal started unpacking his leather satchel, taking out his Wiccan tools.

"Hey, Jenna," Matt said, since she had ignored him upstairs. His usual pressed appearance had taken a downslide in the last few days: his hair was no longer brushed smooth, his clothes looked less carefully chosen.

Jenna met his gaze squarely, then turned away from him with no expression on her face. Matt flinched. I'd always thought of Jenna as being kind of needy and dependent on Matt, but now I was beginning to suspect that she'd always been the stronger one.

"Last Wednesday, I asked you to choose your correspondences," Cal said as we settled on the floor around him. "Did anyone have any success?"

Jenna nodded. "I think I did," she said, her voice firm.

"Let us have it," said Cal.

"My metal is silver," she said, showing us a silver bracelet on her wrist. "My stone is rose quartz. My season is spring. My sign is Pisces. My rune is Neid." She lifted her hand and drew Neid in the air. "That's all I have."

"That's plenty," said Cal. "Good work. Your rune, standing for delay and the need for patience, is very apt."

He fished in his satchel and took out a squarish chunk of rose quartz the size of an egg. It was pale pink, mostly clear, not milky, and inside were cracks and flaws that looked like broken windowpanes, trapped inside. I thought it looked like pink champagne, frozen in time. Cal handed it to Jenna. "This is for you. You'll use it in your spells."

"Thanks," Jenna said, looking deeply into it, pleased.

"Your rune, Neid, will also become important. For one thing, you can use it as a signature, either on your spells or even in notes and letters."

Jenna nodded.

I sat forward, excited. This was cool stuff—this was what I really loved about Wicca. In my Wicca books the use of quartz in various spells had come up again and again. It had been used religiously for thousands of years. In particular, pink or rose quartz was used to promote love, peace, and healing. Jenna could use all three.

"Robbie?" Cal asked.

"Yeah," he said. "Well, I'm a Taurus, my rune is Eoh, the horse, which also symbolizes travel or change of some kind. My metal is copper. My herb is mugwort. My stone is emerald."

"Interesting." Cal grinned at us. "This is really interesting. You guys are doing a great job of feeling your way to your essences. Robbie, I didn't even associate emerald with you, but as soon as you said it, I thought, yeah, of course." He reached into his bag, rejecting several stones, then brought one out.

"This is a rough emerald," he said, holding it toward Robbie. It was about the size of a pat of butter, a dark, greenish lump in his hand. Robbie took it. "Don't get excited—it's not gem quality. No jeweler would buy it from you. Use it in good health," said Cal, and I was oddly reminded of taking communion at church. Cal went on,

"Emerald is good for attracting love and prosperity, to strengthen the memory, to protect its user, and also to improve the eyesight."

Robbie turned and wiggled his eyebrows at me. Until about a month ago, he'd worn thick glasses. My healing potion had had the unexpected side benefit of perfecting his vision.

"So do you just have every stone possible in that bag?" Ethan asked.

Cal grinned. "Not every one. But I have one or two of the most typical."

I had been wondering the same thing myself.

"Okay, Matt?" Cal prompted

Matt swallowed. "I'm a Gemini," he said. "My rune is Jera. My stone is tourmaline."

"Jera, for karma, a cyclical nature, the seasons," said Cal. "Tourmaline."

"The kind with two colors," Matt said.

"They call that watermelon tourmaline," said Cal, and took one out. It looked like a hexagonal piece of quartz, about an inch and a half long and as thick as a pencil. It was green on one end, clear in the middle, and pink on the other end. Cal handed it to Matt, saying, "Wearing this balances the user. Use it in good health."

Matt nodded and turned the stone over in his hand.

"I can go next," said Ethan. "I know what Sharon's are— should I tell them to you?"

Cal shook his head. "She can tell us at the next circle or at school."

"Okay, then, mine," said Ethan. "I'm a Virgo. My season is summer. My stone is brown jasper. I don't have a plant or anything. My favorite jellybean flavor is sour apple."

"Okay," said Cal, smiling. "Good. I think I have a piece of brown jasper . . . hang on." He looked at the stones in his bag and pulled out one that looked like solidified root beer. "Here you go. Brown jasper is especially good for helping you keep your feet on the ground."

Ethan nodded, looking at his stone.

"I think for your rune, you should use . . ." Cal considered Ethan thoughtfully while we all waited. "Beorc. For new beginnings, a rebirth. Sound okay?"

"Yeah," Ethan said. "Beorc. Cool."

Cal turned to me with a special look. "Last but not least?"

"I'm on the Scorpio-Sagittarius cusp," I said. "Mostly Sagittarius. My herb is thyme. My rune is Othel, which stands for an ancestral home, a birthright. My stone is bloodstone."

I might have been the only one to see Cal's pupils dilate and then contract in an instant. Was my choice wrong? Maybe I should have run my ideas by him first, I thought uncertainly. But I had been so sure.

Cal let a stone drop unseen into his bag; I heard it click faintly. "Bloodstone," he said, trying it out. I met his gaze as he looked at me. "Bloodstone," he repeated.

"What are its properties?" Jenna asked.

"It's very old," said Cal. "It's been used in magick for thousands of years to give strength to warriors in battle, to help women through childbirth. They say it can be used to break ties, open doors, even knock down barriers." He paused, then reached into his bag again, rummaged around, and pulled out a large, dark green stone, smooth and polished. When he tilted it this way and that, I could see the dark, blood-colored flecks of red within its darkness.

"Bloodstone," repeated Cal, examining it. "Its ruling

planet is Mars, which lends it qualities of strength, healing, protection, sexual energy, and magick involving men."

Jenna grinned at me, and I felt my cheeks flush.

"It's a fire stone," Cal went on, "and its associated color is red. In spells you could use it to increase courage, magickal power, wealth, and strength." His eyes caught mine. "Very interesting." He tossed me the stone, and I caught it. It felt smooth and warm in my hand. I had come across another bloodstone among the things in Maeve's toolbox. Now I had two.

"Okay, now let's make a circle," said Cal, standing. He quickly drew a circle, and we all helped cast it: purifying it, invoking the four elements and the Goddess and God, linking hands within it. Without Sharon there were only six of us. I looked around and realized that I was starting to feel like these people were my second family.

Each of us held our stones in our right palm, sandwiched with the left palm of the person next to us. We moved in our circle, chanting. Looking forward to the rush of ecstatic energy I always got in a circle, I moved around and around, watching everyone's faces. They were intent, focused, perhaps more so than during other circles: their stones must be at work. Jenna looked lovely, ethereal as delight crossed her features. Wonderingly she glanced at me, and I smiled at her, waiting for my own magick to take me away.

It didn't. It was a while before I realized I was deliberately holding it down, not letting it go, not letting myself give in to the magick. It occurred to me: I didn't feel safe. There was no reason I could think of not to, but I simply didn't. My own magick stayed dampened, not the enormous outpouring of power that it usually was. I let out a deep breath and put my trust in the Goddess. If there was danger here that I couldn't see, I hoped she would take care of me.

Gradually Cal took us down, and as we slowed, my coven members looked at me expectantly. They were used to me having to ground myself after a circle, and this time, when I shook my head, they seemed surprised. Cal gave me a questioning look, but I just shrugged.

Then Jenna said, "I feel kind of sick."

"Sit down," Cal said, moving to her side. "Ground yourself. All of you may feel some increased sensations because of your stones and the inner work you did over the week."

Cal helped Jenna sit cross-legged on the carpeted floor, her forehead touching the floor, both hands out flat. He took her chunk of pink quartz and placed it on the back of her slender neck, exposed because her ash blond hair had slipped down on both sides.

"Just breathe," he said gently, keeping one hand on her back. "It's okay. You're just getting in touch with your magick."

Robbie sat down, too, and assumed the same position. This was amazing. The others were finally picking up on the kind of magickal energy I'd been overwhelmed by since the beginning. Forgetting about my own weird feelings, I met Cal's eyes and smiled. Our coven was coming together.

An hour later Cal ended the circle. I stood and got my coat from the hall.

"It was a great circle tonight, guys," Cal said, and everyone nodded enthusiastically. "School starts again Monday, and we'll all be distracted again, so let's try to keep focused. I think you'll find it's easier to do now that you have your working stones. And just remember, we have a rival coven,

Kithic. Kithic is working with witches who are untrustworthy, who have an agenda. For your own sake, I want you all to stay away from anyone associated with them."

I looked at Cal in surprise. He hadn't mentioned his intention of telling us this, but I supposed it was only natural, given the connection between Hunter and Sky, Sky and Kithic.

"We can't just be friends with them?" asked Jenna.

Cal shook his head. "It might not be safe. Everyone, be careful, and if anything feels strange or you feel things you can't figure out, please tell me right away."

"You mean like spells?" Ethan asked with a frown. "Like if they put spells on us?"

"I don't think they will," Cal said quickly, raising his hands. "I'm just saying be alert and talk to me about everything and anything, no matter how small."

Robbie looked impassively at Cal. I doubted he planned to quit seeing Bree. Matt looked completely depressed—he didn't seem to have a choice about seeing Raven or not: she wanted to see him, and so far he hadn't been able to say no.

Cal and I went out to the car, and I was silent with thought.

14

Finding

December 2000

My petition to become a Seeker has gone to the top. Yesterday I met with the seven elders of the council. They once again turned me down. What to do now?

I must curb my anger. Anger cannot help me here. I will ask Uncle Beck to intercede on my behalf. In the meantime I am taking classes with Nera Bluenight, of Calstythe. With her guidance I can school my emotions more and petition the council once again.

—Giomanach

On Sunday morning I realized that one week ago today I had turned seventeen. Looking back, it had been an intensely unhappy day: trying to appear normal while reliving the horror of watching Hunter go over the ledge, the dismay over Cal's wounds, the temporary loss of my magick. This week was going better. Thank the Goddess and God, Hunter was alive. I felt reassured by knowing that he wasn't inherently evil—and neither was I. Yet there were still huge, unresolved issues in my life. Questions about Cal and the things he might or might not be hiding from me, questions about myself and the depth of my commitment to Cal, to Wicca itself . . .

I went to church with my family because I knew my mother would make a fuss if I tried to duck out for the second week in a row, and I just wasn't ready to fight that battle. I sleepwalked through the service, my mind churning ideas incessantly. I felt I was two people: Catholic and not Catholic. Part of my family and not part of my family. In love with Cal, yet holding back. Loathing Hunter and yet full of joy that he was alive. My whole life was a mishmash, and I was being divided in two.

When the time for communion approached, I slipped out of our pew as if I was heading for the bathroom. I stood in the drafty hall behind the organist's cubby for a couple of minutes, then came back and fell in line with the people who had just taken communion. I took my seat, dabbing my lips as if I'd just sipped from the chalice. My mother gave me a questioning look but didn't say anything. Leaning back, I let my thoughts drift away once again.

Suddenly Father Hotchkiss's booming voice startled me. From the pulpit he thundered, "Does the answer lie within or without?"

It was like a bolt of lightning. I stared at him.

"For us," Father Hotchkiss went on, gripping the pulpit, "the answer is both. The answers lie within yourselves, as your faith guides you through life, and the answer lies without, in the truth and solace the church offers. Prayer is the key to both. It is through prayer we connect with our Maker, through prayer we reaffirm our belief in God and in ourselves." He paused, and the candles glowing behind him seemed to light the whole nave. "Go home," he went on, "pray thoughtfully to God, and ask him for guidance. In prayer will be your answer."

"Okay," I breathed, and the organ started playing, and we stood to sing a hymn.

After church my family had lunch at the Widow's Diner as usual, then headed home. Up in my room I sat on my bed. It was time to take stock of my life, decide where I was going. I wanted to follow the path of Wicca, but I knew that it wouldn't be easy. It would need more commitment from me than the things I was doing. It had to be woven into the everyday cycles of my life. I needed to start living mindfully in every moment.

Serious Wiccans maintain small altars at home, places to meditate, light candles, or make offerings to the Goddess and God, like the one in Cal's *seòmar*. I wanted to set one up for myself as soon as possible. Also, I had been meditating a bit, but I needed to set aside time to do it every day.

Making these simple decisions felt good—they would be outward manifestations of my inner connection to Wicca and my witch heritage. Now for another outward manifestation. Quickly I changed into jeans and a sweatshirt. When the coast was clear, I retrieved Maeve's tools from behind the vent and threw my coat over the box.

"I'm going for a drive," I told Mom downstairs.

"Okay, honey," she replied. "Drive carefully."

"Okay." Out in Das Boot, I put my coat on the seat

beside me and cranked the engine. A few minutes later I was approaching the edge of town.

Surrounding Widow's Vale are farmlands and woods. As soon as we had gotten our driver's licenses the year before, Bree and Robbie and I had gone on many day trips, exploring the area, looking for swimming holes and places to hang out. I remembered one place not too far out of town, a large, undeveloped tract that had been cleared for lumber back in the 1800s and was now covered with second-growth trees. I headed there, trying to remember the turns and forks, looking for familiar landmarks.

Soon I saw a field I remembered, and I pulled Das Boot over and put on my coat. I left the car on the shoulder of the road, took Maeve's box, and set off across the field and into the woods. When I found the stream I remembered, a sense of elation came over me, and I blessed the Goddess for leading me there.

After following the stream for ten minutes, I came upon a small clearing. Last summer, when we'd found it, it had seemed a magickal place, full of wildflowers and damselflies and birds. Robbie and Bree and I had lain on our backs in the sun, chewing on grass. It had been a golden day, free of worries. Today I had come back to partake of the clearing's magick again.

The snow here was deep—it had never been plowed, of course, and only faint animal tracks disturbed it. With each step I sank in over my ankles. A boulder at the edge of the clearing made a convenient table. I set Maeve's box there and opened it. Cal had said that witches wore robes instead of their everyday clothes during magickal rites because their clothes carried all the jangled, hectic vibrations of their lives. When I had worn Maeve's robe and used her tools a few days ago, I had felt nauseated, confused. It had occurred to me today that perhaps it was because of the clashing vibrations of my life and my magick.

Father Hotchkiss had advised us to pray, to look within for answers before we tackled outside problems. I was going to take his advice. Witch style.

Luckily for me, it was another one of those weird, warm days. The air was full of tiny dripping sounds as snow melted around me. I shucked my coat, sweatshirt, and undershirt.

It might have been warm for late autumn, but still, it wasn't summer. I began to shiver, and quickly pulled Maeve's robe over my head. It fell in folds to midcalf. I untied my boots, took off my jeans, and even my socks.

Miserably I peered down at my bare ankles, my feet buried in the snow. I wondered how long I would have the guts to stick this out.

Then I realized I no longer felt even the tiniest bit cold.

I felt fine.

Cautiously I lifted one foot, it looked pink and happy, as if I had just gotten out of the bath. I touched it. Warm. As I was marveling about this, I felt a focused spot of irritation at my throat. I touched it and found the silver pentacle Cal had given me weeks ago. I was so used to wearing it that I hardly noticed it anymore, but now it felt prickly, irritating, and regretfully I took it off and put it on the boulder with my other things. Ah. Now I was completely comfortable, wearing nothing but my mother's robe.

I wanted suddenly to sing with joy. I was completely alone

in the woods, enveloped in the warm, loving embrace of the Goddess. I knew I was on the right path, and the realization was exhilarating.

I set up the four cups of the compass. In one I put snow, then took out a candle. Fire, I thought, *flame,* and the charred wick burst into life. I used that candle to melt the snow into water. It was harder to find earth, but I dug a hole in the snow and then scraped at the frozen ground with my athame. I'd brought incense for air, and of course I used the candle for fire.

I made a circle in the snow with a stick, then invoked the Goddess. Sitting on the snow, as comfortable as an arctic hare, I closed my eyes and let myself sink through layer upon layer of reality. I was safe here; I could feel it. This was a direct communion between me and nature and the life force that exists within everything.

Slowly, gradually, I felt myself joined by other life forces, other spirits. The large oak lent me its strength, the pine, its flexibility. I took purity from snow and curiosity from the wind. The frail sun gave me what warmth it could. I felt a hibernating squirrel's small, slow heartbeat and learned reserve. A fox mother and her kits rested in their den, and from them I took an eager appetite for survival. Birds gave me swiftness and judgment, and the deep, steady thrumming of the earth's own life force filled me with a calm joy and an odd sense of expectation.

I rose to my feet and stretched my bare arms outward. Once again the ancient song rose in me, and I let my voice fill the clearing as I whirled in a circle of celebration.

Both times before, the Gaelic words had seemed like a call to power, a calling down of power to me. Now I saw that it was also a direct thread that connected me to Maeve, Maeve to Mackenna, Mackenna to her mother, whose name, it came to me, had been Morwen. For who knows how long I whirled in a kaleidoscope of circles, my robe swirling, my hair flying out in back of me, my body filled with the power of a thousand years of witches. I sang, I laughed, and it seemed that I could do it all at once, could dance and sing and think and see so startlingly clearly. Unlike the last time, I felt no unease, no illness, only an exhilarating storm of power and connection.

I am of Belwicket, I thought. I am a Riordan witch. The woods and the snow faded around me, to be replaced by green hills worn smooth by time and weather. A woman strode forward, a woman with a plain, work-lined face. Mackenna. She held out tools, witch's tools, and a young woman wearing a clover crown took them. Maeve. Then Maeve turned and handed them to me, and I saw my hand reaching out to take them. Holding them, I turned again and held them out to a tall, fair girl, whose hazel eyes held excitement, fear, and eagerness. My daughter, the one I would have one day. Her name echoed in my mind: Moira.

My chest swelled with awe. I knew it was time to let the power go. But what to do with it, where to direct this power that could uproot trees and make stones bleed? Should I turn it inward, keep it within myself for a time when I might need it? My very hands could be instruments of magick; my eyes could be lightning.

No. I knew what to do. Planting my feet in the churned snow beneath me, I flung my arms outward again and came to a stop. "I send this power to you, Goddess!" I cried, my throat hoarse from chanting. "I send it to you in thanks and blessing! May you always send the power for good, like my mother, her mother, her mother before her, and on through the generations. Take this power: it is my gift to you, in thanks for all you have given me."

Suddenly I was in the vortex of a tornado. My breath was pulled from my lungs, so that I gasped and sank to my knees. The wind embraced me, so that I felt crushed within strong arms. And a huge clap of thunder rang in my ears, leaving me shaken and trembling in the silence that followed, my head bowed to the snow, my hair wet with perspiration.

I don't know how long I crouched there, humbled by the power I myself had raised. I had left this morning's Morgan behind, to be replaced by a new, stronger Morgan: a Morgan with a newfound faith and a truly awesome power, gifted by the Goddess herself.

Slowly my breathing steadied, slowly I felt the normal silence of the woods fill my ears. Both drained and at peace, I raised my head to see if the very balance of nature had shifted.

Before me sat Sky Eventide.

15

Visions

February 2001

They have accepted me at last. I am the council's newest member—and its youngest, the most junior member of the third ring. I'm one of more than a thousand workers for Wiccan law. But my assigned role is that of Seeker, as I requested. I've been given my tools, the braigh and the books, and Kennet Muir has been assigned as my mentor. He and I have spent the past week going over my new duties.

Now I have been given my first task. There is a man in Cornwall who is accused of causing his neighbor's milk cows to sicken and die. I'm going down there today to investigate.

Athar has offered to come with me. I didn't tell her how glad I was of her offer, but I could see that she understood it nonetheless. She is a good friend to me.

—Giomanach.

Sky was perched on a snow-covered log about fifteen feet away from me. Her eyes were almond-shaped pools of black. She looked pale with cold and very still, as if she had been waiting a long time. Kicking in after the fact, my senses picked up on her presence.

She casually brushed off one knee, then clasped her gloved hands together.

"Who are you?" she said conversationally, her English accent as crisp and cool as the snow around us.

"Morgan," I was startled into replying.

"No. Who *are* you?" she repeated. "You're the most powerful witch I've ever seen. You're not some uninitiated student. You're a true power conduit. So who are you, and why are you here? And can you help me and my cousin?"

Suddenly I was chilled. Steam was coming off me in visible waves. My skin was damp and now turning clammy with sweat, and I felt vulnerable, *naked* beneath my robe.

Keeping one eye on Sky, I dismantled my circle swiftly and packed away my tools. Then I sat on the boulder and dressed, trying to act casual, as if getting dressed in front of a relative stranger in the woods was an everyday thing. Sky waited, her gaze focused on me. I folded Maeve's robe and put it back in my box, and then I turned to face Sky again.

"What do you want?" I demanded. "How long have you been spying on me?"

"Long enough to wonder who the hell you are," she said. "Are you really the daughter of Maeve of Belwicket?"

I met her eyes without responding.

"How old are you?"

A harmless question. "I just turned seventeen."

"Who have you been studying with?"

"You know who. Cal."

Her eyes narrowed. "Who else? Who before Cal?"

"No one," I said in surprise. "I only started learning about Wicca three months ago."

"This is impossible," she muttered. "How can you call on the power? How can you use those tools without being destroyed?"

Suddenly I wanted to answer her, wanted to share with her what I had just experienced. "I just—the power just comes to me. It *wants* to come to me. And the tools . . . are mine. They're for me to use. They *want* me to use them. They beckon me."

Sky sighed.

"Who are *you?*" I asked, thinking it was time she answered some questions herself. "I know you're Sky Eventide, you're from England, you're Hunter's cousin, and he calls you Athar." I thought back to what I had learned during the *tàth* thing with Hunter. "You grew up together."

"Yes."

"What are you doing with Bree and Raven?" I demanded.

After a pause she said, "I don't trust you. I don't want to tell you things only to have you tell Cal and his mother."

I crossed my arms over my chest. "Why are you even here? How did you know where to find me? Why do you and Hunter keep spying on me?"

Conflicting emotions crossed Sky's face.

"I felt a big power draw," she said. "I came to see what it was. I was in my car, heading north, and suddenly I felt it."

"I don't trust you, either," I said flatly.

We looked at each other for long minutes, there in the woods. Sometimes I heard clumps of snow falling off branches or heard the quick flap of a bird's wings. But we were in our own private world, Sky and I, and I knew that whatever happened here would have far-reaching consequences.

"I'm teaching Bree, Raven, Thalia, and the others basic Wiccan tenets," Sky said stiffly. "If I've told them about the dark side, it was only for their protection."

"Why are you in America?"

She sighed again. "Hunter had to come here on council business. He told you he's been doing research about the dark wave, right? He's combining his research with his duties as a Seeker. I get worried about him—all our family does. He's treading on dangerous ground, and we didn't want something bad to happen to him. So I offered to keep him company."

Remembering what Hunter's council duties were, I felt my fists clench. "Why is he investigating Cal and Selene?"

Sky regarded me evenly. "The council suspects they've been misusing their powers."

"In what way?" I cried.

Her dark eyes gazed deeply into mine. "I can't tell you," she whispered. "Hunter believes you're not knowingly involved with their plan. He saw that when you two were in *tàth meanma*. But I'm not so sure. Maybe you're so powerful that you can hide your mind from others."

"You can't believe that," I said.

"I don't know what to believe. I do know that I don't trust Cal and Selene, and I fear they're capable of more evil than you can imagine."

"Okay, you're pissing me off," I said.

"You need to face the facts. So we need to figure out the facts first. Hunter thinks Selene has a big plan that you're a key element of. What do you think they'll do to you if you don't want to be part of it?"

"Nothing. Cal loves me."

"Maybe he does," Sky said. "But he loves living more. And Selene would stop at nothing to have you—not even her own son."

I shook my head. "You're crazy."

"What does your heart tell you?" she asked softly. "What does your mind tell you?"

"That Cal loves me and accepts me and has made me happy," I said. "That I love him and would never help you hurt him."

She nodded thoughtfully. "I wish you could scry," she said. "If you could see them . . ."

"Scry?" I repeated.

"Yes. It's a somewhat precarious method of divination," Sky explained.

I nodded impatiently. "I know what it is. I scry with fire."

Her eyes opened so wide, I could see the whites around her black irises.

"You don't."

I just looked at her.

Disbelieving, she said, "Not with fire."

Not answering, I shrugged.

"Have you scryed to see what's happening in the present?"

I shook my head. "I just let the images come. It seems to be mostly the past, and sometimes I see possible futures."

"You can guide scrying, you know. You focus your energy on what you want to see. With water you'll see whatever your mind wants to see. A stone is the best, most accurate, but it offers less information. Do you think you could control scrying with fire?"

"I don't know," I said slowly, my mind already leaping with possibilities.

Ten minutes later I found myself in a situation I never could have dreamed up. Sky and I sat cross-legged, our knees touching, our hands on each other's shoulders. A small fire burned on a flat stone I had unearthed in the snow. It crackled and spat as the snow in the cracks of the burning branches boiled. I'd lit it with my mind, and had felt a stealthy surge of pride at the way Sky's eyes widened in shock.

Our foreheads touched; our faces were turned to the fire. I took a deep breath, closed my eyes, and let myself drift into meditation. I tuned out the fact that my jeans were getting wet and my butt would probably never thaw again. I had never scryed while doing the Wiccan mind meld, but I was into trying it.

Gradually my breathing deepened and slowed, and sometime later I sensed that Sky and I were breathing in unison. Without opening my eyes I reached out to touch her mind, finding the same suspicious brick wall that I had with Hunter. I pushed against it, and I felt her reluctance and then her slow acceptance. Cautiously she let me into her mind, and I went slowly, ready to pull out if this was a trap, if she tried to attack. She was feeling the same fear, and we paused instinctively until we both decided to let down our guards.

It wasn't easy. She had always rubbed me the wrong way, and she just about hated me. Surprisingly, it hurt to see the depth of her dislike for me, the rage she felt over what I had done to Hunter, her suspicion of my powers and their possible sources. I didn't realize witches could transfer their powers to another until I saw her worry that Selene had done this to me.

We breathed together, locked in a mental embrace, looking deeply into each other. She loved Hunter dearly and was very afraid for his safety. She missed England and her mother and father terribly. In her mind I saw Alwyn, Hunter's younger sister, who looked nothing like him. I saw her memory of Linden, how beautiful he had been, how tragic his death was.

Sky was in love with Raven.

What? I followed that elusive thought, and then it was there, in the forefront, clear and complete. Sky was in love with Raven. Through Sky's eyes I saw Raven's humor, her strength, her gutsiness, her determination to study Wicca. I felt Sky's frustration and jealousy as Raven chased Matt and flirted with others and had no reaction to Sky's tentative overtures. To Sky, slender, blond, restrained English Sky, Raven was almost unbearably lush and sexy. The bold way she spoke, her vivid appearance, her brash attitude all fascinated Sky, and Sky wanted her with a frank desire that took me aback and almost embarrassed me.

Then Sky was leading me, asking questions about Cal. Together we saw my love for him, my humiliating relief that someone finally wanted me, my awe at his beauty and respect for his power. She saw my uncertainty about and fascination with Selene and my discomfort about Cal's *seòmar*. As Hunter had, she saw that Cal and I hadn't made love yet. She saw that Hunter had almost kissed me, and she nearly broke off contact in surprise. I felt like she was paging through my private diary and began to wish I'd never agreed to this. My mind told Sky I had been shocked to find out I was Woodbane and extra shocked just four days ago to learn Cal was Woodbane also.

Now, together, she thought, and I opened my eyes. After looking at each other for a moment, weighing what we had learned, we turned, staying connected, and looked into the fire.

Fire, element of life, Sky thought, and I heard her. Help us see Cal Blaire and Selene Belltower as they are, not as they show themselves to us.

Are you ready to see? I heard the fire whisper back to us seductively. Are you ready, little ones?

We are ready, I thought, swallowing hard.

We are ready, Sky echoed.

Then, as it had for me in the past, the fire created images that drew us in. I felt Sky's awe and joy: she had never scryed with fire before. She strengthened her mind and concentrated on seeing the here and now, seeing Cal and Selene. I followed her example and focused on that also.

Cal, I thought. Selene. Where are you?

An image of Cal's huge stone house formed within the flames. I remembered how I could never project my senses through its walls and wondered if that applied to scrying. It didn't. The next time I blinked, I found myself in Selene's circle room, the huge parlor where she regularly held her coven's circles. It had once been a ballroom and now seemed like a grand hall of magick. Selene was there, in her yellow witch's robe, and I recognized Cal's dark head standing out from a group of people I didn't recognize.

"Do we really need her?" a tall, gray-haired woman with almost colorless eyes asked.

"She's too powerful to let go," said Selene.

An icy trickle down my back told me they were speaking of me.

"She's from Belwicket," a slender man pointed out.

"Belwicket is gone," Selene said. "She'll be from anywhere we want her to be."

Oh, God, I thought.

"Why haven't you brought her to us?" asked the gray-haired woman.

Selene and Cal met eyes, and to me it felt like they fought a silent battle.

"She'll come," said Cal in a strong voice, and inside me I felt a piercing pain, as if my heart were being rent. "But you don't understand—"

"We understand that it's past time for action," another woman said. "We need this girl on our side now, and we need to move on Harnach before Yule. You had an assignment, Sgàth. Are you saying you can't bring her to us?"

"It will be done," said Selene in a voice like marble. Again her gaze seared Cal, and his jaw set. He gave an abrupt nod and left the room, graceful in his heavy white linen robe.

I can't see any more, I thought, and then I said the words aloud. "I can't see any more."

I felt Sky pulling back as I did, and I shut my eyes and deliberately came back to the snowy woods and this moment. Opening my eyes, I looked up to see that the sky was darkening with late afternoon, that my jeans were soaked through and miserably uncomfortable, that the trees that had made a circle of protection around me now seemed black and threatening.

Sky's hands slid off my shoulders. "I've never done that,"

she said in a voice just above a whisper. "I've never been good at scrying. It's—awful."

"Yes," I said. I looked into her black eyes, reliving what I had just seen, hearing Selene's words again. Shakily I uncoiled and stood, my leg muscles cramped, my butt beyond feeling, and an unsettling feeling of nausea in my stomach. As Sky stood, stretching and groaning under her breath, I knelt and scooped up some clean snow, putting it in my mouth. I let it melt and swallowed the cold trickle of water. I did this again, then rubbed snow on my forehead and on the back of my neck under my hair. My breath was shallow, and I felt shaky, flooded with fear.

"Feel ill?" Sky asked, and I nodded, eating more snow.

I stayed on all fours, melting small mouthfuls of snow while my brain worked furiously, trying to process what we had seen. When Bree and I had fought over Cal and I had realized that we were no longer friends after eleven years, it had been shockingly painful. The sense of betrayal, of loss, of vulnerability had been almost unbearable. Compared to what I was feeling now, it had been a walk in the park. Inside, my mind screamed, No, no, no!

"Were those images true?" I choked out.

"I think so," Sky said, sounding troubled. "You heard them mention Harnach? That's the name of a Scottish coven. The council sent Hunter here to investigate evidence that Selene is part of a Woodbane conspiracy that's trying, basically, to destroy non-Woodbane covens."

"She's not the dark wave?" I cried. "Did she destroy Belwicket?"

Sky shrugged. "They don't see how she could have. But she's been linked to other disasters, other deaths," she said, hammering my soul with each word. "She's been moving around all her life, finding new Woodbanes wherever she goes. She makes new covens and ferrets out blood witches. When the coven is solid, she breaks it up, destroying the non-Woodbane witches and taking the Woodbanes with her."

"Oh my God," I breathed. "She's killed people?"

"They believe so," Sky said.

"Cal?" I said brokenly.

"He's been helping her since he was initiated."

This was all too much for me to take in. I felt frantic. "I have to go," I said, looking around for my tools. It was now almost dark. I grabbed Maeve's box and shook some of the snow off my boots.

"Morgan—" Sky began.

"I have to go," I said, more strongly.

"Morgan?" she called as I took the first step into the woods. I turned back to look at her, standing alone in the clearing. "Be careful," she said. "Call me or Hunter if you need help."

Nodding, I turned again and made my way back to my car. Inside, my heart began screaming again: No, no, no . . .

16

Truth

I've always wondered if my mother killed my father. After all, he left her, not the other way around. And then he had two more kids right away with Fiona. That really freaked Mom out.

Dad "disappeared" when I was almost nine. Not that I'd seen anything of him before that. I was the forgotten son, the one who didn't matter.

When Mom got the phone call, she just told me that Dad and Fiona had vanished. She didn't say anything about them being dead. But as the years have worn on and no one's heard from him—that I know about, anyway—it seems safe to assume he's dead. Which is convenient, in a way. It means Giomanach doesn't have Dad's power behind him. But still, I wish I knew what really happened. . . .

—Sgàth

The sun had faded away. My wheels crunched ice on the road as I drove past old farms, fields of winter wheat, silos.

Cal and Selene. Selene was evil. It sounded melodramatic, but what else do you call a witch who works on the dark side? Evil. Woodbane.

No! I told myself. I'm Woodbane. I'm not evil. Belwicket wasn't evil; my mother wasn't. My grandmother wasn't. But somewhere along the line, my ancestors had been. Was that why Selene wanted me? Did she see the potential for evil in me? I remembered the vision I'd had of myself as a gnarled crone, hungry for power. Was that my true future?

I choked back a sob. Oh, Cal, I screamed silently. You betrayed me. I loved you, and you were just playing a *part.*

I couldn't get over this. It was a physical pain inside me, an anguish so devastating that I couldn't think straight. Tears rolled down my cheeks, leaving hot tracks and tasting of salt when they touched the edges of my lips. A thousand images of Cal bombarded my brain: Cal leaning down to kiss me, Cal with his shirt open, Cal laughing, teasing me, offering to help me with Bakker, making me tea, holding me tight, kissing me hard, harder.

I was flying apart inside. I began to pray desperately that the scrying had been a lie, that Sky had tricked me, made me see things that weren't there, she had lied, had lied. . . .

I needed to see him. I needed to find out the truth. I'd had my questions answered by Hunter and by Sky, and now only Cal remained to fill me in on the big picture, the dangers I was blundering into, the reasons I needed to be careful, to watch myself, to rein in my power.

But first—I had to hide my mother's tools. With all my

heart, I hoped that Cal would convince me of his innocence, convince me that Sky was wrong, convince me that our love was true. But the mathematician in me insisted that nothing is one hundred percent certain. I had bound my mother's tools to me, they were mine, and now I had to make sure no one would take them away or make me use them for evil.

But where to stash them? I couldn't go home. I was already almost late for dinner, and if I went home, I wouldn't be able to turn around and leave. Where?

Of course. Quickly I made a right turn, heading to Bree's house. Bree and I were enemies: no one would suspect I would hide something precious in her yard.

Bree's house looked large, immaculately kept, and dark. Good—no one was home. I popped the trunk on my car and took out the box. Whispering, "I am invisible, you see me not, I am but a shadow," I slunk up the side yard, then quickly ducked beneath the huge lilac bush that grew outside the dining room window. It was mostly bare this time of year, but it still hid the opening to the crawl space beneath Bree's house. I tucked the toolbox out of sight behind a piling, traced some fast runes of secrecy, and stood up.

I was opening my car door when Bree and Robbie drove up in Bree's BMW. They pulled up beside me and stopped.

Ignoring them, I started to swing into the driver's seat of my car. The passenger window scrolled down smoothly. Crap, I thought.

"Morgan?" said Robbie. "We've been looking for you. We were talking to Sky. You've got to—"

"Gotta go," I said, climbing in and slamming the door shut before he could say anything else. I had already talked to Sky, and I knew what she'd said.

Robbie opened his door and started toward me. I peeled off, watching him get smaller in the rearview mirror. I'm sorry, Robbie, I thought. I'll talk to you later.

On the way toward the river, thoughts of exactly what I would say to Cal raced through my mind. I was in the middle of my ninth hysterical scenario when—

Morgan.

My head whipped around. Cal's voice was there, right beside me, and I almost screamed.

Morgan?

Where are you? my mind answered frantically.

I need to see you. Please, right away. I'm at the old cemetery, where we had our circle on Samhain. Please come.

What to do? What to think? Had everything he'd told me been a lie? Or could he explain it all?

Morgan? Please. I need you. I need your help.

Just like that night with Hunter, I thought. Was he in trouble? Hurt? Blinking, I wiped away some stray tears with the back of my sleeve and peered through the windshield. At the next intersection I turned right instead of left, and then I was on the road leading north, out of town. Oh, Cal, I thought, a new wave of anguish sweeping over me. Cal, we have to have it out.

Five minutes later I turned down a side road and parked in front of the small Methodist church that had once shepherded the people who now lay in its graveyard.

Shuddering with leftover sobs, I sat in my car. Then I felt Cal, coming closer. He tapped gently on my window. I opened the door and got out.

"You got my message?" he said. I nodded. He examined my face more closely. Then he caught my chin in his hands and said, "What's wrong? Why were you crying? Where were you? I tried going by your house."

What should I say?

"Cal, is Selene trying to hurt me?" I asked, my words like shards of ice in the night air.

Everything in him became still, centered, and focused. "Why would you say that?"

I felt his senses reaching out to me, and quickly I shut myself down, refusing him entrance.

"Is Selene part of an all-Woodbane coven that wants to erase non-Woodbanes?" I asked, pushing my hair out of my face. Please tell me it's a lie. Please convince me. Tell me anything.

Cal gripped my hair in his hand, making me look at him. "Who have you been talking to?" he demanded. "Dammit, has that bastard Hunter been—"

"I scryed," I said. "I saw you with Selene and other people. I heard them talking about your 'assignment.' Was I your assignment?"

He was silent for a long time. "Morgan, I can't believe this," he said at last. "You know you can't believe stuff you see in scrying—it's all nebulous, uncertain. Scrying shows you only possibilities. See, this is why I always want you to wait until I guide you. Things can be misunderstood—"

"Scrying showed me the possibility of where my mother's tools were," I said, my voice stronger. "It's not always lies— otherwise no one would use it."

"Morgan, what's this all about?" he asked in a loving voice. He gently pulled me to him so that my cheek rested against his chest, and it felt wonderful and I wanted to sink into him. He kissed my forehead. "Why are you having doubts? You know we're *mùirn beatha dàns*. We belong together; we're one. Tell me what's wrong," he said soothingly.

With those words the pain in my chest intensified, and I took deep breaths so I wouldn't cry again. "We're not," I whispered, as the truth broke over me like a terrible dawn. "We're not."

"Not what?"

I tilted back my head to look into his gold eyes, his eyes full of love and longing and fear. I couldn't bring myself to say it outright.

"I know you slept with Bree," I lied instead. "I *know* it."

Cal looked at me. Before Bree and I had broken our friendship, she had been chasing Cal hard, and I knew from past experience that she always got whatever guy she wanted. One day she had been happy, saying she and Cal had finally gone to bed, so now they were going out. But they hadn't started going out, and he had come after me. I'd asked him about it before, and he had denied sleeping with her, with my best friend. Now I needed to know the truth of it, once and for all, even as I was being hit with other painful truths from every direction.

"Just once," Cal said after a pause, and inside, I felt my heart cease its pumping and slowly clog shut with ice.

"You know what Bree's like," he went on. "She won't take no for an answer. One night, before I really knew you, she jumped on me, and I let her. To me it was no big deal, but I guess she was hurt that I didn't want more."

I was silent, my eyes locked on his, seeing in their reflection all my dreams exploding, all my hopes for our future, all shattering like glass.

"The only powers she had were reflections coming from

you," he said, the barest trace of disdain in his voice. "Once I realized you were the one, Bree was just ... unimportant."

"Realized I was the one what?" My voice sounded tight, raspy, and I coughed and spoke again. "The one Woodbane around? The Woodbane princess of Belwicket?" I pushed him away. "Why do you keep lying to me?" I cried in anguish. "Why can't you just tell me who you are and what you want?" I was practically screaming, and Cal winced and held up his hands.

"You don't love me," I accused him, still pathetically hoping he would prove me wrong. "I could be *anyone*, young or old, pretty or ugly, smart or stupid, as long as I was *Woodbane*."

Cal flinched and shook his head. "That isn't true, Morgan," he said, a note of desperation in his voice. "That isn't true at all."

"Then what *is* true?" I asked. "Is anything you've told me true?"

"Yes!" he said strongly, raising his head. "It's true that I love you!"

I managed a credible snort.

"Morgan," he began, then stopped, looking at the ground. His hands on his hips, he went on. "This is the truth. You're right. I was supposed to find a Woodbane, and I did."

I almost gasped with pain.

"I was supposed to get close to her, and I did."

How could I still be standing, I wondered in a daze.

"I was supposed to make her love me," he said quietly. "And I did."

Oh, Goddess, oh, Goddess, oh, Goddess.

He raised his head and looked at me, my eyes huge and horrified.

"And you were the Woodbane, and you didn't even know

it. And then you turned out to be from the Belwicket line, and it was like we'd hit gold. You were the one."

Oh, Goddess, help me. Help me, please, I beg you.

"So I got close to you and made you love me, right?"

I had no answer. My throat was closed.

Cal gave a laugh laced with bitterness. "The thing is," he said, "no one said I had to love you back. No one expected me to, including me. But I do, Morgan. No one said I had to fall for you, but I did. No one said I had to desire you, enjoy your company, admire you, take pride in your strength, but I do, dammit! I do." His voice had been rising, and he stepped closer to me. "Morgan, however it started, it isn't like that now. I feel like I've always loved you, always known you, always wanted a future with you." He put his hand on my shoulder, gently kneading and squeezing, and I tried to back up. "You're my *mùirn beatha dàn*," he said softly. "I love you. I want you. I want us to be together."

"What about Selene?" My voice sounded like a croak.

"Selene has her own plans, but they don't have to include us," he said, stepping closer still. "You have to understand how hard it is to be her son, her only son. She depends on me—I'm the heir to the throne. But I can have my own life, too, with you, and it doesn't have to include her. It's just—first I have to help her finish some things she's been working on. If you help us, too, it will all go so much faster. And then we can be free of her."

I looked at him, feeling a cold, deadly calm replacing the panic and wretchedness inside me. I knew what I had seen in my vision, and I knew Cal was either lying or kidding himself about Selene's plans. They didn't include letting him—or me—be free.

"I'm free of her now," I said. "I know that Selene needs me for something. She's counting on you to sign me up. But I'm not going to, Cal. I'm not going to be part of it."

His expression looked like he had just watched me get hit by a car.

"Morgan," he choked out, "you don't understand. Remember our future, our plans, our little apartment. Remember? Please just help us with this one thing, and then we can work out all the details later. Trust me on this. Please."

My heart was bleeding. I said, "No. Selene can't have me. I won't do what she wants. I won't go with you. It's all over, Cal. I'm leaving the coven. And I'm leaving you."

His head snapped up as if I had hit him, and he stared at me. "You don't know what you're saying."

"I do," I said, trying to make my voice strong, though I really wanted only to crumple in misery on the ground. "It's over. I won't be with you anymore." Each word scarred my throat, etching its pain in acid.

"But you love me!"

I looked at him, unable to deny it even after all this.

"I love *you*," he said. "Please, Morgan. Don't—don't force my hand. Just come with me, let Selene explain everything herself. She can make you understand better than I can."

"No."

"Morgan! I'm asking you, if you love me, come with me now. You don't have to do anything you don't want to. Just come and tell Selene herself that you won't be part of her coven. That's all you need to do. Just tell her to her face. I'll back you up."

"You tell her."

His eyes narrowed with anger, then it was gone. "Don't

be unreasonable. Please don't make me do anything I don't want to do."

Fear shot through me. "What are you talking about?"

His face had a strange look, a look of desperation. I was suddenly terrified. The next second I whirled, broke into a run, and was digging my car keys out of my pocket. I ripped open the car door, hearing Cal right behind me, then he yanked the door open, hard, and shoved me in.

"Ow!" I cried as my head hit the door frame.

"Get in!" he roared, pushing against me. "Get in!"

Goddess, help me, I prayed as I scrambled to let myself out the other side. But when I grabbed the door handle, Cal put his hand on my neck and squeezed, muttering words that I didn't understand, words that sounded ancient and dark and ugly.

I tried to counter with my Gaelic chant, but my tongue froze in my mouth and a paralyzing numbness swept over me. I couldn't move, couldn't look away from him, couldn't scream. He had put a binding spell on me. Again.

I'm so stupid, I thought ridiculously as he started Das Boot with my keys.

17

The Seòmar

February 2001

I did it. I put a witch under the braigh.

The fellow in Cornwall was mad, there is no question of that. When I came to question him he first tried to evade me, then when he saw that I would not give up, he flew into a frenzy. He gibbered about how he would curse me and my whole family, that he was one of the Cwn Annwyn, the hounds of Hell. He began to shout out a spell and I had to wrestle him to the ground and put the braigh on him. Then he began to weep and plead. He told me how it burned him, and begged me to let him go. At last his eyes rolled back in his head and he lost consciousness.

I put him in the car, and Athar drove us to London. I left him with Kennet Muir. Kennet told me I'd done well; the man might be mad but he also had true power and was therefore dangerous. He said my task was done, and now it was the seven elders' job to determine the man's future.

I left, and then Athar and I went to a pub and got very drunk. Later, she held me while I wept.

—Giomanach

"You just don't get it, do you?" Cal said angrily, taking a corner too fast. I slumped against the car door helplessly. Inside, my mind was whirring like a tornado, a thousand thoughts spinning out of control, but the binding spell he had put on me weighted my limbs as thoroughly as if I were encased in cement.

"Slow down," I managed to whisper.

"Shut up!" he shouted. "I can't believe you're making me do this! I love you! Why can't you listen to me? All I need is for you to come talk to Selene. But no. You can't even do that for me. The one thing I ask you to do, you won't. And now I have to do this. I don't want to do this."

I slanted my eyes sideways and looked at Cal, at his strong profile, his hands gripping Das Boot's steering wheel. This was a nightmare, like other magickal nightmares I'd had before, and soon I would wake up, panting, in my own bed at home. I just needed to wake up. Wake up, I told myself. Wake up. You'll be late for school.

"Morgan," Cal said, his voice calmer. "Just think this through. We've been working with witchcraft for years. You've only been doing it a couple of months. At some point you'll just have to trust us with what we're doing. You're only resisting because you don't understand. If you would calm down and listen to me, it would all make sense."

Since I was in essence deadweight right now, his telling me to calm down seemed particularly ironic. Cal kept on talking, but my brain drifted away from his monologue. Focus, I thought. Focus. Get it together. Make a plan.

"I thought you would be loyal to me always," Cal said. My eyes were just above the window ledge, and I saw that we were just entering Widow's Vale. Were we going to Cal's house? It was so secluded—once he got me there, I'd never get out. I thought about my parents wondering where I was and wanted to cry. Focus, dammit! Think your way out of this. You're the most powerful witch they've ever seen; surely there must be something you can do. Think!

Cal flew through a red light at the edge of town, and involuntarily I flinched as I heard the squeal of brakes and an angry horn. I realized he hadn't even put my seat belt on me, and in my present helpless state I couldn't do it myself. Fresh, cold fear trickled down my spine when I pictured what would happen to me in an accident.

Think. Focus. Concentrate.

"You should have just trusted me," Cal was saying. "I know so much more than you do. My mother is so much more powerful than you. You're a student—why didn't you just trust me?"

My door was locked. If I could open it, I could maybe tumble out somehow. And get crushed beneath the wheels since I probably couldn't leap out of the way. Could I unroll my window and shout for help? Would anyone in town recognize my car and wonder why I wasn't driving it?

I tried to clench my right hand and saw with dismay that I could barely curl up my first knuckle.

The night of my birthday, when Cal had put the binding spells on me, I had somehow managed to break free. I had—pushed, with my mind, like tearing through plastic, and then I had been able to move. Could I do that now?

We raced through downtown Widow's Vale, the three stoplights, the lit storefronts, the cars on their way home. I peered up over my window, hoping someone, anyone, would see me. Would Cal get stopped for speeding? I almost cried as a moment later we passed through downtown and were on the less-traveled road that led toward Cal's house. Panic threatened to overtake me again, and I stamped it down.

Bree's face floated suddenly into my mind. I seized on it. Bree, Bree, I thought, closing my eyes and concentrating. Bree, I need your help. Cal has me. He's taking me to Selene. Please come help me. Get Hunter, get Sky. I'm in my car. Cal is desperate. He's going to take me to Selene. Bree? Robbie? Hunter, please help, Hunter, Sky, anyone, can you hear me?

Working this hard mentally was exhausting, and my breath was coming in shallow pants.

"You don't understand," Cal went on. "Do you have any idea what they'd do to me if I showed up without you?" He gave a short, barking laugh. "Goddess, what Hunter did to me that night was child's play compared to what they would do." He looked at me then, his eyes glittering eerily. He looked belovedly familiar and yet horribly different. "You don't want them to hurt me, do you? You don't know what they could do to me. . . ."

I closed my eyes again, trying to shut him out. Cal had always been so in control. To see him this way was sickening, and a cold sweat broke out on my forehead. I swallowed and tried to go deep inside myself, deep to where the power was. Bree, please, I'm sorry, I thought. Help. Help me. Save me. Selene is going to kill me.

"Stop that!" Cal suddenly shouted, leaning over and shaking my shoulder hard.

I gasped, opening my eyes. He glared at me in fury.

"Stop that! You don't contact anyone! Anyone! Do you hear me?" His angry voice swelled in the car's interior, filling my ears and making my head hurt. One hand shook me until my teeth rattled, and I clenched my jaws together. I felt the car making big swerves on the road and prayed to the Goddess to protect me.

"Don't you wreck this car," I said, unclenching my lips enough to speak.

Abruptly he let go of me, and I saw the glare of headlights coming at us and then the long, low blare of a truck horn blowing. It swept past us as I drew in a frightened breath.

"Shit!" Cal said, jerking the steering wheel to the right. Another horn blared as a black car screeched to a halt just before ramming my side. I started to shake, slumped against my door, so afraid, I could hardly think.

You, afraid? part of me scoffed. You're the Woodbane princess of Belwicket. You could crush Cal with the power in your little finger. You have the Riordan strength, the Belwicket history. Now, save yourself. Do it!

Okay, I could do this, I told myself. I was a kick-ass power conduit. Letting my eyes float closed again, trying not to think about the chaos raging around me, I let the music come to me, the timeless music that magick sent. *An di allaigh an di aigh,* I thought, hearing the tune come to me as if borne on a breeze across clover-covered hills.

An di allaigh an di ne ullah. Was that my voice, singing in a pure ribbon of glorious sound that only I could hear? My fingers tingled, as if coming awake. *An di ullah be nith rah.* I drew in a deep, shuddering breath, feeling my muscles twitch, my toes curl. I am breaking this binding spell, I thought. I am smashing it. I am tearing it like wet tissue. *Cair di na ulla nith rah, Cair feal ti theo nith rah, An di allaigh an di aigh.*

I was myself. I had done it. I stayed exactly where I was, opening my eyes and gazing around. With a flare of alarm I recognized the tall hedges that surrounded Cal's property. He swung Das Boot into a side road, skidding a bit, and we began to crunch on icy gravel.

Bree, Sky, Hunter, Robbie, anyone, I thought, feeling my radiating power. Alyce, David, any witch, can you hear me?

The side road to Cal's driveway was long, with tall, overhanging trees. It was pitch-black except where moonlight glistened off snow. The dashboard clock said six-thirty. My family was sitting down to eat. At the thought I felt a surge of anger so strong it was hard for me to hide it. I couldn't accept the possibility that I might never see them again, Mom, Dad, Mary K., Dagda. I would escape. I would get out of this. I was very powerful.

"Cal, you're right," I said, making my voice sound weak. I couldn't even feel the effects of the binding spell anymore, and a surge of hope flamed in my chest. "I'm sorry," I said. "I didn't realize how important this was to you. Of course I'll go talk to your mom."

He turned the wheel and paused, reaching out his left hand and pointing it ahead of him. I heard the metallic rumbling of heavy gates, heard them swing on hinges and clunk open with a bang.

Then, as if he had finally heard me, Cal looked over. "What?" He stepped on the gas, and we rolled through the gate. Ahead of me was a dark roofline, and I realized we were in the backyard, and the building in front of me was the little pool house. Where Cal had his *seòmar*.

"I said, I'm sorry," I repeated. "You're right. You're my *mùirn beatha dàn*, and I should trust you. I do trust you. I just—felt unsure. Everyone keeps telling me something different, and I got confused. I'm sorry."

Das Boot rolled slowly to a halt, ten feet from the pool house. It was dark, with the car's one headlight shining sadly on the dead brown ivy covering the building.

Cal turned off the engine, leaving the keys in the ignition. He kept his eyes on me, where I leaned awkwardly against the door. It was all I could do to keep my hand from grasping the door handle, popping the door, and running with all my might. What spell could I put on Cal to slow him down? I didn't know any. Suddenly I remembered how his pentacle had burned at my throat when I used Maeve's tools. I'd felt better without it on. Was it spelled? Had I been wearing a spell charm all this time? I wouldn't doubt it at this point.

With agonizingly slow movement, I slipped my right hand down into my pocket and pulled out Cal's pentacle. He hadn't noticed I wasn't wearing it yet, and I let it slip from my fingers to the floor of the car. As soon as it left my hand, my head felt clearer, sharper, and I had more energy. Oh, Goddess, I was right. The pentacle had been spelled all this time.

"What are you saying?" Cal said, and I blinked.

"I'm sorry," I repeated, making my voice a little stronger. "This is all new to me. It's all confusing. But I've been thinking about what you said, and you're right. I should trust you."

His eyes narrowed, and he took hold of my hand. "Come on," he said, opening his door. His grip on my hand was crushing, and I dismissed the possibility that I could slip out suddenly and run. Instead he pulled me out the driver's-side door and helped me stand. I pretended to be weaker than I was and leaned against him.

"Oh, Cal," I breathed. "How did we get into such a fight? I don't want to fight with you." I made my voice soft and sweet, the way Bree did when she talked to guys, and I leaned against Cal's chest. Seeing the mixture of hope and suspicion cross his face was painful. Suddenly I pushed hard against him, shoving with every bit of strength in my arms, and he staggered backward. I raised my right hand and shot a spitting, crackling bolt of blue witch fire at him, and this time I didn't hold anything back. It blasted Cal right in the chest, and he cried out and sank to his knees. I was already running, my boots pounding heavily toward the metal gates that were swinging closed.

The next thing I knew my knees had crumpled and I was falling in slow motion to land heavily, face-first, on the icy gravel. The breath left my lungs in a painful whoosh, and then Cal stood over me, cradling one arm against his chest, his face a mask of rage.

I tried to roll quickly to shoot witch fire again, the only defensive weapon I knew, but he put his boot on my side and pressed down, pinning me to the cold ground. Then he grabbed one of my arms, hauled me to my feet, and squeezed the back of my neck, muttering another spell. I screamed, "Help! Help! Someone help me!" but of course no one came. Then I sagged, a deadweight.

"*An di allaigh*," I began in a choking voice as Cal hauled me toward the pool house. I knew where we were going, and I absolutely did not want to go there.

"Shut up!" Cal said, shaking me, and he pushed open the changing room door. Bizarrely, he added, "I know you're upset, but it will all be okay. Everything will be all right soon."

Reaching out, I grasped the door frame, but my limp fingers brushed it harmlessly. I tried to drag my feet, to be an awkward burden, but Cal was furious and afraid, and this fed his strength. Inside we lurched through the powder room, and Cal let me slump to the floor while he unlocked the closet door. I was trying to crawl away when he opened the door to his *seòmar*, and I felt the darkness come out of it toward me, like a shadow eager to embrace.

Goddess, I thought desperately. Goddess, help me.

Then Cal was dragging me by my feet into his room. With my magesight I saw that it had been cleared of everything, everything I could have used for a weapon, everything I could have used to make magick. It was bare, no furniture, no candles, only thousands and thousands of dark spells written on the walls, the ceiling, the floor. He'd prepared my prison in advance. He'd known this would happen. I wanted to gag.

Panting, Cal dropped my feet. He hovered over me, then narrowed his eyes and grabbed at the neck of my shirt. I tried to pull away, but it was too late.

"You took off my charm," he said, sounding amazed. "You don't love me at all."

"You don't know what love is," I croaked, feeling ill. I raised my hands over my eyes and clumsily brushed my hair out of the way.

For a moment I thought he was going to kick me, but he didn't, just looked down at me with the devastating face that I had adored.

"You should have trusted me," he said, sweat running down his face, his breathing harsh.

"You shouldn't have lied to me," I countered angrily, trying to sit up.

"Tell me where the tools are," he demanded. "The Belwicket tools."

"Screw you!"

"You tell me! You should never have bound them to you! How arrogant! Now we'll have to rip them away from you, and that will hurt. But first you tell me where they are—I didn't feel them in the car."

I stared at him stonily, trying to rise to my feet.

"Tell me!" he shouted, looming over me.

"Bite me," I offered.

Cal's golden eyes gleamed with hurt and fury, and he shot out his hand at me. A cloudy ball of darkness shot right at me, hitting my head, and I crashed headlong to the floor, sinking into a nightmarish unconsciousness, remembering only his eyes.

18

Trapped

June 2001

Litha again. It's now fully ten years since my parents disappeared. When they left, I was a boy, concerned only with building a working catapult and playing Behind Enemy Lines with Linden and my friends.

At the time we were living in the Lake District, across Solway Firth from the Isle of Man. For weeks before they left, they were in bad moods, barking at us children and then apologizing, not having the time to help us with our schoolwork. Even Alwyn started coming to me or Linden to help her dress or do her hair. I remember Mum complaining that she felt tired and ill all the time, and none of her usual potions seemed to help. And Dad said his scrying stone had stopped working.

Yes, something was definitely oppressing them. But I'm sure they didn't know what was really coming. If they had, maybe things would have turned out differently.

Or maybe not. Maybe there is no way to fight an evil like that.
—Giomanach

When I awoke, I had no idea how much time had passed. My head ached, my face burned and felt scraped from the gravel, and my knees ached from when I had fallen on them. But at least I could move my limbs. Whatever spell Cal had used on me, it wasn't a binding one.

Cautiously, silently, I rolled over, scanning the *seòmar*. I was alone. I cast out my senses and felt no one else near. What time was it? The tiny window set high on one wall showed no stars, no moon. I crawled up on my hands and knees, then unfolded myself and stood slowly, feeling a wave of nausea and pain roll over me.

Crap. As soon as I stood, I felt the weight of the spelled walls and ceilings pressing in on me. Every square inch of this tiny room had runes and ancient symbols on it, and without understanding them, I knew that Cal had worked dark magick here, had called on dark powers, and had been lying to me ever since the day I met him. I felt incredibly naive.

I had to get out. What if Cal had left only a minute ago? What if even now he was bringing Selene and the others back to me? Goddess. This room was full of negative energy, negative emotions, dark magick. I saw stains on the floor that had been hidden by the futon the first time I was here. I knelt and touched them, wondering if they were blood. What had Cal done here? I felt sick.

Cal had gone to get Selene, and they were going to put spells on me or hurt me or even kill me to get me to tell them where Maeve's tools were. To get me to join their side, their all-Woodbane clan.

No one knew where I was. I had told Mom I was going for a drive more than six hours ago. No one had seen me meet Cal at the cemetery. I could die here.

The thought galvanized me into action. I got to my feet again, looking up at the window, gauging its height. My best jump was still two feet short of the window ledge. I pulled off my jacket, balled it up, and flung it hard at the window. It bounced off and clumped to the floor.

"Goddess, Goddess," I muttered, crossing to the door. Its edge was almost invisible, a barely seen crack that was impossible to dig my nails into. In the car I had my Swiss Army knife—patting my pockets quickly yielded me nothing. Still I tried, wedging my short nails into its slit and pulling until my nails split and my fingers bled.

Where was Cal? What was taking so long? How long had it been?

Panting, I backed up across the room, then launched myself shoulder first at the small door. The impact made me cry out, and then I slid down to the floor, clutching my shoulder. The door hadn't even shuddered under the blow.

I thought of how my parents had been so devastated when I took up Wicca, how afraid they had been for me after what happened to my birth mother. I saw now that they'd had good cause to worry.

An unwanted sob choked my throat, and I sank to my knees on the wooden floor. The back of my head ached sickeningly. How could I have been so stupid, so blind? Tears edged from my eyes and coursed down my bruised and dirty cheeks. Sobs struggled to break free from my chest.

I sat cross-legged on the floor. Slowly, knowing it was pointless, I drew a small circle around myself, using my index finger, wetting the floor with my tears and my blood. Shakily I traced symbols of protection around me: pentacles, the intersected circles of protection, squares within squares for orderliness, the angular runic þ for comfort. I drew the two-horned circle symbol of the Goddess and the circle/half circle of the God. I did all these things with only the barest amount of thought, did them by rote, over and over, all around me on the floor, all around me in the air.

Within moments my breathing calmed, my tears ceased, my pain eased. I could see more clearly, I could think more clearly, I was more in control.

Evil pressed in around me. But I was not evil. I needed to save myself.

I was the Woodbane princess of Belwicket. I had power beyond imagining.

Closing my eyes, I forced my breathing to calm further, my heartbeat to slow. Words came to my lips.

"Magick, I am your daughter,
I am following your path in truth and righteousness.
Protect me from evil. Help me be strong.
Maeve, my mother before me, help me be strong.
Mackenna, my grandmother, help me be strong.
Morwen, who came before her, help me be strong.
Let me open the door. Open the door. Open the door."

I opened my eyes then and gazed before me at the spelled and locked door. I looked at it calmly, imagining it opening before me, seeing myself pass through it to the outside, seeing myself safe and gone from there.

Creak. I blinked at the sound but didn't break my concentration. I was unsure whether I had imagined it, but I kept thinking, Open, open, open, and in the darkness I saw the minuscule crack widen, just a hair.

Elation, as strong as my earlier despair had been, lifted my heart. It was working! I could do this! I could open the door!

Open, open, open, I thought steadily, my focus pure, my intent solid.

I smelled smoke. That fact registered only slightly in my brain as I kept concentrating on opening the door. But I realized that my nose was getting irritated, and I kept blinking. I came out of my trance and saw that the *seòmar* was becoming hazy, and the scent of fire was strong.

I stood up within my circle, my heart kicking up a beat. Now I could hear the joyful crackling of flames outside, smell the acrid odor of burning ivy, and see the faint, amber light of fire reflected in the high window.

They were burning me alive. Just like my mother.

As my concentration broke, the door clicked shut again.

Panic threatened to drown me. "Help!" I screamed as loud as I could, aiming my voice at the window. "Help! Help! Someone help me!"

From outside, I heard Selene's voice. "Cal! What are you doing?"

"Solving the problem," was his grim response.

"Don't be stupid," Selene snapped. "Get away from there. Where are the tools?"

I thought fast. "Let me out and I'll tell you, I promise!" I shouted.

"She's lying," said another voice. "We don't need her, anyway. This isn't safe—we have to get out of here."

"Cal!" I screamed. "Cal! Help me!"

There was no answer, but I heard muffled voices arguing outside. I strained to hear.

"You promised she would join us," someone said.

"She's just an uneducated girl. What we really need is the tools," said someone else.

"I'll tell you!" I shouted. "They're in the woods! Let me out and I'll take you there!"

"I'm telling you, we have to leave," someone said urgently.

"Cal, stop it!" said Selene, and suddenly the sound of flames was louder, closer.

"Let me out!" I screamed.

"Goddess, what is he doing? Selene!"

"Get back or I'll torch the whole place with all of us in it," said Cal, sounding steely. "I won't let you have her."

"The Seeker will be here any minute," said a man. "There's no way he won't come for this. Selene, your son—"

I heard more arguing, but I was choking now, the smoke stinging my eyes, and then I heard the popping of the wooden rafters up above. I pressed my ear to the wall and listened, but there were no more voices. Had they all just gone away? If I died in the fire, they would never find Maeve's tools. That wasn't true, I realized. They could scry to find them; they could do spells to find them. The simple concealment runes I had traced around the box wouldn't deceive any of them. They wanted me to tell them only to save time. They didn't really need me at all.

I tried once again to open the door with my mind, but I couldn't focus. I kept coughing and my mind was starting to feel foggy. I slumped against the wall in despair.

It had all been for *nothing*: Maeve hiding her tools to keep them safe, coming to me in a vision to tell me where they were, my finding them with Robbie, my learning how to use them. For nothing. Now they would be in Selene's hands, under her control. And maybe the tools were so old that they had been used by the original members of Belwicket— before the clan promised to forsake evil. Maybe the tools would work just as well for evil as they could for good.

Maybe this was all my fault. This was the big picture everyone kept talking about. This was the danger I was blundering into. This was why I needed guidance, a teacher.

"Goddess, forgive me," I muttered, lying belly down on the smooth wooden floor. I pulled my jacket over my head. I was going to die.

I was very tired. It was hard to breathe. I was no longer panicking, no longer full of fear or hysteria. I wondered how Maeve had faced her death by fire, sixteen years before. With each moment that passed, I had more in common with her.

19

Burn

June 2001

Here's an interesting thing: I went today to Much Bencham, which is the little town in Ireland next to where Ballynigel used to be. No one there wanted to talk to me, and I got the feeling the whole village was anti-witch. Having seen their closest neighbors turn to dust all those years ago, I'm not surprised. But as I was leaving the town square, an old woman caught my eye. She was probably on the dole—making ends almost meet by selling homemade pasties. I bought one, and as I bit into it she said, very quietly, "You're the lad's been asking questions about the town next door." She didn't name Ballynigel, but of course that was what she meant.

"Aye," I said, taking another bite. I waited.

"Odd things," she murmured. "Odd doings in that town, sometimes. Whole town wiped off the face of the earth. It's not natural."

"No," I agreed. "Not natural at all. Did no one survive, then?"

She shook her head, then frowned as if remembering something. "Though that woman last year said as how some did survive. Some escaped, she said."

"Oh?" I said, though inside my heart was pounding. "What woman was this?"

"She were a beauty," said the old woman, thinking back. "Dark and exotic. She had gold eyes, like a tiger. She came here asking about them next door, and someone—I think it was old Collins, at the pub—he told her they were dead, all of them, and she said no, she said that two made it away to America."

"Two people from Ballynigel went to America?" I said, to make certain. "After the disaster, or before?"

"Don't know, do I," said the woman, starting to lose interest. "She just said that two from there had gone to New York years ago, and that's in America, isn't it."

I thanked her and walked away, thinking. Damn me if that tiger woman didn't sound like Dad's first wife, Selene.

So now I am on my way to New York. Is it really possible two witches from Belwicket escaped the disaster? Could they be in New York? I won't rest until I know.

—Giomanach

Dying from smoke inhalation is not the worst way to go, I thought sleepily. It's uncomfortable and gives you a drowning sort of feeling, but it must be better than being shot or actually burned to death or falling off a cliff.

It wouldn't be long now. My head ached; smoke filled my

lungs and made me cough. Even lying on the floor, with my head covered by my jacket, I wouldn't last much longer. Was this how it had been for Maeve and Angus?

When I heard the voices calling my name from outside, I figured I was hallucinating. But the voices came again, stronger, and I recognized them.

"Morgan! Morgan! Are you in there? Morgan!"

Oh my God, it sounded like Bree! Bree and Robbie!

Sitting up was a mistake because even a foot above me, the air was heavier. I choked and coughed and sucked in air, and then I screamed, "I'm in here! In the pool house! Help!" A spasm of coughing crushed my chest, and I fell to the floor, gasping.

"Stand back!" Bree shouted from outside. "Get away from the wall!"

Quickly I rolled to the wall farthest away from her voice and lay there, huddled and coughing. My mind dimly registered the familiar, powerful roar of Das Boot's engine, and the next thing I knew, the wall across from me was hit with a huge, earthshaking crash that made the plaster pop, the window shatter and rain glass on me, and the wall bulge in. I peeped out from under my coat and saw a crack where smoke was rising, pouring out into the sky, grateful for release. I heard the roar of the engine, the squeal of wheels, and the whole building shook as my car rammed the wall violently once more. This time the stone and plaster broke, studs snapped, and then the crumpled, ash-strewn nose of my car was perched in the wall, opening like the mouth of a great white shark.

The driver's door opened, and then Bree was scrambling over rubble, coughing, and I reached out to her, and she grabbed my arms and hauled me out over the wreckage. Robbie was there outside, waiting for us, and as my knees buckled he ran over and caught me. I bent over, coughing and retching, while he and Bree held me.

Then we heard the nearing sounds of wailing fire sirens, and in the next few minutes three fire trucks appeared, Sky and Hunter arrived, and Cal's beautifully manicured lawn was ruined.

And I was alive.

grabbed my arms and hauled me out over the wreckage.

Rob he was there outside, waiting for us, and as my knees buckled he ran over and caught me. I bent over, coughing to stop... while he and Bree held me.

Then we heard the nearing sounds of wailing fire sirens, and in the next few minutes three fire trucks appeared, Sky and Hunter arrived, and Cat's beautifully manicured lawn was a...

And I was alive.